THE UNDERCOVER NAZI HUNTER

EXPOSING THE SUBTERFUGE AND UNMASKING EVIL IN POST-WAR GERMANY

DEDICATED TO THE MEMORY OF WOLFE FRANK

THE UNDERCOVER NAZI HUNTER

EXPOSING THE SUBTERFUGE AND UNMASKING EVIL IN POST-WAR GERMANY

Wolfe Frank

Edited by Paul Hooley

Frontline Books

THE UNDERCOVER NAZI HUNTER
Exposing the Subterfuge and Unmasking Evil in Post-war Germany

First published in Great Britain in 2019 by Frontline Books,
an imprint of Pen & Sword Books Ltd, Yorkshire - Philadelphia

Also by Paul Hooley
Nuremberg's Voice of Doom (Editor)
From Lockington to Gillingham
One Foot In The Grave

Typeset in 10.5/12.5 Palatino and Gill Sans Light
Printed and bound by TJ International Ltd, Padstow, Cornwall

Pen & Sword Books Ltd incorporates the imprints of Pen & Sword Archaeology,
Atlas, Aviation, Battleground, Discovery, Family History, History, Maritime,
Military, Naval, Politics, Social History, Transport, True Crime, Claymore Press,
Frontline Books, Praetorian Press, Seaforth Publishing and White Owl

For a complete list of Pen & Sword titles please contact:
PEN & SWORD BOOKS LTD, 47 Church Street, Barnsley, South Yorkshire, S70 2AS, UK.
E-mail: enquiries@pen-and-sword.co.uk Website: www.pen-and-sword.co.uk

Or
PEN AND SWORD BOOKS, 1950 Lawrence Road, Havertown, PA 19083, USA
E-mail: Uspen-and-sword@casematepublishers.com
Website: www.penandswordbooks.com

CONTENTS

PART ONE
PREPARATION

PART TWO
THE 'HANGOVER AFTER HITLER' SERIES OF ARTICLES

PART THREE
THE CONFESSION OF SS SS-GRUPPENFÜHRER
WALDEMAR WAPPENHANS

PART FOUR
AFTERMATH

LIST OF ILLUSTRATIONS

SELECTED QUOTATIONS

'By early 1949 it had become blatantly obvious to me that we were increasingly reading only what the Germans wanted us to read … An idea began to develop in my mind: could I not go to Germany and gather material, covering a multitude of subjects and write a more accurate account of what was happening? If I did, who would sponsor such an enterprise? Who would print it? And how could I become an investigator without appearing to be one?'
Wolfe Frank

'Misinformation about Germany has led to unpleasant surprises in the past. A true picture of Germany is elusive because Germans often present different aspects to "outsiders." A fresh appraisal of the German question could only be obtained by a German and Mr Frank had all the exceptional qualifications necessary … A one-man poll cannot of course be conclusive. But when conducted intensively by a scientific observer with the exceptional qualifications of Wolfe Frank it can turn a pencil flashlight on to dark places, help to confirm some things that had been only suspected, and occasionally bring some surprises – such as the relative ease with which one of the 2,000 still-missing Nazi VIPs covered his tracks and secured an influential job with the occupation authorities'.
Geoffrey Parsons Jr., Editor of the New York Herald Tribune (NYHT)
European Edition – November 1949

'He [Frank] might not come back; but that would be his and our bad luck. He wants insurance against death or accident'.
'I frankly do not believe we should go into the business of insuring his life. That's his lookout. If he wants to do something safe he'd better forget the newspaper business'.
Exchange of letters between NYHT executives in New York and Paris – 1949

'Before Mr Frank was sent to Germany, his project was first cleared with the Allied Military Authorities in Western Germany. Though they are in no way responsible for his findings, his survey was made with their foreknowledge'.
Geoffrey Parsons Jr., Editor of the New York Herald Tribune (NYHT) European Edition – 1949

'When he appeared, I greeted him with his real name and told him I was an Englishman. His face whitened and his hands shook as he dropped into a chair. I had been prepared for quite a different reaction and felt a little silly about the small automatic I had handy in my jacket pocket … He clasped his hands to his head for a few moments, then muttered (I could barely hear his words): "God – I've kept it up for so long and now I'm caught. What will you do? Hand me over?"'
SS General Waldemar Wappenhans on being apprehended by Wolfe Frank – autumn 1949

'Before the war there were about 600,000 persons of Jewish descent living in Germany. They comprised about one per cent of the population. Today there are 60,000. This means, in effect, that 540,000 more or less were exiled or put to death in one way or another'.
Wolfe Frank – November 1949

'The greatest thing the Fuehrer did, was to finish off the Jews. Unfortunately, 60,000 of them escaped. But don't worry, we'll get them yet'.
Comment by a workman in a Hamburg café to Wolfe Frank in 1949

'There is no less anti-Semitism in Germany than there was ten years ago. The principal differences are that there are fewer Jews against whom to direct it, and occupation authorities who keep it from breaking out in violence'.
Wolfe Frank – November 1949

'Today in West Germany in labour camps where convicted Nazis are doing time, guards are asking prisoners for certificates to show the guards have treated them well during their imprisonment … One of my friends who formerly worked for the Bavarian de-Nazification ministry remarked: "It won't be long now before even the judges will be asking the accused for affidavits

that the judges couldn't have been nicer or more lenient in handling their cases".'
Wolfe Frank – November 1949

'One of the subjects I was to cover was German morality or lack thereof. Obviously I was working on this with considerable relish. First hand experience rates far above hearsay. But there was the problem of Maxine [Frank's wife] who could not be told of [or later read about] my personal research work on the subject'.
Wolfe Frank – in his memoirs

'Ninety per cent of the German women are for sale today. The price varies from a few marks, or a meal, or an evening out, to a mink coat, a diamond bracelet, or a tidy bank account'.
Kurt Kolmsperger, editor of the Munich Catholic newspaper Merkur
– autumn 1949

'Children aged twelve were having sex, mothers were having sex with their sons, and fathers with their daughters. It was a fairly shattering experience to observe all this and it is an eerie thought indeed that among the well-to-do West Germans of today are many who have gone through this soul destroying phase in their lives'.
Wolfe Frank, in his memoirs, referring to his observations in the refugee camps he visited in 1949

'Hitler's masseur disclosed to me secrets of Hitler's physical condition and ménage and his last hours in the Berlin bunker'.
Wolfe Frank – November 1949

'I stayed with Hitler until we got to the bunker ... I shall never be able to forget that experience ... by then Adolf was the most horrible sight I ever hope to see. He walked without lifting his feet off the ground, and his whole body seemed to be made of jelly. The features of his face had sagged monstrously, and his mouth seemed to droop open all the time. His voice was hoarse and his speech blurred ... my orders were to take all the women out excepting, of course, those like Eva Braun and Frau Goebbels who were parties to the suicide pact'.
A. J. Weinert, Hitler's masseur, during an interview he gave to Wolfe Frank – autumn 1949

'The top of the table was blown upward, against his [Hitler's] arm, which was badly sprained and bruised. But that was just about his

x

only injury … I saw Adolf less than five minutes after it happened. His trousers hung in shreds … He sat on the couch and laughed and laughed for quite a long time. And he kept slapping his thigh with his uninjured arm as he laughed. All his entourage crowded around to tell him he had been saved by an act of God. He seemed to believe it'.
A. J. Weinert, Hitler's masseur, during an interview he gave to Wolfe Frank
– autumn 1949

'It was she [Eva Braun] who eventually persuaded Hitler to put an end to it all, Adolf was still listening to those around him, like Goebbels, who kept telling him he could still win. If Eva hadn't worked on him and persuaded him that all was finished, they might have persuaded him to bail out and carry on from somewhere else'.
A. J. Weinert, Hitler's masseur, during an interview he gave to Wolfe Frank
– autumn 1949

'The general view was "Everything he [Hitler] did was fine up to 1939 and then the fool went and lost the war". I heard him referred to a number of times as "that non-smoking vegetarian": seldom by any more derogatory epithet'.
Wolfe Frank –November 1949

PREFACE 2019

The first edition of this work should have appeared seventy years ago! However, due to growing tensions associated with the rapidly escalating Cold War[1], the USA's focus was moving away from Germany and very much onto the threats being posed by Russia. At precisely the same time, the Allied Control Council[2], governments generally, and other responsible bodies – including the world's media – were advocating a softer approach towards Germany. They had been persuaded that the point had been reached where it was wrong to continue inflicting further suffering on a defeated, humiliated and devastated nation. As one leading German politician of the time had pleaded: 'We should not be asked to walk about in the cloak of the repentant sinner forever. No future can be built on that'[3].

These changes in attitude led firstly the copyright holders, and then the authors, to delay publishing the material in book form until times and circumstances were more favourable. The manuscripts were therefore archived and then forgotten about – until their recent, fortuitous, re-discovery.

In 1949 Wolfe Frank, the former Chief Interpreter at the Nuremberg Trials, entered Germany under an assumed name and on false papers to carry out a detailed undercover investigation. His intention was to reveal the true state of the nation to counteract what the Germans in the Western and the Russians in the Eastern occupied zones wanted the world to believe was happening. Frank's enterprise was backed by the *New York Herald Tribune (NYHT)* and resulted in the publication of a highly acclaimed series of articles that appeared in the Paper, during the December of that year, under the generic title *Hangover After Hitler*. The series was then syndicated to ninety other papers around the world.

The Undercover Nazi Hunter is made up of two essential elements. The first consists of the *NYHT* articles together with fascinating accounts of how the series was conceived, written, authorized and prepared. The second element chronicles the astonishing story of how Frank single-handedly tracked down, apprehended and interrogated Waldemar Wappenhans – one of the highest ranked war criminals on the Allies 'Wanted List' – and includes the life story Frank drew out of him.

The Wappenhans testimony, or 'Confession' as it was referred to at the time – a hugely important historical document in its own right – was taken and transcribed by Wolfe Frank. Only two copies of the document were ever produced; one was handed in with the former SS Major General; the other, which also bears Wappenhans' signature, was retained by Frank. Faithfully translated from the German original, the entire, unexpurgated Confession is reproduced herein for the first time in any language.

Parts of what follow in this Preface were incorporated in my Introduction to this book's companion volume – *Nuremberg's Voice of Doom* (NVOD)[4] – they are included again here for the benefit of readers and to provide important details about the background, context and the circumstances that led to the publication of this work.

Three years ago, retired panel beater and paint sprayer Mike Dilliway, in the course of moving home, came across six to eight cardboard boxes, a number of files and two briefcases crammed full of assorted papers that he had squirrelled away and had not thought about for over a quarter of a century.

Mike had inherited this cache from Wolfe Frank whom he had befriended in the Wiltshire village of Mere (where Frank lived and Mike worked) and, not knowing quite what he had or what to do with the documents, had placed them in his attic for safe keeping.

During the course of some of the conversations the friends had over the years, Wolfe had mentioned that prior to the Second World War he had been involved in an underground resistance movement in Germany before escaping to England in 1937. He had also indicated that he had been an interpreter and interrogator at the Nuremberg trials of Nazi war criminals (Hermann Goering, et al.) and that he had once been a successful journalist and businessman. Illness and some unfortunate involvements in both his professional and personal life had however, by 1988, reduced Wolfe's life to a low ebb – both physically and financially – and this had led to him taking his own life.

In 2015, needing to make a decision on what to do with Wolfe's collection of papers, Mike asked me (as a writer he knew who had an interest in historical and military matters) if I would take a look at the material to see if there was anything there that might be of importance.

After two years of sorting, re-sorting, cataloguing, assessing, researching, sequencing, checking and editing several thousand pages of data, and then obtaining many confirmations, I had a complete picture of the life of Wolfe Frank who had, in fact, been Chief Interpreter at the Nuremberg Trials prior to becoming an intrepid investigative journalist for the *NYHT*. So important were my discoveries that I knew by the end of my researches that I had to share the knowledge I had acquired – not only with military historians but also with a much wider audience. This led to the publication of firstly *NVOD* and now this book, which deals with a particular phase in Frank's life that saw him conduct his dangerous undercover survey of what was really happening in post-war Germany.

NVOD consists of a posthumous autobiography of the first half of Wolfe's remarkable life – that stands up to the closest scrutiny – plus a potted biography of his later days based upon his memoirs. Further information has been added that chronicles the life, times and involvements of this brave, dedicated and gifted man whose exploits and achievements should not be allowed to fade into obscurity. *NVOD* is, in fact, a record of two interwoven themes – one of love, adventure and excitement, the other of a former German citizen's fight for the right to become a British soldier and his extraordinary commitment to service, duty and justice throughout what many consider to have been the greatest and most important trial the world has ever seen.

To further assist readers of this book I have included in the Prologue and Epilogue a brief, although I hope adequate, outline of the more important details of Wolfe's life. This, I believe, will prove to be valuable additional material that will fill in gaps and answer many of the questions that might arise in readers' minds.

The two essential, distinct, yet similarly intertwined elements of *The Undercover Nazi Hunter* consist of the highly regarded *Hangover After Hitler* series of articles, together with the Wappenhans Confession and all its ramifications.

In the months following the Nuremberg Trials of 1945–48 Frank had become increasingly alarmed at the misinformation coming out of Germany, so in 1949 he risked his life again by returning to the country of his birth to make his covert survey of the main facets of post-war German life and viewpoints. During his five-month enterprise he worked as a German alongside Germans in factories, on the docks, in refugee camps and elsewhere. Equipped with false papers he sought objective answers to many questions regarding: refugees; anti-Semitism; morality, de-Nazification; religion; nationalism; and, most importantly, what had happened to the 2,000 Nazi war criminals on the Wanted List, many of whom were believed to be in hiding within Germany.

The *NYHT* said at the time: 'A fresh appraisal of the German question could only be obtained by a German and Mr Frank had all the exceptional qualifications necessary. We believe the result of his "undercover" work told in human, factual terms, is an important contribution to one of the great key problems of the post-war world … and incidentally it contains some unexpected revelations and dramatic surprises'.

The Undercover Nazi Hunter is divided into four distinct parts.

Part One records how and why Frank came up with the idea for his project; how he approached and won over the *NYHT*; the fascinating behind-the-scenes discussions and manoeuvrings that went on within the newspaper's corridors of power; and all that was involved in gathering the information and preparing the articles for publication.

Part Two reproduces Frank's *Hangover After Hitler* series in its entirety and how the articles were originally published – save that, for the sake of continuity, I have Anglicized some American spellings – i.e. programme instead of program; labour instead of labor; colour instead of color, etc.

Part Three is the testimony, as recorded by Wolfe Frank, of SS-Gruppenfuehrer Waldemar Wappenhans. This is a unique, wholly absorbing and extremely important military and historical document that gives an insight into the making of a proud, highly decorated, WWI army <u>and</u> air force officer and how he was later seduced by, and recruited into, the Nazi regime that shaped his life throughout WWII. Quite apart from the significant information it contains, the Confession is eloquent, poignant and concise, and it clearly outlines, in human terms, the contrast between the atrocities carried out by the Third Reich (see Chapter 10 Note 5) and the more honourable way both sides, and their respective officers, conducted themselves during the Great War.

Part Four explains how Frank discovered the whereabouts and identification of the Nazi General; how he came to take his Confession; what he did with the document; how he subsequently dealt with Wappenhans; how and why the SS-Gruppenfuehrer came to be betrayed by those he believed to be his friends; and what eventually happened to those involved in these events. It also raises the question – was Frank working for Military Intelligence as well as for the *NYHT?*

The vast majority of the material in this book is reproduced exactly as it was written by Wolfe Frank and the editors and executives of the *NYHT*, together with an accurate translation of the, until now unseen, Wappenhans Confession. These texts are printed in what is known as a serif typeface (Palatino) as is used for this paragraph. [Any text appearing within square brackets, as this sentence, has for the benefit of readers, been added by me].

There are passages however, interspersed within the text, together with this Preface, the biographical Prologue and Epilogue and the Notes at the end of each Chapter (occasionally repeated for continuity and ease of reference), which I have added to clarify matters, explain situations and to add further and better particulars to what Frank and those others involved have written. To clearly show a distinction between the words of those mentioned above, mine are printed in a sans serif typeface (Gill Sans) as is used for this paragraph and indeed for the whole of this Preface (other than the paragraph immediately above this one).

My words are not intended to detract from Frank's or the *NYHT* contributors' writings, or to in any way alter the content or direction of their thoughts or stories. Rather they are included to assist the reader to better understand certain situations as described – or matters that Frank, the *NYHT* or Wappenhans assume were more widely known, or were in common usage, at the time their words were committed to paper at the end of the 1940s.

I believe, and hope, that historians, students, linguists and those interested in military matters will find *The Undercover Nazi Hunter* to be a further valuable record as well as an interesting read. I feel this book will also appeal to a much wider audience that is not so well versed in the facts of these matters or the terminology used. If I seem therefore at times to be 'teaching grandmothers to suck eggs' it is only to assist those who may be less familiar with some of the historical references and jargon used, or to more clearly explain what is recorded, or to expand upon the context or situations described.

The *NYHT* thought so highly of Wolfe Frank's abilities that they signed him up on the same terms as those they had offered to other notable contributors of the time including Dwight Eisenhower (supreme Commander of Allied Forces in Europe and a future President of the USA), American literary giants John Steinbeck and Ernest Hemingway and also the Duke of Windsor.

It had been the *Herald's* intention to publish this book and share the proceeds with Frank – as is explained by Frank and by Geoffrey Parsons Jr., editor of the *NYHT European Edition,* whose original 'Draft Preface' of 1949 has also been included for authenticity. However, by the time the articles appeared in the newspaper, the Cold War was escalating. Changing attitudes towards developing friendlier relationships with Germany, and the world having turned its attention to the threats posed by Russia, led the Paper's executives to decide not to appear to be continuing to expose the kind of weaknesses Germany and its people were suffering as they were trying to rebuild their devastated nation.

The *NYHT* stood aside therefore and passed the publishing rights of this work to Frank for him to 'use the material of the series in any way he likes'. The Paper also gave him the contents of its own internal files, included as part of this book, which in themselves make absorbing and fascinating reading. Frank had every intention of producing the book, initially it seems in conjunction with Wappenhans, and then, following the former Nazi's demise, by himself. It would appear however that he left it too late, only approaching a publisher with his memoirs and unedited manuscripts shortly before he died in 1988.

It is clear however that Wolfe Frank hoped the full story of his covert investigations would be published posthumously. It is with great pleasure therefore that I now present *The Undercover Nazi Hunter* – exactly seventy years after its intended publication date and the times that its contents were originated by the unlikely triumvirate of The Voice of Doom, the editors and executives of a great American newspaper and a Nazi General wanted for war crimes.

Paul Hooley, Editor, *Gillingham, Dorset*

Notes:

1. The 'Cold War' was the name given to the period of rivalry that developed after WWII between the USA and the Soviet Union and their respective allies. It was waged on political, economic and propaganda fronts from the late 1940s until the collapse of the Soviet Union in 1991.

2. The Allied Control Council or Allied Control Authority, was the military occupation governing body of the Allied Occupation Zones in Germany and Austria following the end of WWII.

3. Dr Carlo Schmid, German opposition leader in 1949.

4. *Nuremberg's Voice of Doom: The Autobiography of the Chief Interpreter at History's Greatest Trials*, written by Wolfe Frank and edited by Paul Hooley (ISBN:9781526737519) was published in 2018 by Frontline Books Ltd., a Division of Pen & Sword Books Ltd.

'The Voice of Doom' was the sobriquet the world's press bestowed upon Wolfe Frank following his announcing of the sentences to the Nazi war criminals at Nuremberg, which were simultaneously listened to by a radio audience of several hundred million.

DRAFT PREFACE 1949[1]

Russell Hill[2] came into my office in *The Herald Tribune* building in Paris one day with a dark, stocky man whom he introduced as Wolfe Frank. (Blah-blah – give your account of how this started, briefly[3]).

We in the *European Edition* organization thought it a good idea. Our New York colleagues were not so sure that a one-man etc., etc. – but they agreed to support us and publish and syndicate what we got, provided it turned out the way we thought it would given reasonable luck, plenty of hard work, constructive briefing, and all the rest that it would necessarily take at our end to make our enterprise a success.

We took Wolfe Frank out of Germany at mid-October and spent six weeks in Paris with him working over his mass of notes and recollections and impressions, reducing them all to a series of fifteen[4] concise stories which we thought gave an overall picture as we editorially believed it should be presented for reading not only in the United States but also in countries in the four other interested continents.

We think we made a good job of this. [Other] editors took the same view – at any rate, they bought and published the series. But this job was necessarily a collaboration on the side of selection of material, presentation, and actual writing. It had to be because, while Mr Frank was in some sense our accredited investigator, he was not a trained correspondent or even a professional reporter; he necessarily took a highly personal view of some aspects of the Germany he saw (or did not see), and the Germans he met (or did not meet), and he at times reached conclusions or made statements which we – not entirely unknowledgeable about Germany and the Germans – thought debatable or too sweeping, or needing qualifications or explanations which could not be interpolated for space reasons. Thus from time to time we would have to reach agreed compromises in the actual presentation of material where we were dealing not with fact but with intangibles of which the conclusions and impressions of a number of unprejudiced observers could very well differ in an important degree.

Even at that we thought it best, in Mr. Frank's interests no less than in our own and in the interests of all the editors in so many countries who were using the series, to prelude the series with the statement that Mr Frank's opinions were his own and not necessarily those of the *New York Herald Tribune*, which had sponsored, aided and financed his research mission.

Our responsibility for the sponsored mission ended when we were through with the series produced for the newspapers who wanted it and published it. Every sentence, every term, every phrase, and even a great many hundreds of nouns and adjectives, had been checked on by more than one critical editorial mind, and not infrequently debated and argued with the patient Mr Frank and we were satisfied that we had done our job, discharged our responsibility, and played fair both with our own and all the other papers' reading public, and with Mr Frank.

Now Mr Frank is telling his own story in his own way in this book, and we have had very little to do with it, except to advise him where he has sought our advice, and tell him that he may use the material of the series in any way he likes. We have no responsibility now for any of the views, impressions or conclusions, and very properly so: because this is a personal story, his own story, and a man must tell his story in his own words and in his own way, and it is right that the light and the shade should be strengthened by the injection of personal emotions and inhibitions which are inseparable from a personal narrative yet out of place in a newspaper series produced as the result of a specific assignment to make a 'report on a Germany suffering from the hangover after Hitler'.

Indeed, the writer personally believes that this personal narrative, which is now a one-man and not a substantially organizational enterprise, may very well provide a better 'Report on Germany and the Germans' than our meticulously produced and carefully checked and balanced newspaper series. It will certainly be more moving, vivid, and enduring[5].

Geoffrey Parsons Jr.

Editor, *New York Herald Tribune European Edition [1945–50]*

Notes:

1. This Preface was written by Geoffrey Parsons Jr. whilst he was editor of the *European Edition* of the *New York Herald Tribune (NYHT)*. It is very much a raw

draft produced in the typical and traditional style of a newspaperman of his standing – that is to say that these are first thoughts dashed off, no doubt at speed, on a 1940s typewriter – to be returned to later by the author and then checked by a sub editor and a copy stylist. Individually and collectively the editorial team would, had the book progressed, have ensured a duly amended piece was grammatically correct before approving it for publication. Parsons, the son of a Pulitzer prizewinner, was a gifted and highly respected editor who left the *NYHT* soon after he wrote these words to become Chief Press Officer and Director of Information at NATO. His draft Preface is reproduced here verbatim for authenticity.

2. Russell Hill was a well-known *NYHT* correspondent during World War II who was also a reporter and correspondent for *Radio Free Europe* and the author of a number of important books including: *Desert War; Desert Conquest;* and *Struggle for Germany* – which deals with the same issues of post-war Germany and the emerging Cold War that so concerned Wolfe Frank and Geoffrey Parsons Jr. and prompted the *Hangover After Hitler* series.

3. This was an instruction from Geoffrey Parsons Jr. to Wolfe Frank to provide details of their meeting – details that are recorded later in this book.

4. Eventually sixteen stories plus an introductory article were published.

5. *The Undercover Nazi Hunter* in fact deals only with firstly: the idea, deliberation, formulation, preparation, investigation, undercover reporting, printing and publishing of the *Hangover After Hitler* series of articles that Wolfe Frank produced for the *NYHT;* and secondly his single-handed apprehension, interrogation and handing over (after personally having taken and prepared the Confession) of one of the highest ranking former Nazi officers on the Allies 'Most Wanted' list. The rest of the Wolfe Frank story, to which Geoffrey Parsons Jr. is here referring, is recorded in *Nuremberg's Voice of Doom* (see Preface 2019 Note 4) – the contents of which are outlined in the Prologue and Epilogue of this book.

PROLOGUE

Born on St Valentine's Day in 1913 the man who became known as Wolfe Frank, The Voice of Doom[1], was the son of an industrialist, Ferdinand Frank, and his second wife Ida. His father and grandfather were both Jewish. However Wolfe, like his mother, was a Protestant. He was brought up in the family home, Villa Frank in the village of Beierfeld, Saxony, and he went to the local elementary school before completing his education at the Grunewald Gymnasium in Berlin[2].

Wolfe's childhood and formative years were generally happy and, as the son of a wealthy businessman, he enjoyed a comfortable and privileged lifestyle, clouded only by his father's strictness and infidelities, which eventually led to Wolfe running away from home and going 'underground' in Berlin where he secured an apprenticeship with BMW. Later he joined the Adler Motor Works, then a local garage where he managed over twenty staff before, at the age of twenty-two, going into partnership with a colleague to start a successful car sales and repair company – and a not so successful, short-lived, career as a rally driver[3].

From his teenage years until his final days Wolfe, an exceptionally handsome and charming man, proved to be irresistible to the ladies and in his early adulthood (and indeed throughout his life) he took full advantage of the opportunities that presented themselves to him, whilst at the same time enjoying the lifestyle of the Bavarian 'playboy' he admits to having become.

However two events in 1933 ended Wolfe's idyllic situation and brought home to him the harsh realities of the times. They also highlighted his own vulnerable position. Firstly his father – who had by then lost his several factories and realized what, as a Jew, lay ahead of him – took his own life.

The second event occurred on the evening of 5 March. Frank was present in Munich – 'The Birth Place of the Nazi Movement' – watching the Nazis' triumphant parade through the city as they announced Hitler's coming to power. During the rally he witnessed what was almost certainly the Third Reich's first public beating of a Jew – a middle-aged man standing in front of him was struck to the ground by a Brownshirt[4] simply for not giving the Nazi salute.

PROLOGUE

This incident led Wolfe to resolve that, from that moment onwards, he would never again give the Nazi salute himself, and he managed to avoid doing so for the next three years – even on the many occasions he was in the Fuehrer's presence (see Chapter 31 note 1).

Having seen what was happening to Jews – including the confiscation of their properties and goods; the beatings and humiliations; the internments in ghettos and then concentration camps; and the disappearance of friends and family – Wolfe became an active member of an underground resistance movement and was involved in smuggling large amounts of money and endangered Jewish citizens out of Germany.

In 1936 Wolfe's life changed dramatically again. He met and fell in love with the woman who was to become his first wife – Baroness Maditta von Skrbensky. They were unable to marry in Germany (or elsewhere in Europe) because of Wolfe's non-Aryan ancestry. However, whilst on holiday in Italy the couple were befriended by a British Army officer, Major Humphrey Sykes (see Chapter 31 Note 2), who in April 1937 arranged for Wolfe and Maditta to travel to England and to be married at his home on the army base at Tidworth in Wiltshire.

On the day of his return to Germany Frank was tipped off, by a friend in the Gestapo, that he was about to be arrested the following morning and interned in Dachau concentration camp. Branded 'An enemy of the State, to be shot on sight' he escaped to Switzerland and then (following a cash advance from Humphrey Sykes) to England, leaving behind his bride of six days whom he did not see again for almost ten years.

Arriving in England without money and very few possessions, and unable to speak the language, Wolfe began to immediately and enthusiastically integrate himself into the British way of life. Within two years he had become: fluent in English; risen to the position of Managing Director of two of Sykes's companies; the producer of a West End musical; and an executive with a land corporation of Cape Canaveral, Florida.

In 1938, with the growing tensions in Europe, Frank was advised to somehow formerly disassociate himself from Germany. He did this by marching into the German Embassy in London and insulting Hitler 'with a list of unprintable adjectives' before spitting on a portrait of the Fuehrer. Shortly after he received notification that he had been deprived of his German citizenship as an individual who was 'Hostile to, and an enemy of, the National Socialist German Reich'.

For a short while life could not have been sweeter for Frank. He was officially 'Stateless,' fully established in England, an executive of several companies, had a new luxury apartment in London's exclusive Dolphin Square[5], rented a large house on the Thames[6] and owned his own narrow boat. He had friends in the highest circles of society, government and the theatre and was also in a long-term relationship with a beautiful actress and dancer, Patricia Leonard[7], who was destined to become one of the wealthiest women in the world.

In spite of all this, his known heroism as an underground resistance worker and his having been officially declared an enemy of the Third Reich, at the outbreak of the Second World War Frank was arrested, along with all other former German and Austrian citizens, and interned as an 'enemy alien'.

Having lost everything he had worked so hard for and furious at what the authorities had done to him Frank was determined to clear his name, gain his freedom and join the British Army. Within weeks of his detainment he was appointed Camp Leader (of nearly 2,000 men) and for the next several months he applied pressure on those commanding the various camps he was moved to whilst enlisting the help of Humphrey Sykes, other influential friends and Members of Parliament. Amongst those officers directly involved in his detainment was Sir Timothy Eden, brother of the then War Minister Sir Anthony Eden (who later became Prime Minister).

Frank's persistence eventually paid off and he was not only released, but he and a number of other internees were allowed to enlist in the British Army's Auxiliary Pioneer Corps[8]. Following twenty-three requests to be allowed to join a fighting unit he was transferred firstly to the Royal Armoured Corps and then, in December 1944, having gained a commission, to the Royal Northumberland Fusiliers which he joined as a Second Lieutenant.

During the remaining months of the war Frank distinguished himself in a number of roles and his linguistic skills came to the fore especially whilst training Belgian soldiers (in French) how to use the Vickers machine gun.

Following the Allies' victory in Europe Frank was appointed Staff Captain and instructed to join the British War Crimes Executive[9] where he was informed: 'This unit will be engaged in collecting material for the prosecution of the major war criminals. That's Goering and others, you know. We leave on Sunday'.

Frank was therefore involved with the BWCE from day one of its operations and he was given the very first piece of evidence to translate – Hitler's infamous *Nacht und Nebel* decree[10], which ordered the execution of Allied fliers.

The BWCE moved from London to Paris to Bad Oeynhausen near Hanover where Frank honed his skills as a translator, investigator and interrogator. This led to him being singled out as being an interpreter with exceptional skills and brought him to the attention of Colonel Leon Dostert, Head of the US Language Division who, at their first meeting, immediately had Frank transferred from the BWCE onto the US translating team for the Nuremberg Trials. This eventually led to Frank being appointed Chief Interpreter.

From being unable to speak English in 1937, by the time of the Nuremberg trials Frank was considered to be the finest interpreter in the world. He spoke and understood German better than most Germans did and he spoke English with the depth, clarity and diction of a highly educated British aristocrat. He was also a pioneer of simultaneous translation. First used at Nuremberg the system proved to be more successful than anyone had ever hoped.

Frank's contributions at Nuremberg (fully covered in *Nuremberg's Voice of Doom* – see Preface Note 4) were considered to be major factors in seeing that justice was fairly and meticulously interpreted and translated to all parties in a way that, it is said, shortened proceedings by an estimated three years.

Following the trials the *New York Herald Tribune* stated: 'Wolfe Frank, ex-German and ex-British officer, as chief interpreter for two years at the Nuremberg trials materially contributed to the practical success of those enormously difficult procedures. He won the unreserved tributes of the American and British jurists,' whilst the US Office of Chief Counsel for War Crimes wrote: 'Wolfe Frank … superlative scholarship and administrative assistance … and intellectual integrity … satisfactory alike to the bench, the defense and the prosecution'.

Frank left Nuremberg in November 1947 and spent some time in Switzerland and Paris as a journalist before setting up an import/export company in London.

However he was becoming increasingly concerned about the news coming out of Germany as he expresses in his memoirs:

• I had been involved in the writing of a chapter of human history that would be read, talked about and remembered forever. I had been more totally and decisively immersed in recording the horrors of the war than most of the millions who had fought in it. It had changed me.

• A lifetime is too short for such horrors to be filed away in the annals of history as something destined to be forgotten. As long as there are orphans who remember the extermination of their families, as long as there are men and women mentally or physically crippled by the faithful servants of Hitler's Third Reich, we should not afford ourselves the luxury of burying such ghastly memories.

• How could anyone report that most Germans had not known about Nazi crimes, concentration camps and atrocities?

Haunted by these thoughts and all he had witnessed during 'History's greatest trial' Frank knew he had to do something that foreign governments and journalists were unable to do – assume the identities, lifestyles and characteristics of typical Germans and conduct his own covert investigation and reveal to the world what was really happening in Germany and what had happened to the 2,000 Nazi war criminals whose names appeared on the Allies 'Wanted List'.

He came up with a plan of how that could be achieved:

Could I not go to Germany and gather material, covering a multitude of subjects that came to mind, and write about them? Who would sponsor such an enterprise? Who would print it? And how could I be both an investigator and appear not to be one?

PROLOGUE

What follows is the story of how Wolfe Frank risked his life again to achieve his objective and how this ultimately led to him becoming the Undercover Nazi Hunter.

Notes:

1. Wolfe was originally named Johann Wolfgang Frank, and then Hans Wolfgang Frank. He later became Hugh Wolfe Frank – the name under which he was granted British passports and, in 1948, British citizenship – however he preferred to be known as Wolfe Hugh Frank or just plain Wolfe Frank.

    His mother, a highly superstitious woman, informed him that he had actually been born on 13th of February but that she had persuaded the registrar to record the birth as having taken place on St Valentine's Day.

    In November 1945, as the foremost interpreter at the first, and major, Nuremberg trial of Nazi war criminals Frank was given the task of announcing the sentences of the International Military Tribunal to the defendants – Goering, et al. – and simultaneously to several hundred million radio listeners. This earned him the soubriquet 'The Voice of Doom'.

2. Grunewald Gymnasium, founded in 1903, was, during Wolfe Frank's time there, a grammar and boarding school for boys. Until the Nazis came to power in 1933 approximately one third of the pupils and many of the teaching staff were Jewish.

3. Having purchased and prepared a hand built 'Tracta' racing car that he described as being 'twenty years ahead of its time' Wolfe entered it in an important race on the rally circuit (the Kochelberg Hill-climb) only to lose the vehicle in dramatic circumstances. Coming out of a bend at full throttle he was forced to swerve to avoid one of Germany's top drivers, Ernst von Delius, who had stalled. Frank's car skidded but miraculously he survived. Frank writes of the incident: 'Somehow, I was thrown clear before my five hundred Marks disintegrated on the way down the mountainside. My racing career had lasted just three minutes twenty-three seconds and I had to pay 200 Marks to have the debris taken away. Tony [his business partner] cried for days'.

4. The Sturmabteilung (SA) – Storm Detachment – was the parliamentary wing of the Nazi Party. Its members were known as 'Brownshirts' because that was the colour of the uniform they wore.

5. Dolphin Square is a block of luxury flats, favoured by members of both Houses of Parliament and the Gentry, which were built between 1935-1937 near the River Thames in Pimlico.

the

PROLOGUE

6. *The House on the Creek* at Maidenhead.

7. Patricia Leonard was born in Fulham on 9 November 1914. Her father, Theodore, was an actor from South Africa and her mother, Elena, was a well-known opera singer from Australia. Patricia was a starlet at 17 and became a leading lady in many West End productions in the 1930s and during the war years including *Hi Diddle Diddle (1935)*, *Red Peppers (1938)*, *A Ship at Bay (1939)*, *The Little Dog Laughed (1939)*, *Scoop (1942)* and *I See a Dark Stranger (1946)*. Soon after the war she married the noted American philanthropist Francis Francis, heir to the Standard Oil fortune. The couple purchased Bird Cay, one of the Berry Islands, and transformed it into 'one of the most developed islands of the Bahamas'. They also had a home on Lake Geneva. Patricia retired from the stage in the late 1940s to raise a family and devoted much of her time to animal and children's charities. She died in 2008, aged 93.

8. Members of the Auxiliary Military Pioneer Corps performed a wide variety of tasks in all theatres of war ranging from handling all types of stores, laying prefabricated track on beaches and stretcher-bearing. They also worked on the construction of harbours, laid pipes under the ocean, constructed airfields and roads and erected bridges. (In 1940 the Corps' name was changed to the Pioneer Corps and, following the war, King George VI designated it to be the Royal Pioneer Corps).

9. The British delegation for the prosecution of Nazi war criminals was designated the British War Crimes Executive. Consisting of some 170 persons including: barristers; analysts; translators; secretaries; and typists; the BWCE was responsible for the British legal administration of the trials.

10. *Nacht und Nebel* (Night and Fog) was a decree, issued by Hitler in 1941, which dealt with the elimination of persons in occupied territories. Victims of the decree were said to have disappeared into the night and fog without a trace.

PART
ONE

PREPARATION

'The Germans are the most dangerous people in Europe.
I do not think two defeats have changed them much.'

*Field Marshal Lord Wavell, British wartime commander in
The Middle and Far East (later Viceroy of India) – November 1949.*

THE IDEA OF UNCOVERING
THE TRUTH ABOUT POST-WAR
GERMANY

OVER THE FIFTEEN-MONTH PERIOD following my retirement as
Chief Interpreter at the Nuremberg Trials (where in view of my
having announced the death sentences to the Nazi war criminals the
world media had dubbed me 'The Voice of Doom') I developed a
growing allergy to the kind of reporting that I had been reading on
Germany in the English and international press.

By early 1949 it had become blatantly obvious to me that we were
increasingly reading only what the Germans wanted us to read. Allied
journalists in Germany appeared to be relying more and more upon
what the Germans were telling them and less and less on what they
themselves were discovering, uncovering and observing. One reason
for this was that those reporters did not speak German – or not enough
of it.

How could so many journalists, for instance, record that most
Germans had not known about Nazi war crimes, concentration camps
or atrocities? And why were the Allies permitting so many Germans to
flee from the Russians in the East to the Western occupied zones? In
other words, why was the public not being provided with the true
scenario of the rapidly developing new, post-war Germany that now –
only four years after the end of WWII – was becoming a major feature
of the face of Western Europe.

An idea began to develop in my mind: could I not go to Germany
and gather material, covering a multitude of subjects and write a more
accurate account of what was happening? If I did, who would sponsor
such an enterprise? Who would print it? And how could I become an
investigator without appearing to be one?

A friend of mine knew Russell Hill of the *New York Herald Tribune* (*NYHT*) in Paris. We met and the three of us came up with a rough blueprint for such an enterprise.

I would approach Geoffrey Parsons Jr., the editor of the *NYHT European Edition* with the following project: I would assume the identity of a German and would go to Germany, equipped with the necessary (obviously false) documents, and I would go out in search of facts related to a range of subjects that the newspaper wanted covered.

This was, in fact, about all I put before Geoffrey Parsons Jr. when I met him at the *NYHT* offices in Rue de Berri, Paris. I liked Geoffrey at once. He was a quiet, thoughtful, exceptionally well-read man and he was totally aware of the situation about which I was concerned.

We began to put meat on the skeleton of my idea. False papers would be no problem – enough craftsmen were available at the *NYHT* who had practised the art of forging such papers during the occupation. Something would have to be leaked to the US Military in Germany since I wanted to be covered if the Germans caught me and put me in jail. Parsons knew General Huebner[1] well and an off-the-record arrangement was made whereby I had a contact in the US Army through which I could get myself fished out of any German prison. It was never needed – in fact I discovered an unbelievable lack of curiosity and interest in the identity of others among Germans.

The *NYHT* editorial team would make a list of subjects they wanted covered, but I would have a free hand to add to or omit from it. Once I had gone into Germany, I would cease to be Mr Hugh Wolfe Frank and would become Herr Hans Haag, who actually existed in Munich and who kindly contributed his driving licence to the enterprise for a consideration. The honourable forgers at the *Tribune* built all of my documentation around this driving licence, simply using my picture instead of Haag's, and I learned to imitate his signature, which was included on the licence.

Two questions had yet to be answered before we would sign on the dotted line: top management in New York would have to go along with the idea, and my wife Maxine[2] would have to put up with my being away for several months!

Notes:

1. Lieutenant General Clarence Ralph Huebner (1888 – 1972) was the last Military Governor (acting) of the American Zone in Germany. He held the post from May until September 1949.

2. Wolfe's second wife Maxine was an American actress who continued to use her maiden name – Cooper. She was born in Chicago in 1924 and studied theatre arts at the Pasadena Playhouse. Maxine travelled to Europe in 1946 to entertain US military troops, during which time she met and married Wolfe Frank. She stayed in Europe for five years working in the theatre and television and during this period, as her private letters attest, she and Wolfe were devoted to each other. The couple moved to the US in the early 1950s but divorced in 1952. Maxine continued to perform in the theatre and for US television and made her film debut in 1955 starring alongside Ralph Meeker in the film noir *Kiss Me, Deadly*. She later appeared in another movie classic of the period – *Whatever Happened to Baby Jane?* In 1957 she married Sy Gomberg, a screenwriter and producer, and retired from the acting profession in the early 1960s to raise a family. The couple remained married until Sy Gomberg's death in 2001. Maxine became well known as a photographer and as a Hollywood activist standing up for minority groups in the theatre and human rights and against nuclear weapons and the Vietnam War. Maxine Cooper Gomberg died, aged 84, in 2009. (Amongst its most notable alumni the Pasadena Playhouse lists such names as Raymond Burr, Victor Mature, Eleanor Parker, Tyrone Power, Robert Young, Charles Bronson, Gene Hackman, Dustin Hoffman … and Maxine Cooper Gomberg).

THE PROPOSAL

Editor: To assist in presenting the idea to the American executives of the *NYHT*, whose approval would be required to proceed with such a major project, an enthusiastic Geoffrey Parsons Jr. asked Wolfe Frank to provide a written proposal based on what they had discussed. Wolfe chose to do that by way of submitting the following communication addressed to Parsons and enclosing letters of support (also reproduced on the following pages) from:

The Rt Hon Sir David Maxwell Fyfe, KC, MP, *British Deputy Chief Attorney at the Nuremberg Trials*

Tim Holland Bennett, *Head of Casting at BBC Television*

Brigadier General Telford Taylor, *USA Chief of Counsel for War Crimes*

From: Wolfe Frank

To: Geoffrey Parsons Jr., *Editor, NYHT European Edition*

14 April 1949

Dear Mr Parsons

You may recall that we met in your office about a month ago when I made a proposition to you that I need not reiterate here since the material I am attaching to this letter covers it completely.

I had to delay my writing to you since certain business matters made it quite impossible for me to decide upon a period when I could possibly be absent from London for any length of time. These matters have now been cleared up and I will be in a position to leave London any time after 15 May.

Since talking to you in Paris I have, of course, given the matter considerable thought. The most serious problem would appear to be that once I am in Germany and have become a member of the German population I will have to account for my prolonged absence from that country. It would be no good posing as a returned prisoner of war. This would simply multiply the number of people who might find me out by the number of other ex-prisoners of war who were imprisoned under similar circumstances. In other words it would require a complete knowledge of units, locations, names of officers and so on and so forth, which it would take months to acquire.

To cut a long story short I propose to appear as a young man who, early in 1939, was sent to Switzerland with Tuberculosis. He went to Davos[1], a place known to all Germans, was still there requiring treatment when war broke out and who, being somewhat opposed to the Nazi Regime, had decided not to follow the call to arms of his Fatherland, but to stay on in Switzerland. When his lungs got better he took a job in a sports shop, and during the summer he worked as a keeper of the local tennis courts. In 1949 he got himself into trouble through doing a bit of black marketeering and the Swiss chucked him out of the country.

Having friends in Davos I shall be able to substantiate this tale with some testimonials and it has the advantage that I know conditions there so well that I could not be caught out by any questions. There will also, of course, be the necessary doctor's certificate showing that I was sent there in 1939.

I have also been able to arrange for a perfectly genuine set of German papers belonging to a friend of mine who is at present in England and who will let me have the use of his German documents – which he will report lost if necessary.

Furthermore, as there is a great deal of unemployment in Germany at this stage, I have seen to it that I will not lose too much time in obtaining work once I get there.

During our conversation you asked me for some proof of my integrity and for some evidence that I could write.

I have therefore discussed the scheme with Sir David Maxwell Fyfe[2] and asked him to give me a reference. He suggested that this would hardly be a case of a 'To whom it may Concern' letter, and he suggested that I should write him a letter to which he would reply. Copies of my letter to Sir David and his answer are enclosed.

I adopted the same procedure with Mr Tim Holland Bennett (head of casting at BBC Television) who was formerly a commentator with BBC *Radio Newsreel*[3] and as such reported on the Nuremberg Trials[4]. He later arranged for me to work for *Newsreel* as a Special Correspondent. His answer to my letter (which is similar to the one I sent to Sir David) is also enclosed.

5

Should you require an American reference then I would suggest General Telford Taylor[5] who may, as you said, impress your New York office. I do not know Taylor's address at the moment, but would obtain it quickly for you should you so require.

I also enclose a true translation of an article of mine in a Swiss newspaper, which, you will appreciate, loses some of its fluency through being translated, and a number of scripts I used for my broadcasts for *Radio Newsreel*. I am sure that you will appreciate that the *Newsreel* scripts in particular were designed to serve a definite tendency. A lot of people in this country, who had been appalled at the horror of the crimes which we had to deal with during the big trial, felt very strongly about the complete lack of interest on the part of the British and American public with regard to the Subsequent Proceedings[6]. My own point of view was that whilst the fanfares had stopped playing and the lights had been dimmed after the IMT, it was most important to give some publicity to the Subsequent Proceedings in order to show the depths to which the leadership towards crime of Goering et al. had penetrated. Perhaps you will concede me this point when you look at the amount of space given to the last Nuremberg verdict at this very moment. At any rate it was my job to get Nuremberg on the air and that was done with the broadcasts you will find enclosed.

For the rest I would draw your attention to the sentence in Sir David's letter in which he says: 'I also know that you have kept in touch with and studied the period of transition'. It would be from there that the series of articles under consideration would, of course, carry on.

I hope that the enclosed material will enable you to take the next step. I would suggest that there is a great deal of detail to be arranged and that it might be best if we discussed this in Paris. I shall be glad to come over to see you if this suits you.

Hoping to hear from you soon.

I remain,

Yours very sincerely,

Wolfe H. Frank

Wolfe Frank – Post-educational Background (1933–1949)

The arrival of the Nazis in Germany on the political scene forced me – being half Jewish – to abandon plans for a degree in engineering at Berlin Technical High School. I went into industry and began (in 1933 aged twenty) by taking a master mechanics degree at BMW in Munich.

After a brief apprenticeship with various sales organizations for motorcars in Munich, I became senior salesman, at the age of twenty-two, of a large garage and later took over the running of their service department and workshops. In this capacity I was in charge of more than twenty men and handled everything from accounts to repairs.

Meanwhile, in the summer of 1934, I became a member of a small anti-Nazi group in Munich and handled a total of three assignments for them: two transfers of funds to Switzerland and the removal of a 'wanted' person also to Switzerland. This entailed all necessary preparatory work right up to and including the three actual trips to Switzerland which, in each case, meant risk of life. Eventually, after leaving Germany, these activities were discovered and there was an order that I was to be shot on sight as being a 'highly dangerous individual'. I was deprived of my German citizenship in 1938 as being 'an enemy of the National Socialist Third Reich'.

A warning of impending arrest, which reached me on the 20th April 1937, four days after my first marriage, forced me to leave the country overnight and without funds. I arrived in England one month later but spoke no English worth mentioning.

After learning the language within six months, I joined a friend, Major Humphrey Sykes, in business. I held his Power of Attorney and first of all saved considerable funds for him from an ill-fated theatrical production (Kalman's *Countess Maritza*) by taking over the business management of the show and recasting it for production in London's West End.

I then acted as European representative of the Atlantic Peninsula Corporation of Titusville Florida, which was engaged in the construction of port facilities at Cape Canaveral, Florida. In this capacity I was mostly responsible for raising funds necessary to keep the project going in the US.

Simultaneously, I was appointed Managing Director of the Ace Sand and Gravel Company of London. This small business, consisting of no more than a hole in the ground when I took over, was making a loss by trying to sell building sand from a pit in Kent.

We made a careful study of the supply and demand position in England and it was found that our hope was to develop the sales of glass sand. We therefore developed methods of treating our sand to make it suitable for glass making and, at the outbreak of the war, were in the position to supply Britain's bottle glass industry with sand which was no longer available from its original sources in Belgium and Holland. The Ace Sand Company is the biggest business of its kind in Southern England today. While being in charge I was entirely responsible for running it and in charge of up to forty men and a quarter of a million dollars worth of equipment.

At the same time I started and ran – with Sykes' funds – a small and successful furniture factory which was forced to close down later due to timber shortage in England.

Having first volunteered for military service in England in 1939, I was nevertheless interned, together with all so-called 'enemy aliens' in June 1940. Six months later I was released to join the British Army. After making twenty-three applications for transfer from the non-combatant Military Pioneer Corps, I was finally transferred to the Royal Armoured Corps in June 1943. I passed out 6th best trainee in the history of my training regiment and was recommended for a commission. After passing through Officer Cadet Training Unit (OCTU) I was commissioned in the Royal Northumberland Fusiliers in December 1944. My first assignment was that of training a Belgian machine gun crew in handling the Vickers 303 Machine Gun. The language used was French.

Injured during training in February 1945, I was on sick leave until July of that year and then posted, with the rank of Staff Captain, to the British contingent at the Nuremberg War Crimes Trials. There I was assigned to the interpreting branch which was headed by Colonel Leon Dostert of the US Army. During the big trial I interpreted both from English into German and vice versa.

At the end of the international trial General Telford Taylor, in charge of the Subsequent Proceedings, hired me as chief interpreter for his organisation. I set up and ran the new interpreting branch as an employee of the US War Department. In this capacity I was in charge of all operations and a personnel of thirty-six interpreters.

At the same time, by arrangement with the BBC, I wrote and recorded twice weekly dispatches from the trials for the *Radio Newsreel* service of the BBC in English and wrote and broadcast similar dispatches for the BBC's German service.

From: Wolfe Frank

To: The Rt Hon Sir David Maxwell Fyfe, KC, MP

16 March 1949
(Similar letters were sent to Tim Holland Bennett and General Taylor).

Dear Sir David,

During a conversation I had with Mr Geoffrey Parsons, the Editor of the *European Edition of the New York Herald Tribune*, I proposed to him a plan that I hope will ultimately lead to a comprehensive series of articles on German affairs. Mr Parsons and I agreed that American journalists who are covering Germany, being recognizable as Allied reporters from the outset, are experiencing difficulties in probing into the minds of the German people. My proposition to the *NYHT* is that I should go to Germany where, equipped with a set of German papers, I would become a member of the German population and spend three to six months there working with Germans.

It is the intention of the *Herald Tribune* to clear this matter with General Clay[7] direct – who they thought would be very much in favour of the idea. I have not at this point gone into the question of clearing this matter with the British Zone since this is a matter to be left to the discretion of the editor of the *Tribune*, and will also depend on whether I extend my activities to the British zone of occupation.

I am supplying Mr Parsons with a selection of BBC broadcasting scripts, and a translation of an article I wrote on Nuremberg in the *Zurcher Zeitung*[8], which I think will prove that I can write. Furthermore, the BBC correspondent, with whom I collaborated in Nuremberg, will give his opinion on my journalistic abilities.

Mr Parsons would like to have some corroboration on my integrity in order to be able to take this plan up with the *Tribune's* New York offices and he suggested that I might obtain a letter from you.

I am hoping that during the time in which you have known me you may have been able to form an opinion as to whether I could carry out this assignment, and if that is so, I should be most grateful if you could write such a letter which I can pass on to Mr Parsons.

Yours sincerely,

Wolfe H. Frank

From: The Rt Hon Sir David Maxwell Fyfe, KC, MP

To: Wolfe Frank

17 March 1949

My dear Frank,

Thank you very much for your letter of the 16 March, which I have read with interest.

From my knowledge and daily experience of your performance as a most efficient and capable interpreter during the trial of the major Nazi War Criminals at Nuremberg, I know that you have a profound knowledge of the Nazi background of Germany, both from the historical and personal point of view. I also know that you have kept in touch with and scrutinised the period of transition. I have, therefore, no doubt that you would be able to carry out the scheme outlined in your letter with great ability, and I wish you luck if the proposition materialises.

With repeated good wishes to your wife and yourself,

Yours sincerely,

David Maxwell Fyfe

From: Tim Holland Bennett

To: Wolfe Frank

11 April 1949

My dear Wolfe,

Very many thanks for your letter of 8 April. I must say that I can think of nobody better fitted than yourself to undertake the assignment you mention. Although you were officially employed as an interpreter, I personally found your knowledge of Germany and the German people invaluable, particularly as you seemed to have a natural aptitude for realising the news value and journalistic possibilities of this knowledge. I certainly picked your brains in the most shameless manner and you introduced me to many aspects of life in Germany that would otherwise have passed me by.

Here's wishing you every success in your venture.

Yours sincerely,

Holland Bennett

From: Brigadier General Telford Taylor

To: Whom it May Concern

Mr Wolfe H. Frank was employed by the Office of Chief of Counsel as Chief of the Interpreting Branch from 7 October 1946 to 13 November 1947. During this period, I had frequent occasion to observe his work, including not only the interpreting work which he himself performed, but also the manner in which he supervised the approximately thirty-six interpreters who were under his supervision.

Mr Frank's performance was most excellent and, indeed, may be described as brilliant. He is an outstanding expert in not only simultaneous interpretation, but in the selection and training of interpreters for this very difficult work. I take great pleasure in recommending his performance and his abilities most highly.

Telford Taylor
Brigadier General, USA Chief of Counsel for War Crimes

Notes:

1. Davos, an Alpine town in Switzerland, was Wolfe Frank's favourite place, he loved skiing and visited Davos often over much of his lifetime. He eventually had homes there and following his death his ashes were taken to Davos and buried in his mother's grave.

2. Sir David Maxwell Fyfe (1900-1967) was a Member of Parliament, lawyer, and judge who variously held the offices of Solicitor General, Attorney General, Home Secretary and Lord High Chancellor. He later became the Earl of Kilmuir. At Nuremberg he was Britain's Deputy Chief Prosecutor and his cross-examination of Hermann Goering, which was translated by Wolfe Frank, is regarded as having been one of the most noted in history.

3. *Radio Newsreel* was a nightly half-hour programme broadcast by the BBC that featured political commentaries, eye-witness accounts and short talks.

4. The Nuremberg Trials were the military tribunals held by the Allied forces after the Second World War. The trials were the prosecution of prominent members of the political, military, judicial and economic leadership of Nazi Germany, who planned, carried out, or otherwise participated in the Holocaust and other war crimes. They were held within the Palace of Justice in Nuremberg, Germany. The first and most high profile of the trials were those of the major war criminals (Goering et al.). Held before the International Military Tribunal (IMT) – they were described as being 'the greatest trial in history' by Norman Birkett, one of the British judges who presided over them. Held between 20 November 1945 and 1 October 1946 the IMT tried twenty-four of the most important political and military leaders of the Third Reich.

5. Telford Taylor (1908-1998) was an assistant to Chief Counsel Robert Jackson at the IMT. In October 1946 he was promoted to Brigadier General and appointed Chief Counsel for the Subsequent Proceedings.

6. The 'Subsequent Trials' (ST) or more commonly 'Subsequent Proceedings' (SP) – formally the Trials of War Criminals before the Nuremberg Military Tribunals – were a series of twelve US military tribunals for war crimes against other members of the leadership of Nazi Germany. They were also held in the Palace of Justice.

7. General Lucius D. Clay (1898–1978) was the senior US Army officer responsible for the administration of occupied Germany after World War II.

8. *Zurcher Zeitung* (New Journal of Zurich) is a Swiss German-language daily newspaper.

THE DELIBERATIONS

Editor: ***The New York Herald Tribune*** was a newspaper published in New York. It came into being in 1924 when the *New York Tribune* acquired the *New York Herald.* The paper appeared daily until its closure in 1966 and during its lifetime won nine Pulitzer Prizes. From its inception, until 1958, the *NYHT* remained in the ownership of the Reid family and by 1949, when Wolfe Frank's German project was under consideration, Helen Rogers Reid was controlling the paper and her son Whitelaw 'Whitie' or 'Whitey' Reid was the editor.

The New York Herald Tribune European Edition was a separate English-language daily newspaper owned by the *NYHT* that was published in Paris. The paper became a mainstay of American expatriate culture in Europe, with Geoffrey Parsons Jr. as Editor at the time of the Wolfe Frank project. (Whilst the *NYHT European Edition* closed alongside the *NYHT* in 1966 this part of the Group's business was acquired, in a joint venture, by *The Washington Post* and *The New York Times* and continues today as *The New York Times International Edition*).

The New York Herald Tribune Syndicate was the Group's syndication service which sold-on features, comic strips and radio and television columns to media outlets across the world. The service was managed from New York by Buel Weare, with London based Patrick Thompson appointed as the Syndicate's 'World Representative (excluding the American Continent).'

Whilst Geoffrey Parsons had full control of all aspects of the *NYHT European Edition,* including editorial content, there was of course the closest possible working relationship between the two papers. Parsons' budgets were much more limited than those of the *NYHT* and Wolfe Frank indicates that the fees he received were, he believed, amongst the highest the paper had ever paid. It was natural therefore for Parsons to try to persuade his colleagues in New York to also publish the series and to pay for, or share, the up-front costs. He also needed the *NYHT Syndicate* to agree to sell the series to other publications to recoup the outlay and to hopefully show a profit for the Group. However, Parsons made it clear that as he was convinced the idea was a winner he was prepared, if necessary, to bear all the costs from within its own limited resources.

Geoffrey Parsons Jr. therefore forwarded the Wolfe Frank proposal to his executive colleagues in New York with a recommendation that the project should proceed as soon as possible. There then followed an intense period of discussions amongst the *NYHT's* top decision makers who included:

Whitelaw 'Whitie' Reid, Joint Owner, Editor, Vice President and later Chairman of the *NYHT*.

William E. 'Bill' Robinson, a *NYHT* executive, close friend of USA President Dwight Eisenhower and later president of Coca-Cola.

Buel F. Weare, *NYHT Syndicate* Group Manager.

C. Patrick Thompson, *NYHT Syndicate's* World Representative (excluding American Continent).

Walter Kerr, a senior *NYHT* correspondent and later a Pulitzer Prizewinner.

John T. Dema, *NYHT* Sales Director.

William H. Wise, *NYHT* General Manager.

Following publication of the *Hangover After Hitler* series of articles in the *NYHT* the whole file of the executives' internal and external correspondence concerning these matters was given to Wolfe Frank. Those communications, which make fascinating reading, are reproduced in chronological order (apart from the first two letters) on the following pages.

From: Geoffrey Parsons Jr., *Editor, NYHT European Edition*

To: Buel Weare, *NYHT Group Syndicate Business Manager, New York*

Paris: 9 May 1949 (printed out of chronological order for the sake of clarity)

Dear Buel

I think I've got a good idea for a feature for the early or late fall which, the way things are developing about Germany, may fall in a most timely way.

Briefly, it is this: Wolfe H. Frank, who was chief interpreter during the Nuremberg trials, an ex-German, fairly young, who is now a British citizen, came to Russell Hill and me, some time ago with a proposal. He suggested that neither the American military government nor the American correspondents in Germany had any true, inside, idea of what the Germans were really thinking because the Germans never really told them the truth. He has an idea that we are probably being taken in by what the Germans tell us. He suggested that he go into Germany, with German papers and work there for three to six months, in the American, the British and possibly the French zones, and then come out and write a series about 'What the Germans Really Think'. Frank is more than a superb interpreter. He has done considerable work for the BBC, has the highest British and American testimonials as to his personal character, and seems to me to be an extremely alert intelligent guy, with no very set political prejudices – except that he is not pro-German.

Pat Thompson thinks the idea has natural syndication possibilities, as do I. Our initial commitment need be next to nothing – a contract to split fifty-fifty all world syndication profits, after deduction of our expenses. The guy, once in Germany, will live on the Germany economy and will need no real money, if any. It is possible, since I believe he is married, that we might have to help his wife out in England while he is doing the job, but this would be a comparatively small advance.

I haven't found anyone who doesn't think this is a natural, and in addition a public service. My idea is that we should clear the project with the Allied Military Governments in advance, so that we can claim a certain amount of official backing, which would then in turn validate Frank's findings. Frank is an unusually brilliant guy, and naturally a lot depends on him, and how he does the job. Some of his recommendations, copies of which I enclose, as well as his latest letter to me, will give you a fill on his background. Talking to him on the telephone the other day, I asked him for a personal dossier on himself, which he had given me verbally when I first met him.

He is going to see Pat Thompson this week in London and is coming over to Paris the following weekend. If you and the rest of the people in New York approve the project, let's try and get him going as soon as possible.

I think we have an idea here and I believe we have the man to produce the goods, particularly if we can give him sufficient advance guidance, and we are in a position to do so. Among the inducements that we can hold out, of course, is the finding of an American publisher

15

for the book on his six months among the Heinies[5] that Frank wants to write out of the material he gathers for us.

Please let us know as rapidly as possible the New York reaction to this project. Walter Kerr, incidentally, will be over here in time to talk to Frank and give you additional impressions of the guy.

I gather from a letter my father wrote my mother, who is staying with us now, that you and he may be going to Cuba to see Hemingway[6] in June. May I reiterate what I emphasized in my letter on my own visit to Hemingway in Italy a few months ago, that you go armed with some good advice and dope on the tax situation, which may well prove vital.

Let me hear from you soon, Buel,

With very best wishes

Geoff

Memo from: C. Patrick Thompson, *World Representative NYHT Syndicate*

To: Geoffrey Parsons Jr., *Editor, New York Herald Tribune European Edition and*

   Buel Weare, *NYHT Group Syndicate Business Manager, New York*

London: c.12 May 1949 (printed out of chronological order for clarity)

Frank: German Project

1. All seem now agreed this is a good proposition if successfully realized.
2. I had a long and close talk with Frank at my Sussex place Sunday, 8 May, and am sure now his mind runs with ours: i.e., he knows as well as we do what is needed.
3. Buel had in mind the importance of briefing Frank on just what to look for, I had this in mind too. Frank knows what to look for, I believe, better than we do: he is a naturalized citizen: he knows Germany better than our people there do. But I think the point is to brief him on what editors, American especially, would want him to look for. The questions in their minds they would want answered. I explained this to him and stressed that this would enable him to 'target' his activities and reduce to a minimum his guesses of what we want especially.

Points that occurred to me and that I mentioned to him were:

(a) Check the student mind in a university city.
(b) Check the old-military-caste mind.

(c) Try and get to Kiel or some navy-tradition spot, or alongside the navy equivalent of the Junker[1], and find out what goes on inside that mind – are they dreaming of navies or snorkel fleets again?

He has various highlights in his own mind: among them, what has become of sundry Nazi-big-shot relatives and henchmen, what they're doing now. I told him you, Geoff, and Russell Hill, would brief him on questions that interest you, to which you'd like answers, and believe the public would like to know. Might be an idea to jot down a list.

4. I went over the writing-technique and presentation angles with him. He agrees that if what he writes on coming out does not seem to us to ring the bell, he will work over the stuff with us in the sort of editorial collaboration that Eisenhower[2] submitted to.

5. He plans a stay of about four months June-September. He would accumulate notes. He agrees it would he best to get the series done as soon as he gets out, and leave the book for later. I told him I thought a series about the Gunther *Inside Europe*[3] size, twelve pieces of 1,500 words each, would about do the trick; but that this was a personal view.

6. He broached the question of finance and I discussed this with him in a general way. He said he had mentioned to you, Geoff, or there had been mentioned, a $1,500 advance against ultimate proceeds. He had in mind taking care of his family expenses while away. His wife is a young actress who goes into a new play end of this month: but the play might fold: I mentioned that when we used Steinbeck[4] we put him on regular correspondent's pay, and the rest was speculation. Actually I think a $1,500 advance is reasonable if we go into this. Maybe we could arrange to send a monthly cheque to his wife. All this finance business is outside my province. But I'm sure enough that taking the pessimistic view, looking for something that falls far short of our expectations when we get it, we could do enough with the thing to get our money back, and then some. We know that the man himself has a powerful incentive to do an all-out, full-stretch job (he wants to make a name with this thing), and that he is a capable and highly intelligent guy, and very specially equipped for this job.

7. He might not come back; but that would be his and our bad luck. He wants insurance against death/accident. He has in mind that when he registers for work he may be sent to a coal mine. Not too safe.

8. He goes to Paris between 15–18 May for a talk with you, Geoff. As he wants to start in around 1 June it seems we must get down to business now, and reach decisions.

9. I don't know whether you have done any thinking about the specific agreement – presumably there will have to be one – but in case you have not, and I have after talking to you, Geoff, and Frank, I have

rough-drafted the heads of an agreement which may help if, as and when you have to get down to one. I have not shown this to Frank or mentioned a contract. Actually, the *Syndicate* may have a common form of agreement to cover projects of this kind, and a routine insurance; I wouldn't know. But I have a feeling that we should take care to set down clearly what this is all about; that we should limit our responsibility and liability; and that we should make sure that there is no chance of any material escaping us in any way before we get through with our syndication.

From: Buel Weare, *NYHT Group Syndicate Business Manager, New York*

To: C. Patrick Thompson, *World Representative NYHT Syndicate*

New York: 4 May 1949

Dear Pat:

Subject: "Inside Germany": Special Series Project

Thank you for your letter of April 25. This idea is a good one. In my opinion a successful realization of it in a series would sell widely in this country. I think we should be very careful, however, to brief Frank before he goes into Germany on just what to look for. This would have to be done by our most experienced people who know Germany, such as Marguerite Higgins, Russell Hill and others.

 I too hope this project works out,

Sincerely,

Buel Weare

From: C. Patrick Thompson, *World Representative NYHT Syndicate*

To: Geoffrey Parsons Jr., *Editor, New York Herald Tribune European Edition*

London: 13 May 1949

Dear Geoff,

Frank Project

I had further speech with Frank today. I told him that Walter Kerr would be in Paris, making a neat conference party for the briefing: you, Frank, Kerr, Hill. I have contributed all I can think of in this department. The story to a certain extent should tell itself; and while it's vital that Frank knows just what American editors want, I don't think we shall do much good and may do harm by over-briefing. I'd therefore suggest that you three Americans confer first and when you sit down with Frank, a German-Briton, a man who was 26 years a German, who was all through Nuremberg, and who knows his Germany and Germans better than we do, you should have a compact set of high-light directives, which should be useful to him, though maybe only as tentative targets to keep in mind; because the guy to a considerable extent is geographically limited and has to take many things as they come, and use his opportunities.

We checked the time factor, and it looks as though this would be something for mid-November, if all goes to plan. He thinks of coming out in October. It will add to the costs if he then has to sit down in Paris and get his stuff sorted, and written. We shall have to pay for his Paris keep. But if he comes back to London, there's no cost. I could be back to keep contact with him and look over his stuff at that time; and I could keep daily mailings of stuff and comments or notes going to you if necessary. Or when the whole series was roughed, he could hop to Paris for forty-eight hours, or you could hop to London. I think we should plan ahead on this, and that back-to-London is the logical thing.

On finance, checking your letter to Buel, and my earlier memo to you after talking to him, I sounded him out today, and this may suit everybody: Working on the basis of eighteen weeks in Germany, and a $1,500 advance-royalty being a reasonable risk in all the circumstances, pay his wife the dollar equivalent of ten pounds a week (say $40) in dollars in New York (she's an American and has an American bank account, I understand), and pay him the balance of $1,500 when he comes out of Germany and we have seen his material and know we can use it (or alternatively pay him the balance when he comes out of Germany, committing ourselves to the risk that he will do his stuff successfully, as I feel sure he will).

We may be able to work some sterling ultimately into the pay-off on his share of syndicate proceeds, since as a British citizen any dollars we pay him personally he has to turn over to the Treasury for conversion into sterling anyway. Such sterling payments will be useful to the syndicate, which has a problem relating to utilizing sterling. We need not discuss this latter point with Frank, I think, at this stage; we need not stipulate payment in dollars, except in so far as the weekly or monthly payments to his wife are concerned.

I can if you wish take care of this detail once I know what advance payment is agreed.

Frank may also be agreeable to taking francs for the French sale, against an equivalent dollar drawback on American sales. He would not have to pay British tax on francs paid to him in Paris: a considerable inducement. This again is a detail which need not be taken up until later.

I have told him we would help him find a publisher for the book in America. It might be a spring book proposition.

Yours,

Pat

From: Buel Weare, *NYHT Group Syndicate Business Manager*

To: C. Patrick Thompson, *World Representative (excl. Americas) NYHT Syndicate*

New York: 13 May 1949

Dear Pat:

Subject: Frank: German Project

Thank you for your memo on this subject which is undated but which we received on 12 May.

Please refer to your Paragraph 3. I have discussed this carefully with Walter Kerr and we are of the opinion that Frank, no matter how well-posted, will require substantial briefing by Russell Hill, Geoff Parsons and Walter Kerr before he goes. He will waste a lot of time and effort unless he has very clearly in mind just what the things are to look for. Luckily, Walter Kerr is starting for Paris on May 16 to attend the Council of Foreign Ministers so he will be able to talk the thing thoroughly out with Geoff Parsons.

As to the advance, we would like to keep it as reasonable as possible. I frankly do not believe we should go into the business of insuring his life. That's his lookout. If he wants to do something safe he'd better forget the newspaper business.

This morning I have a letter from Geoff Parsons dated May 9. This is the first we have on the project from Geoff but I have things started here through your latest report and through your letter of April 25. When Walter Kerr arrives in Paris the first of the week he'll have the full thinking here.

Sincerely,

Buel Weare

From: Buel Weare, *NYHT Group Syndicate Business Manager*

To: Geoffrey Parsons Jr., *Editor, NYHT European Edition*

New York: 16 May 1949

Dear Geoff,

Thank you for your letters of May 9 and May 12. About the proposed German feature by Wolfe H. Frank. By the time you get this letter Walter Kerr will be with you. He and I have talked about this from the start. I think this would be very good if properly done, but Walter has developed some considerable mental reservations which, I trust, you and he will go into thoroughly. If the project could be planned so that Walter's objections were overcome, I think we would have something.

Sincerely

Buel F. Weare

From: Geoffrey Parsons Jr., *Editor, NYHT European Edition*

To: William E. 'Bill' Robinson, *New York based NYHT executive*

Paris: 16 May 1949

Dear Bill,

I enclose a memo on a syndicate feature which we over here believe is sure fire. We need a quick decision on it, however, a decision within the next three or four days if we want to keep it to ourselves. I am sending copy of the memo also to Whitie, as well as the original to Buel.

This should be ready for in mid- or late November publication. I think it's a natural. Will you do what you can to get us a decision?

As ever,

Geoff

From: Geoffrey Parsons Jr., *Editor, NYHT European Edition*

To: Whitelaw 'Whitey (or Whitie)' Reid, *NYHT Editor and Vice President*

Paris: 26 May 1949

Dear Whitie,

I enclose a copy of a long letter I have just mailed to Buel Weare about this Frank German project that we over here have become very

21

interested in. The letter to Buel will, I hope, explain our feelings about it pretty completely. As I suggest, perhaps after you have talked it over in New York and if you are interested, but need some more answers, we can set up a phone call to talk about it. I hope you will show your copy of my letter to George Cornish[7], because I was unable to make a separate copy for him. I've been pretty much out of the office for over a week now, unfortunately, because of being sick. I'm feeling a little better this weekend and am taking advantage of it to get this off. Please tell your Mother that I will get after an answer to her letter tomorrow or the next day. Unfortunately, the decision on this German project must be made in the next few days so I had to get this done first.

We are all delighted that Big Bill is coming over for the annual meeting, but we wish you or Helen[8] could make the trip too.

Sincerely,

Geoff P. Jr.

From: Geoffrey Parsons Jr., *Editor, NYHT European Edition*

To: Buel Weare, *NYHT Group Syndicate Business Manager, New York*

Paris: 26 May 1949

Dear Buel,

I hope we can get a positive decision immediately to go ahead on the Frank project. The time is getting short. If we do not want to work with Frank, we must tell him so quickly so he can make a deal – as he undoubtedly can, and probably on better terms – with someone else.

It is very difficult to answer your doubts and queries about a project as novel as this one in a letter, particularly since I am not too sure what it is that may be worrying you people in New York. I will try, however, to make another pitch in this letter on behalf of this project and try to convince you. (I am sending copies to Whitie and to Bill Robinson).

Wolfe Frank has made two trips to Paris since I last wrote you, to talk to Walter Kerr, Russell Hill, and the rest of us here. All of us, including Walter, are very favorably impressed with Frank as an extremely intelligent guy, exceptionally well-equipped to embark on this job. Walter, however, remains considerably less sold on the project itself than the rest of us.

Walter's point of view, as he summed it up for me to pass on to you, is this: Frank is obviously a capable man. He is not against the project; neither is he for it, though he believes it has a better chance of producing a good story than another German series by Knop that has been under consideration by N.Y. What he would like to do is to arrange with Frank to do his series on the same basis as Knop apparently is going to do his, that is, the *Herald-Tribune* makes no commitment beyond agreeing to look at Knop's material when he comes out, and if it likes the material, will syndicate it on a fifty-fifty basis.

I pointed out to Walter that what Knop apparently proposes to do and what Frank proposes to do are not the same things at all; that Frank is going to try to do something that has not been done at all by anyone yet; that he is in almost a unique position because of his peculiar background and abilities to carry out the job; that what he proposes to do not only involves considerable personal risk to himself (of injury in a coal mine, of being beaten up by Germans if he makes a slip, or being beaten up by German police, etc.); and, finally, that Wolfe Frank could easily get someone else to back him in this project if we turn him down, and that the amount of money involved for us is small as compared with the potentialities.

Walter replied: okay then, let some book publisher give Frank a $5,000 advance, and we will make a deal with a publisher. My reply to this was that if we could get first rights and maintain complete control of the newspaper syndication for such a small initial outlay as we propose we would be stupid to tie ourselves to the timing and controls of a book publisher.

Walter also argued that any series would he difficult to sell, whether to George Cornish or to other editors throughout the country, owing to shortage of space, etc. My counter-argument was that the two people who knew more about selling features than he or I did, Buel Weare and Pat Thompson both agreed that the series was saleable. I also added that I had discussed in the project generally with Eve Curie[9], to test the reaction of a Paris editor, and she said that the series was a natural for her paper. I am sure this would be true generally in Europe. Walter agreed that he would have to bow to your judgment as to the syndication possibilities. My impression is that Walter came over here pretty much dead set against the Frank project, which he had first understood from Pat Thompson's letter to be for the Eastern Zone of Germany, and that he has now 'progressed' to a neutral position. I have been sick in bed with a bad cold and acute sinus for the past ten days which has prevented me from having further talks with Walter on the project. I have a lot of respect for Walter, but I believe he has some for me, and I am sure if we had been able to talk this project through he would become convinced as I am that this is an eminently good risk which we cannot afford to pass up.

So much for the negative side of the picture. On the plus side, we have the fact that Russell Hill, who knows Germany and the conditions of reporting what the Germans think in Germany, even better than Walter, is 100 percent sold not only on the essential validity of the basic conception of the project (which is to tap information not elsewhere or otherwise available), but on Frank's ability to do the job. Ned Russell[10] in London is also completely sold on Frank, as are Eric Hawkins[11] and Bill Wise. In fact, Wise says that if New York has no objections on policy grounds, the *European Edition* would be willing to finance the project if you are not willing. I mention this primarily to indicate the reaction of people on the scene over here.

Walter mentioned another objection which he said had been raised in New York. Supposing, he said, Frank discovers that our present conceptions of what the Germans believe and think are essentially correct, of what value then, he asked, would be the Frank series? On the other hand, he said, supposing Frank's findings are at great variance with our present conceptions, who is going to believe him? I do not think either case presents a problem for us, because they are based on a misconception of what we hope to get and of how it will be handled when we get it. (Walter asked Frank: 'What do you expect to find.' Frank replied, I think quite sensibly, 'If I thought I could tell you what I expect to find, you shouldn't send me to do the job').

The essential argument, it seems to me, is this. To a very large extent, Germany, and the Germans, hold the key not only to post-war Western Europe, but also to the balance of power between the East and the West. Inevitably, Germany, for many months and probably years, is going to play a crucial role in our efforts to reconstruct Europe and organize a peaceful world. It is extremely difficult to get at the truth in an occupied country (good example: the basic contradiction between the official British and American estimates of the extent of French resistance in 1942-43).

I mentioned our project to Foster Dulles[12] at a luncheon Ambassador Bruce was giving for Tom Dewey the other day (to which I took my wife and my sinus) and he said he couldn't imagine a more useful thing that the *Herald Tribune* could do. He said he had discussed with Clay[13] in New York last week this basic question of whether we knew what was in the mind of the Germans. He said he had pointed out to Clay that in as much as all the German officials in the Western Zones really owed their positions to the Allied military governments, that it was extremely doubtful whether it could be honestly said that they represented a true German point of view. He was sure, as I am, that no American correspondent, however well he knows the language nor however diligent, could ever get underneath the surface (Here is another point at which Walter and I disagree; he thinks our own correspondents might do the job).

I think you should know something about the work programme proposed by Frank. As you already know, he intends to enter Germany through Switzerland, picking up the necessary background papers in Davos, on his way through. He has friends near Berchtesgaden who will help him out with forged papers (probably at a cost of $150 to $200). He plans then to work in a factory in Stuttgart or Frankfurt for several weeks toughening up before moving into the Ruhr, where he plans to try to get assigned by the labour exchange to a mine. From there, he hopes to go to Hanover to work in the 'people's car' factory. This, he hears, is so completely dominated by Nazis that from the directors down to the sweepers, every single employee is a member of the Nazi Party. Before he is through he wants to put in a period in Berlin, in the Allied and Russian zones.

He is arranging with a friend in Military Government to act as custodian of his notes. Intra-German mail is not subject to censorship and he plans to write daily, or every other day, notes on his findings and adventures to this friend who will lock them up in a safe until Frank is ready to pull out. In this way he should have a mass of factual material, with names, places, dates, etc., which should answer the objection that Walter raised about his findings. I don't believe that we will find that Frank discovers we are all right or all wrong about Germans, but what he will produce will be important new evidence, so factually presented, that it cannot be disregarded, whether it confirms or contradicts present conceptions. Adding to the reader interest of it all, of course, will be his own personal adventure story of a man who becomes a German again. It might be compared with Ray Spiegel's excellent series on his voyage through the south as a Negro. This is the aspect that I haven't yet been able properly to explain to Kerr and the one on which the whole series has its great strength and value.

I think also we should take into consideration that we are not using an unknown ex-German for the job. He was the chief interpreter at the Nuremberg trials. He has the highest recommendations from top British and American officials. He is a British citizen and he is married to a young, Chicago-born American actress NOW playing in the London production of *The Male Animal*. (Can you imagine the Chicago Sun-Times turning down this series when they know Mrs Frank comes from Chicago and that her father is the General Electric distributor there?)

I enclose a rough draft of an agreement between the *NYHT* and Frank. It is based on an original draft by Pat Thompson, modified after my last two talks with Frank. It is not, of course, in legal form, but at least can give you a basis to go on. Pat told me on the phone the other day that you didn't like the insurance idea. The estimates on the cost of the insurance fall between $140 and $200. I suggest we add an extra $2,000 insurance to cover our investment, naming ourselves as beneficiaries. With the $1,500 advance royalties to Frank, the insurance, the expenses of his trips to Paris and his travelling expenses to Germany, plus something like $200 for his forged papers and starting money in Germany, our total investment should run to not over $2,100 or $2,200. It would include about $75 for me to go up to see General Huebner in Heidelberg and get the whole project cleared, so that they can bail Frank out of a German jail if he gets into trouble because of his papers. This sum would come out of the first amount realized by the syndication. The first $1,500 on top of the advance and the expenses would come to us. After that it would be a fifty-fifty split.

Will you please talk it over with the interested people in New York as soon as possible. If you have additional questions, let's set up a phone call and try to get the thing worked out.

With best regards,

Geoff

From: Geoffrey Parsons Jr., *Editor, NYHT European Edition*

To: C. Patrick Thompson, *World Representative NYHT Syndicate*

Paris: 26 May 1949

Dear Pat:

I have heard nothing further from New York about our German project so I'm writing Buel Weare today requesting immediate authority by cable to proceed along these lines:

1. We advance Wolfe Frank approximately $1,500 – in dollars or sterling or both – as an advance payment for world syndication rights for his series of up to fifteen articles on 'What the German Really Thinks Today' or whatever we plan to call the series. We would agree to divide the profits.

2. That in addition, we advance the comparatively small amount of funds he will need for his travelling and other expenses. (For example,

we agreed yesterday that he should go through Davos, Switzerland, on his way in order to complete his background papers). I should think those expenses can be held down to $300 or $400.

3. That we insure Frank, say to the end of this year for the pound equivalent of something like $25,000. Frank will look up the costs in London this week, but I doubt whether it will amount to very much. In all, I think we can assure New York that our initial investment will not exceed $2,000.

Finally, I will also write Buel that if New York decides it is not interested, the *European Edition* will gladly take the risk and advance the money itself.

Walter Kerr arrived by plane at noon yesterday and was really too tired yesterday afternoon to make a great deal of sense. However he had discussed the project with Buel at some length in NY and NY apparently is depending a good deal on his personal impression of Frank, which was excellent. I, naturally, will pass this on to Buel and try to get Walter to give me a memo to enclose. Hill is very much sold on the project.

Frank has to be in London tonight for the opening of his wife's play, but plans to come back Thursday or Friday night, if possible on our chartered plane, providing Selwyn Lezard can wangle a ride for him. Will you see what you can do to help? By then Walter Kerr, Hill, and I hope to have gotten down on paper the kind of things we think should be covered. I believe we are all pretty much in agreement on this but by setting them down, we are less likely to omit things we might discover belatedly.

Wolfe Frank is taking this memo to you himself.

All the best,

Geoff

Notes:

1. The Junker were members of the landed nobility in Prussia (parts of present day Germany, Poland, Russia, Lithuania, Denmark, Belgium and the Czech Republic). They owned great estates that were maintained and worked by peasants with few rights.

2. Dwight David 'Ike' Eisenhower (1890–1969) served as the Supreme Commander of the Allied Expeditionary Forces in Europe during World War II and then as Chief of Staff of the US Army. In 1953 he became the 34th President of the United States of America.

3. John Gunther (1901–1970) was an American journalist and author who was best known for a series of sociopolitical works known as the 'Inside' books including *Inside USA* and *Inside Europe*.

4. John Ernst Steinbeck, Jr. (1902–1968) was an American author whose works are considered to be classics of Western literature. He was awarded the Pulitzer Prize in 1939 for *The Grapes of Wrath* and in 1962 won the Nobel Prize for Literature.

5. A derogatory term used for German soldiers that originated in World War I.

6. Ernest Hemingway (1899–1961) was a highly acclaimed American novelist who won the Nobel Prize for Literature in 1954. Soon after the events here under discussion Hemingway's wife Mary was giving Wolfe Frank canasta lessons in Paris.

7. George Cornish was Managing Editor of *NYHT*.

8. Whitelaw Reid's mother Helen Rogers Reid – President of *NYHT*.

9. Eve Curie was co-editor of the French daily newspaper *Paris-Presse*.

10. Ned Russell was London Bureau Chief for *NYHT*

11. Eric Hawkins was a senior *NYHT* correspondent based in Paris and London.

12. John Foster Dulles was a US Senator who in 1953 became the 52nd United States Secretary of State.

13. General Lucius D. Clay (1878–1978) was the senior US Army officer responsible for the administration of occupied Germany after World War II.

APPROVAL AND AGREEMENT

Editor: Geoffrey Parsons Jr. in Paris was totally convinced that Wolfe Frank's idea was a good one and was bound to be a 'sure-fire' success. His colleagues in America however needed to be convinced. Parsons worked tirelessly in promoting the project and he was finally rewarded with the support of all concerned – as his notes clearly indicate:

We in the *European Edition* organisation thought it a good idea. Our New York colleagues were not so sure that a one-man expedition of this sort would be successful. But they agreed to support us and publish and syndicate what we got provided it turned out the way we thought it would given reasonable luck, plenty of hard work, constructive briefing, and all the rest that it would necessarily take at our end to make our enterprise a success.

The communications that follow detail and confirm the various agreements made between the interested parties.

From: Jon Dema, *NYHT Sales Director*

To: C. Patrick Thompson, *World Representative NYHT Syndicate*

New York: 24 May 1949

Dear Mr Thompson:

Today we received the following cable from you:

'Kerr approving Frank German project Parsons asks cable authorization to invest two thousand stop I think worthwhile but details agreement need careful watch'.

For your information, Mr. Weare is out of town and will return to the office on Tuesday, May 31. Concerning the Frank German project, Jack

Mearns today explained Buel Weare's absence to Geoffrey Parsons in Paris when he spoke to Geoff by telephone about the arrangement for the midnight file trial service. Mr Parsons informed Jack Mearns that he would airmail Mr Weare a letter tonight outlining the Frank project in detail so that Mr Weare would have the full information on his desk when he returns for his consideration and final approval.

I will attach your cablegram to Parson's letter when it is received here.

Sincerely,

John Dema

Memo: *Unsigned and Undated*

To: C. Patrick Thompson, *World Representative NYHT Syndicate*

Pat: Geoffrey says okay re Wolfe Frank – advance plane ticket for next week and any other expenses. Glad you got together. Please get in touch with him and tell him the fare etc. okayed.

Geoff is sending you copy of cable he's sent Bill Robinson today re a dinner last evening with the Duke of Windsor, re that question.

From: Geoffrey Parsons Jr., *Editor, NYHT European Edition*

To Whom it May Concern

Paris: 3 June 1949

Mr Wolfe H. FRANK has been engaged to do a special series of articles during the next six months for the New York Herald Tribune.

In order to carry out his assignment for this newspaper, it is essential that both our Paris and London offices be able to maintain adequate contact with Mr Frank at his home:

> Front Cottage
> 7 Addison Road
> London W. 14

Anything that can he done to expedite the installation of a telephone in his home would be greatly appreciated.

Geoffrey Parsons,

Editor

From: William H. Wise, *NYHT General Manager*

To: William E. 'Bill' Robinson, *NYHT executive*

Copy to: Geoffrey Parsons Jr., *Editor, NYHT European Edition*

3 June 1949

Dear Bill:

You have probably heard about the project to send an individual into Germany, working as a German, to determine just what the hell these people are thinking about. Last night, Geoffrey talked with Whitie, George and Buel on this subject, and stated that the *European Edition* would underwrite this speculative and potentially profitable operation. The costs involved will run to about $2,300.

Geoffrey reported that all were enthusiastic about the plan in New York, and credited us with the initiative, its development, and now its execution. I based the decision here on a very intimate knowledge of the situation, of the person involved, and on Pat Thompson's very conservative estimation as to the kind of money this story can bring back in Europe. If it is any sort of a job at all, we can come very close to getting it all back in the United Kingdom.

Therefore, we have obligated ourselves from Geoffrey's meager special feature budget in order to put this over. I must confess that I extracted one promise from Geoffrey, viz: that he do the re-write job himself, or allocate someone of very high talent to do the same. It seems to me that this is the kind of thing we should do in close collaboration with you, both administratively and editorially.

Sincerely,

William H. Wise

Memo on the Frank Trip: *Unattributed*

10 June 1949

1 – For the same reason that the best ex tempore speeches are the speeches that have been prepared the most carefully, so the finest series of articles is the series that has been most carefully prepared. To go off on an expedition with a mind that is too open is to come back with a wide variety of information that is difficult to handle.

2 – The thing to do is to start off with a clear conception of the objective, not knowing what you are going to find but knowing what you are looking for.

3 – In this case the idea is to penetrate the German mind, to find out what Germans really are thinking. It is sound to a limited extent but too limited for the reading public in the United States and Western Europe.

4 – I think we should plan a series of from six to eight articles of not more than 1,200 words apiece (1,000 is better). They should explore the six, seven or eight subjects that most interest Americans and Europeans, the whole built around the personal adventures of a former German who goes home, of a man who has worked and lived again as a German.

5 – I would guess that the current German mind should be no more than one of these subjects or at most the train of thought that knits together the whole.

6 – As for the remaining subjects the field is wide open, but I will suggest a number of possibilities. They are in fact nothing more than the questions that people ask themselves every day – the questions to which they want to know the answers, they are:

> A – The life of a German in 1949? Food, clothing, transport?
> B – What Germans are running the country? Who are they?
> C –Estimate of the occupation? Has it worked? Schools?
> D – A German looks at the Ruhr.
> E – The police system, the four freedoms[1], democracy?
> F – Former Nazis? Where are they now?
> G – Your personal experiences?
> H – The Communist Party in West Germany? Its raison d'etre?

Memo on the Frank Trip: *Unattributed (most probably Geoffrey Parsons Jr.)*

11 June 1949

I think it is important to have fairly specific objectives in view; otherwise Frank's findings will be too diffuse, too uncoordinated to be assembled into either a decently organized series of articles or a book. To make his one-man poll of German opinion more than just a series of unrelated interviews or impressions, Frank must get repeated reactions to a more or less constant series of questions. After a time, these reactions should begin to fall into a pattern which in turn begins to mean something.

What are the questions we want answered? Surely a central problem of the post-war world is the incorporation of an adequately prosperous

Germany – or Western Germany – into the economic and political framework of a peaceful Europe. The Germans, in the past, have thwarted or wrecked other attempts to maintain peace in Europe. They can probably do it again. It may be too early to make any judgment or even hazard any guess as to what direction Germany may move in, but for what it is worth, I think the specific questions should try to give clues to this direction.

Obviously, it would be interesting to know now, more than four years after the end of the war, how they feel about the war, about Hitler, and why they think they lost the war. Perhaps they don't even talk about it. Let's find out. What is their attitude toward war in general.

The Germans didn't waste much time in junking the Weimar Republic[2] after the last war. What is their attitude toward the Bonn Constitution[3], toward the elections (now scheduled for August 14), on ultimate unification, (are they more or less resigned to a divided Germany, or what?).

I think there should be one good article on young Germans; those who are twenty-one today were fifteen or sixteen when the war ended. Is there any noticeable difference in their thinking and attitudes with those of older Germans? Are they optimistic about the future, fatalistic, what?

Sex is more interesting to more people than anything else. What has happened to German morality since the war? People living in very crowded conditions, great movements of population, etc.; what has been the result of these conditions? (Here some actual statistics on crime, on marriages and births, may be obtained by Don Cook to buttress Frank's impressions).

How strong is the legacy of anti-Semitism?

I'd be interested if Frank runs into a single German who mentions the concentration camps or any sense of responsibility in connection with them or the war in general.

Germany was certainly a police state under Hitler. How are the police organized now? Are people aware of a change; have they any realization or being somewhat more free, even though occupied, to speak their minds, than they were before their defeat?

What is the attitude of the Germans toward their present political leaders who are doing business with the military governments? Will these men bear the stigma of collaborators with the enemy? Naturally, we would want something on the attitude toward the various occupying forces (what nicknames do they give them; what jokes do they tell on them, etc?).

From: William H. Wise, *NYHT General Manager*

To: Wolfe Frank

11 June 1949

Memorandum of Agreement and Understanding between the New York Herald Tribune S A and Mr Wolfe H Frank.

Dear Mr Frank

It is our understanding that you intend to enter Germany, and work there, operating on a plan of your own, in order to study what the average German in several social categories is thinking and saying, and other relevant data intended to reflect the true state of mind of the German national today. It is our understanding that, based upon this effort, you will obtain material for a series of articles to submit to the New York Herald Tribune S A, for a book, and for other purposes.

It is further our understanding that this is to be a personal enterprise of your own, working in close collaboration with this Company, with particular reference to the collection and the preparation of the material thus gathered. This Company is interested to the extent of having a first lien on the whole of the material gathered, for the purpose of obtaining and publishing a series of not less than eight, and not more than twenty articles. You will undertake to make no journalistic, radio, or other use whatsoever of the aforesaid material, or any part of it, until these articles are written to the satisfaction of this Company, and publication of them is completed by this Company. You agree to provide the finished articles specified above not later than one month after completing the mission in Germany.

In connection with the interests of this Company, it is understood that you agree to accept expert editorial assistance from us if such should be considered necessary by us.

In consideration thereof, we agree to advance to you the sum of $1,400[4], payable to your wife, in monthly installments of $350, the first payment to be made upon your arrival in Germany. In addition, we agree to advance up to $600 for travelling expenses and for insurance taken out on your behalf. After review of these articles in the event that this Company does not begin publication or syndication of these articles within thirty days after their completion, you will be freed of all obligations to the Company, and may attempt to dispose of the material elsewhere. In the event of successful disposal of the material elsewhere, you will agree to repay this Company the sum it will have expended directly up to the completion of the articles by you.

This total of $2,000 shall be recoverable by us as a first share on profits of syndication of the newspaper articles. Any additional costs over and above the sum specified must be approved by this Company, and such additional costs, if any, will be treated similarly to the $2,000 advance set forth herein. In addition to the sum directly expended, there shall also be charged against this project a reasonable sum for technical assistance in writing, which may be required to satisfy us before publication.

The proceeds of the sale of rights to newspapers and magazines, other than ourselves, and the New York Herald Tribune Inc. New York, which are covered by the payments described above, shall be charged fifty-fifty between you and ourselves, after repayment of the advance specified above and other costs of syndication.

The *New York Herald Tribune SA* agreed to attempt also the sale of the book rights on a world basis. On such rights sold, you will receive 75 per cent of the profits from such sales. The Company will have the exclusive right to such sale for 120 days after acceptance of the newspaper articles described above.

This Company shall not have any further responsibility or liability except as specified herewith.

Your signature to this letter will constitute our agreement.

Very truly yours,

William H Wise,

General Manager.

(The letter is countersigned by Wolfe Frank)

Notes:

1. The 'Four Freedoms' were goals that US President Franklin D. Roosevelt proposed ought to be enjoyed 'everywhere in the world' – they were: Freedom of Speech; Freedom of Worship; Freedom from Want; and Freedom from Fear.

2. The Weimar Republic was the unofficial designation given to the German State as it existed between 1919 and 1933. Many Germans blamed the Republic for

the country's defeat in World War I and for the humiliating terms of the Treaty of Versailles. It came to an end in 1933 when Adolf Hitler seized power and founded the single-party state that began the Nazi era.

3. The Bonn Constitution was 'The Basic Law for the Federal Republic of Germany' which was approved in Bonn on 8 May 1949.

4. $1,400 dollars in 1949 would be worth $14,000 in 2018.

PREPARATION AND ITINERARY

IDREW A PICTURE FOR GEOFFREY PARSONS of how I was planning to use existing connections in order to go about my task and from it he and his staff developed a list of headings I was to cover. I think there were seven or eight, but by the time I had become fully involved in covering them, more subjects of vital interest came up and the final number of articles was sixteen.

My first visit to the *NYHT* had taken place in April and Wolfe Frank left his home and a grieving wife in London early in June – to become Hans Haag in Germany shortly afterwards.

It had been agreed that I would not contact anyone in Paris except in an emergency and that no-one would be put into the possibly embarrassing position of knowing where I was and what I was doing – respectable enterprises of the international press do not, it seems, want to be caught sending out spies with phoney papers, even if the unofficial and tacit approval of a high ranking officer of an occupying power has been obtained.

I began living as a German on 14 June 1949 and continued to do so until October 1949 when I emerged with 50,000 words of notes. They could not be mailed to the *NYHT* so I posted them regularly to a lawyer friend of mine in Munich. I retrieved them at the sojourn and eventually transcribed them in Paris.

My notes on the subject say it all: Entered, as a businessman, with military entry permit No. P/69802 – at Basle. In order to provide convincing reasons for my absence from Germany during preceding years, testimonials had been obtained from Swiss friends showing that I had worked there as a mechanic and van driver from 1939 to 1946, but these were not needed at any time.

The route I travelled was: Frankfurt – Munich – Berchtesgaden – Landsberg – Berchtesgaden – Moschendorf Refugee Camp – Starnberg

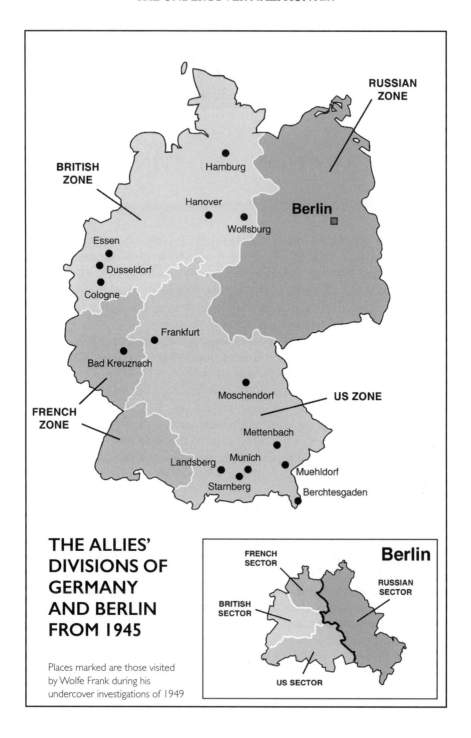

RUSSIAN ZONE

BRITISH ZONE

Hamburg

Hanover

Wolfsburg

Berlin

Essen

Dusseldorf

Cologne

Frankfurt

Bad Kreuznach

Moschendorf

US ZONE

FRENCH ZONE

Mettenbach

Landsberg Munich

Muehldorf

Starnberg

Berchtesgaden

THE ALLIES' DIVISIONS OF GERMANY AND BERLIN FROM 1945

Places marked are those visited by Wolfe Frank during his undercover investigations of 1949

Berlin

FRENCH SECTOR

RUSSIAN SECTOR

BRITISH SECTOR

US SECTOR

– Frankfurt – Hanover – Wolfsburg – Frankfurt – Hanover – Hamburg – Berlin – Bad Kreuznach –Duesseldorf – Essen – Cologne – Frankfurt – Munich – Berchtesgaden – Paris. A total of 3,000 miles, or so – not counting side trips.

The people along the road to whom I talked at length included the following:

Editor: This list, written immediately after his return to Paris in October 1949, records: those people Wolfe Frank interviewed during the months he spent undercover in Germany; where the interviews took place; and the subjects that were covered. The information contained within the square brackets [ ] has been added by me to clarify certain designations, situations and events for the benefit of the reader.

Alfred & Ruth Stoll, *Berchtesgaden*: They supplied all my clothes and arranged for all contacts along my entire route. Ruth Stoll, being related to Richard Schultz [Shultze or Shulze], who was sentenced to death and was awaiting execution, arranged for me to meet him in Landsberg Jail.

Kurt Haegerle, *Berchtesgaden:* Employed by the US Army to operate the lift at Hitler's *Eagles Nest* retreat [on Obersalzberg, a hill rising above Berchtesgaden in Bavaria]. He was formerly on Hermann Goering's personal staff and served Emmi Goering as major-domo [chief steward] and chauffeur.

A. J. Weinert, *Berchtesgaden:* Formerly Hitler's masseur.

Kurt Horchler, *Berchtesgaden:* Refugee Commissioner for the Berchtesgaden area.

Dr Wilhelm Schmidhuber, *Munich:* Portuguese Consul in Munich. Industrialist and banker, and a power within the Bavarian Party [a patriotic political party that advocated Bavarian independence within Europe]. Subjects discussed: Bavarian Party; the French; German politicians and German politics.

Dr Kurt Kolmsperger, *Munich:* Editor of the *Munich Merkur* [a Bavarian daily newspaper] and friend of Schmidhuber. Subjects discussed: As above, plus moral decline and religion.

39

Josef Berghaus, *Munich:* Brother of the well-known armament manufacturer who was then in Switzerland, Spain or Argentina [Bernard Berghaus was a Nazi party member who played an important role in the rearmament of Germany during the Third Reich and was, at the time, being sought by the Allies for using forced labour in his factories]. Subjects covered: black market; gambling.

Doris Haag, *Munich:* Wife of the owner of my [forged] papers, who was a former solo dancer at the Metropol Theatre, Berlin.

Beate Eberbach, *Munich:* Ballet dancer, sister-in-law of Albert Bormann – brother of Martin Bormann [Hitler's all-powerful 'fixer']. Subjects: Dr W. Meyer & De-Nazification [Allied initiative to rid Germany of all remnants of Nazism].

Helene Fischer, *Munich:* A chambermaid, refugee from Silesia and an expert border crosser.

Frau Inez Huebner, *Munich:* My Landlady in Munich who has an English mother and background. Subjects: the housewife's worries; pro-Semitism.

Herbert Wiessler, *Munich:* Formerly one of the kingpins of the Munich blackmarket.

Dr Theobald (Bonzo) Boehm, *Munich:* Solicitor and former member of the SS. Subjects: the SS; resistance groups, antagonism to which friends of occupation personnel are subjected; and other matters.

Herbert Hemmeter, *Munich:* Wealthy owner of Munich distillery, who had stayed for a lengthy period in the USA. Subjects: resurrection of Nationalism, despicable trends of German population.

Herbert Englehardt, *Munich*: Anti-Nazi of exceptionally high integrity; until recently a ministerialrat [ministry councillor] in the Bavarian Ministry for de-Nazification.

Fritz von Dessauer, *Munich:* In charge of cultural matters in Munich schools administration, including arts.

Dr A. Fingerle, *Munich:* School councillor, visited US, informant on all matters of school reconstruction.

Dr K. Ederer, *Munich:* School Councillor. Subjects: school reforms; religion.

Philipp Heilscher, *Munich:* Head of Fiscal Section, Munich Municipal Administration. Subject: currency reform.

Karl Heckner, *Berchtesgaden:* Head of Berchtesgaden Food Office. Silesian refugee. Subjects: food supplies, re-appearance of the Nazis.

Dr Fuchs, *Munich*: Member of the school administration system and my guide during my tour of Munich schools.

Professor Phillip Lersch, *Munich:* Head of the Psychological Institute of Munich University. Subjects: the university and students; school reform; psychology of Communism; reappearance of Nazis; morals; and others.

Dr Wilhelm Gillitzer, *Munich:* An official of the Bavarian Refugee Ministry.

Dr Adam, *Munich:* Under Secretary of State for refugee problems.

Dr E. Hagmann, *Munich:* Dr Adams's executive officer for Upper Bavaria.

Dr Georg Nentwig, *Munich:* Former German army judge; Silesian – my guide, in his capacity as official in refugee ministry, when I toured refugee camps.

Border Commissioner J. Mueller, *Moschendorf:* In charge of Moschendorf Refugee [formerly Concentration] Camp. A former Silesian industrialist.

Dr Peter Dietl, *Moschendorf:* Mueller's assistant.

Dr Weigl, *Kempfenhausen:* 'The Chief' of the group of educators responsible for school reform.

Count Roland Faber-Castell and Countess Nina, *Nuremberg:* Owner of the Faber-Castell pencil works. Subject: The threat of communism.

Dr Rudolf Diels, *Nuremberg:* First Chief of Prussian Gestapo, Government President of Cologne and Hanover, sentenced to death under Hitler, author of *Lucifer ante Portas*. [An important witness and an informant of Frank's during the Nuremberg Trials]. Subjects: team spirit among high former Nazis; the Argentine.

Richard Schultz, *Landsberg Jail:* Death candidate, subject to final approval, accused of putting the Fuehrer's order [killing of allied flyers] into effect.

Major Carol B. Hodges, *CIC Headquarters, Munich:* Contact supplied by CID HQ Heidelberg. Hodges is a psychiatrist by profession, holds a Munich doctor's degree. Subjects: my entire investigation.

Ernst Rosenow, *Munich:* Since the 1920s he has been the barman at the Munich Regina. Was suspected of being a Gestapo spy. Subjects: the slump in the entertainment world.

Edith Schultze-Westrum, *Munich:* Actress who got into trouble under the Nazis for living with a Jew. In trouble now for being married to a Nazi.

Heinz Ickrath, *Planegg:* Former banker and member of the resistance group with which I was connected. Sentenced to five years hard labour by the Nazis, caught tuberculosis in British POW camp.

Alfred Loritz, *Munich:* Leader of Bavarian Reconstruction Group.

Dr Martin Horn, *Munich:* Defence Counsel for Joachim von Ribbentrop [German Foreign Minister sentenced to death at Nuremberg]. Subject: politics.

Dr Alfred Seidl, *Munich:* Defended Rudolph Hess in Nuremberg [third most powerful Nazi under Hitler – sentenced to life imprisonment], due to defend Ilse Koch [known as 'The Bitch of Buchenwald' for her cruelty as wife of Karl-Otto Koch commandant of the Nazi concentration camp at Buchenwald].

Ernst Mueller-Meiningen, *Munich:* Editorial writer for *Sueddeutsche Zeitung* [one of the largest daily newspapers in Germany] and opponent of Minister of Justice Josef Mueller. Subject: the reluctance of the elite in Germany to participate in politics.

Gisela Petzl, *Munich:* A woman with nine husbands. Subject: the difficulty of finding a tenth.

Dr R. M. W. Kempner, *Frankfurt:* German public enemy Number One. [Kempner was a former German lawyer who became the US Assistant Chief Counsel at the Nuremberg IMT].

Clark Denney, *Frankfurt,* Head of legal section of JEIA [Joint Import-Export Agency]. Subjects: refugees and DPs [Displaced Persons].

? Watts, *Heidelberg:* British Liaison officer in *Heidelberg,* Subject: contacts with British Intelligence – warned me not to go to into the East [Russian] Zone of Berlin.

? Pulverkopp, *Frankfurt:* Owner of black market restaurant and uncrowned king of German black market. Subject: the technique of cigarette smuggling.

Dr Heinz Wendt, *Hanover:* VD [Venereal Disease] specialist and friend of Dr Diels. Appointed as my contact man by the latter. Collector of icons. Subject: icons.

Minister Gericke (Agriculture, Lower Saxony), *Hanover*: Subject: Germany and the Atlantic Pact [NATO].

Count E. Westarp, *Hanover:* Background politician, ex-SS member, questionnaire forger, in contact with British Political Intelligence. Subjects: the extermination of a German political elite; the lack of substance on the part of politicians today; and other subjects.

Professor Wilhelm Roepke, *Hanover (from Bern):* Formerly German – well-known economist. Subjects: Germany and the Atlantic Pact, the opening of a 'Second Front' in Europe's East [The Cold War].

Dr Hjalmar Schacht, *Hanover and Bleckede:* Subjects: Dr Hjalmar Schacht [acquitted at Nuremberg]; the Second Front; the refugee problem.

Senor (Herr) Kroenn, *(from Argentina):* Argentine President Juan Peron's envoy who had orders to collect Dr Schacht.

Waldemar Wappenhans, alias, Hans Seemann, *Hanover:* [As Wappenhans] he was an SS General, a former German WWI air force ace and Police and SS leader of Rovno and Brest-Litowsk. [As Seemann] he became Property Control Officer for British Military Government, Hanover. Subjects: Escapes and hiding; His memoirs.

Shirley Ventner, *(from Johannesburg):* A touring tennis player. Subject: the necessity of permitting German sports to return to the international field.

E. B. 'Crash' Abbott, British Military Governor, *Hanover:* Subjects: the entire field of my investigation; German right-wing politics; General Wappenhans.

General V. Minishky, *Hanover:* Formerly a general in the Soviet Socialist Army, later an inmate of Russian Slave Labour Camp. Subject: publication of his anti bolshevist book.

Herr and Frau Kaston, *Hanover:* My landlords. Musicians. Subjects: Kaston's experiences as a British POW; a German housewife's worries.

Heinz Nordhoff, [Managing Director of Volkswagen], *Wolfsburg:* Subjects: the Volkswagen plant, its past and its future prospects; Nordhoff's own interesting personal history.

Frl Loeffler, *Wolfsburg:* Nordhoff's secretary – hard to by-pass.

Helmuth Orlich, *Wolfsburg:* Chief of the inspection department of the Volkswagen plant. Engineering degree of Kiel University. Made arrangements to place me in various sections of the plant. Subjects: workers and their mentality; politics; the German people.

? Kuropp, *Wolfsburg:* First man with whom I worked at Volkswagen plant. Subjects: the Russians; politics; wages; quarters.

Delius, Schaceker, various drivers and one SA Officer with whom I worked subsequently at the Volkswagen plant. Subjects: local politics; anti-Semitism; the occupation.

Hillebrand and his Assistant, who ran the Army repair section at the Volkswagen plant reconditioning British vehicles. Subjects: the British; Communism; politics; anti-Semitism; etc.

Herr Beck, *Wolfsburg and Duesseldorf:* A commercial traveller. Subjects: concentration camps; the British.

Johannes and Otto Wischmann, *Hamburg:* Owners of old established Hamburg firm of cat-gut manufacturers – anti-Nazis, with sane views about anti-Semitism.

Hans Gechter, *Hamburg:* Manager of Messrs. Hinsch & Consorten's warehouse at Hamburg docks – they arranged for me to work there. Subjects: Hamburg and politics.

Nicolai Schmidt, *Hamburg:* Big time operator and now textile manufacturer. Subjects: black market in Russian held Berlin; morality; adventures with the Russians.

Karin Himboldt, *Hamburg:* Schmidt's wife, a film star who played the lead in *Tale of Five Cities.* Subject: films and the theatre.

Helmuth Bungardt, *Berlin:* Schmidt's partner in most major operations – my guide in Berlin.

Gisela Bungardt, *Berlin:* Helmuth Bungardt's wife, until recently Prima Ballerina of the Russian controlled Berlin Opera. Subjects: ballet in Germany; the special treatment the artists used to get from the Russians; black market.

Ursula Herking, *Hamburg:* Recognised star of post-war German cabaret. Supplied most of the material on post-war entertainment's shortcomings.

Anni Hoell, *Hamburg:* The owner of Hamburg's best-known artist's 'pension' [guesthouse].

Dr Laverkuehn and Dr Laternser, *Hamburg:* Both ex-Nuremberg defence counsels, now defending Manstein [Erich von Manstein, a prominent Nazi, was convicted of war crimes and sentenced to eighteen years in prison].

Colonel Gerald Draper, of the Irish Guards, *Hamburg:* Prosecuting counsel in Manstein trial. Subject: the mass extermination of children.

Elwyn Jones MP, *Hamburg:* Prosecuting Manstein. Subject: the trial.

Max Schmeling, *Hamburg:* Subjects: Max Schmeling [former World Heavyweight Boxing Champion] and his mink farm.

Dr Phil Werner Priebe, *Berlin:* The 79 year-old parson who confirmed me in 1927. Subjects: Religion; the Oxford Group [An American Christian group also known as MRA – Moral Re-Armament]; morals.

Dr Ernst Walther, *Berlin:* My history and German teacher. Subjects: schools; youth; education, anti-Semitism; morals; religion.

Lothar Schmid, *Berlin*: Wealthy car dealer. Protected his Jewish partner throughout Third Reich. Subjects: the coming war; escape to the Argentine.

Emi Schernick, *Berlin:* Now the owner of my father's former firm [Frankonia – a large engineering works based in Beierfeld that manufactured lamps, household goods and kitchen appliances]. Subject: the economic difficulties affecting Berlin firms in the West Sector who have to rely on trade with the Russian Zone.

Liselotte Sasse, *Berlin:* Wife of former DNB [German News Bureau] economic editor, now missing, in Russian hands. Subjects: her past; experiences with Russian soldiers; German men.

Ilse Ueberschaar, *Berlin:* Sister of my best school friend. Now blind. Subjects: rape by the Russians; loss of all personal property.

Fritz Wilhelm Benn, *Potsdam:* Announcer and script-writer for Russian controlled *Radio Potsdam*. Subjects: Russia and counter propaganda; the SED [Socialist Union Party of East Germany]; living conditions in the Russian Zone; rape of women; his role as a future agent on our side.

Five bachelors on an evening out, *Berlin:* Subjects: the Berlin Police; nightlife; black market.

Erna Sander, *Berlin:* Journalist and magistrate. Subjects: Berlin's position and fiscal troubles; her own story as an ex-party member and a half-Jew; the lack of firmness on the part of Western Powers in their dealings with the Soviets.

Michael Oppenheim, *Mainz:* One of fifty-eight surviving Mainz Jews. A civil servant (town administration) in charge of cultural matters. Subjects: the story of his own survival; French policy in Germany; anti-Semitism.

Josef Boeltes, his wife and Philip Schneider, *Bad Kreuznach:* Owners and members of a firm of wine merchants. Subjects: the history of the French occupation of Germany; the great progress made by their firm; their undeniable admiration for the French.

Ernst Liegel-Seitz, *Bad Kreuznach:* One of the owners of the Seitz works – manufacturers of wine-making machinery. Subjects: the occupation; French policy in Germany.

Annemarie Lohrer, *Bonn:* My guide through the Bundeshaus [Parliament House of the Federal Republic of Germany 1949 – 1999]. Subjects: gossip about the delegates.

Heinz Ehrlich, *Essen:* Road construction engineer, engaged on building ammunition depots for the British who arranged for contacts re dismantling.

Ernst Heinrichsbauer, his son and Herr Weber, *Essen:* Owners and manager of the firm dismantling the Thyssen plant and Ruhrchemie. Subject: all aspects of dismantling.

Dr Hille, *Munich:* Chief of Munich Labour Exchange, an old SPD [Social Democratic Party] man and an ex-Mayor of Saxony. Subjects: return of the Nazis; antagonism shown to their opponents.

Various other contacts that I interviewed (some of whom were aware of my identity and some who were not) included: customs officers; policemen; pupils in several schools; thirty chimney sweeps in a trade school; prostitutes; forty to fifty refugees in various camps; approximately ten newly returned POWs from Russia; hitchhikers and vagrants; drunks in pubs, inns and nightclubs; the unemployed outside a labour exchange; thirty-odd workers at the Volkswagen plant; guests on sidewalk cafes; fellow passengers in trains; Americans, British, French, Dutch and Belgian visitors to Germany. In other words, a fairly representative group from whom information was collected.

TRANSCRIBING, EDITING AND MARKETING

M Y TIME IN GERMANY WAS UP – a message came from Paris [in October 1949] to come back. I went to Munich, picked up my 50,000 words of notes and returned to Paris where the mountains of notes were transcribed and sorted out.

The series was born and the first article appeared on Monday 5 December and finished on 23 December.

From: Geoffrey Parsons Jr., *Editor, NYHT European Edition*

To: Buel Weare, *NYHT Group Syndicate Business Manager, New York*

Paris: 11 October 1949

Dear Buel

To keep you au courant on our projected series by Wolfe Frank, I have to report to you that he is due to arrive in Paris tomorrow. Our present schedule is that he will spend the next three or four days dictating his notes to one or two stenographers here. I will then take him down to my place in the country for the next couple of weeks and try to get into shape for publication the excellent material that he has accumulated. I went up to Frankfurt in August and spent two days with Frank going over the material, and on the whole, it lived up to expectations. Some of his pieces are complete entities, and will write themselves. Others are more complex and will take a good deal of work. Tentatively, at that time we outlined the following possible pieces in a series which we planned to run – from between twelve and fifteen articles. The order in which they are listed is not necessarily the order in which they should appear.

1. An outline of his project – the conditions under which he made it, etc. This might conceivably be done in a precede by us.

2. German Refugees from New Poland and Czechoslovakia.

3. De-Nazification.

4. The Hitler legend – pinned around an interview with Hitler's masseur.

5. A visit to the Landsberg camp [jail] for Nazis – the first by any newspaperman.

6. Children, schools, school reforms, etc.

7. Morality, Crime and Sex.

8. Anti-Semitism.

9. Games, entertainment and sport.

10. Working in the Volkswagen factory where he discovered an ex-SS General working for the British Intelligence [On Geoffrey Parson's typed copy Wolfe Frank has circled the words 'British Intelligence', doubled underlined 'Intelligence' and added in pen 'Ha-ha!'].

Since then, he has been to Hamburg, Berlin and The Ruhr. He operated partly under his own name and openly; partly with papers forged by ex-members of the French Resistance in Paris under a German pseudonym. Only once, he wrote me, was his story of how he happened to be in Germany challenged. Since I saw him, he has worked in a storehouse on the Hamburg docks for a while, and he was fired from that job at the request of the Workers' Council. Actually, this was the only case where anyone poked a nose into his background. Berlin, where he went to school and which he knows well, he feels is a good story for him, particularly since he got hold of a man who works the Russian-operated Potsdam radio. He has also been in the French Zone, and has been working this past week in the Ruhr. Our only worry is getting the material into proper shape, and I am confident that we can.

I see that we are starting our Asiatic series on the nineteenth of October. Joe Newman should have his series ready to begin around November first. I hope we will be ready to deliver to you about

November first Wolfe Frank's series which can follow after Newman's. During this next week I will try to get you a draft of an announcement of the Frank series with several suggested titles.

As soon as he arrives, we will work out a definite synopsis, and I will forward this to you. In any case, I see no reason why our early optimism about the possibilities of the project is not fully justified.

I'm sending a copy of this note, care of you, to Pat Thompson and another copy to Walter Kerr. Please let me hear of any suggestions you may have, or any additional information you may acquire.

With best regards,

G. Parsons

THE
'HANGOVER AFTER HITLER'
SERIES OF ARTICLES

'Every sentence, every term, every phrase, and even a great many hundreds of nouns and adjectives, had been checked on by more than one critical editorial mind, and not infrequently debated and argued with the patient Mr Frank and we were satisfied that we had done our job, discharged our responsibility, and played fair both with our own and all the other papers' reading public, and with Mr Frank'.

Geoffrey Parsons Jr.,
Editor of the New York Herald Tribune, European Edition, 1949

Editor: At the time Wolfe Frank wrote the following articles in 1949 he was unable or it was unsafe to disclose who many of those he mentions were and he has sometimes referred to them under unidentifiable names. However he did record many of their names, and other details about them, in his contemporaneous notes (see list in Chapter 5), and, once he was free to do so, in the further information he later included in his memoirs. Wherever possible I have therefore identified those to whom he refers and included their names in square brackets [ ].

THE *NYHT* INTRODUCTION TO THE SERIES

WHEN I RETURNED TO PARIS and the *Tribune* offices, in October 1949, 50,000 words of notes had to be sorted out, filtered and turned into newspaper articles. This was done in Geoffrey Parsons's delightful chateau near Paris and took many weeks.

Finally, a title had to be found for the series. It came to me, one Sunday morning, after the fourth of Geoff's superbly prepared dry martinis – 'Hangover After Hitler'.

The title page of the *European Edition, New York Herald Tribune*, No. 20,794 of Saturday 3 December 1949 bore my picture and ran the following introduction to the series:

HERALD TRIBUNE WILL PUBLISH *'HANGOVER AFTER HITLER'* SERIES

German-Born Briton Lived Four Months Under Cover in Native Land

The European Edition of the *New York Herald Tribune* announces the publication, beginning Monday, of a series of articles, entitled *Hangover After Hitler* by Wolfe Frank.

The writer of the articles, which deal with many of the major aspects of post-war Germany, was born in Germany and lived there until he was twenty-four years old, when he escaped arrest by the Gestapo by fleeing to Switzerland. He served in the British Army as an officer during the recent war and later became chief interpreter at the Nuremberg war-crimes trials.

From June until October of this year Mr Frank lived again as a German, worked as a German in many parts of the Western Zones and talked to Germans as a fellow German. As a result, he emerged with

50,000 words of notes on what Germans are saying when they are talking among themselves and not to impress Military Government officials or Western Allied correspondents. These notes form the basis of his series.

His fifteen [eventually sixteen] articles cover many important topics, including de-Nazification, anti-Semitism, sex and morals, entertainment, politics and the tremendous German refugee problem.

He uncloaked a 'wanted' SS (Elite Guard) officer who was working under an assumed name for the Western Allies and visited Landsberg prison as a 'relative' of a Nazi sentenced to death. He worked in the Volkswagen plant, and played the part of a refugee in a refugee camp.

Publication of this unusual survey of Germany today will begin on Monday. Readers are urged to reserve their copies of the *European Herald Tribune* immediately.

Elsewhere the *NYHT* published the following:

Wolfe Frank won the unreserved tributes of the American and British jurists at Nuremberg. The Office of Chief of Counsel for War Crimes[1] acknowledged their debt to him 'for superlative scholarship and administrative assistance … and intellectual integrity … satisfactory alike to the bench, the defence, and the prosecution.

Equipped with false papers to use if necessary, he [Wolfe Frank] sought objective answers to many questions – his enterprise was assisted by the *New York Herald Tribune* for these reasons:
- Misinformation about Germany has led to unpleasant surprises in the past.
- A true picture of Germany is elusive because Germans often present different aspects to 'outsiders.'
- A fresh appraisal of the German question could only be obtained by a German, and Mr Frank had all the exceptional qualifications necessary.

We believe that the result of five months 'undercover' work, told in human, factual terms, is an important contribution to one of the great key problems of the post-war world … and incidentally, it contains some unexpected revelations and dramatic surprises.

Synopsis of the Series

After World War I there were many illusions about Germany and the German mind. People thought that defeat had changed the German people. Many were convinced that the influential elements had modified their secret aspirations. The collapse of the Weimar Republic[2] and the rise of Nazism came as a shock and a surprise mainly because people outside Germany had been seeing only the mask which the Germans presented to them, and to visitors and foreign correspondents in Germany, and had failed to discern the true face and mind behind.

Since World War II ended one facet of this pattern has re-emerged. It has become apparent that there is a sharp line between what Germans say to foreigners and what they say among themselves. Helpful in the first occupation phase, the Germans are steadily tending to close their ranks; and consistently, when it suits them, they have two versions of their views – one for the Allies, and one for themselves.

For this unprejudiced factual survey Mr Frank used many of his pre-war connections, together with contacts he had made during the two years he occupied a post at Nuremberg which brought him alongside key Germans and gave him an insight into what lay back of the Nazi phenomenon. He worked as a German alongside Germans in Ruhr factories, on the Hamburg docks, in Berlin and elsewhere. Some of his investigations were aided by top German state officials; others, knowingly or unknowingly, by such persons as ex-SS members, Hitler's former masseur, Emmi Goering's former major-domo and chauffeur, Dr Schacht, armament industrialists, factory managers, foremen and workmen, prostitutes, Berlin entertainers, an SS general in hiding, black marketeers, housewives, lawyers, school-masters, university professors, parsons, food officials, refugee camp commanders, a former Gestapo chief, editors and writers, Jew survivors, customs officials, policemen, refugees in various camps, etc.

The general pattern of these investigations was set by the *Herald Tribune, European Edition* editors and *Herald Tribune* correspondents, with special knowledge of Germany, in conference with Mr Frank before he went into Germany. They were designed to provide objective answers to many questions which so far have remained unanswered or inadequately answered as for instance:

- Did anti-Semitism die with Hitler, or is it a real quirk of the Germanic mind?
- What is the real nature and extent of the problem of eleven million refugees in Germany, how does it affect German life, and are conditions in the refugee camps as terrible as we hear?
- Is it true that in some big industrial plants, such as the Volkswagen factory, a worker doesn't last long unless he has a Nazi party card?
- Is it true that many of the 2,000 Nazi VIPs on the 'Wanted' list are still at large in Germany, and if so how do they manage to hide their identities, and live?

- Is de-Nazification thorough or superficial, and do the Germans really help or hinder it?
- What do the Germans really think about the Nuremberg trials? And about Hitler, Goering, and the Buchenwald Bitch?[3]
- Is German sex life and morality really as demoralized, as a result of the three factors war-Nazism-occupation, as is reported?
- Is religion reviving or declining among the German people?
- Is the reported German resistance to arms plant dismantling effective, and if so how?

A one-man poll cannot of course be conclusive. But when conducted intensively by a scientific observer with the exceptional qualifications of Wolfe Frank it can turn a pencil flashlight on to dark places, help to confirm some things that had been only suspected, and occasionally bring some surprises – such as the relative ease with which one of the 2,000 still-missing Nazi VIPs covered his tracks and secured an influential job with the occupation authorities.

The main objective of the mission in Germany was to obtain an entirely new approach, a fresh appraisal of the German question; and the resultant highlights, constituting a summarized report in human terms, are presented as a useful contribution to the understanding of one of the great key problems of the post-war world.

Notes:

1. The Office of Chief of Counsel for War Crimes (OCCWC) was officially established in October 1946 and formally deactivated in June 1949. The OCCWC was the successor to the Subsequent Proceedings Division of the Office of the US Chief of Counsel for the Prosecution of Axis Criminality.

2. The Weimar Republic is an unofficial historical designation for the German State as it existed between 1919 and 1933. It was named after the city of Weimar where its constitutional assembly first took place.

3. Ilse Koch (1906-1967), known as the Buchenwald Bitch, was the wife of Karl-Otto Koch, commandant of the Nazi concentration camps Buchenwald and Majdanek. In 1947 she became one of the first prominent Nazis to be tried by the U.S. military. Her abuse of prisoners was described as being sadistic, and the image of her as 'the concentration camp murderess' was current in post-war German society. She was sentenced to life imprisonment. However, to the public's consternation, the term was later reduced to four years.

HANGOVER AFTER HITLER SERIES:
INTRODUCTION

Published Monday 5 December 1949

MY BRIEFING BEFORE I SET OUT for Germany last June was clear enough, but it presented me with a tall order.

'Find out what problems dominate life in Germany today', I was told. 'Find out what the Germans say about these problems when they are talking among themselves. Try to get at what their real attitudes are toward the major questions, the past and the future, the allies, de-Nazification, anti-Semitism, and so on.

'You make your own plans and work out your own programme. Go where you like, or where you can. Try to get back, whole, by mid-October'.

Since then I have spent nearly five months in the three occupied zones of Western Germany and in all the sectors of Berlin. I travelled more than 4,000 miles. I talked at length with hundreds of Germans, among them politicians and doctors, actors, industrialists, students, children, workers, housewives, artists, bankers, prostitutes, murderers, clergymen, Jews and SS men.

False Papers

My first step was to provide myself with documents which would permit me to move freely as a German. I obtained a German identity card and a driving license, both of which bore my photograph and a labour-registration slip. Former members of the French resistance in Paris helped me alter the documents so that they were able to pass inspection. They fixed my photos on the identity card and the driving licence and then affixed the proper rubber-stamp seal on top of the picture. They apologized because it took them several hours to find the right colour of ink.

'During our occupation by the Germans,' they said, 'we would have had the right colour readily available'.

I had certain misgivings regarding my documents. My age was given as forty-two, whereas I am thirty-six. My eyes were listed as grey-blue, but mine are brown. The fingerprints of course, weren't mine at all. I had practiced the signature of the original owner of the papers, but my efforts were not very convincing.

As it turned out, however, my qualms were superfluous. I passed road checks twice and even entered Landsberg jail with my borrowed papers. Nobody ever gave them more than a cursory glance.

As another precaution I had arranged an elaborate and 'provable' story of my background. I was worried lest someone become curious about where and what I had been doing during the war. I had worked out a story about having been exempted from military service because of tuberculosis and having been sent to Davos[1], in Switzerland, for a cure. According to my story, I had no great desire to return to Germany and be sent off to the Eastern Front after my cure and remained in Switzerland until this year. I had even supplied myself with references from Davos.

Assumed Roles

It turned out to be time wasted. I couldn't have told my story if I had wanted to. Everybody in Germany has a story, and people are so tired of hearing them that they have become completely incurious about each other. Furthermore, there has been such a tremendous influx of German refugees from the East – more than nine million – that a newcomer arouses no suspicion.

I had anticipated from the outset that the Germans from whom I could obtain information would fall into two main groups. The first would be old friends who knew me. But after spending two and a half years in Germany in the occupation forces and at Nuremberg, I knew I would have to treat what they told me with caution, for they would be inclined to adjust their sentiments for an outsider, however friendly.

The second group would be the Germans whom I could approach as a fellow German. I travelled roughly 80 per cent of the time as a German, 20 per cent under my own identity as a German-speaking British subject. To these two main sources of information there was added a third which I had not reckoned with in advance. These were German officials, refugee camp commandants, factory managers, who felt they had a case which needed only to be reported objectively to the outside world.

Worn Clothes

In order to assume the outward appearance of a German I needed a set of clothes, shirts, underwear, toilet articles and a suitcase, well-worn and recognizably German. I obtained these from friends in a small Bavarian village. Without the help of these friends the expedition would have been far more complicated.

Franz and his wife Regine [Alfred and Ruth Stoll] not only supplied me with the necessary equipment, but also with a long list of their friends all over Germany, who helped me directly or through further introductions in carrying out the mission. For many years Franz and Regine have kept their house open to a flow of visitors ranging from film stars to penniless travellers. Consequently, anyone coming from them was assured of a favourable reception. Their friends saved me an immense amount of time and effort. The journey took me from Munich to Frankfurt, Hanover, Hamburg, Berlin, Mainz, Dusseldorf, Essen, Cologne, and back to Frankfurt, with many intermediate stops and short trips. It covered the three Western zones of occupation and Berlin including the Russian sector.

Incuriosity

In the course of my travels, I assumed the role of a lecturer at schools, the relative of a condemned man in Landsberg jail, a German reporter, an unemployed worker, and a refugee from the Soviet Zone. I became a mechanic in the Volkswagen plant, an apprentice in a Hamburg warehouse and an applicant for dismantling work.

A large amount of information came from casual acquaintances in cafés, restaurants, dance-halls and cabarets, friends made on trains or hitch-hiking along the Autobahns.

At the end of each day I recorded my experiences and conversations. These notes amounted to over 50,000 words. They form the basis for the articles which follow.

[NYHT] Editor's Note on the Author

The European Edition of the New York Herald Tribune today publishes the first of a series of articles on post-war Germany by Wolfe Frank who was born in Germany and lived there until 1937, when he was twenty-four, and who became an officer in the British Army during the war and served as chief interpreter at the Nuremberg war-crimes trials. Mr Frank is now a British subject, married to a young American actress, the former Maxine Cooper, of Chicago.

Material for this unusual series, entitled 'Hangover After Hitler' was gathered by Mr. Frank during five months spent in Germany this summer and early fall. During the greater part of this period, Mr Frank lived again as a German, worked as a German, and talked to other Germans as one of their fellows.

He had suggested this project to the **Herald Tribune** last spring on the theory that in talking to Allied correspondents and Military Government officials the Germans frequently put on a quite different face from the one they wear among themselves. He pointed out that Germany is still an occupied country, that no formal peace treaty has yet been signed with the Germans, and that a useful journalistic service could be performed by a report which sought to go beneath the surface of the country which, for better or for worse, may hold the key to Europe's future.

Before Mr Frank was sent to Germany, his project was first cleared with the Allied Military Authorities in Western Germany. Though they are in no way responsible for his findings, his survey was made with their foreknowledge.

Mr Frank was born in Beierfeld, Saxony, Germany, Feb. 14. 1913. His father was head of a number of motor accessories, cutlery and enamelware factories. He was educated by private tutor in Berlin and in Munich. In 1934 while working in the sales department of a Munich automobile firm, he joined an anti-Hitler group which was particularly active in helping Jews and others pursued by the Nazi regime to escape to Switzerland. Warned of his imminent arrest by the Gestapo in April 1937, Frank, in turn, himself fled to Switzerland and eventually to England.

He entered business there, becoming managing director of two companies, which he continued to direct until June, 1940, when he was interned as an 'enemy alien.' After six months' internment, during a considerable period of which he ran a camp of 1,900 internees under British control[2], he was permitted to enlist, as a 'safe' alien in the military Pioneer Corps[3], he won transfer to the Royal Armoured Corps[4], where he was passed out sixth-best trainee in the history of the training center. He was accepted as an officer candidate, and in December 1944, became one of the first 'enemy aliens' to be regularly commissioned in a fighting unit of the British Army and was posted to the Royal Northumberland Fusiliers[5].

After the German surrender, he was assigned to the British War Crimes Executive[6] and in September 1945, went to Nuremberg with the rank of captain. He wound up, after his demobilization, as chief interpreter on the staff of the American chief of counsel for war crimes, Brigadier General Telford Taylor[7].

He married Miss Cooper in Nuremberg in February 1947 and after six months in Switzerland, returned to London. Mr. Frank was on leave of absence from his position as export adviser to a firm of London aircraft brokers while doing the research for this series.

The conclusions reached and opinions expressed in Mr Frank's articles are his own.

Notes:

1. Davos, an Alpine town in Switzerland, was Wolfe Frank's favourite place, he loved skiing and visited Davos often over much of his lifetime. He eventually had homes there and following his death his ashes were taken to Davos and buried in his mother's grave..

2. Wolfe Frank was 'Camp Leader' of the internees at several alien civilian internment camps including Southampton, Bury in Lancashire and Peel on the Isle of Man – a small, self contained, township that accommodated male internees only.

3. Members of the Auxiliary Military Pioneer Corps performed a wide variety of tasks in all theatres of war ranging from handling all types of stores, laying prefabricated track on beaches and stretcher-bearing. They also worked on the construction of harbours, laid pipes under the ocean, constructed airfields and roads and erected bridges. In 1940 the Corps' name was changed to the Pioneer Corps and, following the war, King George VI designated it to be the Royal Pioneer Corps.

4. In July 1943 Frank joined the Royal Armoured Corps Training Regiment at Farnborough in Hampshire.

5. Frank was commissioned in December 1944 as a Second Lieutenant in the Royal Northumberland Fusiliers.

6. In July 1945 Frank was informed 'you've just been posted to a thing called the British War Crimes Executive (BWCE) … the unit will be engaged in collecting material for the prosecution of the major war criminals. That's Goering and others, you know'.

7. Telford Taylor (1908-1998) was an assistant to Chief Counsel Robert Jackson at the IMT. In October 1946 he was promoted to Brigadier General and appointed Chief Counsel for the Subsequent Proceedings.

9

WHAT HAPPENED TO THE NAZIS?

Hangover After Hitler Series: Published Tuesday 6 December 1949

TODAY IN WEST GERMAN labour camps where convicted Nazis are doing time, guards are asking prisoners for certificates to show the guards have treated them well during their imprisonment. It is becoming more and more difficult to find prosecution witnesses in de-Nazification[1] cases. One of my friends who formerly worked for the Bavarian de-Nazification ministry remarked: 'It won't be long now before even the judges will be asking the accused for affidavits that the judges couldn't have been nicer or more lenient in handling their cases'.

From all the evidence I collected during my summer living as a German among Germans, the de-Nazification process has become worse than useless. It is now having results contrary to those intended. Obviously drastic changes in the whole de-Nazification programme, if not its complete abandonment, are inevitable in the near future. The East German Parliament[2] has already unanimously passed a law restoring full citizenship rights to ex-Nazis.

Except in Berlin, where the de-Nazification programme had been completed and superseded by such topics as the blockade, politics, and the proximity of the Red Army, de-Nazification was a favourite subject of conversation everywhere I travelled in Germany. The talk ran nearly always along the same lines, from which the following generalizations may safely be drawn:

1 – There is widespread disgust among Germans with the way the de-Nazification programme has worked out, with its creeping pace and uneven execution, with its inconsistent and often unjust results.

2 – There is no longer any opprobrium in the German mind connected with persons convicted or suspected of Nazi affiliations, except perhaps for top people blamed for losing the war or for the unpleasant consequences of Nazi atrocities.

3 – Real non-Nazis were so few, comparatively, and so unimportant in the life of the German community, that even with the Allies trying to help them win precedence in reorganizing Germany after the war, they were hopelessly unequal to the task.

Ex-Nazis in large numbers had to be called on to do the job.

4 – Although there is no real Nazi party today and no real Nazi leadership, there is a Nazi 'esprit de corps,' a solidarity that has been strengthened rather than weakened by the de-Nazification programme. There is evidence, as I shall point out later, that former members of the SS are regrouping, although at the moment primarily for social rather than political purposes.

A Hard Look

Now, obviously, it is not entirely to the point whether the Germans are satisfied with the way de-Nazification has worked out. A conquered nation cannot be expected to be wholly happy about measures imposed by the conquerors in an attempt to make its people peaceful members of the European community. But it is certainly high time, four and a half years after the war, to take a good, hard look at what these measures are accomplishing – or failing to accomplish.

I had an unusual opportunity to observe the early stages of the de-Nazification programme. The first de-Nazification court (Spruchkammer[3] No. 1) was established in Nuremberg, where it could have easy access to the war-crimes files in the Palace of Justice. After Franz von Papen[4] and Hans Fritzsche[5] were acquitted by the International Military Tribunal (see Plates 10,11 & 15) they became the first prominent Germans to be tried by German courts for their Nazi affiliations.

At the time, the president of the Nuremberg de-Nazification court, Dr Camille Sachs[6], came to me with a tale of woe about his difficulties with Alfred Loritz, then de-Nazification minister for Bavaria. Loritz insisted on an immediate trial and maximum sentences for Von Papen and Fritzsche over Dr Sachs's objections that they should be allowed a reasonable time to prepare their defence. I made a report to the American authorities suggesting that we could hardly hope the Germans would learn new standards of justice if ex-Nazis were given the same treatment in court that they had meted out when they were in power. Two American judges I took to sit in on the trial of Fritzsche expressed themselves as shocked at the proceedings.

This was one extreme. Even then de-Nazification trials ranged all the way to the other extreme. There was a Bavarian case in which the defendant was merely forbidden, during the next five years, from spreading National Socialist propaganda! Now, in 1949, early severity has given way to more lenient punishment for identical offences.

The Nazi of exceptional cunning who hid out or otherwise escaped early trial today gets a much better break. There is another source of injustice. A number of important Nazis were tried early, have already served their sentences and are today back in circulation. Meanwhile, tens of thousands of lesser fry, particularly in the civil-servant class, are still waiting their turn to be tried. Until they are tried, they are barred from returning to their jobs or from drawing pensions.

Nazis Judge Nazis

The fervour of anti-Nazi sentiment, fairly powerful in 1945, has become so dissipated that anti-Nazis with suggestions for improving the de-Nazification programme consider it unwise to make such suggestions publicly. The ex-Nazis and pro-Nazis are too well established in positions where they can be nasty again. One of my oldest Munich friends, till recently an official in the Bavarian de-Nazification ministry, was one stout anti-Nazi I encountered who had interesting comments to make on the programme.

'The original idea of assessing the degree of guilt of the active Nazis was good,' he told me, 'but it failed because, in order to put it into practice, we had to find people who could prove convincingly that they were not themselves Nazis.

'That was the first obstacle.

'Mere non-membership in certain Nazi organizations could never be proof that a man was not a Nazi ideologically, although it often was considered sufficient proof. A lot of undesirable elements crept into the de-Nazification ministries. Many were refugees from Eastern Germany. Their replies to questionnaires could not be checked. We would find, a little later, or sometimes a long time later, that we were actually employing members of the SS and other Nazi organizations to de-Nazify others.

'The inadequacy of the salaries paid to the staff of de-Nazification ministries left the staff wide open to bribes or favours. An investigator, for example, received only 200 Reichsmark[7] a month. Before the revaluation of the mark, that meant about $20 at the official rate, one dollar at the black rate or, roughly, two packs of cigarettes. Even the prosecutors, with 700 Reichsmarks, weren't much better off. Seven packages of cigarettes a month hardly represent a liveable income for a family'.

Bacon and Eggs

My friend, then, with a broad Bavarian dialect, re-enacted what he said might be a typical encounter between a rich farmer and a de-Nazification investigator.

'You from the ministry, eh?' asks the farmer, rubbing his hands together. 'Well, my friend, when did you last see a side of bacon? Not since 1939? We'll fix you up.

'Woman, get this man a side of bacon, two kilos of butter and three-dozen eggs! And now what did you want to see me about?'

The result of the investigation was a foregone conclusion.

'The next thing that went wrong,' said my friend, 'was that the Americans began to get fed up with the slow progress that was made. They wanted speed. Speed could be obtained only by sacrificing thoroughness and by generally relaxing the whole operation. The judges became more lenient. And the Nazis became cheekier. Witnesses became hard to find. Witnesses who had volunteered to testify in 1945 can't be dragged into court today, or if they arrive in court, they can't seem to remember a thing'.

The average Nazi appears in court with old clothes and a hard-luck story. My friend suggested that the only way to insure a proper trial would be to march defendants into court wearing the uniforms of the highest rank they attained, complete with all the decorations they were once so proud of. They should be made to salute the tribunal with a resounding 'Heil Hitler!'

'Then,' said my friend, 'you could be sure that they would get justice. The sentences would be a lot stiffer!'

Typical Failure

While passing through Munich, I came across a case of de-Nazification, which, I was told, typified the failure of the programme. It was the case of one Dr Waldemar Meyer, who had been chief of the Munich branch of the Adler Motor plant, where I once worked. Meyer, a loud-mouthed man, had become a member of the SS as early as 1934 and forced his unwilling son also to join.

Meyer's Nazi affiliation, and the anti-Semitic policies he maintained in the Adler plant, did not prevent him in 1934 from selling a large red convertible Adler car to a Jewish lawyer, Dr Friedl Strauss. Almost immediately thereafter Dr Strauss was sent to Dachau concentration camp – his story later became part of the Nuremberg trial record. Strauss's mother had been told that if she turned over to the Gestapo 'benevolent fund' of Munich all of her son's property, she would be able to retrieve him late one night outside of the Dachau barbed wire. Strauss was shot in the back as he tried to escape, according to instructions given him, and his mother died later in an insane asylum.

Meyer, meanwhile, remained in the SS, and the Adler works carried on. As late as April, 1945, Meyer, then an SS major, was leading a last-ditch convoy from Munich to Hamburg.

But it was not until last April [1949] that Dr Meyer finally appeared before a de-Natzification tribunal. He had spent a year in an internment camp in the British Zone, and then remained inconspicuous in Munich until things had quietened down. At what he considered a likely moment he turned in his de-Nazification questionnaire.

I managed to see his file (against regulations) and it suggests that Meyer had no records prior to 1939, except on the credit side. The prosecution never even asked for his police file. There was not a single compromising document or prosecution witness at his trial.

Instead, there were letters signed by officials of the Vatican to the effect that Meyer had gone to Rome in 1942 and had voiced protests against certain brutal aspects of Martin Bormann's policies. On a Vatican letterhead in his file appeared a statement that at one point Meyer had been earmarked for a post of special envoy.

The result was that SS Major Dr Waldemar Meyer was ruled a mere fellow traveller and was fined only 2,000 Deutsche Marks, about $500.

An old man I know who, it is true, joined the Nazi party in 1933, was barred from his job for more than four-and-a-half years, and used up his life savings and went into debt in the mean while. He was quickly de-Nazified when his case finally came up for consideration, but he considers that he paid far more heavily than Dr Meyer, and with far less reason.

Happy SS Rallies

I do not know whether Dr Meyer has joined one of the groups of former members of the SS that have been organized recently, but I know that those groups exist. I know, for example, that former SS men are approaching other SS members in the Munich area and urging them to attend meetings of their 'club'. The reunions are held in a villa near Feldafing, on Lake Starnberg, fifteen miles from Munich. For the moment, I was told, the emphasis is on reminiscences of the 'good old days'.

Another SS group meets regularly in the house of an elderly lady in Wiesbaden, also in the American Zone. She is the widow of a professional officer who fell in the German Army in World War I, and her two sons died in Hitler's army. She may merely be providing the innocent background for her SS visitors, but the chairman of the group is reported to be Radl, an Austrian and former adjutant of Otto Skorzeny[8], the rescuer of Mussolini, and kidnaper of the son of the Regent of Hungary.

These meetings were described to me as 'happy get-togethers of the veterans'. There is no evidence that, as yet, any attempt has been made to link up these groups, which may be presumed to be far more widespread than the two instances I know about. Linked together into a national organization, with aggressive leadership, they might easily become a political force to be reckoned with in Germany.

NYHT Reader's Comment:

Good and Bad Nazis?

To the Editor, European Edition, NYHT:-

The failure of the de-Nazification policy does not root in a German unwillingness to accuse the culprits. The causes of the failure originate in the Allied policy of assuming too much and not observing the real situation after the surrender. The bulk of the party members felt themselves liberated by the Allies and happy to escape an intolerable yoke. Remember the easy way the Allied forces went through the inner provinces of Germany after the crossing of the Rhine at Remagen! [see Chapter 24 Note 3].

The bulk of the party members was prepared and determined to give account of the many crimes of local and general party criminals. Look into the party programme. There is no word in it of concentration camps, of poisoning Jews and others, of burning and murder, of breaking windows. Until the summer of 1934 and the slaughter of Roehm and his followers there were even Storm Troop leaders, SA leaders who never allowed their men to sing those disgusting anti-Jewish songs pointing out the poor minority of 500,000 Jews against 70 million Germans and the nonsense of crying about them.

And now the de-Nazification laws.

The party members of 1937 and later were as good as wholly pardoned. The followers before that year, and especially those of 1933 and earlier, were overcharged. What an injustice! said the people. The man who joined after 1935 knew of the illegal brutality and so on, in most cases knew only a bit, but really enough, about Dachau. The man who joined in 1933 or before didn't know that he was being led into human darkness. Many of them objected, and never got party offices ...

FRANZ LEHNHOFF

Cologne-Sulz, Dec. 7.

Notes:

1. After the war the Allied Powers initiated a comprehensive 'de-Nazification' programme. Its purpose was to eradicate National Socialist thought from political, economic, intellectual and cultural life. Nazi laws were abolished and all signs and symbols of National Socialism were removed. The main focus of the programme was the systematic screening of all former members of the NSDAP – party membership was defined as the criteria for their dismissal from executive positions in industry and from public office.

2. The East German Parliament, officially the Parliament of the German Democratic Republic, existed from 1949 until 1990. It administered that section of Germany occupied by Soviet forces after WWII.

3. Spruchkammer was a court-like institution that was used for de-Nazification.

4. Franz von Papen (1879-1969) was a former Chancellor of Germany who stood trial at Nuremberg on two counts but was acquitted. It was Wolfe Frank who translated and announced the court's verdict to both Papen and Fritzsche (below).

5. Hans Fritzsche (1900-1953) was Head of Propaganda and was charged on three counts and acquitted. However he was later charged by a de-Nazification Court and sentenced to 9 years imprisonment. He died soon after release.

6. Camille Sachs was Secretary of State in the Bavarian Ministry.

7. The Reichsmark was the currency in Germany until June 1947 when it was replaced by the Deutsche Mark. Inflation had rendered the Reichsmark almost worthless and it was supplanted by a barter economy known as 'cigarette currency'.

8. Otto Skorzeny was a lieutenant colonel in the Waffen-SS who led an operation that liberated Italian dictator Benito Mussolini following his arrest and imprisonment by the Italian government.

HITLER, GOERING LIVE IN GERMAN MEMORY

Hangover After Hitler Series: Published Wednesday 7 December 1949

TWO DAYS AFTER I ARRIVED in my old home-town of Munich last June, I walked through the famous Odeonplatz, with its wrecks of buildings on all sides, to the newsstand on the corner of the Briennerstrasse. There I saw a sight which was to disturb and shock me each time I encountered it during the rest of my summer in Germany. The faces of all the top Nazis seemed to be staring at me from the covers or the German picture magazines. Hitler, Rommel[1], Himmler[2], Goebbels[3] and Goering[4] all appeared to have found their apotheosis in the illustrated weeklies strung about the newsstands.

Once the German editors discovered that the occupation authorities raised no objection to the publication of personal reminiscences about top-ranking Nazis, a veritable rash of memoirs broke out. Servants and relatives rushed to cash in on their connection with the Hitlerian hierarchy. Hitler's sister, Hitler's secretary, Goering's secret-police chief and Himmler's chauffeur were among those who were persuaded to tell inside stories about the private lives of these figures who were so well able to shield themselves from this sort of publicity while they were alive and in power. Now of course they were no longer around to suppress such stories or to insist on their own interpretation of the facts.

German readers seemed to lap up these revelations of the intimate lives, hitherto denied them, of the architects of their disaster. A little late, the Nazi leaders were being presented to their followers more or less as human beings. I could discover no earth-shaking new facts in these memoirs, but they certainly could be regarded as proof of a continuing and lively popular interest in the leaders whose promised 1,000-year Reich had foundered in twelve years.

'That Vegetarian'

The name of Hitler very rarely entered spontaneously into my hundreds of conversations with Germans this past five months. When occasionally I prodded the name of the Fuehrer into a conversation, the average reaction was that everything he did was fine up to 1939 and then the fool went and lost the war. I heard him referred to a number of times as 'that non-smoking vegetarian': seldom by any more derogatory epithet.

One fact that hit me in the face time after time as I talked to Germans was that of all the key Nazis, Reichsmarshall Hermann Goering today still retains the greatest hold on the admiration and affection of the German people. No one I met appeared to remember that Hitler on 23 April 1945 had shorn Goering of all his authority and denounced him as a traitor to the Third Reich[5].

I had got an insight into this development of a Goering legend just three years ago. On 15 October 1946, shortly before midnight, I had left the courthouse in Nuremberg with a feeling of some dissatisfaction because I had failed to get an assignment as interpreter for the hangings of Goering and the other war criminals. I had been the one to translate for them the words 'Death by hanging' fifteen days earlier when the sentence was pronounced, and I had rather expected to see the gruesome job through to the end.

At 6:45 the next morning, listening to a newscast of the American Forces Network. I heard 'Hermann Goering committed suicide in his cell by taking poison'. I dressed and hurried out of the Grand Hotel into the busy railroad station square to see what, the German reaction would be to this news. I grabbed the first German I bumped into and said: 'Have you heard – Goering committed suicide last night? They didn't hang him after all!'

'Did he really? Hermann? That's incredible!' For a second the man's eyes lit up. Then he checked himself and went on his way. I stopped a woman, and the reaction was the same.

Goering Legend

Now, after spending months among the Germans I think I understand why Goering holds this position. During his trial at Nuremberg, in his thirteen-hour speech in his own defence, he had restated without equivocation the whole Nazi philosophy which had been so widely accepted among the German people. The fact that he had not backed down and tried to change colours to save his skin and the fact that he

70

had contrived to cheat Germany's conquerors of carrying out their sentence on him had made a tremendous impression on many Germans.

Even if they could not all cash in by selling their memoirs and back-stairs gossip to the picture magazines, most of the servants and others who performed personal services for the top Nazis I found to have made their transition into the post-war period quite easily. Goering's valet, for example, works for the American Special Services in Bavaria and can sometimes be seen driving Frau Emmi Goering about in a borrowed car. I spent an evening in Berlin with the barman who officiated at the Nazi big wig parties, and I met Eva Braun's[6] hairdresser who is at work again in Berchtesgaden. In most cases, these people had little trouble getting de-Nazified (see chapter 9 Note 1). They had worked so close to the top figures in the Nazi party that they were never compelled formally to join any of the party organizations. The result was that their negative answers on the de-Nazification questionnaire automatically cleared them.

The Masseur's Tale

I found Hitler's masseur, A. J. Weinert, a good-looking fellow, working at the hospital at Reichenhall, twelve miles from Berchtesgaden. During the two hours that he pummelled me one day last summer he told me how he happened to go to work for Hitler and recounted the story of his last days with the Fuehrer in the famous bunker shelter under the Reichschancellery in Berlin.

The Germans have so overdone their efforts to reconstruct the private lives of their late Nazi leaders that the reminiscences of the survivors have become the target for cabaret jokesters. One satirical paper kidded the whole process with a story about 'a man who had talked with Blondi, Hitler's dog'. Nevertheless, the masseur's story, so far as I know hitherto unpublished, seems to me to deserve recording to help round out a picture. I noted it down immediately after my session with Weinert.

The masseur had first met Hitler during the 1936 Olympic Games in Berlin, while working for the German team. The chairman of the German Olympic Committee had presented Weinert to the Fuehrer at that time.

'Even back in 1936,' Weinert said, 'I was surprised at the contrast between the Hitler that existed in pictures and the real one in the flesh. He held himself badly and looked as if he took no exercise. But his very light blue eyes had a penetrating quality that impressed me deeply'.

In 1943, Weinert was serving as a non-commissioned officer in the army when his commanding officer told him that he was being transferred to Hitler's headquarters.

'Like most NCOs,' he said, 'I didn't like the idea of a top headquarters job at all. I had been trying to get a transfer to a base hospital in Berlin, but now there was nothing I could do about that.

'Off I went to Hitler's HQ, but I got there only after a lot of security nonsense, changing automobiles, riding with the curtains pulled down and so on. The first HQ I joined was at Rastenburg in East Prussia. Later I travelled everywhere with Hitler: to Russia, back to Rastenburg, to Berlin, to Berchtesgaden, and finally to the bunker in Berlin'.

Flabby Fuehrer

According to Weinert, it was Theodor Morell, Hitler's favourite doctor, generally regarded as a colossal quack, who was responsible for naming the masseur to work on Hitler.

'Morell advised me at the outset that Hitler had fired eight previous masseurs', Weinert told me, 'and Morell warned me that I had better make a success of the job.

Morell said Hitler needed massaging badly, since it was impossible to get him to take any exercise.

'I was promoted to the rank of temporary captain and saw Adolf the day after I arrived at his HQ. Hitler's memory was incredible: he remembered meeting me at the Olympic Games seven years earlier.

'We got along fine from the beginning. Sometimes he liked to talk. At other times he was gruff and kept his mouth shut. We never talked politics, which suited me fine, mostly just personal matters and trivial things'.

Weinert said that Hitler in 1943 was already in poor shape. He had sloping shoulders and a bad posture. He never walked a step if he could help it.

'He always looked unhealthy,' according to Weinert, 'with a pallid, sallow complexion. His features were flabby and got flabbier as time went on. As a rule, I massaged him frequently, though there were also fairly long intervals when I did not see him.

'I met everybody around headquarters of course and treated many of them. Martin Bormann[7] (who succeeded Rudolf Hess as Deputy Fuehrer) was one of my clients. He was a tough customer and hard to get along with. I always thought him a deep and sinister character. I am convinced, though I confess I lack evidence to support my conviction, that Bormann was in with the Russians and is in Russia today, together with Pilot Hans Bauer (for many years Hitler's personal air pilot and one of the "bunker party") who vanished as Berlin fell, at the same time as Bormann'.

Busy Bormann

Bormann had an amazing capacity for work, Weinert said, and he often operated on a schedule of twenty hours a day. He slept only three or four hours. He kept six secretaries hustling; not one of them was able to keep up the pace for more than six months. By the end, Weinert said, Bormann had extended his control into every sphere of the Nazi government, so that nothing was done without his knowledge and approval. Generally, he added, everyone at headquarters was afraid of Bormann and happy to stay out of his way.

'I also treated Keitel (Field Marshal Wilhelm Keitel, executed after the Nuremberg trials). In my opinion, he was the most responsible for our disaster. He never told Hitler the truth when things were going wrong. I've heard him say to his adjutant: "Now, remember, the Fuehrer must not hear of this" … which was typical of the way he operated. But it was Frau Keitel who wore the pants in that family. She controlled the field marshal completely. When I treated him for varicose veins, she arranged everything: time, treatment and so on, as if he had no responsibility of his own!'

Assassination Attempt

'I was at Hitler's Rastenburg headquarters', Weinert continued, 'at the time of the attempted assassination of 20 July 1944[8]. I must say I haven't much respect for the people who bungled that affair. If you plan to pull off something like that, you should go ahead boldly, prepared to go down the drain yourself. But Graf von Stauffenberg[9] wouldn't have it that way. He simply plonked the briefcase containing the bomb down on a chair in Hitler's conference room, and beat it.

'What happened next was miraculously lucky for Adolf. He somehow pushed the chair with the loaded briefcase on it under the heavy conference table and stood behind the chair while talking to the assembled group.

'At the moment the bomb exploded, Hitler's hand was outstretched over the table, making a gesture. The top of the table was blown upward, against his arm, which was badly sprained and bruised. But that was just about his only injury. By some freak, the main force of the explosion was directed away from Hitler and blew the legs off some of the people who were standing on the other side of the table. Four people were killed in the explosion.

'I saw Adolf less than five minutes after it happened. His trousers hung in shreds. In fact, all the horizontal threads seemed to have been blown away, leaving only the vertical ones hanging down. He controlled himself pretty well, I must admit, under the circumstance. He sat on the couch and laughed and laughed for quite a long time. And he kept slapping his thigh with his uninjured arm as he laughed. All his entourage crowded around to tell him he had been saved by an act of God. He seemed to believe it ...

'I stayed with Hitler until we got to the bunker in the Reichschancellery in Berlin. I shall never be able to forget that experience. Eva Braun had arrived in Berlin in March. There had been some talk of my massaging her, but Adolf vetoed it: jealous scruples, I suppose.

'I had always imagined that she was running around with him for financial gain and prestige, but I changed my mind when we were all together living in the cramped and crowded quarters of the bunker.

'It was she who eventually persuaded Hitler to put an end to it all, Adolf was still listening to those around him, like Goebbels, who kept telling him he could still win. If Eva hadn't worked on him and persuaded him that all was finished, they might have persuaded him to bail out and carry on from somewhere else'.

Eva Braun

The masseur said that it was about the date of Hitler's birthday, 20 April, that Eva Braun finally won Hitler over to suicide. He said that from that date on there was a great deal of talk of suicide in the bunker, where most of Hitler's immediate court shared one big communal room, adjoining Adolf and Eva's private suite. At that time the Red Army was directly threatening Berlin.

'By then,' said Weinert, 'Adolf was the most horrible sight I ever hope to see. He walked without lifting his feet off the ground and his whole body seemed to he made of jelly. The features of his face had sagged monstrously, and his mouth seemed to droop open all the time. His voice was hoarse and his speech blurred.

'You see, in those few days he realized that not only had he lost the war and driven Germany into disaster, but – and I think this was the worst blow – he realized also that nearly all the people whom he had trusted had turned against him or deserted him.

'He used to rave a lot about those who had proved unfaithful and he would order executions. Some, like that of his brother-in-law, Fegelein[10],

74

who was married to a sister of Eva Braun's, were actually carried out. (Fegelein was shot in the garden directly above the bunker). Other executions ordered, like that of Goering, were not carried out.

'During his last few days in the bunker, before I left, he used to invite members of his staff to drink and be merry while the world collapsed. By that time, arrangements had been made to evacuate a number of persons from the bunker, and my orders were to take all the women out excepting, of course, those like Eva Braun and Frau Goebbels who were parties to the suicide pact.

'On 24 April I was ordered to get aboard a Condor twenty-two-seater transport plane at Tempelhof Field. It was one of the last planes to take off from Tempelhof before the Russians arrived. When I climbed into the plane I found it full of quite unimportant people and no women. Our undercarriage was shot off by Russian ack-ack shortly after our take-off. We were headed for Berchtesgaden, but we ran out of gas over Munich, and our pilot put us down there with a perfect belly landing'.

Weinert then made his way to Berchtesgaden, mainly on foot, only to run into an accusation of desertion when he reported to the officer in command there.

Communications with Berlin were cut, said Weinert, and there was no way of confirming his orders. He was told to get back to Berlin, and he set off for Munich.

'I kept praying,' he told me, 'that Hitler's suicide would quickly become a reality. I certainly had no desire to return to that hell in that bunker. In Munich, I found all flying had stopped, and soon afterward, during a brief spell when radio communications were re-established with Berlin, I heard that Hitler had finally killed himself'.

Added footnote: In view of the countless reports of Hitler's last days I quote the masseur, A.J. Weinert, without comment, except that he supplied so many details he could not have invented it all. Nor had the accounts of Hitler's last days then appeared. He was quite happy for me to take notes because, it seemed, I was the first person who had wanted to hear his story – my fellow historians seemed to have missed out on him.

Notes:

1. Erwin Rommel (1891–1944), popularly known as the Desert Fox, was a German general who earned a strong reputation for chivalry amongst the Allies. Implicated in the plot to kill Hitler, the Fuehrer gave him the choice of

committing suicide and keeping his family alive and his reputation intact or facing a trial that would result in disgrace and execution. He chose the former and committed suicide by using a cyanide capsule.

2. Heinrich Himmler (1900–1945) was Reichsfuhrer-SS, Chief of German Police, Director of the Reich Main Security Office and Minister of the Interior. Arrested by British forces in 1945 he committed suicide (see Plates 3, 6 & 15).

3. Paul Joseph Goebbels (1897–1945) was the Nazi Reich Minister for Propaganda and a leading advocate for the extermination of Jews in the Holocaust. Goebbels succeeded Hitler as Chancellor of Germany on 30 April 1945. The following day he and his wife committed suicide after poisoning their six children with cyanide.

4. Hermann Wilhelm Goering (1893–1946) was President of the Reichstag, Vice-Chancellor of Germany and Hitler's designated deputy and successor. Convicted of war crimes and crimes against humanity at Nuremberg he was sentenced to death by hanging, but committed suicide the night before his scheduled execution (see Plates 3, 6, 8, 10 & 11).

5. The Third Reich (Realm) is the name given to that period of German history under the dictatorship of Adolf Hitler through the Nazi Party (1933–1945). The First Reich was the period known as the Holy Roman Empire (962–1806) and the Second Reich the German Empire (1871–1918).

6. Eva Braun (1912–1945) was Hitler's long time partner and his wife for less than two days. They committed suicide together in a bunker in Berlin on 30 April 1945.

7. Martin Bormann (1900-1945): was Deputy Leader of the Nazi Party and was found guilty in absentia of War Crimes and Crimes against Humanity at Nuremberg and sentenced to death by hanging. However it was later established that he had died trying to flee the Allies after Hitler's suicide in May 1945.

8. On 20 July 1944 a plot by senior German military officials to murder Adolf Hitler and take control of his government failed when a bomb planted in a briefcase went off but did not kill the Nazi leader. Hundreds of people thought to be involved in the conspiracy were arrested and brought before the Nazi People's Court – around 200 were executed.

9. Claus Philipp Maria Schenk Graf von Stauffenberg (1907–1944) was a colonel in the Wehrmacht (unified forces of Nazi Germany) and a leading member of the failed assassination attempt on Hitler's life. He was executed by firing squad shortly afterwards.

10. Hans Otto Fegelein (1906–1945) was a commander in the Waffen-SS. He was shot for desertion two days before Hitler's suicide.

NAZIS KEEP UP MORALE IN PRISON

Hangover After Hitler Series: Published Thursday 8 December 1949

CHILDREN IN THE PICTURESQUE BAVARIAN TOWN OF LANDSBERG are playing a new game. They call it *haengerles* – the hanging game. They know that in the prison[1] nearby, where Hitler did time after the unsuccessful 1923 putsch[2], hundreds of men have been hanged by the Americans for their crimes against humanity. Daily they can see the labour squads of prisoners march through the town to their places of work.

But there are prisoners, those who wear dark-red jackets, who never leave the prison building. They are the men waiting to be hanged.

A few of them have been waiting in solitary confinement for as much as two years. Yet by letters and other means they have made their influence felt beyond the prison walls – sometimes even after death. The man I visited in the jail [now known to have been Richard Schulz or Schulze] had once been on his way to the gallows when his execution was postponed. Friends of his had shown me a letter he had written a few days before the rope was to be placed round his neck. He wrote:

> 'Dear Mrs F…
> As the end of my earthly life is now a matter of a few days I want to say farewell to you and your daughter. All efforts to obtain justice must be regarded as having failed.
>
> This is a dreadful blow indeed but there is no point in bickering and asking why. Those fifteen of us who remain of the Dachau trial[3] have died 150 deaths in these last weeks when, time after time, our comrades set out on the journey from which there is no return. This is such torture to the mind, such horror that it could not have been contrived more efficiently, but we shall summon our last ounce of

strength to be upright and brave when we cross the threshold to our death.

I myself shall step across it knowing that I am innocent of any crime. My sentence is a mistake caused by human failure. It seems that only our highest judge in heaven will make the right amends. Yet, before this, there has to be the sacrifice of a human life!

Inge, my wife, has written me a letter of farewell and she is still hoping for a miracle and that justice will prevail. But I fear that human decency has sunk so low in this world of ours that truth and justice will not assert themselves.

My last greetings. Yours …'.

Prison Visit

I learned that distant relatives of his lived in Munich. I phoned the prison: he had not yet been hanged. Two days later I was on my way with four loaves of black bread and a large slab of bacon as a gift for the prisoner. I planned to visit him as a relative.

Driving a borrowed little car down the winding road into the town, I was selfishly worried in case some inquiry into my relationship to the condemned man involved a test of my 'borrowed' German papers. This would be the first test of them and it could bring my German mission to a premature end. The prison is strictly barred to all newspaper men.

But it was worth the risk. Considerable controversy had centred around the Dachau war-crimes trials. Allegations had been made that the American interrogators had forced prisoners into confessing crimes they had not committed. The German clergy, Catholic and Protestant, had protested publicly and in notes to Washington against these alleged methods and the judges' sentences. There was much talk about this in Germany, and now a Unified States Senate investigative committee had arrived. While I knew that no coercion had ever been used in Nuremberg, I had not been to the war-crimes trials at Dachau.

I stopped the car in the old cobbled market square at the bottom of the slope into the town, and asked on old man the way to the jail. 'You mean the *Kriegsverbrecher Anstalt* (war-criminals institute)?' The old man gave me detailed directions without showing any curiosity.

I soon found the building, a grey functional structure, arranged like the wings of a windmill, pierced by narrow, barred windows. Its large oak doors were closed. A sign told me that visiting hours were daily, from 3 to 5 p.m., and that no one arriving after 3:30 p.m. could be admitted. I was nearly thirty minutes late.

Plea

A working party was marching toward the entrance. I beckoned one of the Polish guards, immaculate as an occupation MP in his black uniform and white helmet.

I explained that I had come 200 miles to see a condemned man, my cousin. A breakdown had delayed me. My cousin had accumulated several visiting hours (prisoners are allowed visitors weekly for one hour). Could the guard not have a word with the guard commander?

The guard shrugged, went off, and shortly an NCO appeared and explained in broken German that the rules were unbreakable I insistently repeated my story, adding that my cousin might be hanged before I could return. The NCO looked thoughtful and told me to wait.

Returning, he took me to the reception office, and handed me over to a German, a young man with a sunken, tubercular face, and dark, suffering eyes. Once again I repeated my story, explaining that, although we had never met, the prisoner would know who I was: I had married his cousin's sister.

The young German shrugged. 'The rules are very strict, but I always try to help. I will see what I can do'.

He picked up the phone and explained my case to someone he addressed as 'captain.' He hung up. 'It's all right. The captain will make an exception because the prisoner hasn't had visitors this month. You can only see him for half an hour. Please wait'.

He took my food parcel, saying it would have to be searched and then shared out – the prisoners were well fed.

I sat on a bench in the small waiting room. A collection box on the table bore the inscription: 'To our relatives and friends! For some time many of our comrades have been unable to raise the postage for the two letters they are allowed to write every week. We therefore appeal to all those who have not forgotten us and want to help us for a contribution to our postage collection. The Prisoners of Landsberg'.

I dropped a mark into the box.

The door to an adjoining room opened and I had a glimpse of several men and women talking to prisoners through a fine-meshed wire partition.

The young German came back to say the prisoner was waiting.

'There's no room in here. You'll see him in another room in the main building'.

Interview

We left and walked across a courtyard, where flowers and lawns were being tended by prisoners, into the main building. My guide opened a door at the end of the entrance hall, gleaming and spotless as a hospital ward: 'I'll be back for you in half an hour, or as late as I can make it'.

In the room I looked around. There was the same wire partition, and behind it, the prisoner. His guard, another of those immaculately uniformed Poles, had turned his back, and was looking out of the barred window.

'Gruess Gott[4],' I said, advancing to the wire, 'I suppose you know who I am?'

He put the palm of his right hand flat against the wire. I placed my right hand against the wire. Our hands touched. This was the prisoners' handshake.

He was a tall, slim man with thin white hair, and very clear whites to his brown eyes. I knew him to be nearly sixty, but except for his white hair he looked younger. His colour was healthy, his carriage erect.

We looked at each other. 'How have you been?' I asked, fumbling for an opening.

'As well as can be expected. We are treated well. The food is quite good and there's enough of it'.

In answer to a question he said that he was still in solitary confinement, and this he found the hardest part to bear. 'No one to talk to. But it's better than during the trial. You know what happened to us then? They forced confessions from us. I was sentenced to death although, before God, I committed no crime. I was accused of ordering the shooting of Allied flyers. I did no such thing'.

I asked about the chances of a pardon.

He said he had lost all hope. 'We won't get justice even if they set the trial aside, they wouldn't pardon us. They might commute the death sentence to life – I just don't know'.

Hope

I asked him if he knew about the American investigating committee which had just arrived. Yes, the prison grapevine had passed the news around. He thought that a moving of prisoners to other cells was a measure to prevent communication between potential committee witnesses. That morning there had been hammering in another wing of the prison. Workmen had taken down the gallows.

'That has been the greatest ray of hope yet, for two years Friday has been hanging day here. There can't be any hangings next Friday unless' – he grinned – 'they rebuild the gallows'.

He was sure that if the American Senators got the truth, the gallows would not go up again. X-rays would prove injuries inflicted by interrogators on 'my comrades'.

Puffing a cigarette which I had pushed through the wire he went on:

'It has been worse hearing the footsteps of my innocent comrades at dawn on those hanging Fridays than to think that my turn would come next. But they've been magnificent. Not one broke down.

'One nearly succeeded in committing suicide the night before his execution. For months he saved sleeping pills prescribed by the prison doctor. When they came for him he was unconscious. As they could not wake him up they strapped him to a stretcher. They carried him past my cell to the gallows and hanged him. He was lucky – he never knew that death had come'.

He emphasized that the Americans were much concerned to take good care of live prisoners. 'They treat us strictly according to the rules. Food is good and sufficient and we get daily exercise. I am perfectly fit physically. Mentally, it's different. It needs iron self-discipline to keep going. But although we can't talk to each other, no one will be able to say he has seen any of us weaken. We have that determination in common'.

Encounter

Just then the door opened and another prisoner entered. I recognized a Nuremberg defendant whose testimony I had translated in court. I ducked, coughing, hand to my face. If I was recognized, reported, taken before the commandant, my mission in Germany might come to a premature end. But when I peered up, the man was emptying the ashtray into a bucket and walking out. I handed another cigarette through the wire and asked about recreation.

He said they had an excellent prison orchestra, which gave a concert every Sunday. 'They play from the prison tower'. He pointed through the barred window. 'We can't leave our cells, but it is wonderful to hear the music. We have more than enough to read. German publishers have sent us over 8,000 new books. We probably have the best library in Germany'.

A glance at my watch showed me that I had exceeded my time. The prisoner caught the movement.

'When you write to Inge (his wife)', he said, rising, 'tell her that my comrades and I have gathered new hope that justice may still be done. But if we die it will be because we were National Socialists, and obeyed orders. We shall die as soldiers'.

When I asked him if there was anything else I could do he said that when he expected to be executed, one Friday morning, he had asked the Protestant prison chaplain, Eggert, to see that his ashes were sent to his wife for burial. There was nothing more.

The door behind me opened. The young German was back to tell me that I had overstayed and must go now. The prisoner smiled, thanked me for coming, asked me again to tell Inge not to worry. He pressed his hand against the wire. Our palms touched. 'Auf Wiedersehen'. He left quickly, the guard at his heels.

The young German led me across the pretty little courtyard and a Polish sergeant, selecting a key from his huge bunch, let me out of the gate. Just then the clock in the tower struck five.

I had been there only an hour ...

Outside

In the little town of Landsberg Germans were going about their daily business. Behind them lay twelve years of Hitler's possessive thousand-year Reich—one Reich, one Volk, one Fuehrer. No more than a memory of those exciting days remains. But behind the walls of Landsberg prison that memory is strong. The men we have sentenced for crimes committed under Hitler's orders are keeping their loyalties and the legend alive, and there is no doubt they derive from it a strength it would be unwise to underestimate.

A month after my visit to the condemned man I found this death notice in a German paper:

> 'After serious illness, Otto Steinbrinck died at Landsberg at the age of sixty-one. In him there died an upstanding German man. He lived for his love for his country, devotion to his family, the fulfilment of his professional tasks, and his faith in his friends.
>
> His death is all the more tragic because the longed-for reunion with his family was denied.
>
> It is with heartfelt remembrance of our common achievements in Berlin, and comradely memory of our joint experiences in Nuremberg and Landsberg that we say farewell to our most faithful friend Otto Steinbrinck.
>
> We shall never forget him'.

Otto Steinbrinck is described in another death notice as: 'Captain, retired, of the German Navy, bearer of the Pour le Mérite[5], and honorary citizen of the town of Lipstadt'.

83

The second notice ends: ... 'we all who have known this honest, gallant German man will honour him in our memory'.

The second death notice is signed by members of Steinbrinck's family. To understand its full implications one must know that the dead man was serving a seven-year term imposed by the American Military Tribunal at Nuremberg for war-crimes.

But it is the first notice that is important. It is signed by fellow prisoners, making their collective voice heard beyond the prison wall, and, by implication, criticizing and denouncing the judges who sentenced them.

In the little town of Landsberg Germans, who, like myself, have carefully studied their newspaper, are going about their daily business.

NYHT Readers' Comments:

Esteem

To the Editor, European Edition, NYHT:-

From what I have so far read of this series, I estimate it to be quite the most important contribution I have yet seen to our information on the utterly perplexing problem of Germany's future. With which, of course, is intimately connected the future of all the rest of us ...

I should like you to know that your newspaper, of which I have recently become a regular reader, is in my view quite the best daily published in Europe.

F. E. MORGAN

London, Dec. 12, 1949.

(Lieutenant General Morgan was Deputy Chief of Staff of SHAEF and in 1945-46 chief of UNRRA operations in Germany. –Ed.)

Disappointment

To the Editor, European Edition, NYHT:-

Wolfe Frank's articles on Germany have turned out to be a sad disappointment to your readers. Those who hoped to gain novel insights into the German situation of today were served a mixture of gossip and rumour, interspersed only too scantily with facts …

CARL F. BAUMGAERTEL

Rueckersdorf, Dec. 12, 1949.

Notes:

1. During the Occupation of Germany the Allies used Landsberg Prison in Bavaria to hold Nazi War Criminals and it was the place of execution of 288 of them – 259 by hanging and twenty-nine by firing squad.

2. A putsch is a secretly plotted and suddenly executed attempt to overthrow a government. The Beer Hall Putsch, also known as the Munich Putsch was a failed coup attempt by the Nazi Party leader Adolf Hitler to seize power in Munich. Hitler was found guilty of treason and sentenced to five years imprisonment in Landsberg Prison but was released after nine months.

3. The Dachau trials, held within the former Dachau concentration camp in Bavaria, tried those war criminals caught in the United States zones of Occupied Germany and Austria and those accused of committing war crimes against American citizens and military personnel.

4. Gruess Gott is a Bavarian greeting that can range in meaning from deeply emotional to casual.

5. The *Pour le Mérite* is a German order of merit that was established in Prussia as a decoration for exceptional military valour equivalent to the Victoria Cross (VC). Worn on the collar its cross was sky blue in colour which gave it the nickname 'The Blue Max'.

BREAKDOWN OF GERMAN MORALS[1]

Hangover After Hitler Series: Published Friday 9 December 1949

WHEN I WENT INTO GERMANY, there were a good many things I wanted to find out about, and most of them cost me considerable effort. Some things the Germans hated to talk about to strangers and some things they hated to talk about at all; many phases of German life never come to the surface, and it takes a good bit of hunting around to find them. But in every part of the country there was one subject that I never had to go out of my way to investigate, and that was sex. It was no trouble at all, thank you.

For one thing, there are seven women to every five men in Germany and, travelling alone as I was, I had all the earmarks of a bachelor. In Germany, a bachelor is first prize. And being in this rare position, he is expected to shop around, which in this case means not only studying the products set out for his delectation, but also tasting them now and then.

And the products come packaged for quick sale. The man who invented the sweeping neckline can by-pass New York and Paris and Rio, if he wants to see his invention on display. Bavaria is the area for his investigation. In Munich there were times when it appeared that the neckline had been swept away entirely and was rapidly becoming a waistline. On chilly days the girls wear sweaters, which they apparently borrow from their little sisters. 'Why not?' said a girl to me in a cafe in Briennerstrasse. 'we have to show what we're selling. What you're looking at is our working capital'.

The war, by the way, has done well by the female German figure. The chunky, thick-legged, thick-waisted fraulein has been the butt of continental humour since time immemorial, but the war took away their starches and put them on rations; it took away their automobiles and trams and perched them on bicycles or set them on their feet. The result is good, and when it is displayed with the head back, the shoulders squared and the chest well out, the product in question is not to be scorned.

Catholic View

But perhaps you think I am referring to the German equivalent of the girls you see trying to rustle up a profitable evening along the Champs-Elysees. To dispel this idea I give you Kurt Kolmsperger, editor of the Munich Catholic newspaper *Merkur.*

'Ninety per cent of the German women are for sale today,' he said to me. 'the price varies from a few marks, or a meal, or an evening out, to a mink coat, a diamond bracelet or a tidy bank account. You realize that there are very few men in Germany who can provide such things as a fur coat, whereas a woman's desire for a fur coat remains constant. Consequently, really desirable women turn themselves into corporate assets, in which the shares are held by several men who come to an amicable arrangement among themselves for the lady's estimable services'.

That is what the editor said to me and I didn't believe it either, particularly the figure '90 per cent'. But I copied it down carefully, and asked Herr Kolmsperger if that was really what he had said, and then repeated it to every likely person I saw during the remainder of my stay in Germany: school teachers, and doctors who treat venereal diseases; clergymen and black marketeers, husbands and wives. There was no substantial difference of opinion. An editor, for once, had been accurate.

It wasn't anything that had happened overnight, he told me. Even before Hitler, sexual customs had become looser among the Germans than the world at large considered desirable. Hitler only regularized it, with his breeding farms for good Aryan bullies and flaxen-haired, unmarried Aryan girls. No small contribution was made by the rigorous regimentation of youth in the organisations like the Hitler Youth for the boys, and the German Girls. They were held in these organizations until they were eighteen and then went away to mixed labour battalions.

Nazi Youth

'All these youngsters,' Kolmsperger said, 'were passing more and more time in these organisations and less and less with their parents and their neighbours. And remember, in these camps their leaders were chosen for Nazi background, and not moral qualifications. The best of them were likely to be careless of their charges; the worst of them exploited the hold they had over them'.

On this subject he could tell me little. In 1945 I was called upon to screen Gestapo files in Westphalia, some of which contained data on Nazi youth leaders charged with homosexual offences against their wards. I found nearly 100 such cases.

'Then came the War', Kolmsperger continued, 'and the inevitable consequences. The men went to war and left their women behind; the population began to float and there was a trend toward utter irresponsibility. Foreign workers were brought in, and wherever they replaced German men in industry they tended to replace them at the hearth as well. Then the air raids, the bombs, the destruction, the horror, and the need of a woman for a man – any man at all – who would be with her.

'And finally, the collapse; no work, no money, no food; millions of men prisoners of war or dead. Women had to live and feed their children. And the victors had arrived: rich Americans, rude Russians, hesitant British, reticent French and, as time went on, more and more Germans who were thriving on the black market. What would you expect? The women sold themselves for anything they could get: a little food, shelter for a night, a few cigarettes'.

Anyone who was in Germany during 1945 knows that there is no exaggeration in this account. I remember picking my way across the rubble of a West German town and meeting a girl, perhaps thirteen or fourteen years old – a beautiful child with long blond hair and large soft eyes – pushing a baby carriage. Almost inaudibly, in bad English, she whispered, 'Please – chocolate for baby'.

I told her to wait, doubled back to my billet. She took the chocolate I gave her and put it in the pram, murmured thanks, turned the pram and raced off as fast as she could among the bomb craters and the debris. I saw her again ten days later. She was strolling along, her waist tightly encircled by a British Tommy.

Self-Support

But this was four years ago. 'Since those days', Kolmsperger said, 'things have become little better. Money is scarce and hard to earn. There is much unemployment, and even the wage earner is not always able to support his family. Mothers and daughters, sisters and widows are going out today to provide for themselves, and I do not have to tell you how. Only actresses and entertainers lead proper lives today – it has become daring and advanced to be proper'.

The situation is bad everywhere, he said, and worst among refugees who are utterly unable to survive on the few D-marks a day they are granted by the state.

I have quoted a good deal from Kolmsperger because he put into words the things I checked later with others throughout Germany. There were some matters I did not have to check. German women, I quickly found, are far easier to get along with than German men. They are anxious to please and their requirements are modest.

They constantly set about discovering whether I was a bachelor, not insistently but wistfully. I had only to say that I was a bachelor, as I have already mentioned, to become involved in an affair, with absolutely no commitments on my side. No German would agree, or could reasonably be expected to agree, to a marriage in which he had not first investigated the suitability of his chosen partner. 'Unfortunately', a young widow told me at a party one evening, 'the men know very well it would be stupid to put an article in stock when you need only take a franchise'.

There are no 'torch songs' in Germany – songs in which a man laments the coquetry or the cruelty of his loved one. An audience in Germany would laugh at such a song. There are disappointed lovers, yes – but who can stay disappointed long with the opportunity of a German bachelor?

When moral decay has set in as deeply as all this, no one escapes. Even the happily married woman discovers, in too many cases, that her husband is willing to take advantage of the situation. The wife can look the other way, or sue for divorce only to find herself without a husband and without any hope of finding one. (I had one conversational titbit that made me the centre of attraction in any German cocktail party: it had been discovered in America, I would tell my audience, that a woman who has been divorced once stands a better chance of remarrying than a single girl stands of capturing husband No. 1).

Mariage á Trois

Most women shrug their shoulders and try to ignore extra-marital escapades. Some go even further to hold the husbands they have – the 'mariage á trois' has a firm hold in Germany. In any country where the women outnumber the men by such a tremendous margin the three-cornered marriage is likely to be found; in Germany the concurrent circumstances make it almost inescapable. No one is very shocked about it any more.

No one is shocked, because no one thinks very much about sex any more in Germany. An account like this one begins to give the impression that the country is sex mad, and exactly the opposite is true. Germans are worrying about work and housing and the occupation and food and clothes and a great many pressing matters. When they have their attention directed to sex, they say, in effect, 'Oh that!'

They find the Americans preoccupied with sex, and it startles them. But that doesn't prevent them from considering an American a prize catch as a husband, although not as a lover. They have in mind the fact that in American homes a woman has a position she cannot hope to attain in Germany.

In the whole picture, the only change for the better is the drop in outright prostitution and in venereal disease. Both soared with the beginning of the occupation, and even today in the larger German cities the number of street walkers – many of whom were not yet born when Hitler took power – astonishes a visitor from outside.

But with the attenuation of the black market and the new rate of exchange for the D-mark, occupation personnel are not nearly as rich as they used to be, and they are looking for less expensive pleasures. Time, too, has permitted many to enter regular liaisons with German girls. Accordingly, the prostitute is less sought after, the venereal disease rate is back to normal and this problem – which is really hardly a moral problem at all – is nearer some kind of solution.

As for the rest of it, how is it to be cured? No one in Germany had any substantial suggestions. The roots of the disease go all the way back to the First World War and the chaos that followed the collapse of the monarchy and the inability of the republic to cope with its problems. It may be that only a long period of stability will provide a cure – and unhappily for the Germans, such a period seems farther off today than it has ever seemed before.

NYHT Readers' Comments:

Jobs Available

To the Editor, European Edition, NYHT:-

We admit that after the war a considerable number of women and girls used 'the easy way out,' accepting food, clothing, cigarettes and other things that were hard to get at the time, by anybody who was able to offer them. However, even during the darkest days, the number was by no means so high as 90 per cent. There were enough jobs available for girls who wanted to work, although it meant a hard struggle to live on a month's salary. We know many girl-students, who in order to finance their studies, took up a job besides going to lectures at the university.

Mr Frank seemingly, like most foreigners who come to Germany, has met only the class of women whom every country is ashamed of. Did he bother to visit discussion groups, sports clubs or accept private invitations by decent and well-educated middle-class families?

LOTTE WICHMANN and SONJA SCHMIDT

Hamburg, Dec. 16, 1949

All to Blame

To the Editor, European Edition, NYHT:-

As an officer who served with the British forces occupying Germany after World War II, I believe it to be true that prostitution and venereal disease both went up during the period of occupation. No one can possibly say in fairness that only one nationality is to blame for this state of affairs. I and other British ex-service men feel thoroughly ashamed of that part for which the British forces can fairly take responsibility …

MAJOR R. L. GARRATT

Woking, Surrey, Dec. 10, 1949.

Indignation

To the Editor, European Edition, NYHT:-

I have just read with the utmost indignation the most insulting article in your number of Dec. 9 – 'Breakdown of German Morals,' by Wolfe Frank. Please tell these writers, both Frank and Kolmsperger, that they are damned liars. They say that 90 per cent of the German women are for sale today. That is preposterous. That is a tremendous insult for the whole German people. Of course, morals have suffered considerably in consequence of the lost war. But that is in the main the consequence of the starvation to which the German people has been submitted through the Morgenthau plan. The rate of 90 per cent implies that nearly every German woman is for sale. This is a tremendous exaggeration. The rate is by no means higher than 50 per cent …

FRIEDRICH BACHMANN.

Frankfurt, Dec. 13, 1949

Personal letter to Wolfe Frank

I worked with you [during the Nuremberg Trials?] and I respect you as a good boss, who took care of his subordinates, including the Germans and hope you will not be offended by my disagreeing with you.

I believe if other countries had suffered the same 'sad fate' as Germany there would have been similar situations among women and I do not believe your estimate [90 per cent of German women are for sale] is justified ... I love my country and know what morals mean ... I think I am one of the '10 per cent of respectable German girls' but believe there are far more.

HANNELUISE GIERING.

Nuremberg, Dec. 19, 1949

Personal letter to Wolfe Frank

I have enjoyed your series of articles especially those on refugee camps and the Volkswagen factory.

If your acquaintance's remark that '90 per cent of German women are for sale' was really made, then he is wrong. ALL women, in fact all humans are for sale in a time of need, especially one such as Germany has just experienced. The price has sunk to a few pounds of butter, or cigarettes.

I also find your comment that '90 per cent of Germans approved of Hitler until he lost the war' exaggerated and not objective. You would not take offence at this criticism if you knew my political beliefs.

I am a former teacher and [many?] of my young pupils went in [to the forces?] to my great sorrow. They were brainwashed and despite the most loving upbringing, came to a miserable end.

FR. CARMEN HUBENER

Munich, Jan. 6, 1950

Note:

1. In the 1949 *NYHT* printed article (above) Frank suggests he is reporting entirely the accounts and experiences of third parties. However in his memoirs (written many years later and long after his divorce from his then wife Maxine) he writes: 'One of the subjects I was to cover was German morality or lack thereof. Obviously, I was working on this with considerable

relish. First hand experience rates far above hearsay. But there was the problem of Maxine who could not be told of my personal research work on the subject. But a way out presented itself. A man I had known before the war, a member of the small resistance group in Munich in which I had been involved, suggested the Editor of the *Munich Merkur* [Dr Kurt Kolmsperger] as an authentic source of information. A devout catholic, sociologist and cosmopolitan, he could be a marvelous source, if, indeed, he were willing. I went to see the savant, now deceased, and, after some preliminary fencing, disclosed my identity and purpose. He was enthusiastic. But before we turned to the subject in hand, I asked him clearly and in very formal terms "Herr Doktor, will you allow me to quote you?" And yes he would, because only by being outspoken could this terrible decline of morality, this terrible disintegration of morality of German women be halted. My own observations and feelings in the matter were expressed in the article'.

THE BEST-RUN ZONE IN GERMANY

Hangover After Hitler Series: Published Saturday 10 December 1949

NOT FAR FROM KOBLENZ – or perhaps I should say Coblence – in the French Zone of Germany I have an old friend named Fritz Berger [Josef Boeltes], who has built up, over the years, one of the finest businesses as a wine producer in that rich wine-growing country.

It was his business, he says, which kept him completely out of politics during the years of the Third Reich. A man who makes good wine tends to drink good wine, and 'there is simply not enough time', Fritz maintains, 'to drink and to take part in politics too'. Fritz drank his way through 1933 to 1945.

I had visited him before, in 1946, and he told me that a French official had arrived and requisitioned 100,000 litres of his wine. In addition, there was the threat to impound Fritz's 'Schatzkammer' – his treasure cellar – where every wine grower in the Palatinate[1] keeps his finest and his most precious vintages. Fritz protested vigorously against this.

The French officer answered quite politely. 'Monsieur', he said, 'this is just what the Germans did to us in France. We had to learn how to fix things so there was enough for them and enough for us as well. That is what you will have to learn now'. I might add that Fritz learned well and quickly.

When the 100,000 litres were collected, he was horrified to see the French empty the wine into huge steel tankers without regard for vintage or quality. He has never forgiven them. But the French knew what they were doing. The wine went to France and was distilled. The alcohol was used in making perfumes, which were sent to America and brought back dollars for France. In one operation the French earned hard currency and disposed of some important competition.

Best Run Zone

This strange blend of urbane brutality marked the first years of the French occupation, and it was modified, as I soon discovered, only when it was in French interests to modify it. The result is that the French Zone is the best run of all three Western zones in Germany, according to a majority of the Germans I talked to, and that the French themselves, although the Germans may not like them as individuals nor fear them as a nation, are thoroughly respected as occupying powers.

The French, after all, started with three advantages. Having been themselves occupied, they were familiar with the problems of the occupying power, and the devices of the occupied people. They knew where to apply pressure and how to apply pressure and the exact steps that would be taken to resist pressure.

They possessed a large reservoir of German-speaking Frenchmen from Alsace and Lorraine. The British and Americans were frequently caught in the dilemma that resulted from the lack of such nationals; officials who spoke no German or who had only an acquired knowledge of German never understood fully what was going on around them, while officials who were naturalized immigrants were too close to the Germans to command their respect.

Finally, the French had a clear idea of what they wanted to achieve. More directly than any nation in the world, they wanted to prevent the resurgence of a dangerous Germany. This consideration was so completely overriding that it enabled the French to subordinate, for the greatest part, even their natural desire for vengeance.

They were working unashamedly for the good of France. Where this ran parallel to the good of Germany, they did things for the Germans with an alacrity and an efficiency that neither the British nor the Americans have been able to match.

Schools

They decided, for example, that French security demanded the suppression of the Nazi school system and the establishment of a system that would include education in French culture. They did a first-rate job of reforming the schools, and it is already in operation. In the United States Zone a committee of thirty men and women has been developing plans for school reform for more than a year, and is not expected to submit a final report for still another year.

In their relations with individual Germans, they have been chilly and correct. The British and the Americans dine with 'good' Germans[2] – the

French would not think of doing so. 'The Americans are jovial to do business with, the British are haphazard', a German told me. 'The French know what they want and say so. I prefer to do business with the French'.

Their first actions, when they entered Germany, were to make it clear that the Germans were a defeated nation and that France was an occupying power. The principal directing signs on railroad stations, highways and other public places are printed in French – Koblenz is Coblence; Mainz is Mayence. The German name appears underneath, in small print.

But to get back to my friend Fritz Berger and his wife Martha. I had been very eager to get back to them, and visited them again as soon as I could. They greeted me jubilantly.

Fritz, I noticed, had put on weight, and he was beaming from ear to ear. They were still living in their little flat over the plant, but Martha announced that they would soon be moving to a new apartment and that their furniture, requisitioned years before by the French, was to be returned to them.

The larder was bursting with eggs, butter, meat – and it was strange to recall how grateful they had been, a few years before, when they embarrassed me with thanks for a few American cigarettes and some coffee. While France was hard up for food the French had drawn ruthlessly upon the Germans for their needs; now that things were better for France they were better for the French Zone as well.

Good Wine

The wine was excellent and abundant. No more had been taken away, and he had received payment for the 100,000 litres that had been requisitioned. The French were not only leaving him in peace; they were storing some of their own wines in his cellar and were negotiating to make him distributor for French wines in Germany.

I invited the Bergers to dinner at my hotel – it had been stripped bare by the French when I was last there; but now it was newly decorated and thriving. Over the Rhine wine and the Cognac, Fritz gave me his theory, as a businessman, for the change in French policy.

'It began', he said, 'when the currency was reformed and the new deutsche mark began to circulate. The French saw at once that this was a solid currency, and that some day it would be fully negotiable.

'And they realized that, with the position they had established here, they would be in a position to benefit if the German economy began to thrive – they would share in the profits as we became a going concern. They have common sense, the French. They have built a market here for French products, and they have watched the Germans begin to produce many things the French can use. They are all anxious to do business with us'.

Later, Fritz introduced me to one of his acquaintances [Ernst Liegel-Seitz] – a manufacturer whose factory was badly hit during the war. 'Today', he said, 'I employ 1,200 workers again and we have a sizable backlog of orders. One of our representatives abroad has set up his own plant and is exploiting our patents. We had to redesign all our products, but in the process we have improved them until we are again the leaders in our field.' We were drinking white wine from his own vineyards, and he raised his glass of choice 1945. 'Here's the best of luck to you in England', he said to me. 'I think you are going to need, it'.

Manipulation

It was strange to realize, but I discovered, talking to this man and to others, that the French have actually created an *esprit de corps* among the Germans in the French Zone. They discuss occurrences in other parts of Germany and then say, with a good deal of satisfaction: 'Of course, that could never happen in our zone'.

One gets the impression, steadily, that in Bizonia[3] there is always the fear that certain Germans are manipulating the occupying powers. In the French Zone, the original manipulation is firmly in the hands of the French. There is counter-manipulation among the Germans of course – an occupation is a sort of subterranean warfare in itself – but the French call the tune.

Politically, the French support those Germans who seek a federal government rather than a centralized French government, and as in the case of Loritz [see Chapter 18] these are not always the most desirable Germans. The French, in effect, put separatism above democracy in their programme. Their goal is a Germany which will be no threat to France.

I have given a good deal of space to my visit with Fritz. I was elsewhere in the French Zone, and if I write only about the Bergers it is because what I found there was typical of what I found elsewhere.

On my way out I noticed something that epitomized my visit. I had boarded the train for Frankfurt and settled myself in a compartment reserved, as large signs advertised, for Allied personnel. It was my privilege, for I had a British passport. And, alone in my compartment, I rode through the French Zone.

There are similar signs on trains in the British and American Zones. Few heed them. 'We don't have to read the signs', I heard a German say once as he settled himself firmly in his seat. But in the French Zone they have to read them – unless they want to be ejected bodily from their seats.

I am not trying to say that this is a pleasant way to do things. But the French, having decided to do them that way, are carrying out their intentions, and they are respected for it. The Americans and British gain absolutely nothing by permitting their programme to be ignored.

I remembered a speech made a few days earlier in the Bundestag by an opposition speaker, Dr Carlo Schmid, and I looked it up to re-print some of it here:

'We should not be asked to walk about in the cloak of the repentant sinner forever. No future can be built on that. Nor can we possibly ask the French that they should simply forget. Only if we, ourselves, are prepared to supply the evidence and proof that we are not forgetting why things have happened as they did, only then will we be able to turn to the French and say "The time has come for you to forget some of what has occurred".'

It will be the French, and not the Germans, who will decide when that time has come. Meanwhile, they are running their Zone of occupation with cold courtesy and utter firmness. Decision and firmness have always impressed the Germans. They are impressed with it still, even though they might have assured you that the last people from whom they would have expected it were the French.

NYHT Readers' Comments:

French Zone

To the Editor, European Edition, NYHT:-

To be complete, Mr Frank's article 'The Best-Run Zone in Germany' should have 'for France' added in italics. For surely whatever is being accomplished in the French Zone is being done 100 per cent for the French and not at all for the Germans. Whereas in the American Zone the whole intent is to get the country on its feet …

The average uninformed traveller cannot help compare the three zones to the disadvantage of the French. This is most obvious along the Rhine, where the French area looms like a poorhouse between fresh paint, *va-et-vient*, and gay air of the other two territories. One sees little but through traffic in the French Zone and over it, in Rhineland and Schwarzwald, there hangs a general feeling of gloom which most tourists are glad to leave behind them. Perhaps what makes the poorest impression is the widespread, haphazard forest cuttings at points which seem unlikely ever to be receptive to reforestation and which may produce soil wastage, crop damage, and flooded roads. These careless ravages will for a long time remind Germans of French revenge, deserved or not ...

OLD GERMANY HAND

Frankfurt, Dec. 11, 1949.

(In fairness to Mr Frank, his point was that the French in their zone are 'working unashamedly for the good of France,' and that the Germans prefer the disciplined, practical French policy to the more liberal American and British behaviour. 'Decision and firmness,' he concluded, 'have always impressed the Germans.' –Ed.)

Objectivity

To the Editor, European Edition, NYHT:-

Is Mr Frank too closely related to Germany to be objective? Can anyone believe that in Hitler's Germany a smiling wine-grower was 'too busy making wine to be interested in politics?' No one who has spoken with Germans honestly can come to such a conclusion.

But the important question now is: 'What are the beliefs of the wine-grower today?' Let us determine whether the wine-grower is our friend or not. It is possible that this particular wine-grower believes that the French Zone of Occupation is the best in which to live. But it is not possible to believe that he desired to remain under foreign occupation indefinitely. What are this German's hopes and plans for the future? This is a vital question, for upon millions of such people depends the future of Germany.

I, too, have conversed with Germans. These people have very definite ideas concerning every phase of present-day political, social and economic problems... I believe an insight into the true conditions in Germany *is* necessary and is not being supplied.

RICHARD M. FAND

Paris, Dec. 13, 1949.

Notes:

1. Palatinate is the territory of the German Empire ruled by the Count Palatine of the Rhine.

2. A 'good German' was a euphamism during and after WWII for one who claimed not to have supported the Nazi regime or to have known about the Holocaust or German war crimes.

3. Bizonia was the combination of the American and the British occupation zones from 1 January 1947 during the occupation of Germany after World War II.

14

NINE MILLION WITHOUT A FUTURE

Hangover After Hitler Series: Published Monday 12 December 1949

NINE MILLION OF THE FORTY-SEVEN MILLION GERMANS living in the three Western Zones today are people who have been expelled from their homes in the East or who have fled from them. One of every five Germans in the Western Zones is an uprooted, transplanted German, generally unwelcome if not actively resented by his already overcrowded, under-housed, job-short, fellow Germans of the West.

It is difficult to grasp in human terms what nine million people mean. The combined population of the five New England states, plus Nebraska, comes to about nine million. So does the combined population of Greater Paris and Greater Berlin. New York City's five boroughs have a population of about eight million.

The number of refugees is growing rapidly, as the mass migration from East to West continues day and night. The experts estimate that the number of German refugees in the Western Zones will shortly total eleven million. Pessimists among the experts say the figure will reach fourteen million, more than one in every four people in an already densely populated area of Europe. In some ways, today's German refugee problem outstrips the tremendous Nazi-created problem of the displaced persons after the war.

The overwhelming majority of the refugees have no work, no homes of their own, no future they can discern. No international organizations are worrying about their care. They have no place to go; they are at the end of the road.

Today there are nine million hapless and disorganized individuals. Tomorrow, with leaders, they could become an army, still unarmed perhaps, but an army nine million strong. Or eleven million; maybe fourteen million.

Revisionism

At Bonn, only a few weeks ago, a Bundestag[1] delegate, who said he represented seven million German refugees, announced that refugee brigades (fluechtlings brigaden) were being formed. Their aim would be, he said, to fight for the return to the lands from which they had been expelled. The report from Bonn was accompanied by a statement from an unidentified Allied spokesman, who said that the movement would certainly be banned if it proved to have a military character. It was a significant straw in the wind.

The refugees, one can be certain, will be clamouring ever more stridently for their former homes east of the Oder-Neisse Line[2]; for their old homes in Silesia and Pomerania, in former East Prussia, in the Czech Sudetenland[3] and in Austria, Hungary and Yugoslavia, from which they have been expelled since the war. They will be crying too for the homes in the Russian Zone of Germany from which they have fled.

The German political parties have already shown they are aware that the refugees constitute a huge pool of potential voting strength, and in their various ways have been moving to exploit it. The competition among the political parties for this vote can quickly become a very disturbing factor in the heart of Europe.

Promises to the refugees, like the promises of many politicians in many countries, have not been kept, and this has contributed to the hopelessness among the refugees about their future. Already these people believe they have nothing to lose and, much as they are sick of war, have drifted into a feeling that their only hope for the future is a conflict between the East and West. Yet, generally speaking, I found little appreciation anywhere of the explosive nature of the German refugee situation.

Chimney Sweeps

My attention was directed to the refugees in the course of one of the most emotion-charged experiences of my life. It came, curiously, in the course of a visit to a class for chimney sweeps at a Munich trade school. I had passed most of the afternoon touring secondary schools with a member of the municipal school council, talking to, and answering questions from polite, well-brought-up boys and girls who had exhibited a lively interest in Great Britain and manifested a widespread desire to go to England to live. (America, they said, was too far away).

At the end of the afternoon, the principal of a recently re-roofed school took me into a classroom where thirty men, between the ages of

102

twenty-two and thirty-five and dressed in ordinary work clothes, sat behind school desks. The principal had warned me that the men were in a bad mood. Upsetting an ancient German tradition, the Americans had instituted competitive free enterprise into the chimney-sweep profession. It had previously been the custom in Bavaria for master chimney-sweeps to be assigned districts in which they would have monopolies, carrying on their trade with assistants and apprentices. When a master sweep died or retired, his chief assistant would take over. Now the Military Government had scored a victory against cartelization in the chimney-sweep field, and the 'trust' didn't like it.

The teacher of the class, whom I had met in the principal's office, introduced me to the class as someone who had recently come from England. As I spoke, I looked at the faces of the men. Hostility was evident.

'Look', I heard myself saying, 'I'm not only *from* England: I *am* English. I want to have a frank talk with you. Please say what's on your minds: there won't be any repercussions. You've probably guessed that I was born in Germany. I have come back to write about the Germany of today. That includes your problems. Please, meine Herren (gentlemen), don't hold back'.

German Views

For maybe fifteen seconds there was no reaction. Then three of them began at once. Two yielded and the third loudly asked: 'Why must the Americans interfere with life in Germany so much that they mess up our professional tradition?'

To this I was unable to give any specific answer that could satisfy them. It was the same with other questions that followed.

The next man on his feet, pale, thin, blond, wrought-up, spoke in a trembling voice: 'I come from Silesia, I am a refugee. How can the Americans and British stand by and watch the brutal things the Poles are doing to us? What about the crimes committed in the Russian Zone? I was a prisoner in England, you understand? Finally, when I came home to Silesia secretly, I found my family had been driven from their home. I can't find them'.

His voice broke. He fell back into his seat. They followed one another, asking questions, often accusing, assertive questions, such as: 'Why don't the Western powers stay where they were at the end of the war? Do you really expect us to believe the Allies didn't know what the Russians were all about in 1945? Are you trying to tell us that the British Empire was built on that sort of ignorance?'

I heard someone in the rear of the room say that we were trying to sell the idea of freedom to the Germans, but, by God, we had deprived them of the last remnant of freedom remaining to them. There was contradiction, and they began arguing among themselves. One said that at least they could talk freely now, as they were doing to me.

German Claims

One little man jumped up, very pale and tense, and in Saxon dialect stated: 'I am not a National Socialist. But this one must admit: the Fuehrer was right when he said that what is German must remain German. Those peoples in Europe who are German by origin, who speak German, belong to the Reich. The Polish Corridor had to be abolished. The Saar[4] is German and always will be'.

The class was quiet now, except for a few who were shaking their heads and muttering. The little Saxon continued.

'Austria, too, is German. And the Sudetenland. It all belonged to us, and they wanted to be with us. That's a fact. If Hitler had got our colonies back, there would have been no war' …

He stopped suddenly, apparently exhausted. Considerable discussion about Russia ensued.

'We knew what to expect of Russia', said one 'and we were close enough to them for you to find out from us. Why, it wasn't too late even in the very last days of the war. If you had joined forces with us we could have pushed them back where they belong, and there would have been peace, real peace, in Europe today'.

The teacher was looking at his watch. Time was up. A pleasant looking young man in the front row who had been unable to break through the talk still obviously had something on his mind. I approached and asked what he had to say.

'Promise me something', he said, 'whatever else you do, visit a refugee camp near the Czech border and see for yourself what misery some of us Germans are enduring.

I know. I've been through it all myself. I've been in a refugee camp'.

He was tearful with emotion. I promised. The classroom was stuffy on that summer's day, and as I left, I was unsure whether it was the heat or the tense, antagonistic atmosphere that had me sweating. It was one of the few occasions that summer that I was to see Germans really worked up and angry.

I had been in Germany a month when I encountered the students of chimney sweeping. The refugee problem had not been mentioned to me. I had met a few refugees, but they had jobs and were not part of the problem.

The next morning I called at the Billeting Commissioner's office in the Leopoldstrasse, in Munich, and saw Dr Wilhelm Gillitzer. He struck me as highly intelligent. He certainly had an articulate understanding of the refugee situation.

He told me that at that time the Refugee Ministry owed the food suppliers a million marks (then around $330,000). The crisis was so serious that he feared the suppliers would be unable to extend credit. Then thousands of children would go milk-less. Their parents had no money and no means of getting milk. He urged me to visit several camps and observe conditions for myself.

He arranged a conference with leading officials of the refugee section of the Bavarian Ministry of the Interior. I explained frankly what I was doing and said I wanted no conducted tours or press hand-outs. I wanted to go to a camp as a refugee. There was some objection to this. It was however overruled by Dr Adam.

Dr Adam was the ministerial director, a bespectacled human dynamo who seemed to be running two conferences and three jobs on the phone simultaneously. Quickly he introduced me to his chief statistician, several colleagues, and to Dr Georg Nentwig. Dr Nentwig was instructed to show me several camps and arrange for my admission to one as a refugee. All the time the busy Dr Adam kept brandishing an outsize mauve pencil, like the one Hermann Goering fancied in his days of glory.

Next day I was to go to the refugee camps.

NYHT Reader's Comment:

Hangover After Hitler

To the Editor, European Edition, NYHT:-

Mr Wolfe Frank chose a very descriptive title to his interesting series of articles on Germany. 'A Hangover,' that it is, with an unusual subsequent headache of broken hearts and lives. Many of the expellees have known better days, especially during the Nazi orgy that caused the headache. Did the expellees of today learn to show compassion to the expellees of yesterday-Hitler's? Is there no other reaction on the part of 'the pale, thin, blond, wrought-up' young man from Silesia, than to ask, 'How can Americans and British stand by and watch the brutal things the Poles are doing to us?' Or might he, from his own experience, show a little compassion to 'the pale, thin, blond victim of the Nazis, beaten soft in the course of ten horrible years ...'

E.A.B.

Rome, Dec. 15, 1949.

Personal letter to Wolfe Frank

I am a new senior official in the West German Ministry of Refugee Affairs and I have followed your reports in the *NYHT* with great interest. For four years I have been trying to co-ordinate the refugee assistance groups in all the German states and this has succeeded in spite of the different political and economic developments of the different zones.

I am particularly interested in helping refugee journalists, editors and publishers to make a living in the West. The Press and publishers have offered help, but the people lack the essential tools of their trade – typewriters.

I wondered if foreign correspondents who are leaving Germany might be willing to donate their now unneeded machines to help their refugee colleagues make a living? Would you be willing to put this suggestion to your colleagues perhaps in the form of another article?

WERNER MIDDELMANN

Bonn, Dec. 13, 1949

Notes:

1. The Bundestag is the German federal parliament. It was founded in 1949 at Bonn.

2. The Oder-Neisse Line is the international border between Poland and Germany as drawn after WWII.

3. Sudetenland is the name for the northern, southern and western areas of Czechoslovakia.

4. The Saar or Saarland is one of the states of the Federal Republic of Germany. From 1947 to 1956 the Saar was occupied by the French.

LIFE IN
A GERMAN REFUGEE CAMP

Hangover After Hitler Series: Published Tuesday 13 December 1949

CAMPS, WHETHER OF THE CONCENTRATION, or refugee variety, I shall never like. I spent six months interned behind barbed wire in Britain as an 'enemy alien' after the outbreak of the war, so my personal experience contributes to my prejudice.

As chief interpreter in the Nuremberg war-crimes trials, I listened to (and translated) a great deal of testimony about the horrors of the Nazi concentration camps. In spite of this preparation, I was shocked at the conditions I found in the refugee camps, where the German government is doing its poor best to provide board and lodging for tens of thousands of fairly ordinary folk.

Camp Anzenbach at Berchtesgaden was the first I went to, wearing well-worn Bavarian clothes (faded khaki with green piping and deer-horn buttons). I went along ostensibly as a minor member of an official party that was visiting the camp. On our way there, I was told that the camp barracks, really nothing more than temporary huts, had been condemned as uninhabitable and that the purpose of the official visit was to advise the inmates of their impending transfer to Camp Winkl, five miles away on the other side of town.

The barracks, on a bleak and barren site, were prevented from total collapse by makeshift repairs. You could see daylight through some of the roofs. Some huts were in such disrepair that they had been abandoned, adding to the over-crowded condition that already prevailed in the remaining huts. Like so many others of the 500 refugee camps in Bavaria this one was located in an area where opportunities for employment were virtually non-existent.

Cubicles

Inside the huts families lived in cubicles made with blankets strung from wires. Food was stored on shelves in each cubicle, and the flies swarmed thicker than any swarms I had ever seen before. One such 'room', for example, served as living room, sleeping quarters and kitchen for the widow of a Sudeten-German shoemaker, her three small children and a grown son and daughter. The shoemaker had died a few days earlier, and his widow was trying to carry on his trade, as he had done, in this same crowded cubicle.

The widow began to weep almost as soon as we invaded her cramped quarters. She showed us a photograph of an attractive white cottage in the Sudetenland.

'We live for the day when we can go back', she said. During the next ten days that I spent in refugee camps these words were to become an echoing refrain.

In another hut we met a master blacksmith, a powerful man with a rugged face and a heavy crop of black hair. He was one of the luckier inhabitants of the camp, having found employment in an American vehicle-repair shop at Berchtesgaden. He argued that the hatred and dissent that developed between the Sudeten Germans and the Czechs had been 'sown from above'.

'We never had any trouble of our own making. Our only hope and all that keeps us going is the thought of going back. We know that only a war can bring that about. No one is interested in us, or what happens to us. We are strangers here in Bavaria and will always remain strangers. The Allies expect the German government to help us, but they can't, even if they wanted to'.

Refusal

Meanwhile, word had been passed around that the ministry officials had called a meeting in the assembly room, an empty hut, with the camp administrators office partitioned off at one end. The room filled quickly with people of all ages, including babies only a few weeks old, held in their mothers' arms. The heat was stifling, the flies were everywhere and the atmosphere was one of distrust and suspicion.

The ministry representative began to explain that the camp had been condemned. He urged the people to prepare for the impending move to Camp Winkl, which, he pointed out, they knew to be a far better place than Camp Anzenbach. He was quickly interrupted by many voices.

The blacksmith emerged as camp spokesman. He was very agitated. 'This is now our home', he said, 'we have become used to it and attached to it. We believe that things can get only worse if we are made to move again. One German government brought us our misery. It is up to the present one to see that we stay right here. I warn you that you'll have to use force to move us. We're staying here'.

A very old lady, who looked over seventy, was sitting on a stool in the front row. She said she would jump in the lake if they tried to move her. She began to cry.

They offered suggestions to try to stave off the move. They wanted to rebuild the camp, put up new huts, start a small industry. They would never leave. Confronted with the unreasoning stubbornness of these people, the ministry spokesman, to my surprise, backed down. He would take the matter up once again with higher authority, he said. And we left Camp Anzenbach for Camp Winkl.

Winkl was beautifully located, in a green countryside on the main road to Munich. It was indeed a far better camp than Anzenbach. The buildings were of permanent construction. There were a nursery, a cinema, showers, a hospital and a number of shops. I was told that all the inhabitants of Camp Anzenbach had, at one time or another, visited Winkl. Their determination to cling to their own dilapidated, unsanitary camp in preference to Camp Winkl is difficult to understand unless one assumes that after having once been uprooted from their homes they preferred a present misery which they knew to any change. My first day with the refugees had been tiring and depressing.

Camps

The next morning, Dr Georg Nentwig, himself a refugee from Silesia who was serving as administrative director for the refugee section, showed me a map of Bavaria, with each of the 500 camps spotted with a coloured pin. We picked out three camps to visit. The first was at Dachau [near Munich], not far from the notorious concentration camp; the second was Camp Mettenbach, near Muehldorf, in Upper Bavaria and the third was Camp Kruemm, not far from Mettenbach. Although there were exceptions, filth, demoralization and degeneracy were the rule at all of them.

At the Dachau camp, where were lodged 300 Germans and 800 non-Germans, among them Poles, Bulgars, Hungarians, Ukrainians and Yugoslavs, the picture varied dramatically from barracks to barracks. It was 10:30 in the morning when we visited the first hut, which was occupied by Ukrainians. Half a dozen occupants were still lounging in their bunks, sleeping, reading, or talking to neighbours. In the next room, there were more men still in bed, and in one bunk a man and woman clung to each other, oblivious to their neighbours or to us. In the next hut a young woman was sleeping peacefully, while several men were shaving, making beds, or getting dressed.

Both huts were untidy and filthy.

Only a few yards away a completely different atmosphere reigned. Here, Hungarians and Yugoslavs who were awaiting Australian visas lived in a climate of hope which was reflected in their individual attitudes. Their quarters were clean and under the direction of their room leader, a young Yugoslav law student. It was obvious that a healthy and willing self-discipline was maintained.

But at the adjoining barracks, a few yards further on, occupied by Polish refugees who for one reason or another had been turned down for emigration, the story was different. The hut was appallingly dirty.

Camp Mettenbach, located in an agricultural area where work is scarce, had a reputation as a trouble spot.

Nentwig told me that most of the inhabitants had been there for a long time, and they included some criminal elements. It housed Spaniards and South Americans who had been stranded in Germany, Ukrainians and Sudeten Germans.

Crime

A considerable group of the Spaniards had just been jailed for housebreaking and were awaiting trial. As we walked through the camp one of the directors, a Bavarian in leather shorts told us that his police were currently investigating an alleged case of incest between a thirty-year-old woman and her twelve-year-old son. The camp officials were struggling desperately to bring venereal disease in the camp under control. Prostitution was common.

We entered a hut at random. It was neatly divided in two sections, sleeping and living room. It belonged to a family of three Sudeten Germans, an elderly couple with a grown daughter. The daughter held a fourteen-month-old baby in her lap. We asked if her husband had found work.

'I have no husband', she said simply, grinning. She did not know who the father of her child was.

Nentwig asked her how she lived. She said she was trying to subsist on her dole of eight marks ($1.90) per month. 'That doesn't even pay for the child's milk', she said. 'The farm work around here pays only six marks a week. The working day starts at five in the morning during harvest time and lasts until ten at night. And it's hard work, too. The food is good, but the clothes I wore out cost more than I was earning'.

She shrugged her shoulders. The camp director confirmed what I had already guessed, she earned her living as a prostitute.

The camp director insisted that conditions had lately improved. He had organized camp police, who checked all the huts at 10.00 p.m. and evicted all the men from the women's huts and vice versa.

Children

There were eighty children in the camp. One teacher was trying to give them a sketchy education. I had never heard children talking the obscene language of these youngsters.

'There is nothing they haven't heard from the grown-ups,' said the camp director, 'or worse, nothing they haven't seen. Their sex life begins at twelve, sometimes earlier. I was nearly knocked off my balance yesterday by a young lad of about twelve. I asked where he was going in such a hurry. "There's a couple of girls over there in the woods" the kid said, "I'm going over to join them".'

The director said that there were no punitive or corrective steps to change conditions.

'After living in one of these camps for four years, our people have lost all purpose in life. The only remedy would be to find work for them and give them a hope that some day they will have a home of their own. There isn't a ghost of a chance of that in this area, or with the inadequate funds that the government is providing'.

Camp Kruemm, the next one we visited, presented a happier picture. It was inhabited by German refugees from the Patschka country of Yugoslavia. They were descendants of pioneer farmers who had emigrated from Swabia at the beginning of the last century. They had remained a closely knit community, retained their German character and prospered greatly in the land of their adoption. They had mingled little with the Yugoslavs and intermarried almost not at all. After the liberation of Yugoslavia they were sent back to the fatherland of their grandparents and their great-grandparents.

In broad Swabian accents, they talked cheerfully about their problems. They had stayed put in Yugoslavia when Hitler had called upon German minorities abroad to return to the fatherland. Now they were trying to make the best of their new life. Their camp, smaller and better situated than most, knew few moral or social problems. 'If only these blockheaded Bavarian farmers would let us help them', one rugged-looking old man remarked, 'we could soon show them a thing or two about farming.

But they're too stubborn and belligerent. Well, it's their loss as much as ours'.

Tiny, neat gardens surrounding the camp demonstrated that they knew how to make green things grow.

FUGITIVES FROM URANIUM MINES

Hangover After Hitler Series: Published Wednesday 14 December 1949

I REACHED HOF, last town before the frontier of the Russian Zone, and close to the westernmost tip of Czechoslovakia, at 7.00 p.m. These summer days were hot. I had hitch-hiked from Munich – two days to cover 220 miles.

Shortage of cash since the currency reform of June 1948 has made hitch-hiking a popular, if uncertain, method of transportation in the Western Zones of Germany. I gave the driver of a truck carrying fresh fruit from Munich to Ingolstadt, three cigarettes for moving me fifty miles on my road to Hof. He seemed content with this 'pay.' Another hitch-hiker, who looked like a commercial traveller, boarded the truck with me at the slow-down bend of the Munich-Nuremberg road where the local road joins the autobahn[1]. I don't know how he paid the driver who took us into his cabin.

It was four in the afternoon before I managed to get another ride, but this time a used car dealer, towing an automobile, took me all the way on to Nuremberg. The last twenty miles I covered next day by diesel truck and on the back of a motorcycle.

Next day I was a refugee – No. 3347, in the camp at Moschendorf.

Hidden Identity

Overnight I had looked up Mueller, head of the camp, and presented a letter I had obtained from the director of the refugee administration of Bavaria. This letter instructed Herr J. Mueller to admit me, keep my identity secret, make me free of the camp as an ordinary inmate, avoid conducted inspections, and treat the matter as entirely confidential.

Mueller, a tall, slight man in his forties, promised to get me in next morning. He told me he had owned a ceramic factory in Silesia before he was expelled. Now he had started up his ceramic business again in Hof and divided his time between his business and running the camp at Moschendorf, four miles away. Of the 3,346 persons at Hof-Moschendorf, the largest Bavarian border camp, 2,130 came from other parts of Germany, or from territories annexed by Hitler, while the remainder were non-Germans and included Hungarians, Lithuanians, Yugoslavs, Poles, Latvians, Dutch and stateless persons.

I got from Hof to the camp by train. Before the war the Hof station had been an important rail junction. Today it is virtually the end of the line. Trains move regularly to and from the west, but the rails are rusting and grass grows between the track ties that stretch toward the east and the Russian-occupied zone. An occasional trainload of repatriated prisoners of war moves into Hof from the east; but that's all. The official train crossing point between the West and East zones is to the north, on the border of the British Zone, at Helmstedt.

Refugees

Nevertheless, Hof station is crowded with travellers. They come from the Russian Zone, brought by the money-exchange bureau in Hof station. Most of these people cross the border on foot, illegally. They get only one West mark for six East marks at the Hof exchange office, and this may account for a certain stunned look I noticed on several faces as their owners came out of the bureau. It takes just as much work to earn one mark in the East zone as it does in the West zone.

These travellers from the east stand in front of the newsstand in the station devouring with their eyes the headlines of newspapers they are unable to buy. They stare hungrily at the ham sandwiches and pies in the restaurant.

These East Germans have crossed the border for other reasons besides mark exchange. They come shopping for a rucksack of potatoes, some fat or meat or a little coffee to smuggle back. Sometimes they come to prepare the way for a permanent escape from the Soviet Zone. If they can get past the asylum commission – refugees filter into the camp through a counter-intelligence interrogation, and an asylum-commission interview – they will become inmates of Moschendorf camp.

Checking In

Now, after visiting five refugee camps, I moved into one as an inmate. Mueller's twenty-one-year-old assistant, a former member of the Hitler Youth[2], took me to a girl typist who entered my personal data on an index card: my real name, date and place of birth (the place is now in the Soviet Zone), time and place of supposed illegal border crossing. No further questions were asked.

I received a card for the camp registry. At the registry they took this in, and handed out a white slip called a health card, with spaces for the doctor's report, my compound assignment, and the number of blankets issued to me. There were also meal coupons for three days. Presumably, after three days I was to be entered on the permanent camp rolls.

At the camp dispensary the doctor, who spoke with a Sudeten German accent, asked if I had a venereal disease. I said no. 'Have you had VD?' I said no, 'Okay; you're in'. He signed my health card. My 'medical examination' was over.

The blankets I then picked up at the storeroom had been liberally sprayed with DDT[3] but were so filthy that I always slept with my clothes on, my trouser ends stuffed inside my socks, and I used my raincoat as a pillow.

Hut 78, to which I was assigned, was furnished with twelve double-tier bunks, six stools, and two tables. Each bunk had a straw-filled mattress made of burlap [hessian] which barely held in the straw. Two beds were taken and their owners, both quite young men, were playing cards at a table in the far end of the hut. I dumped my rucksack on a bunk near a window and joined them with the German equivalent of: 'What goes on?'

As I watched the card game two more men, both elderly and very thin, entered the hut. Battered briefcases were their only luggage. Their dialect disclosed them as coming, presumably, from the Russian Zone. They selected bunks and sat down. They looked dog-tired. I soon found out they had crossed the border illegally the night before. They had made more than fifty miles on foot, leaving behind their families and all their belongings.

One was an insurance salesman from Zwickau, in Saxony. He had had a row with the SED (the Socialist Unity Party, as the Communist Party in the Russian Zone is called). The other was an office employee of a uranium mine in the Ore Mountains [the Erzgebirge] that run along the German-Czech frontier. He had quarrelled with the manager of the uranium mine.

Both these men had thought it wise to flee.

When, later, the hut filled up, I found that a number of the inmates were refugees from the Russian-operated uranium mines. Their stories shaped a comprehensive and gruesome picture. I gathered that the Russians have conscripted between 100,000 and 130,000 Germans to work in these mines. This does not include Russian and German defaulters who worked in a 'punitive' mine at Johann-Georgenstadt, near the Czech border. Conditions are such that men and women alike in the Russian Zone have the greatest fear of being sent to the mines. As more and more businesses in the East zone are merged and nationalized as 'Volkseigene Betriebe [publicly owned operation],' more people are freed for work in the mines. Any man or woman guilty of misconduct in the eyes of the Russians, or of German stooges working for the Russians, may expect to find himself en route for Aue, centre of the mining area, as punishment.

Accidents

There was general agreement that safety precautions in the mines were almost unknown. One of the men in my hut, when I turned the talk to the mines, said he had been in three accidents in fourteen months. Once he had suffered a double fracture of an arm from a fall of rock. Next a pit-car had run over his foot and taken off a toe. Finally he had fallen fifty feet down a shaft and fractured his skull. He had been a dairy-farm hand before he went to the mines. Now he was grey and shrunken and looked far older than his twenty-five years.

Several men who had worked as drillers confirmed that drilling is done dry. Inhaling rock dust causes a high rate of silicosis. Some men come down with it in three months or even less. For this reason a driller is automatically admissible to the American Zone after three months in a mine.

The mine workers are given a daily work quota, I was told. On its completion depends their food ration and pay. This runs through the office as well as the mine grades. The general complaint I heard at this camp, which contained many refugees from the mines, was that the quotas are set so high that the Russian controllers are believed to do it systematically to block the possibility of a man drawing his full rations or pay.

Overcrowding

A man has no time to go hunting for food after work, even if he had the energy. He may have to spend three hours traveling to and from his job. This is owing to overcrowding and consequent distribution of the worker force over a wide area. One district I knew, since it was where I was born. The village of Beierfeld had a population of 4,200 in 1939. Now, I was told by a man who had been moved there for mine work – and had escaped – 25,000 people have been dumped down in and around my birthplace village, which is jammed with workers' barracks.

Until lately the whole district, far into Saxony, was fairly tightly sealed, but the seal has now been loosened for a good reason. The Russians need replacements for miners who have fled, and want to get them from outside. Each miner carries a special miner's card as identification and if he is found outside his assigned area it means jail and subsequently the penal mine at Johann-Georgenstadt.

The clerical worker in my hut told me he had crossed the border when his boss made life too tough. This boss, a recent arrival at the mine offices, was a German named Schulz. On his arrival Obersteiger (under manager) Schulz had called a conference of his staff and addressed them thus: 'Men, you probably know my reputation and that I was an SS officer. I'm proud of having been an SS officer. I will run this shaft as I used to run things when I was an SS officer. You will work as I direct, and those who fail will be punished without pity, I will make it hard'.

SS Methods

Soon after, one of his men was charged to complete a job within twenty-four hours. It might have been possible, but certain materials were needed, and these were not provided. Schulz sent for the man when the job was not completed on time. The man excused himself by referring to the lack of those essential materials and pointed out that Schulz himself should have provided them. Schulz's answer was: 'No excuses! You got your orders, you failed to carry them out, you will be punished'. And he stopped the man's ration card and pay for a week.

This was not an isolated case. It is pretty evident than the kind of Germans who found their vocation in the SS organization have become the willing tools of their Russian masters and show the same sadistic tendencies that distinguished this corps in Hitler's day.

I asked a number of the refugees from the mining district about output. But answers were so contradictory as to indicate that these men had no way of knowing or no interest in the subject. The clerical worker alone was definite. He said that tens of thousands of tons of blend have been mined, in the Erzgebirge and shipped by rail and road to washing plants as far away as Zwickau, Chemnitz and even Berlin. But the uranium extraction rate was very low. He thought it had something to do with the quality of the blend.

Notes:

1. The Autobahn, equivalent to motorway in the UK and freeway in the USA, is the federal controlled access-highway system in Germany.

2. Hitler Youth was the youth organization of the Nazi Party.

3. Dichlorodiphenyltrichloroethane, commonly known as DDT, was an insecticide used extensively during and after WWII to control diseases such as malaria and typhus among troops and civilians. In his memoirs Frank adds: 'During the four or five days I spent at the camp I was thoroughly bitten by fleas and bed bugs which seemed to thrive on DDT, became extremely hungry and filled forty or so pages with notes on the tales of woe which poured out from every person I was talking to'.

Also included in his memoirs, but not in the NYHT articles, is Frank's depressing observations of the incest that was taking place within the camp: 'Children aged twelve were having sex, mothers were having sex with their sons, and fathers with their daughters. It was a fairly shattering experience to observe all this and it is an eerie thought indeed that among the well-to-do West Germans of today are many who have gone through this soul destroying phase in their lives'.

INVESTIGATING
THE VOLKSWAGEN PLANT

Hangover After Hitler Series: Published Friday 16 December 1949

IF ANYONE OWNS A VOLKSWAGEN – an automobile I can normally recommend – which shows such odd quirks of behaviour as a movement backward when put into second gear – I can explain all. Although, during the eight days I worked in the Volkswagen factory the production curve may have risen sharply, I have no illusions about the efficiency curve. I am not a mechanic.

It seemed a good idea at the time.

'There's a rumour', the *New York Herald Tribune* briefing editor had told me in Paris, 'that you need a Nazi-party membership card even to hold a sweeper's job in that plant'.

Later, in London, a German friend advised me that the Volkswagen plant 'Is a regular hive of Nazis: you can't get a job there unless you carry the Nazi party brand'.

Finally, in Munich, I was informed by a contact, who seemed to speak with authority, that the German Right-wing party had land-slided the factory election. 'Everyone there is a "verkappter Nazi" (a camouflaged Nazi). It's common knowledge'.

Obviously if this were 100 per cent true the Nazi organization would be tight enough to block entry into the plant of an undercover man like myself, equipped only with flimsy 'manufactured' papers which would not stand efficient investigation. Equally obviously I had to give it a try. Failure alone would prove something. Nazi 'security' would be operating, and effectively.

Job Hunt

After more than three months in Germany, and with my prior background of knowledge and experience, I knew that with my documents I had small chance of getting work anywhere through routine channels. I could only go to work on a personal basis with the man in charge knowing who I was, and hope that he would be able and willing to help. Accordingly, I found that the man to reach at Volkswagen was plant director Heinz Nordhoff[1]. I phoned him from Hanover.

A female secretary [Fr. Loeffler] guarded the director. Herr Nordhoff was a very busy man. She would try to find out when he could talk. A second call gained no ground. I pulled strings, and on the third call reached the elusive Herr Nordhoff. 'In two weeks, perhaps', Herr Nordhoff said.

I asked casually if I might quote him, adding that this delay in itself could answer some of my questions.

Herr Nordhoff's reaction was rapid. 'But don't be ridiculous. Shall we say, tomorrow?'

Tomorrow it was. At the Volkswagen plant I made some unexpected discoveries and lost some illusions. The first was that Herr Nordhoff's stalling was soundly based. He is in fact one of Germany's busiest men, and guards his time and energy like any other capable top executive. Once he knew what I wanted, he immediately agreed to provide facilities for a personal investigation.

Interview

'Rumours?' He shrugged them off. 'No comment. You find out for yourself. You'll have every opportunity you want'.

This knocked at least one chip off my shoulder.

A nutshell history of the Volkswagen plant needs interpolating here. It was the Nazi promise that an American dream, 'an automobile for everyone at a price everyone can pay,' would come true in Hitler's wonderland. The Messiah contracted to provide a serviceable, if small, automobile for 999 marks (then about $240). Payment would be in small monthly instalments.

Hitler himself laid the cornerstone of the Wolfsburg plant in 1938. The blueprint showed Europe's most modern mass production plant. At the start, 1,000 cars a day would run off the giant assembly belt, at peak production, 3,000 a day. The workers' town would house 20,000 men and their families. There were to be canals, rail sidings, and an enormous power plant.

Meantime, the Nazi machine got busy collecting down payments on the cars to be delivered. Hundreds of thousands of wage and salary earners paid the required instalments. It was more than *lèse majesté*[2], it was practically treason, to doubt that the Fuehrer might fail to deliver in reasonable time.

War arrived. The war's demand on materials, resources and labour came first. 'Once the war's won, you'll get your car'. The war wasn't won. After it was over, German instalment-payers sued. They lost their test cases.

War Production

At the beginning of the war the plant had been converted for military production. Eighteen thousand workers – a large proportion slave labour from conquered countries – ultimately were employed there. They made German jeeps, amphibian vehicles, mines, bazookas, aircraft parts – the usual run of any mass-production automobile plant converted for arms production. In 1944 the plant was bombed four times and more than half of it was destroyed. As Germany was smashed down, the machines in the plant dragged to a stop. Then came surrender, and the plant emptied as the slave labourers made their weary way home. The Americans came, and left. The British came, and stayed.

Nordhoff told me that through all this time he had worked solely on the manufacture of automobiles and trucks. He said he had not joined the Nazi party. He had Jewish associates and I was told that he used his position to protect them.

The Americans classified him at the end of the War as an 'industrialist,' and decided he was unemployable. He sought work, failed to find it, ultimately drifted into the British Zone and he found the British only too anxious to secure a competent man to get the Volkswagen plant into production again to bother with the Americans' 'unemployable' classification.

Nordhoff had been with General Motors' Opel plant for a long time. That was enough. 'You're in charge,' said the British colonel who interviewed him.

4, 500 a Month

Nordhoff took over in January, 1948, and now heads a plant turning out 4,500 cars a month. He aims at an output of 6,000 a month. Export has priority. The cars earn hard currency for Germany: $1,100 for the standard model, $1,300 for the deluxe. They are serviceable little runabouts, identifiable by the sharp slope of the hood, under which is the gas [petrol] tank. The engine is in the rear.

Last October the plant was turned back to the German government.

I was to work there. Accommodation was provided at the Hotel Steimker Berg – probably the worst hotel in all Germany – and in my room there I changed my clothes and name.

I then reported to Herr Helmuth Orlich, chief of the Plant Inspection Department. This executive, a short, agile man with greying hair, had been briefed about me by Nordhoff. When I again name the rumours I wanted to check, he, like his chief, refused comment. 'Find out for yourself'.

But he did offer comment on the Right-wing victory in the county elections. He attributed it to an unfortunate decision on the housing problem. When the plant began running again the factory had offered to rebuild homes damaged by the air raids. But they demanded that the county give them control over 80 per cent of the new accommodations thus created. The administration, mostly Social Democrats had turned this down, thereby antagonizing the house-hungry workers. Soon after, in 1947, the newly formed Right-wing party contested the county elections on a better-housing programme. They won a victory so resounding that they lacked candidates to fill all the posts they had won.

British Mistake

This political trend disturbed the British Military Government, which made the mistake of coming out against the Right-wing party and declaring the election void. Interference of that kind can have only one result in Germany today: it won popular sympathy for the Right-wing party.

'The British did the Rightists the greatest possible favour,' said Herr Orlich. 'If they had kept out of it, the rascals and their stooges would have been thrown out in six weeks'.

His statement is supported by the elections for the plants workers' council, which took place only a few months later – the council consists of one Communist and the rest Social Democrats.

But all this was not getting the Volkswagen built, and Orlich conducted me into the plant. He had decided that I would not be advantageously placed on the assembly line, since this would mean routine work and no talking. Instead he intended to assign me to the measuring section, spot-checking the products of the assembly line and parts contracted for outside the plant. He took me to the foreman: 'We are thinking of employing this man', he said. 'Try him out. Give him some problems'.

Two days later the foreman delivered his verdict: 'Quite useless. Doesn't try. Talks too much. No technical knowledge.' Orlich winked at me and turned me over to a workman, who was told to supervise and assist me.

The foreman gave me a mysterious grooved bolt to take along with me. 'Take all its measurements', he said, 'and make a drawing. I want the groove and the rate of climb, diameter, over-all length and everything else. Use the Puppi-taster over there'.

Puppi-taster

'Jawohl,'[3] I replied. It seemed as good a reply as any. The Puppi-taster turned out to be a device which measures to hundredths of a millimetre any surface along which it is run. If this explanation is vague, so is my entire attitude toward the Puppi-taster. I sincerely hope all my results were thrown away.

The workman whose activities I was about to obstruct was named Kuropp, and turned out to be a kindly and helpful person who was a refugee from Berlin. He had been head of a large workshop there, and the Puppi-taster held no terrors for him. He had left Berlin after getting in trouble with the Russians, who had wanted more output than he was able to supply.

'Those Russians', he said, 'you can't reason with them. One day a Soviet colonel inspected my shop. A blacksmith was banging away on a piece of red-hot iron; it was quite a sight, and the colonel marched right up to the man and gave him 100 cigarettes. But iron doesn't stay hot forever: a few minutes later the colonel turned around and the blacksmith was standing quietly, waiting for the iron to heat in the fire. The Russian was furious. "You no work you no food!" he shouted, and had the man's ration card stopped for three days'.

I Puppi-tasted away for two days without getting far with my programme. Under the watchful eye of the foreman it was not easy to strike up conversations, but at last I discovered the secret. There were a few men – not many – who stole off to the lavatory now and then for a smoke, and I began to join them. In the end, I talked to about thirty of them, and did all I could to work up a political conversation. They were simply not interested. They would talk about housing, food, clothes, dentists, dogs, sports, and – of course – they would talk about women. When politics came up they were not cautious – they were just bored. I gave it up as at bad job.

Conversation

I had a little better luck when Orlich shifted me to the transfer drivers section. When a car leaves the assembly line, it is driven to a large square for a final check-up, and then to a railroad siding for shipment. It was exhausting work and the weather was hot; by the end of each day I had earned my keep. But it supplied an opportunity for chatting as we made our way back to the factory after dropping each car.

In fact, we chatted all day – and still no Nazis. The drivers were sharp and interested. They knew what was going on in Germany and they were willing to talk about it. But only two men ever made any remarks that could be considered suspect.

'Ah well,' said a former army officer, stretching himself at the end of a trip. 'We used to be well off. Now we're supposed to be better off. I wish we were well off again.' This sounded promising, and I attached myself to him at lunch. He talked about the plant and the car and riding horses and the army. I struck my first spark when I mentioned to him that I had recently been at the Hofbrauhaus[4], in Munich, and had seen a three-year-old boy there in Bavarian dress, but half Negro.

He thought this was horrible. 'I can't see,' he said, 'why the Catholic Church can't stop that sort of thing. You know – in '39 we had just managed to get it under control. In two more generations we would have been all right. And then the damned fool messed it all up and started a war'.

Ex-Nazi

My other suspect had held high rank in the SA[5], and had been in nominal charge of the factory under the Nazis. We got into a conversation, and I played the part of an agent provocateur for a moment – those were the good old days, I implied, and wouldn't it be nice if they were back again.

'What do you want?' he answered. 'The impossible? Those days are gone. But I'm not worried – I'll make out. When the British first got here I had a rough time; they put me in jail and they searched my papers. In the end they were damned decent. They even apologized for locking me up'.

He shrugged his shoulders. 'I've been decent to people and I helped where I could. The British found that out. Politics? Hell, no! I'm through with that'[6].

The rest of the time I drove cars and heard jokes and the usual nonsense, and became certain that all these men had on their minds was the little, sloping car they were handling. Every scratch was laboriously polished out; a trifling fault in the performance meant the car went back to the factory. 'The customer', they told me, 'is entitled to a 100 per cent product', and they worked as if they meant it.

I slipped off one day and drove around the factory. There are no ships in the canal, because three miles away the canal runs into the Russian Zone. Some of the buildings are still in ruins. But men are working hard, and well. They live in crowded houses and they are poor because they started with nothing. But step-by-step they are rebuilding their factory and rebuilding their lives.

Hitler's blueprints called for a much vaster factory, and they called for a 1,000-year Reich. The men who work there now know that the blueprints have become only vain dreams. They have their noses to the grindstone and they are done with dreaming. They have a full-time job that takes all their energies, and they appear to have neither the time nor the inclination for politics.

Notes:

1. Heinz Nordoff (1899–1968) was appointed Managing Director of the Volkswagen plant at Wolfsburg in 1948 following the recommendation of British Army Major Ivan Hirst who had been directing the plant. During his first year in charge, Nordhoff doubled production to almost 20,000 cars. By the end of 1961 annual production exceeded a million vehicles. He became legendary for turning the Volkswagen Beetle into a worldwide phenomenon; he developed export markets and ultimately manufacturing facilities abroad. Within six years of taking over at Volkswagen, Nordhoff reduced the number of man-hours to produce a single car from 400 to 100. His commitment to improving the workmanship made the Beetle famous for its reliability. In 1955, shortly before the Wolfsburg factory celebrated its millionth Volkswagen, Nordhoff was awarded a Federal Service Cross with star (The Order of Merit of the Federal Republic of Germany).

2. *Lèse majesté* is a crime committed against a sovereign power.

3. 'Jawohl' is a German word, used as a strong affirmative. It doesn't have a specifically Nazi background, but one of its main uses has always been in the military.

4. The Staatliches Hofbrauhaus (public Royal Brewery) is a brewery in Munich owned by the Bavarian state government.

5. SA is the abbreviation for Sturmabteilung (Storm Detachment).

6. In his memoirs Wolfe Frank adds a little more about his investigations in the Volkswagen plant:

'Finally, puffing away at a cigarette in the lavatory, it seemed that I had struck oil: a tall, bespectacled type with a Silesian accent was sounding off to a pal about the beaten Germany"

"What we need," he said "is a strong man. A man who can inspire us. A man who can show us the way into the better future the German nation deserves. We need a man like" – ah here it comes I thought triumphantly, the first strike – "Churchill" said my informant.

'I gave up!

'Volkswagen was certainly not the haven for fleeing top Nazis. I could write that with a clear conscience. Heinz Nordoff grinned when I said my goodbyes'.

A DEMOCRACY THAT IS
BUILT ON SAND

Hangover After Hitler Series: Published Saturday 17 December 1949

A POLITICIAN IN HANOVER[1] – no dignified statesman but a bitter man whose background makes it impossible for him to work openly for power – sat with me and spoke his mind.

'There are some men in this country,' he said, 'who have the intelligence and the strength to become leaders of Germany. You will notice that I do not speak of their integrity. Only of their intelligence and strength.

'How many? Perhaps 400. And if the Allies had the courage of their convictions, they would send these men to the gas chambers in Auschwitz. It would prevent no end of trouble.

'These 400 men do not even know of one another's existence. In time they will. Sooner or later they will begin to discover one another, and to find that they speak the same language and have mapped the same road'.

'You understand,' the politician continued, 'that I am not speaking of the Nazis and the nationalists who are meeting, more or less in secret, all over Germany today. They are the rank and file, or at best the non-commissioned officers, of the party that is to be. The 400 men of whom I speak are the leaders, the elite. They mean disaster for Germany'.

He stopped there, perhaps because he was afraid he had said too much already. As for me, I have no way of knowing whether his '400 elite' are creatures of his imagination or whether they do, indeed, lurk somewhere in Germany.

But five months in Germany convinced me that his theory was not unreasonable. Politically, the situation could not be more grave. The Allies have sought to build a democracy, and they have built on sand.

Exiles

Hitler achieved power in 1933. In the years before that date and the years that followed it, men with visions of a German democracy fought his influence and were defeated. Many of them died at Hitler's hands; many went into exile and died as the years passed. Younger men who came along either avoided politics altogether, or were forced by circumstances to work, if not earnestly with the Nazis, at least in association with them.

The result was inevitable. With the fall of Hitler, Germany could turn only to these aged democratic leaders who had already tried and failed, or to those potential democratic leaders whose association with Hitler made them arbitrarily suspect. The Allies – probably with entire justice – ruled the second group out. It is the first group – mediocre men, lacking utterly any public appeal – who are governing Germany today.

The German citizen does not need to be told this. The minority that is politically aware – in general, the upper classes – worries about it. The mass of Germans responds by displaying a general political inertia. But my conversations with Germans in all walks of life convinced me that the politically aware and the politically inert are united in one common sentiment: they have little but contempt for the Bonn government[2].

In the words of Dr Ernst Mueller-Meiningen, editor of the leading independent Munich newspaper, 'Why do we regard politics, in all its aspects, as being bad, amateurish, insufficient, and why is it often no better than its reputation? Surely because often – at least in the German sphere – politics is practiced by mediocre, amateurish and ambitious persons, and not by men regarded as the best by the people. If we had an instrument to detect the percentage of those who have turned to polities out of a sense of responsibility, and compared this with the number who have become politicians for dubious motives, we would most certainly arrive at a frightening result'.

Disciplined Votes

So the Germans drift and wait for the 'capitulation government' (the term of contempt pinned on the Bonn government by the opposition leader Dr Kurt Schumacher) to die in a flurry of ineptitude. They vote dutifully when they are told to. 'The Germans have a high sense of discipline,' Dr Hjalmar Schacht[3] said after the August elections. 'They were told it was their duty to vote: so they voted'.

In the eyes of most of the Germans I talked to, their government has no real significance for contemporary Germans. Men who associate themselves with it destroy automatically their political future: most Germans consider them the willing tools or the Allied powers, doing Allied bidding within a meaningless government imposed on Germany as part of the German punishment.

The political future of Germany, if current appearances have any significance, will be entirely unrelated to the activities of the Bonn government. How will it be shaped? No one exactly knows. Perhaps by the Hanover politician's '400 dangerous men'.

Or, for another possibility, come with me to Bavaria and meet 'the blond Hitler,' Alfred Loritz. During the August election, a surprisingly large number of Bavarians voted for Loritz and his Wiederaufbau Vereinigung (Economic Reconstruction Party), popularly known as WAV.

Loritz was a lawyer in pre-Nazi days – a rabble-rousing advocate noted for a bullying belligerency in court. Early in the Hitler regime he experienced a stroke of luck. He came into conflict with the Nazis, and was forced into exile. Thus, although he could not know it at the time, he was assured of a favourable reception by the Allies at the end of the war.

WAV

He was quick to return to Bavaria. There he formed the WAV. Securing the post of de-Nazification director in the Bavarian government, he could trade on the rumour that he was high in the favour of the military occupation. As head of de-Nazification, he proved to be a dictator in his own right. It was then the Germans began calling him 'the blond Hitler'.

Then Loritz stumbled. He was arrested on charges of being involved in the black market. While under arrest and in a hospital, he managed to escape. For almost a year he was 'lost'. From a hideout, he supplied his party with political material in writing and on phonograph records.

Ultimately he reappeared and was rearrested. This time he was found to be in possession of foreign currency. Black-marketing was an offence against the Bavarian government. Possession of foreign currency rendered him liable to trial by the Military Government[4]. But all charges were mysteriously dropped.

Loritz was not satisfied to let well enough alone. In speeches, he charged that the Bavarian judicial administration had imprisoned him under conditions as bad as in a Nazi concentration camp, and that he had been ill-treated. The Bavarian Minister of Justice sued him for libel.

To make the suit possible, the Bavarian Diet[5] voted to suspend his immunity. A hearing was scheduled to take place a few days before the August election. The Military Government found this improper, and ordered the trial postponed. In the ensuing squabble with the Bavarian government the Military Government won. The election was held. Loritz was elected to the Bonn Assembly. Once again he was immune from suit.

He still enjoys this privileged position. Today he works from WAV headquarters in Munich. I passed an afternoon there, amid the atmosphere of a madhouse. Men and women rushed about screaming, and out-screaming them all was Loritz – pale, dynamic, choleric. After a few moments I began taking notes on a curious portion of his performance. I am able to report that in eighteen minutes he employed twenty-three juicy Bavarian objurgations [severe rebukes]. During the twenty-five minutes he was in his headquarters he never found time to take off his hat or set down his briefcase.

Brief Interview

Refused an interview by his secretary, I walked into his empty office, furnished with a primitive bench and table, a rusty iron stove and two empty beer bottles. When he came in I began to talk to him. He stared at me wordlessly, obviously not hearing a word I was saying. Finally he honoured me with a few words.

'Get out. I have important election matters to attend to.'

This concluded the interview.

Loritz has directed his campaign at the two million refugees in Bavaria. His party publishes a periodical for them, which started slowly but has been picking up since it began to rely on pornographic headlines. He collected a substantial number of votes.

How important is Loritz? As an individual, not very important at present. But if the Bavarian Party (allegedly supplying some of Loritz's funds) and the WAV were to coalesce (it's possible, and it might not displease the French, the Bavarian Party being separatist), that coalition would control Bavaria. Affecting that screaming, hysterical oratorical style which appeals to the German masses, Herr Loritz would make a beautiful Fuehrer.

Any way you look at Loritz he remains significant as a symptom. The Germans who turn to him and others like him do so because there is nothing better to turn to. This is in some part due to an unfortunate situation which a distinguished German psychologist [Professor Phillip Lersch] summarized to me thus:

130

'Even if we disregard the fact that the word "democracy" has by now assumed the aspect of an aged and worn-out prostitute, we still have three different occupying powers in Western Germany trying to teach us Germans three different versions of democracy. None has been, or is, convincing the man in the street that it is the effective road to a secure, hopeful and, above all, a peaceful future'.

Allied Failure

Considered and authoritative comments of this kind plainly accuse the Allies of some kind of important failure. By this I mean a failure separated from the factors of Germany's ruined cities and the debris of war. Not that those factors can he minimized, since defeat can ruin both a people's government and a people's capacity to govern.

I would extract two related kinds of failure. One is the toleration of mediocrity, because the mediocre men are 'safe and unsullied'. The other is the failure to block off such men as Major General Remer[6]. It is a matter of record that Remer played a major part in putting down the abortive 1944 revolt against Hitler. Yet Remer has been allowed by the Allies, and by the Germans themselves, to reappear effectively on the political scene. He is openly active as a member of a group of Nationalists agitating for German unity.

On the other hand I would say that the Allies have been too persistent in blocking the return to active pubic life and administrative responsibility of able men who put their brains and energies at the service of the Hitlerite regime, but were not ideologically or integrally a part of it. Such men, whatever they think of a regime, must pursue their careers, or perish of inertia, or leave the country – if they can.

Schacht

Dr Schacht [see Plates 10, 11 & 15] is an illustrative case. He is a financial and economic organizer of the highest order. Before the War he was internationally known among central bankers and government economists, and respected. But he was a key administrator in the Nazi state, and he was brought to trial at Nuremberg. He was then brought to trial by his own countrymen at Ludwigsburg. He was acquitted there too – it was the only one of the de-Nazification trials that had any substance.

The Allies stand squarely behind convictions: but the wry remark was made to me: 'Why don't they stand squarely behind acquittals too?' The implied criticism is not unjustified.

Schacht's real trouble seems to be that he was prominent, rather than that he did evil things. Schacht is more unfortunate than many a figure in German public life today who was much more deeply integrated and involved with the Nazi 'way of life' during Hitler's period of power, but whose lack of ability kept him inconspicuous.

I spoke to a great many Germans of the wage-earning and lower-middle-class groups about the European Recovery Programme[7], only to discover that few of them had any knowledge of the aid Germany is receiving through ERP, while a substantial proportion did not know what the initials meant.

In Munich I saw a handicraft fair, and an ERP exhibition, running simultaneously. The first was attracting record crowds; the second was doing a very thin business. Its empty halls depressed me and I wandered into the bar and held converse with a lonely bartender. He was disgruntled, but he had what seemed to me a good idea.

'Herr Hoffman[8] should fish out Hans Fritzsche[9] and get him to handle the advertising for the thing'.

Fritzsche was the prize radio propagandist in the Goebbels stable. Although acquitted at Nuremberg, he is now serving an eight-year de-Nazification sentence in a labour camp. He probably deserves it, but meanwhile Germany lacks comparable talent to fill gaps.

All this is secondary to the primary problem: Who is to lead Germany, today and tomorrow? I recall vividly the bitter words of a mechanic in the Volkswagen plant in Wolfsburg: 'Our politicians are a bunch of senile old stooges who proved their weakness when they let the Nazis seize power. They are the same old men who failed us in 1933. They won't last'.

The mechanic, like so many Germans, looks forward with feelings ranging from disquiet to dread to the day when new leaders appear. He has no confidence in the kind of leaders they are likely to be.

Notes:

1. Recorded elsewhere by Frank as being Count E. Westarp.

2. Bonn became the de facto capital, officially designated the 'temporary seat of the Federal institutions,' of the newly formed Federal Republic of Germany in 1949. Known as the Bundestag (the equivalent of the UK's House of Commons and the USA's House of Representatives) the Bonn government drafted and adopted the German constitution and affirmed Berlin's status as the German capital.

3. Hjalmar Schacht (1887–1970) was a German economist, banker, centre-right politician, and co-founder, in 1918, of the German Democratic Party. He was never a member of the Nazi party but served as President of the National Bank (Reichsbank) and Minister of Economics under Adolf Hitler. He was tried at Nuremberg, but was fully acquitted (see Plates 10, 11 & 15).

4. The Office of Military Government, United States (OMGUS) was the United States military-established government created shortly after the end of WWII. Under General Lucius Clay, it administered the area of Germany and the sector of Berlin controlled by the US Army.

5. In this sense a 'Diet' is a gathering of members who use parliamentary procedures to make decisions.

6. Otto-Ernst Remer (1912 –1997) was a German Wehrmacht officer who played a decisive role in stopping the 20 July 1944 plot to assassinate Adolf Hitler. During the war he was wounded nine times in combat. After the war he co-founded the Socialist Reich Party (SRP) and advanced Holocaust denial. He has been referred to as being the 'Godfather' of the post-war Nazi underground.

7. The European Recovery Programme (ERP), also known as the Marshall Plan, was an American initiative to aid Western Europe after WWII. The USA gave over $13 billion ($140 billion in today's money) in economic assistance to help rebuild Western European economies. The plan was in operation for four years from 1948 and the aims of the programme were to rebuild war-torn regions, remove trade barriers, modernise industry, improve European prosperity, and prevent the spread of Communism.

8. Thought to be a reference to Heinz Hoffman (1910–1985) first Vice President of the German Administration of the Interior and Head of the Department of Political Culture with the rank of Inspector General.

9. Hans Fritzsche (1900-1953) was Head of Propaganda and was charged at Nuremberg on three counts and acquitted. However he was later charged by a de-Nazification Court and sentenced to nine years' imprisonment. He died soon after release (see plate 15).

POVERTY AND LUXURY IN GERMANY

Hangover After Hitler Series: Published Monday 19 December 1949

TRAVELING AROUND THE WESTERN ZONES of Germany, I lived the way the Germans themselves live as much as I could. I stayed in private houses whenever it was possible (although it is actually against the law to have a spare room to rent) and in German hotels otherwise. I ate in German restaurants and shopped in German stores and rode in German conveyances. I think I came out of it with a fairly good idea of how Germans live.

A fairly good German worker, with no particular skills, will put together something like 200 to 300 marks a month. I know that's a wide range, but wages vary that widely in Germany. At the official rate, that comes to $47.50 to $71; at the black-market rate to something less. But neither rate means very much to a German inside Germany; he counts his salary in marks because he spends it in marks, and if the government economists think differently about it he is unmoved.

At the lower of those two rates, he will have to work nearly a week to buy himself a pair of shoes; about a month to buy a radio and six months to buy a Volkswagen, the little German runabout. He could do this if he had no other expenses, but, believe me, he has.

Even if he is single, he will get into the habit of eating most of his meals at home. The cheapest meal he can find in a restaurant will set him back 1.50 marks, which would come to 45 marks a month if he did it daily and is simply too much of a chunk out of his 200 or 300. He wouldn't even bother to stop outside the more expensive restaurants, even on a gala occasion; a steak with potatoes, vegetables and mixed salad would be more than a weeks pay.

Diet

Not that eating at home will be luxurious. Meat is four to five marks a pound, and a rarity. Most of his diet will be bread, potatoes and vegetables, with little milk and that most horrible of all potations, ersatz coffee[1].

And he will not eat in particularly gay surroundings. In most parts of the country there must be two residents for every available room. Clothing and furnishings went up in flames under bombing. Coal is scarce, and although he may spend a good deal of his spare time in the summer scrounging for firewood, he can hardly hope to amass and store enough to see him through the rough German winter.

A single woman is not even as well off as a single man. A friend of mine, earning 200 marks a month as a secretary, gave me a rough idea of her budget for the month:

Rent for furnished single room	25
Two baths weekly	2
Laundry	10
Fares	6
Food	112
Clothing	8
Entertainment	12
	—
Total	175

She has 25 marks a month left over for savings, emergencies, stamps, telephone calls, newspapers and everything else that goes to make up routine living.

She explained to me that the budget for entertainment (about $3 a month) was high. 'Sometimes a man takes me out for an evening', she said, 'But there are too many women in Germany today. I have to pay my own way most of the time'.

A man with a family finds it almost impossible to support them on his salary. His wife and his children must help out. But employment is hard to find, and his life is likely to be a constant struggle to keep even, with the spectre of losing his job always before him. Whatever savings he may once have had were wiped out by the war and the currency crises; he has nothing to fall back on but his own two hands.

Shops

Yet, strangely enough, in the face of all this squalor the shops in Germany give the impression of prosperity and luxury. All over the towns, where homes are in rubble, rows of one-story commercial buildings have sprung up. Rents may run as high as '$400 a month. In Dusseldorf's beautiful Koenigsallee, one display of luxury goods after another holds the eye of the stroller. There is exquisite Rosenthal china, jewellery, leather goods and clothing – everything, it sometimes seemed to me, except customers.

I asked about this paradox and was told it all went back to the currency reform in 1948, when the new West mark was put into circulation. Backed to some extent by the good faith of the Western powers, and apparently free from the danger of Soviet manipulation, the currency became immediately desirable, and accordingly took on a purchasing power that the old mark never had. For the first time since the end of the war, a German preferred currency to goods, and he was willing to put his goods on the market, or to exchange his services for marks instead of in barter.

People with savings became intoxicated with this new purchasing power and set out to make their savings swell. Shops were built and stocked with the owners' last reserves, in the face of widespread grumbling that housing should take priority over leather-goods emporia.

But the one thing that was lacking, and is still lacking, was a healthy economy that could make such shops pay. The Germans simply do not have that kind of money to spend, excepting always those Germans who continue to thrive at illegal activities.

The shops will remain, because they are fairly well built and their stocks are desirable. But more than one thoughtful German assured me that there would be a general shaking out before profits are shown, and the first people into the field are likely to be heavy losers.

Diversions

The same sudden burst of activity characterized the entertainment industry after the currency reform. The Germans have had a hard time since 1933, and they are eager to break loose and enjoy themselves. Entrepreneurs were quick to appreciate the desire, and they responded by building or refurbishing cinemas, cabarets, theatres, bars and sports arenas. The only thing lacking is Germans with enough money to take advantage of entertainment facilities.

The biggest crowds, as usual, turn out at the sports events. Soccer draws fantastic crowds, and motor and cycle racing have regained their pre-war popularity. Even the Volkswagen has been souped up into a fast, if somewhat insecure, racing vehicle.

Tennis is back on the way up, although in Germany it has always been rather an aristocratic sport. Roller-skating has gained tremendously because it is cheap; there is even a rink next to the Parliament building in Bonn, over an air-raid shelter. I tried it.

The crowd was no more distinguished than at any other rink, 'None of the delegates have used it yet', I was told, 'It's too dangerous to roller skate when you can't decide whether to turn Right or Left'.

The Germans have radio, too – and the most popular stations of all, without even a close suspicion, are those run by the United States Army – AFN, the American Forces Network. When Ralph Moffat, the popular disc jockey, left the network, his German fans were heart-broken. They still get their Bing Crosby, Frank Sinatra and Betty Hutton, but the country of Brahms, Beethoven and Bach misses the way Moffat had of presenting them.

Radio

At a German party, the entertainment is almost certain to be supplied by AFN, or by a survival from AFN days. When the Army radio had its all-night *Midnight in Munich* programme, it was the most listened to station in Germany in the early morning hours.

Now that AFN shuts down at midnight the programme is carried over the German transmitter as *Mitternacht in Munich*. And it broadcasts 'Die Zehn der Woche', otherwise known as 'The Hit Parade'.

The German stations lean heavily on instructive programmes, such as the proceedings of the provincial and national Parliaments. Professor Carlo Schmid, a member of the opposition, has won by means of the radio the reputation of being a brilliant speaker and the Germans, still capable of being drugged by oratory, gather around loud-speakers indoors and out when his voice is heard.

The theatres and cabarets, I am prepared to report, are almost without exception dull.

The acting is bad in the theatre, and the material is worse. The only cabaret I attended that was worth the price of a drink was the Bonbonniere in Hamburg and that was entirely attributable to Ursula Herking[2] and the material supplied her by Erich Kaestner[3]. Afterward I complained about other shows I had seen.

'But darling!' Ursula cried. 'Surely you know why! They have no heart, they have no soul'. She went on to tell me why. When Hitler came to power, the cabarets lost some important performers, the Jews. 'You must remember them: Felix Hollaender, Kurt Nelson, Kurt Bois, Margo Lion and many others. They toned down German exuberance with *savoir faire* and a light touch. They had wit and irony. When they went German cabaret went with them'.

So among other things Hitler can be blamed for are the present dull evenings in Germany.

Notes:

1. Ersatz is a coffee substitute made from roasted rice, roasted peas, and roasted chicory.

2. Ursula Herking was a German actress who appeared in over 130 films between 1933 and 1972.

3. Emil Erich Kaestner was a German author, poet, screenwriter and satirist, known primarily for his humorous, socially astute poems and for children's books including Emil and the Detectives.

ANTI-SEMITISM IN GERMANY

Hangover After Hitler Series: Published Tuesday 20 December 1949

THERE IS NOTHING PARTICULARLY FRIGHTENING in the word 'Endloesung' – it means simply the final disposition of a problem, and it is no more offensive than the average German word of that length. But there is an element of horror in the use that Hitler made of it. The problem in question was 'the Jewish problem[1],' and the disposition was mass murder.

The facts are well enough known. Before the war there were about 600,000 persons of Jewish descent living in Germany. They comprised about one per cent of the population. Today there are 60,000. This means, in effect, that 540,000 more or less were exiled or put to death in one way or another.

This was Hitler's most frightful political instrument. But in Germany, anti-Semitism is a political instrument no longer. There are laws against it. Instead, it is merely a national characteristic. There is no less anti-Semitism in Germany than there was ten years ago. The principal differences are that there are fewer Jews against whom to direct it, and occupation authorities who keep it from breaking out in violence.

This is not a pleasant conclusion, but I found it inescapable after five months in Germany. I tried to find out upon what it was feeding, and I discovered that there were many well-springs.

Well-Springs

There was, for example, the discussion in Nuremberg among members of a German Youth Association group. A man who had served as interpreter at Nuremberg was giving the boys and girls an account of the world of deceits that Hitler had practiced upon them and, somewhat didactically, he ended his discourse with the question: 'Now who do you think was responsible for the war?'

There was a brief pause. Then an eighteen-year-old girl gave the reply: 'The Jews'.

I met a lot of eighteen-year-olds in Germany. They were just out of the nursery when Hitler came to power; their entire education and environment was dictated by the Fuehrer. A few years of occupation will never recondition their reflexes. They give the questioner the answers they were told to give during their formative years.

What of the older people? The picture is little better. Time and time again I heard the Jews blamed for all the ills that assail Germany today, and almost every time the discussion was rounded off something like this: 'After all, what can you expect? There is no way of punishing the Jews for the things they are doing; they are in with the Americans'. And occasionally, confidentially, 'Of course, in America all the important positions are held by Jews'.

Black Market

And then there is the difficult problem of the black market. This is most difficult to write about. I can give you the bare facts first, as I discovered them at first hand in Munich.

There are Jewish and non-Jewish shops in Munich. Some of them sell black market goods from under the counter. Of those that do so, some are Jewish and some are non-Jewish, which is exactly what you might suspect.

But to the Germans, a man dealing in the black market is 'the Jew'. In Murnau, near Munich, for example, I pretended to want some coffee and was directed by friends, who are neither Nazi nor anti-Semitic, to 'the Jew'. I took him aside and asked him if he were Jewish. 'Not a single ancestor', he said. 'But the name has nothing to do with ancestry', and he smiled.

There is, however, more to it than that. In most large German cities, there are colonies of DPs – displaced persons – and the Jews among them tend to create settlements of their own. Many of them engage in the Black Market – some because they have no other recourse, others because they are the sort who deal in mildly illegal activities. Germans do the same thing for the same reasons.

Concentrations

But the Jews are concentrated. Their activities are displayed in the same quarter, where anyone may go and permit himself to combine the concept of Jew with the concept of black market. Worst of all, for the Jews themselves, it tends to be more openly done because German authorities are afraid to clamp down. 'If we do', I was told 'the occupation authorities will say we are anti-Semitic'. Accordingly, the greatest service they could do the German community goes undone.

A friend of mine in the De-Nazification Ministry told me how upset he was over the problem. 'There are 60,000 left; normally you would have to pass 1,000 men for every Jew you saw. But they concentrate, and their faults stand out in a country where people are looking for every fault they can find'.

I don't see any point in recounting all the stories I was told about the sins of the Jews – the same stories that are current in every country where virulent anti-Semitism lies just beneath the civilized veneer. They would have a familiar sound to anyone who has ever listened to an anti-Semite anywhere – and I am afraid that is everyone.

Vengeance

There is one other factor specific to Germany. The trials that are going on in Germany today – from the trials of minor offenders to the Nuremberg trials themselves – do not sit well with the Germans. And more than once I have been told: 'But after all, it was the Jews who ran them and one can hardly blame the Jews for wanting vengeance'.

I knew it would have been better for the Jews, in a sense, if Jewish lawyers and prosecutors had not been involved in these trials, and if the occupation had employed no Jewish help. And I know even better that, from a more substantial point of view, it would have been worse for the Jews and for Germany and the world to have not done it that way. That would have been a thoroughgoing concession to Hitler and Hitlerism, and there would have been no decent way to justify it. I suppose it is just one of those problems for which no clear-cut solution exists. I can say, on the basis of first-hand knowledge, that it is being used against the Jews in Germany today.

This is not a cheerful report, and I cannot make it so. There were many people in Germany who gave me the other side of the picture, and I remember many Jews who are living placidly in communities whose utter respect and confidence they hold. But I must admit I think of them as exceptions, and I remember far more sharply, and consider far more typical, the workman in a Hanover cafe who said to me: 'The greatest thing the Fuehrer did, was to finish off the Jews. Unfortunately, 60,000 of them escaped. But don't worry, we'll get them yet'.

Unless they are prevented, they will.

Note:

1. 'The Jewish Problem' or 'The Final Solution' was a Nazi plan for the extermination of the Jews during WWII.

TEARING DOWN GERMAN FACTORIES

Hangover After Hitler Series: Published Wednesday 21 December 1949

'YOU WILL LOSE THE RIGHT to find employment if you insist upon continuing this dismantling work you are doing.

'Dismantling[1] will only last a few more months. Would you not prefer to live longer than that?'

These are extracts from a letter signed 'Adolf Behnke,' a fictitious name, and received by a firm in Essen which was engaged in dismantling the August Thyssen steel plant.

It was dated September 7, 1949. The accuracy of the writer's prediction is astounding. It continued:

'All decent businessmen in the Hamborn-Duisburg area and beyond that in all Germany have turned down with disgust requests to carry out dismantling. They do not want to become demolishing profiteers whose activities will never be forgotten. Do you not wish to keep your name clean for all time?'

I had found it extremely difficult to locate this little firm which had been forced to disregard such a warning for fear of going broke.

On arrival in Essen I had attempted to contact firms who were doing this work. A friend had got on the telephone and called a dozen contacts in the building trade.

'Dismantling?' they had said, 'Not on your life! Try Meyer'. Meyer had said: 'Try Mueller', and Mueller had told us to get on to Schulze.

I tried a few myself. In the end my eardrums were aching. 'That sort of thing is a crime'. Herr Schu, of Essen, had yelled at me. 'Who the hell told you I was doing it? I'll tear him apart! You come out here and I'll tell you all you want to know about dismantling!'

143

So-and-So

At last I found the firm which had received Adolf Behnke's letter. It was tucked away among rubble in the centre of Essen. I got there by following abusive direction signs which, painted on houses along my route, had been ineffectively covered up with whitewash. 'So-and-so is a dismantling scoundrel', they read. It will have to be 'so-and-so [Ernst Heinrichsbauer]'. I couldn't get a word out of the owner of that firm until I promised on my honour that I wouldn't mention his name. Even then he called my friend to ascertain if I could be trusted.

The firm of So-and-So had been let down over a number of vital contracts, according to Herr Frei (not his real name), the manager [Weber Heinrichsbauer, the owner's son].

'We took on dismantling because we knew that 5 per cent, at most, of the stuff we were tearing down could be used again. Even then we were abused and threatened by both the local builders, who have formed a sort of "anti-dismantling ring," and the population. There were threatening phone calls and smashed windows'.

I checked him there.

'Can you prove that only five per cent of this dismantled material is any good?'

He thought he could. Would I like to look at the Thyssen plant myself? I would like to very much.

The next morning found me applying to the administrative office outside the Thyssen plant for a visiting pass. 'Object of visit: to apply for work'. My papers were checked more carefully than ever before. Herr Frei, waiting for me in his office inside, was consulted and affirmed that I should he admitted.

I walked through the gate. Never in my life had I seen anything like this.

Thyssen

The August Thyssen plant is roughly four miles long and four miles wide. There are sixteen square miles of utter and complete destruction. Not even by the widest stretch of my imagination could I visualize that this endless expanse of twisted girders and rusty fragments could ever have been Germany's largest steel-producing plant.

What used to be a series of rolling mills was now a towering mass of rusted, roofless girders. Unobstructed by walls or equipment, the eye could rove for thousands of yards down the entire length of a steel mill.

144

Grass grew everywhere. Bomb craters had been bridged with boards. Occasionally a cloud of steam rose from the ground. It came from an underground pipe-line, still functioning in connection with a gas-producer plant; miraculously left intact.

Signposts in English and German led me to Frei's office. There were slogans, too, painted carefully on walls: 'Dismantling is a crime.' 'Dismantling deprives us of our daily bread.' The British, in charge of the plant, had left them alone.

I located Frei, and my first question was about the total amount of scrap iron in that plant. He could not be certain, but was sure that it was over one million tons.

Some 2,000 men were pulling it down. Or at least they were pulling down what had been earmarked for re-erection elsewhere. In this huge labyrinth it was difficult to see any of them. I would have guessed that there were not more than a couple of hundred.

In one place Frei's workers were busy with oxy-acetylene burners. A huge sheet of steel crashed to the ground in a cloud of dust. 'Good', said a foreman – 'that means tonnage.' (Frei is paid by the ton).

Machinery

We came to a former engine-house with enormous ventilating turbines. There were eight of them, with giant flywheels each weighing several tons.

'You need this whole set to supply air for one medium-sized smelting oven', Frei told me.

'Two of them have been damaged by a bomb. The rest are being dismantled. The parts are carefully painted, numbered, indexed and listed. A team of draughtsmen is preparing blueprints so that they can he reassembled.

'One day a mission from some foreign country will turn up to inspect this machinery which has been allocated to them. They will look at it and say: "God no! We wouldn't touch this junk with a barge pole!" They will know this aggregate could only be used if it is complete, which it isn't, and that the missing pieces can't be replaced with new ones. We've had this happen many times'.

I wanted to know why it had been listed as usable.

'The British did that at the end of the war. I imagine that someone put it on the list as "Plant, blasting, furnace for the use of – six machines intact, two damaged." Somewhere a high-ranking officer saw the list and ticked off the item, "six machines intact." And now we're taking them down'.

We walked through the plant, past smelting ovens with gaping wounds in their sides, torn railway tracks and cranes dangling dangerously from severed rails.

'I've shown you all there is to see', said Frei alter four hours. 'I think you will agree that my "five per cent" is a justifiable figure'.

Without committing myself. I asked what the situation was elsewhere. He admitted that there had been 'genuine' dismantling.

Competition

'But there have been other cases which were clearly aimed at the competition of peaceful industries. They've taken down the "Knirps" umbrella factory at Hilden, which used to export ninety-nine per cent of its production.

'They've taken down a part of the Henkel soap factory. That particular section had stood still since 1911. Even so, Henkel printed a gorgeous, multi-coloured pamphlet on the finest glossy paper, protesting against this dismantling. They sent that to all their agents abroad and stressed that Henkel's soap-flakes were the best. It was done during the worst paper shortage and got them a reprimand from General Sir Brian Robertson[2].

'They took down a plant in Gelsenkirchen which used to make some substance needed for the production of synthetic gasoline. But Germany is prohibited from making synthetic gas, so that plant could never again be operated.

'The management of the Rheinpreussen chemical works, on the other hand, knew how to get along with the British. Dismantling started, but they persuaded the British to take a lot of important items off the list'.

I asked him if he knew about the riot which had resulted in the beating up of British officers outside the Ruhrchemie plant at Holten. Frei had been present.

'We went there in trucks, led by a Colonel Cleghorn in a British car. He was in civilian clothes. We were received by a rebellious mob. The workers' council[3] had got them there to stage that demonstration. It included war veterans who had left their artificial legs and arms at home for the occasion.

'We drove up to the gate and our convoy was hemmed in. There were angry shouts from the crowd. One Englishman, Captain Blakesley, also in civilian clothes, was recognized. "Here's Blakesley, the dismantling swine!" they shouted. The British car was turned over and Blakesley was severely kicked as he lay on the ground.

Retreat

'We Germans had dropped to the floor of our truck. But Colonel Cleghorn did a very brave thing. He walked alone ahead of the truck as it backed up and directed it to a point where it could turn. We managed to retreat from there, but that was an unnecessary defeat for the British. You couldn't imagine the German Army making a mistake like that when it was occupying a foreign country!

'Colonel Cleghorn could have found out that this demonstration was going to happen. All he had to do was to bring one jeepload of MPs. They would have got us into that factory. There would have been no demonstration by the Germans, and no retreat for the British'.

Herr Frei, unlike the writer of the abusive letter, thought that dismantling would continue for a long time yet. His was obviously the wishful type of thinking.

'Dismantling is creating work for 7,000 men in the Essen area alone. It isn't really doing any harm to the German economy. The stuff they're taking down now is useless. The best thing that can happen to those plants is to have their bombed sites cleared'.

But from the political point of view he thought that dismantling had dragged on far too long.

'The German politicians are making capital out of it,' said Herr Frei. 'Relying on the ignorance of their listeners, they are making flaming speeches about these crimes committed against the German people by the Allies. They aren't telling about the useless scrap we're pulling down.

'The British missed an opportunity there. They should have made propaganda for this programme and told the Germans what needed pulling down as war-potential equipment and what was scrap.

'I know for certain that a leading German politician was paid 800 marks by the workers' council of a plant for coming here and stirring up public feeling against its dismantling'.

He smiled sadly. 'As far as our firm is concerned, we're just hoping that the whole programme is carried out. It would keep us going for another three years. But then, you know the old German proverb: *"Was dem einen sein Uhl ist dem anderen sein Nachtigall"* (What to one man is an owl is a nightingale to another)'.

Notes:

1. At the end of World War II the occupying forces put in place a programme, known as Dismantling, which intended to permanently disable Germany's war

147

making capabilities. This included demolishing factories and removing and prosecuting the owners. Pressure to end the programme was already building at the time of Frank's investigations in 1949 and it came to an end in 1951.

2. General Sir Brian Robertson was Chief of Staff and Military Governor of the British Occupation Zone of Germany.

3. A workers' council in Germany is a 'shop-floor' organisation that functions as a complement to, but is separate from, trade unions. They have three main functions: to reduce workplace conflict by improving and systematising communication channels; to increase bargaining power of workers at the expense of owners by means of legislation; and to correct market failures by means of public policy.

THE GERMANS AND
THE CONQUERORS

Hangover After Hitler Series: Published Thursday 22 December 1949

A TALL, HANDSOME, BUT SOMEWHAT DRUNK American soldier was amused by a little German boy in Munich who was unquestionably a few inches shorter than a boy his age is expected to be. 'Youngster', he said, 'if you can stretch up high enough to light my cigarette, I'll give you a trip to the United States'.

The urchin looked up at him boldly. 'And if you can bend down low enough to shine my shoes', he said, 'I'll let you stay in Germany'.

A few hundred yards away, a German telephone worker was making some repairs at a street corner when an American jet plane, glittering in the sun, went into a power dive. Germans usually refrain, very deliberately, from looking at planes directly overhead, but this one looked. He followed the aircraft as it swept down, then mumbled, 'I hope this one dives right into the ground'.

In Berchtesgaden, a mechanic changing a wheel on an automobile: 'Why the hell a lousy little American lieutenant with his idle little wife should have a ten-room villa in Munich, while my brother and his wife and six children are crowded together in two rooms ... Democracy my foot! The war ended four and a half years ago. These people ought to go home, damn it. But they won't – they'll never be willing to go home. They know they'll never have anything like this again'.

A hotel keeper on Lake Starnberg: 'Until this week we were under the Allied Joint Export-Import Agency[1] and full of damned Americans. They ruined the hotel, broke up furniture and drew pictures on the walls. Thank God we're through with those savages. From now on we have room only for Germans'.

Those are four sets of quotations picked up more or less at random. They all concern Americans, largely because the Americans have been more noticeable in the sections where they were collected. In their own zones, the French and the British come in for much the same sort of comment from the average German.

Violations

Then, too, the British and the French do not violate the average German's idea of what is right nearly as much as the Americans can do. Living standards are part of it; the American is well paid and demands the best, which contrasts violently with what the Germans are getting. The British, with considerably smaller pay cheques and far less subsidization by their army, live in comparative austerity. The French go their own correct way, coming into contact with Germans as little as possible. They are so correct, in fact, that even though they are permitted in the French Zone to share apartments with Germans, they never actually come close to German life.

Since I travelled as a German, I was able to share conversations that would never have taken place if the other speaker had suspected I was carrying a British passport.

Even a suspicion that, whether a German national or not, I was working with the Allies would have been enough. During a studio party I attended in Frankfurt, which I attended as a German, someone inquired after a friend he had not seen for some time. There was a moment's silence; then a voice: 'That swine has no business among us. He has worked for the American Counter Intelligence Corps. The time will come soon when he will be taught a lesson'.

I was taught one myself. In my Bavarian disguise I had been invited to the American Press Club in Munich for a cup of coffee. As I left, I passed the blonde at the desk and dropped her a friendly 'Gruess Gott,' [God bless] which was the customary farewell before it was replaced by 'Heil Hitler'.

A week later, this time in a very British blue suit, I was back, and approached the blonde with a question. 'Has Mr Cook arrived yet?' I asked.

'Nein,' she said, 'Er ist noch nicht da.' [No, he is not here yet].

'I would like to leave a message for him'.

'Da ist Papier und Bleistift'. [There is paper and pencil].

'Is Miss Thompson in?'

'Sie ist in der Bar'. [She is in the bar].

I had had enough of this. 'You are employed by the American Press

Club', I said angrily. 'When you are addressed in English, you will reply in English. Is that clear?'

It was. She mumbled an acknowledgement. But though she usually had a word for Americans when they entered the club, she never spoke to me again.

Disapproval

Nor is the traveller who is recognizable as being of German extraction ever quite safe from the subtle disapproval of his former compatriots. My passport shows, of course, the place of my birth, and to emphasize the situation the British Foreign Office has decorated the first page with a large stamp reading 'BRITISH SUBJECT BY NATURALIZATION'. Whenever a German customs official or any other German official, even though he was working in an entirely English-speaking position, noticed that stamp, I was addressed in German.

More than once I was assured by Germans that the Allies had been welcomed as liberators, but that after four and a half years they were all hated.

Another thing I learned a little about was the various operations by which the military occupation authorities were deceived. I did not get much of this first hand – it was, after all, usually highly illegal and no man was to be expected to put his head in a noose by being too informative with a stranger.

But once, I was introduced by a good friend to a self-dethroned head of a smuggling ring [Herbert Weissler] who now owns a restaurant in Cologne and is going comparatively straight. He had made a fortune smuggling cigarettes into Germany, but 'I have withdrawn from operations,' he told me. 'Only last week, customs men caught us and pinched millions of cigarettes. That's nothing, but hell, I might as well retire.

'We used to ship in cigarettes on heavy trucks coming from the West and labelled to show that they were en route for Czechoslovakia. They were weighed at the border and sealed for transit. Once inside the country we would find a quiet spot, rip off the floorboards of the truck or take up the roof and unload the tobacco'.

Smuggling

'Then we made up the weight with the goods shown on the truck's manifest: usually kitchenware or china. Strangely enough, that paid us well, too, because the stuff was cheap in Germany and was worth a good profit in Czechoslovakia. At the border the truck would be weighed again and passed along. It was a good racket.

'But it's all over now. The customs people have too many cars, and if they suspect us they tail us right through Germany'. Our conversation was interrupted by a man who wanted to change 2,000 military occupation dollars into marks. My acquaintance fished the money out of a drawer and went on talking.

'It's become more trouble than it's worth. I think I'll settle down to running my restaurant. Recommend me. I have the freshest meat in all Germany. I kill my own pigs. That isn't quite legal either, you understand, but what can I do? The customers come first'.

Abusing the Allies, and outsmarting them, is one of the principal pastimes in Germany. The man who abuses them is, like most Germans, usually very poor; the man who can outsmart them is likely to be the only well-off man in his section of town. No part of this is likely to change until the Allies leave. And that will be a sad day for the German, whatever his intentions, who neither abused them nor outsmarted them, but made the mistake of co-operating with them.

Note:

1. From the end of WWII until 1949 German exports were controlled by the Allied Joint Export-Import Agency (JEIA), which was loathed by the Germans, who saw it as being bureaucratic and incompetent.

BERLIN:
A RUINED AND DIVIDED CITY

Hangover After Hitler Series: Published Friday 23 December 1949

BERLIN IS MORE THAN SIMPLY A CITY TO ME – more than a small inked portion of the map that indicates the place where West and East are in most direct conflict. To me, Berlin represents the streets and houses where I grew up; the building where my father had his place of business; the boys and girls I went to school with; the first girl I ever fell in love with.

The first morning I was in Berlin I picked my way through the rubble that used to be the suburb of Grunewald, and for the first time in twelve years I stood before the Grunewald Gymnasium [gymnasium is the German word for secondary school]. Much of it was still standing, and it was clear that the school was still in use. Almost fearfully, I asked the old caretaker about my teachers. The old history teacher [Dr Ernst Walther] was still alive, he said, and I waited by the door until class was over. At last it opened and he came waddling out. For a moment he peered at me: then his face lighted up. 'You are Frank,' he said, 'you left school in 1930. You've lost weight – you used to be rather fat'.

Over the years, he had kept his files up to date, although most of them were pigeonholed only in his retentive memory. Warmly, sympathetically, he went through the roster of my friends and acquaintances:

Of my classmates, twenty-four were dead or missing.

My chemistry teacher had starved to death in the Russian Zone.

My philosophy teacher had slashed his own and his wife's wrists and, dying, they had walked together into the Havel River.

The girl I had been in love with when I was fifteen [Ilse Ueberschaar] had gone blind.

Suicide

More than buildings had been ruined in Berlin.

Strolling through the school, he went into detail. 'You remember what Professor Grunert looked like'. he said, 'a huge man, well over 200 pounds. When the war ended, he was living in the Russian Zone. 'There was no food, and he simply wasted away and died in his sleep. He was lucky.

'Professor Grunow was not so lucky. The Russians stormed into his little home. What they did there I do not know. After they left, the old man opened the arteries in his wife's wrists and then in his own; then they walked into the lake. You knew the old professor, a philosopher and a deeply religious man. You can understand what they must have done to have driven him to suicide'.

As for the school itself, 'I miss the Jewish boys', he said. 'They used to bring life into the class. But I don't suppose there will ever be any again. The boys I have are harder to handle today than they were in your time. They don't have the home life you used to have. Many of them are fatherless, and their mothers have to earn a living. The boys aren't looked after'.

He told me a little about my first love. Her brother had been my best friend; he had died early in the war during an experimental flight in a new aircraft whose pilot, eighteen years old, was drunk. His sister married soon afterward, then began to go blind; her husband had divorced her on the grounds that her illness 'hindered his contribution to the German war effort'.

Religion

'You should go see your old parson [Dr Phil Werner Priebe]', the history teacher said. 'He can tell you more about Eva. I walked back along Bismarck Allee toward the Grunewald Church. It was gone, but the doctor still lived in the vicarage, a few doors away. He remembered me vaguely, and led the way into his home, where the living room had become a lecture room and chapel, with an improvised altar salvaged from the wreckage of his church.

'The German people are in a morass,' he said. "They have turned their backs on God and on religion. It will be many, many years before we can change that – far longer than I have still to live. But we must carry on. Somebody must'.

He gave me Eva's address. There was no hurry about seeing her, and I took a tram down the Koenigsallee and got off to stroll down the Kurfuerstendamm, once the Piccadilly of Berlin. Ruins, only ruins.

As I sadly made my way toward the Gedaechtniskirche I noticed a familiar shop: I remembered it well and I remembered, too, that one of the partners had been a Russian Jew. The other partner received me in a room full of priceless antiques. He assured me he remembered me, and asked at once if I thought a war was coming. I pleaded ignorance, and in my turn asked about his colleague.

'He stayed until March 1945', he told me. 'It was difficult, you understand, because he was not only Jewish but Russian. Believe me, it cost a lot of money, but we had good connections. Finally he went to Italy and managed to get to the USA. He is about to be naturalized. I think he must have been one of the last living Jews in Berlin. As for me, I am making plans to get to Argentina. We have had a taste of the Russians, you understand – nothing could make me stay here'.

Barber Shop

I wished him luck and continued on my way. My next stop was a barber shop. The barber, in the old tradition, was talkative, and we were soon chatting about the occupying powers.

'Here in Berlin you can make comparisons', he said. 'If you go out at night and get into a place full of Americans, anything can happen. You may have a pleasant evening, you may see the place torn apart. French? You get hostile contempt. Russians? You may walk out naked, you may walk out loaded with gifts. British? You never notice them'.

Business, he said, was non-existent. 'You are my first customer today. Everyone changes their West marks at the rate of six to one, and goes over to the Russian sector for haircuts. We are going broke'.

I think I was also the first customer his manicurist had ever had. I wiped the blood from my mutilated fingers as I left the shop. At the Zoo station I took an elevated train to Zehlendorf, where I was living. But first I had to pick my way through a crowd of men and women who whispered into my ear, 'East against West'. They are the money-changers trading the depreciated East mark against the solid West mark.

My train went from the American sector to Potsdam, in the Russian Zone. My papers were not good enough for me to leave Western Germany, but on the trains I could see the shocking difference between East and West-zone inhabitants. Day after day I would select a poor, hungry, shabby man or woman and strike up a conversation. I never missed. The train was used mostly by American-sector passengers, but I had chosen an East-zone resident every time. Drawn faces, eyes shut in restless sleep during much of the trip, and when they awake they are cowed and hopeless.

Rape

I saw Eva that evening; in spite of everything she looked well. She had harrowing stories to tell me. 'Mother and I were near Kuestrin when the Russians came. They raped me, my mother, my eighty-two-year-old grandmother – not once'. There was more of this; from Eva, from others who told stories of the first days of the German defeat; from still others who saw these things happening today in the Russian Zone. But there is no point in retelling the stories. They will not be believed[1].

When I told her my mission in Germany, she spoke to a friend [Fritz Wilhem Benn] who lived in the Russian Zone and worked for a Russian-controlled newspaper. She gave me his telephone number, and I called him up early the next morning.

But I was calling from an American telephone, and as the operator put the call through she addressed me once in English. I hung up at once. One does not endanger the safety of a German in the Russian Zone by linking him to an English-speaking source. I booked the call later from a German restaurant – there was a five-hour delay and finally my acquaintance, forty miles away, was on the line.

'Eva says you come to town sometimes', I said.

'Occasionally', he replied.

'If you are coming in soon, I will be at, so-and-so's house, at such and such an address', I said.

'I expect to be in the day after tomorrow', he replied.

'It will be nice to see you again', I told him. He was looking forward to it, he answered. We hung up. He had not asked my name, nor what I wanted. It was like the Germany of the Hitler days when everyone spoke like that over the phone. Now it was the NKVD[2] one was aware of, instead of the Gestapo.

Russian Sector

We met at the house of my friends, and left immediately for my own house, in the American sector. We sat silently in the taxi. I had begun to tell him what I was doing in Germany and he had interrupted me brusquely with 'Not here'.

I had a good look at him in my house. He wore an old raincoat over a frayed suit – his white collar was in a fashion that had gone out twenty years ago. He wore mended grey socks and open sandals. 'My shoes have 'been at the shoemaker's for eight weeks'', he explained apologetically.

156

We talked late into the night, while he ate and smoked and drank like a man who is not sure when he will have an abundance set before him again. In the end, he stayed over night. No German dared go home alone late at night in the lonely section where he lived.

He told me much about the Russian Zone, about the hunger and hopelessness and cruelty of the Russian occupation; about the 'Peoples Police[3],' which is little more than a thinly disguised army; about the propaganda upon which he, like so many others, was hard at work for Russian masters.

The next day, in the Russian sector of Berlin, I saw something of what he meant. Rubbish everywhere, starvation in peoples eyes, and posters, posters, posters: 'Russia fights for peace.' 'Russian leaders will bring peace.' Pictures of Stalin[4] smiling, and more pictures of Stalin.

I ended my trip, one evening, in Ciro's, once Berlin's most fashionable nightclub. There was an excellent band, the inevitable ladies behind the bar, and aside from my own party seven drunk customers. The proprietor joined us for a drink. 'Berlin,' he said. 'It's not a city anymore – it is two villages. I wish I knew where we were going'.

Well, I thought, so do I. I loved Berlin because I can remember Berlin. I, too, would like to know.

Notes:

1. In his memoirs Frank goes further in explaining Russian cruelty: 'I had corroborated evidence of Russian soldiers raping highly pregnant German women and then nailing them to doors by their wrists and ankles so they died in childbirth under incredible suffering. My mind, thoroughly accustomed to atrocity through the testimony about German atrocities, boggled once more'.

2. NKVD – Narodnyy Komissariat Vnutrennikh Del – was the People's Commissariat for Internal Affairs or the interior ministry of the Soviet Union.

3. The Deutsche Volkspolizei (German People's Police), abbreviated to DVP or VP, and colloquially known as the VoPo – was the national police force of the German Democratic Republic (East Germany).

4. Joseph Stalin governed the Soviet Union from the mid-1920s until his death in 1953.

A HIGH NAZI OFFICER
IS RUN TO EARTH

Hangover After Hitler Series: *Published Thursday 15 December 1949*

'WOHLSEIN' [WELL-BEING] TOASTED THE TALL and rather distinguished looking German. He raised the bottle of schnapps (price: 10 marks or $2.30) in a gesture toward me before lifting it to his lips for a healthy swig.

'Good luck', I replied, taking over the bottle, 'during your time in jail'.

The guest in my small attic bedroom in a West German town [Hanover] last September was a former SS officer [Waldemar Wappenhans], one of nearly 2,000 VIPs of the Third Reich whose names are still on the Allies 'Wanted List'. In this group, headed by the missing Martin Bormann, Hitler's sinister deputy, are mass murderers, Gestapo chiefs, SS generals, gauleiters[1], and concentration-camp commandants. Many on the list no doubt are dead. Some have escaped from Germany to more accommodating climes. It is fairly certain, however, that many more are still alive, like my guest, and like him living fairly happily and prosperously under the noses of the occupying powers in Germany today.

I first heard of this SS officer while talking to another member of the Nazi hierarchy I had come to know well during the Nuremberg trials [Rudolf Diels][2]. The two men had quarrelled and when I met No. 2 again last summer, he let slip, in anger, a hint of the undetected existence of the SS officer. I probed him until I got from him a direct line on the identity and whereabouts of the wanted man.

He was living under an assumed name [Hans Seemann]. His real identity was a secret, I discovered, only so far as the Allied authorities were concerned. Lately a number of his fellow Germans had become aware, in one way or another, of his true identity, but none of them had betrayed him to the occupation authorities. This as the wanted man later explained to me, was a significant fact, illustrating a changed attitude on the part of the German people toward prominent Nazis. For a period after Germany's defeat, his fellows would have handed him over promptly to 'the enemy'. That mood has largely gone. Today there is a growing sense of solidarity among Germans, and my man had felt his secret reasonably safe among his countrymen.

Unhappy Meeting

When I reached the town where the SS officer was living. I phoned him and arranged a meeting. When he appeared, I greeted him with his real name and told him I was an Englishman. His face whitened and his hands shook as he dropped into a chair. I had been prepared for quite a different reaction and felt a little silly about the small automatic I had handy in my jacket pocket. Five years of war, several serious wounds and nearly five years of living under a false identity had left him without much spirit. He was in his early fifties but looked older.

He clasped his hands to his head for a few moments, then muttered (I could barely hear his words): 'God – I've kept it up for so long and now I'm caught. What will you do? Hand me over?'

I had read the chief extracts from his dossier in the 'Wanted List.' If the charges against him were true, his case was a serious one. But I gave him no direct answer at the time; I wanted primarily to hear his story. We had the first of several long talks that afternoon. When he had told me of some of his war-time assignments and exploits I appreciated immediately that, whether or not the charges against him were soundly based, Allied Intelligence would want this man for special questioning. Later that day I passed on to the proper authorities an account of our conversation. I am still not free, however, to disclose his name.

The Allied authorities are now dealing with his case, and he fully expects to serve a term in jail. But he hopes, with considerable reason, that his fate will be less severe today than it would have been if he had been caught four years ago. When I saw him several weeks after our first encounter, he gave me his life story and asked me to try to interest a book publisher in it. His idea was that his tale might earn him money to help his wife and daughters while he is serving time.

His story not only tells how he was able to remain unrecognized and free for more than four years, it also casts an interesting light on the dream world in which the German leaders were living in the last months of hostilities, even while the German war machine was falling to pieces about them.

Nazi Autobiography

Here are some relevant extracts from his autobiographical notes:

'Shortly before the end of the war' he wrote. 'I received a summons from Heinrich Himmler. I was recovering from wounds I had received on the Western Front, and he had sent a car to bring me to headquarters. We went for a drive in his Mercedes, and he sat at the wheel, talking incessantly – about our glorious future, about new secret weapons, and about his confidence that victory was imminent. When we parted, he told me: "Take your time and get well. I have important assignments for you. Brush up your English, most of all. We are forming a British Legion at this moment, and I want you to take charge of it when you are fit again".

'On my way home I tried to find the explanation for what I had just heard. So far as I knew, we were still [in January, 1945] at war with the British. Were we, perhaps, recruiting prisoners of war? Was there some truth in the rumours of new, decisive secret weapons, and would they come in time to turn the tide? Suddenly I felt quite optimistic.

'As soon as I reached the hospital, I asked the doctor for my discharge. The answer was disappointing: four more weeks of rest. Impatiently I waited out my time. I called Himmler on the phone. He agreed to my immediate assignment to the Western Front.

'Even the train journey to my new unit was a nightmare. In Munich I was caught in a heavy American daylight raid, and things were crashing all around me. The train services were in a state of chaos. Whenever there was a train, it was continuously attacked by low-flying aircraft. I had to walk for miles to find another train, only to have that one shot up too. The Ruhr was in ruins when at last I got there.

'I joined my new unit, and our orders were to hold the Rhine at all costs until our new weapons were ready. There was talk of new jet fighters, the snorkel submarine and the atom bomb. But all that was futile. Soon after I arrived, the Americans forced the crossing of the Rhine at Remagen[3]. The bridge had been left standing. All attempts to destroy it from the air had failed'.

Bradley's Advance

'There was no halting now the rapid advance of General Bradley's army[4]. He linked up with the British in our rear, and we were encircled. This, it seemed to me, was the end.

'I had lived the life of a soldier, and as a soldier I wanted to die. With two volunteers, armed with Panzerfaust[5], I set out on a sortie against American tanks that were holding a near-by crossroads.

'As I crawled through the dark toward the enemy, my life was passing before my eyes: my childhood, my military training, my days in service, and all the happiness my wife had given me, the smiling faces of my children. Then, we were upon the enemy, and the Panzerfaust went off with a tremendous whoosh. Three hits: three burning tanks. This would be it. There was no counter-fire.

'Once again my luck had stood by me. My time to die had not yet come.

'When we got back to our dugout, we found we were the only survivors of our unit. That night I was listed as dead …

'Immediately afterward, however, I found that there were orders for me to get through to Berlin. I was to let the Americans overrun that area, and I was to get out in civilian clothes. I carried blank identity papers in my pocket against just such an emergency. I had to tear up the first set I made out, I had filled them out carefully for a hypothetical German with an invented name, and then, out of force of habit, when it came to affixing my signature on the dotted line, I had signed my real name!'

Cross-Country Flight

'With my new papers and a new identity I set out for Berlin. I travelled through the fields and forests, hidden by farmers, sleeping in barns or in the open, and living only on a little bread or on the milk I got from cows in the fields. There were American vehicles everywhere, but I kept out of their way. Occasionally some German soldiers joined me, but they soon tired of tramping cross-country and took to the roads, where they were promptly taken prisoner. On I went alone, always to the east, working with map and compass.

'Once or twice I ran into American patrols, but after showing my fake papers I was allowed to proceed. One patrol took me to the mayor of a small town. He checked my papers, winked at me behind their backs, and let me pass. There were still some decent Germans left.

'Another time a man arrived home while his wife was getting me some bread and sausage. He screamed at me, called me a tramp, a Nazi swine, and accused me of being "one of those officer-bastards who had brought war on Germany". I gave him back his bread and sausage and went on my way'.

Ten days later this officer [Wappenhans] was deep inside Germany but, as he writes in his story, 'It had become obvious by now that there was no longer any point in trying to reach Berlin. The Russians were already there, and Hitler was dead. So I decided to head for L … [Hanover]. That was where I found him four and a half years later.

The Hunted

He found his wife and children penniless, and his first concern was to find work. His first job, as a farm labourer, proved too much for his weakened body and he collapsed. An old comrade sheltered and cared for him in the cellar of a ruined house. Even there the wanted man was not safe. A suspicious policeman came and checked his papers. His wife sent word that Allied investigators had made inquiries and seized all the pictures of him from his home.

'It was clear'. he writes, 'that I must find another and safer plan if I were to remain free. It was then that I decided that I would be safest in the lion's den. I would try to find work with the occupying forces.

'My good luck stood by me once again. By chance I heard that the Military Government offices in the next town were looking for someone with just my educational and business background. With the help of a letter from the local labour exchange I got the job at once – and I am still there today [British Property Control Board]. My superiors were pleased with my work and promotion came quickly.

'I developed friendships outside the office with officers of the occupation forces, and there were happy pleasant days when we hunted and rode together. They even invited me to spend Christmas with them at their homes. They behaved decently, generously, and treated me fairly. I would not embarrass them by disclosing their names.

'There were some nasty moments when the German authorities tried to check up on me once again. They might easily have uncovered my real identity if my friends among the Allied authorities had not objected vigorously to German intervention in the affairs of members of their staff who were doing their jobs properly'.

Optimism

The rest of his story is brief. I discovered that he knew the rather incomplete contents of the security file folder bearing his name in the Allied security section. He always knew beforehand of impending check-ups. There is little question that no one on the Allied side had any idea of his real identity. His hiding out in an Allied office was fully successful.

If he had been caught in 1945, this SS officer told me, he would surely have been hanged. His notes contain this final paragraph:

'I have faced death often and even sought it once, during the night of that suicidal sortie on the Western Front. But it was God's will that I should live to fill other tasks.

'I would have hanged most certainly, as have many of my comrades, without reasonable justice, if I had been made a prisoner in 1945. Today, when senseless hatred against National Socialists and soldiers has abated, and when objective thought and reason are coming into their own again, I need no longer fear the light of day.

'Now I shall he free among my beloved family and ready to work and live with a happy heart'.

He wrote this after I had told him he would he tried by the Allied authorities, and it may be that his optimism will prove justified, that he will be able to prove that he has not been a bad man.

Others on the wanted list, however, can expect rougher treatment if caught. Take, for unpleasant instance, Dr Josef Mengele[6], doctor at Auschwitz concentration camp.

Testimony at Nuremberg labelled him as the greatest mass murderer in history – three and a half million victims. Dr Mengele under another name and most probably in a different profession, may be enjoying life in Germany today. You might run across him there, as your taxi driver, or porter, or the waiter who brings you breakfast in your hotel room. He is still on the wanted list.

Notes

1. A gauleiter was the head of a Nazi administration district.

2. Under Frank's personal protection and interrogation Rudolf Diels had provided the Allies with much valuable information during the Nuremberg trials and it was Diels who drew Frank's attention to the whereabouts of Waldemar Wappenhans, alias Hans Seemann. According to Frank, Wappenhans was, at the time, ranked 'fourth' on the Allies 'Most Wanted' list of Nazi war criminals.

3. The battle to which Wappenhans refers here was the battle at Remagen, which, in 1969, was made into a film – *The Bridge at Remagen* starring George Segal, Ben Gazzara and Robert Vaughn. The film – which was based on the book *The Bridge at Remagen: The Amazing Story of March 7, 1945* by writer Ken Hechler – was a fictionalized version of actual events during the last months of World War II when the 9th Armored Division (the Phantom Division) of the US Army approached Remagen and captured, intact, the Ludendorff Bridge.

4. General Omar Bradley was Commander of the Twelfth US Army Group, which comprised forty three divisions and 1.3 million men. It was the

largest body of American soldiers ever to serve under a single field commander.

5. A Panzerfaust (tank fist) consists of a small, disposable pre-loaded launch tube firing a high-explosive anti-tank warhead.

6. Josef Mengele was a member of the team of doctors responsible for the selection of victims to be killed in the gas chambers and for performing deadly human experiments on prisoners. He vanished from Auschwitz in January 1945, shortly before the arrival of the Russian Army and fled to South America where he evaded capture for the rest of his life. He drowned after suffering a stroke while swimming off the Brazilian coast in 1979 and was buried under a false name. His remains were disinterred and positively identified by forensic examination in 1985.

REGARDING THE CAPTURE OF THE WANTED SS GENERAL

Editor: At the time Wolfe Frank wrote his 1949 article on SS-Gruppenfuhrer Waldemar Wappenhans, the then unnamed Nazi in his *Hangover after Hitler* series, British Intelligence and other military authorities, including those of the USA, Russia and Poland, were all keen to take him into custody. To protect him, and because of the on-going investigations, Frank was unable or unwilling to disclose the identities of Wappenhans or others mentioned in the article. However he did record who they were, and other details about them, in his contemporaneous notes, and, once he was free to do so, in the further information he later included in his memoirs. The information reproduced below is taken from those two manuscripts.

The tip-off as to the true identity of the undercover Nazi came from former SS-Oberfuhrer (Senior Leader) Rudolf Diels (see Plates 10 & 11), the protégé of Hitler's deputy Hermann Goering who had appointed Diels to be the first head of the Gestapo. During the Nuremberg trials (1945–47), Frank had helped Diels retain his freedom and avoid being charged with the most serious offences. In turn Diels had been of great assistance to Frank and his fellow interrogators in the preparation of evidence gathered for the prosecutions of the Nazi war criminals.

Frank proclaimed Diels to be 'one of the most fascinating men I had ever encountered' and in his notes and memoirs he goes on to describe the man and to disclose details of their meetings during the weeks and months leading up to the Nuremberg trials:

HE, [DIELS] WAS TALL, very dark haired and had heavy dueling scars[1]. He was extremely intelligent and spoke beautiful cultured German. He was also emaciated, dreadfully nervous whilst being sure of himself, and he was courteous without being servile or afraid … in a few sentences, he gave an outline of his activities in the Third Reich, which were as follows:

He was married to a cousin of Goering and he had been Chief of the Prussian Gestapo at the time of van der Lubbe's burning down of the German Reichstag[2] – the parliament building in Berlin. He had been Chief of the Shipping Division of the Hermann Goering Works (a national industrial unit engaged in a multitude of economic and production activities) and also Lieutenant Governor of the City of Hanover. He had been denounced as having been involved in the 20 July 1944 plot against Hitler[3] but had been spared execution following Goering's intervention. Instead he had been sent to the Russian Front as a private in a 'Strafkompagnie' (penal company) where he ought to have been killed. He had however escaped to the West and had been captured by the British … He did not claim ignorance of the horrors of the time, only the impossibility for anyone to swim against the monstrous tide … as a source of information Diels proved himself to be inexhaustible, infallible and completely accurate … His property near Hanover, a beautiful 17th century farmhouse and farming operation, had been confiscated by the British and was held by the British Property Control Office in Hanover. I went up to the farm with him on one occasion – I was still in uniform and didn't have to ask anyone's permission.

Editor: So important was Diels to those preparing for the Nuremberg trials that he fell into a special category, as Frank records 'he was not a witness, not a prisoner, not a potential defendant, not a free man'. The Russians were anxious to interrogate him, as were the Germans, and he would not have been safe outside British custody. So Frank, having solicited a gentleman's agreement from Diels that he would not try to abscond, took the unprecedented step of placing him, not in a prison cell, but in Frank's own quarters under a fairly loose house arrest. 'This was, of course, monumentally irregular', recalls Frank, 'and pleased me enormously since breaking rules was, and still is, one of my favourite pastimes'.

Later, once the Nuremberg trials had started, it became impossible for Diels to continue living in the British compound and Frank, again in a highly irregular move and on the same gentleman's agreement, arranged for Diels to be allowed to stay with one of the Gestapo Chief's own former mistresses and her husband – and Diels continued to live there for several years with Frank joining them regularly as a house guest. 'During my long stay in Nuremberg', wrote Frank, 'I spent many a happy weekend in that house and it is regrettable that, for reasons of tact and discretion, no more than that can be told'.

(A fuller version of Frank's dealings and relationship with Rudolf Diels appears in Frank's autobiography *Nuremberg's Voice of Doom*, whilst the life and times of

Rudolf Diels are recorded in the former Gestapo Director's own autobiography *Lucifer ante Portas*). Frank met up with Diels again in June 1949 – he was still living at the home of his former mistress – and Frank explained to him his undercover mission in Germany, especially the task he had been set by the *NYHT* to try and discover how 2,000 Nazi war criminals on the Allies 'Wanted List' had been able to evade capture. Frank's notes and memoirs reveal what then occurred:

Diels and I went for a lengthy walk and he told me of the long, uphill struggle he had had trying to avoid a harsh verdict under the still functioning de-Nazification proceedings. His farm near Hanover was still being held by the British Property Control Board[4]. He had wanted to go there one day and had called the German head of that organization [Waldemar Wappenhans posing as Hans Seemann] who had informed him bluntly that he was not granting permission to him, Diels, the 'Erznazi' (arch-Nazi) to set foot in the place. Diels took it calmly and visited an old friend, still at the head of the Criminal Investigation Division of the Hanover Police. Who was this man, Seemann, he inquired, who was being holier than the pope and more unrelenting than the British?

The Chief Inspector had the answer. The name certainly wasn't Seemann. And now Diels was offering me the gentleman, as an interesting subject for my series of articles – as a service rendered, no doubt, in appreciation of quite a lot of trouble I had helped him to avoid.

Seemann became the subject of an extremely interesting article in the *NYHT* series. Not all of the story could be told then, but now all the facts can be recorded.

To begin with, armed with an introduction from Diels, I called on Dr Heinz Wendt, specialist for venereal diseases and collector of icons – on which he was one of the world's leading authorities. He was host, at regular intervals, to a small group of rather illustrious men who met for coffee after lunch in his house. Herr Seemann attended frequently and I was invited the next day. There I met: Professor Wilhelm Roepke, the famous economist; a member of the Royal House of Hanover, Count Gustav Westarp; a Senor (Herr) Kroenn, who had been sent by the Argentine Government to try and persuade Hjalmar Schacht to move to that country and, of course, Herr Hans Seemann. The conversation was on a very high level: the extermination of the political elite in Germany; the lack of intellectual substance on the part of the politicians of the day; Germany and the Atlantic Pact; the opening of a 'second front', in Europe's east; the benefits of dismantling for Germany's industrial recovery; icons; and more of the same.

During the whole of it I was studying Seemann. I had a complete dossier on him, his past and real identity, of course, partly supplied by Diels via the Chief Inspector of Hanover and partly by old friends who were still working in Nuremberg.

He had been, so the files stated: 'German Airforce Ace; SS General; Police and SS Chief at Rovno [Rivne] and Brest-Litovsk; and, of late, Property Control Officer for the British Military Government at Hanover'.

His real name was Waldemar Wappenhans and he occupied a place high up[5] on the Allies 'Wanted List' of 2,000 VIPs of the Third Reich. It was headed then, and still is, by Martin Bormann, Hitler's Deputy, and Dr Josef Mengele, Chief Medical Officer of the Auschwitz concentration camp. And here I was, inviting a member of this infamous group for a drink at my lodgings.

I greeted him by his real name and he stared at me in horror. His face whitened and his hands shook as he dropped into a chair. I had been prepared for quite a different reaction and felt a little silly about the small automatic I had handy in my jacket pocket. 'God', he said. 'I've kept it up for so long and now I'm caught. Who are you, what will you do?'

So I told him who I was, what I was doing and that I didn't know what I would do with him, but I wanted to hear his story [outlined in the previous chapter and reproduced in full in Wappenhans's testament which is to follow].

He told me he was born on the 23 November 1893. He came from the German regular army originally, joined the SS following a call from Himmler and fought in both World War I and World War II.

He had been appointed trustee for Diels's farm. Having been treated rather badly over the telephone by Seemann, Diels had enlisted the assistance of some former police officials and had discovered that he was in reality General Wappenhans. Diels sent for him and called him by his real name. Wappenhans turned pale and then asked Diels not to give him away for the sake of his family. Diels, although he now denies this, did, I think, give Wappenhans such an undertaking. However, he broke his word and gave me the data I required.

I explained to Wappenhans that the reason why I was interested in his story was because the Allied 'Wanted List' still contained nearly 2,000 names and that it would be interesting indeed if one had a clear case, complete with all the details, of how it was possible for him and the other 2,000 people alike, to keep underground, and unmolested, for such a long period of time.

In the course of a number of conversations I had with Wappenhans in Hanover, it was then arranged that I would negotiate with British

Intelligence (BI) some sort of a deal, according to which he would hand himself over at a time which suited him best, and that the British would make every possible effort to prevent his extradition to Poland. There was a little reluctance on the part of BI at the beginning, until I pointed out, somewhat tactfully, that he had been working for them for a period of four and a half years, basing himself on the somewhat correct assumption that he would be safest in the 'lion's den'.

Wappenhans had supplied me with either names, or clues to the names, of a number of senior British officers, with whom he had at one time or another, hunted, ridden, shot, celebrated Christmas, sung carols, and generally had a good time, and they were, in fact, so fond of him that they had told him at one point (when the German authorities looked as though they might become difficult) that if the Germans should try and touch their boy, they, the British, would soon get the matter straightened out.

I supplied BI with some clues with regard to Wappenhans's wartime activities, which included air reconnaissance over the British Isles and keeping check on the British fleet, air reconnaissance over Scapa Flow[6], and further air reconnaissance over Holland, Belgium and France, prior to the invasion of those countries by the German army. BI then announced that it would probably, on the strength of the military importance of Wappenhans's knowledge, be prepared to make a deal.

Finally, it was arranged that Wappenhans would write down details of his military experience – to be submitted to the British military intelligence side. If they were as interested as we thought they would be, we would then give him the undertaking of letting him be at large until the end of October1949, whereupon he would be taken into custody, probably charged with violation of the questionnaire rules and regulations, by giving a false name, and possibly sentenced to six months or so in jail. He would then be let out for German consumption [de-Nazification] which by that time would in all probability, amount to nothing at all in his case.

At one point Wappenhans brought his wife to a meeting. She is a tall, good looking blonde, obviously much younger than he is, very composed, but rather hard. He was wearing 'those boots' meaning SS boots, which somewhat disturbed my peace of mind. She, a blue, rather shiny, tailored costume. There are two children of eleven or so who have to be kept in ignorance of his whereabouts and who, although they know he is alive, always have to tell the other children in their school that he is dead. Actually, he has been reliably reported dead, which was a matter of an arrangement he must have made somewhere and proves that there is still a feeling of solidarity amongst some Germans.

When talking he always kept returning to the happy memories he had of war, since he loved fighting and one of the most enjoyable memories, so far as he was concerned, was his fight against the British in Palestine.

He told me, and this was confirmed by Dr Wendt, that a number of high-ranking SS officers are working and living in Hanover, one of them, for instance, as a brick layer, under his real name – a simple matter since they do not register with the police but live on the black market, which today, of course, is identical with the legal market.

I then wanted to know how he had got himself this high-ranking job with the British Military Government?

Having assumed the identity of Hans Seemann, he told me, his first job as a farm worker proved too much for his weakened body and he collapsed. An old comrade sheltered and cared for him in the cellar of a ruined house. Then his wife sent word that Allied investigators had made enquiries and taken all the pictures of him from the house.

'It was clear', he told me, 'that I had to find a safer plan if I were to remain free. It was then I decided that I would be safest in the lion's den. My luck held and I got a position with the British Military Government and I am still there today. My superiors were pleased with my work and my promotion to chief of the service came quickly'.

He made friends with those British officers who mattered. He spent very many hours in their company. He had been teaching the daughter of the head of the organization how to ride and had been invited to their home as a guest for Christmas dinner. He confirmed British officers had also prevented the German authorities from looking too closely into his background. He refused to reveal the names of those British officers who had helped him.

I had heard him out, and now I answered his earlier question. 'What will I do?' You've asked me that Herr Wappenhans. I can't tell you, yet. For the moment I will do nothing whatsoever. But do one thing, please. Sit down and write down every detail of that part of your military service that involves Britain. I think I am going to need that'.

And we parted company in the early morning hours.

I flew to Nuremberg and got hold of a friend in the documentation centre. We dug out the file on Wappenhans and, with our very thorough knowledge of SS activities in Poland, we decided that Wappenhens, in the positions he had held there could not, under normal circumstances, have perpetrated atrocities. The Polish extradition request was based on his positions, however, and did not bother to cite any specific criminal actions[7].

Said my American lawyer friend: 'You know, Wolfe, we've been involved in justice being doled out with a golden ladle. The Poles will certainly kill this guy, and can you blame them? But I don't think we ought to let them. We certainly wouldn't hang him. Well – now that you know where you are with him, you figure out what to do'.

I did. Back in Hanover, I collected a large brown envelope which contained the account of Wappenhans's activities.

'Then I called on his Christmas dinner host. I introduced myself. 'Major,' I said, 'would you be good enough to send this envelope to Naval Intelligence at the Admiralty in London? It happens to contain the autobiography of a man whose name is high on the Allied Wanted List. And it so happens that he is your most trusted employee – only I must ask you not to do anything to him. You see, the Poles want him extradited, and I honestly believe that they ought to wait until London decides what to do with him'.

The major was in a towering rage.

'I will do no such thing', he thundered. 'And you will tell me, right now, who he is. I will have him arrested. And you. For protecting a wanted criminal'.

'I wouldn't, Sir', said I. 'You see, there is this story of how the Germans came to see you about him – Seemann, it is, of course – and you practically threw them out on their ears. You probably didn't want your daughter's riding teacher, or your Christmas guest troubled, did you? Well now, you see, Sir, the *New York Herald Tribune* people in Paris have a sealed envelope which contains an article I've written about it. If you arrest anyone around here, they open the envelope and print the article, you see. So wouldn't you, please, Sir, hold your horses for a bit?'

'Give me the damned document you have there Frank', said Major X. 'I'll send it. We'll see what happens'.

What happened was that Wappenhans was sent for within forty-eight hours. He spent six weeks being interrogated by the Admiralty – debriefed, as it is now called – and he was treated hospitably and honourably. Somehow, an opinion must have found its way into the file [Frank's?] that he ought not to be extradited, and he wasn't. I felt this to be just.

Wappenhans was a brave man and, first and foremost, a soldier. It would have been a distortion of history or even a miscarriage of justice, if the avalanche of Russian retribution had swept this man away.

When he came back from London, he went through his de-Nazification trial and was sentenced to serve one year in some camp.

Notes:

1. A dueling scar or 'bragging scar' was seen amongst upper-class Germans and Austrians, especially those involved in academic fencing, as being a 'badge of honour' that emphasized one's class and status in society. German military laws permitted men to wage duels of honour until World War I, and in 1933 the Nazis legalized the practice once more.

2. Marinus van der Lubbe (1909 -1934), a Dutchman, was tried, convicted and executed for setting fire to the Reichstag building in Berlin on 27 February 1933, an event that became known as the Reichstag Fire.

3. On 20 July 1944, Claus von Stauffenberg and others attempted to assassinate Adolf Hitler in his field headquarters near Rastenburg, East Prussia.

4. Following the war many German owned properties and estates were seized by the British Property Control Board and handed over to reliable Germans or were held by the Board until the Control Council decided how to dispose of them in the interests of peace.

5. At one point in his memoirs Frank states that Waldemar Wappenhans was ranked fourth on the Allies 'Most Wanted' list of Nazi war criminals.

6. Scapa Flow is a body of water in the Orkney Islands, Scotland. It was the main British naval base during World War II.

7. Between 1941 and 1944 over 1.4 million Ukrainian Jews were killed by the Nazis, including tens of thousands in Rivne (Rovno) and Lutsk. In the book they edited: *The Shoah (Holocaust) in Ukraine* Ray Brandon and Wendy Lower record: 'The killings were carried out exclusively by the KdS [Chief of SS and Police or SSPF] Rivne and its outposts, the Gendarmerie, and the indigenous police. The SSPFs in Lutsk and Zhytomyr, Waldemar Wappenhans and Otto Hellwig respectively, coordinated their various police forces accordingly. They also oversaw the Orpo [Order Police] officers deployed as "SS and police base leaders" in Brest and in Berdychiv and Vinnytsia'. The RKU [Reichskommissariat Ukraine – civilian occupation regime] administration in Rivne was not the only decisive force behind the campaign of total annihilation on such short notice; the county commissars also contributed significantly to organising the individual massacres'.

THE CONFESSION OF
SS-GRUPPENFÜHRER
WALDEMAR WAPPENHANS

'In the afternoon he [Himmler] asked me to come with him to
Berchtesgaden to meet the Führer – we could talk on the way.
Himmler was at the wheel of a small Mercedes. I sat beside him
and in the back were two aides ... [Himmler said] I ought to
brush up my English. We are forming a British Legion [SS] at
this moment, and I want you to take charge of that when you are
fit again ... The Rhine must be held, that is, until the most recent
weapons were operational. There was talk of jet fighters, U-
boats with snorkels and the atomic bomb'.

Waldemar Wappenhans, October 1949

Editor: The Testimony (Confession) of Waldemar Wappenhans, alias Hans Seemann*, was taken and transcribed by Wolfe Frank following his meetings with and interrogations of the SS-Gruppenführer between August and October 1949 and from notes provided to him by Wappenhans.

Two identical copies of the Testimony were compiled in German by Frank and then signed by Wappenhans one of which was passed to British Navel Intelligence at the Admiralty in London – who then spent six weeks interrogating the SS Major General – the other copy was retained by Wolfe Frank and forms part of his archive.

The Frank copy has been translated into English by Frank Mercer[60] and is reproduced for the first time, in its entirety, on the following pages. To assist with the integrity and authenticity of the document, and unlike the rest of this book, German spellings of names, titles and places have been retained as Frank and Wappenhans had recorded them (i.e. Göring instead of Goering, Führer instead of Fuehrer).

To assist readers and to clarify certain names, titles, situations, locations, etc., I have, in addition to the sub headings, added:

(a) In the testimony itself a minimal amount of information [shown, as this, within square brackets] and reference numbers that correspond to the Notes included at the end of the testimony;

(b) Plates 1 to 4 which record Wappenhans' known Army, Air Force, Police and SS ranks, honours and awards; the structure of The Wehrmacht (Germany's Unified Armed Forces) with particular reference to the SS; and a table showing SS ranks and their German and British Army equivalents;

(c) Maps at Plates 12 and 13 indicating the various locations to which Wappenhans refers – using the titles and boundaries as they existed when the testimony was compiled in 1949. Modern day titles of some of the more important towns and cities are shown in square brackets.

* Hans Seemann is the equivalent of the English nickname 'Jack Tar'. Hans being the shortened version of Johannes – John – Jack, and the translation of Seemann being Sailor – Tar.

THE TESTIMONY (CONFESSION) OF
SS GENERAL
WALDEMAR WAPPENHANS

THE EMPEROR'S VILLA was what people called the little town of Plön. An old-fashioned chest with many compartments, a garden of wonderful fruit trees, which leaned against a hillside like a terrace.

Here lived my father, Headmaster and Professor Friedrich Marinack-Wappenhans, tutor of the imperial princes Oskar, August-Wilhelm and Joachim. [Kaiser Wilhelm II's three youngest sons]. At that time, in the year 1899, the Professor was still young, only forty years old. A well-brought up, smart and sporty man, he had spent half his life in England. His father was a German, living in England, his mother (born Wulkow) was English. In the records of Oxford he was well known as a batsman, and winner over Cambridge, and this was a passion he did not abandon back in Germany. The Luisenstadt Modern High School in Berlin, where he worked as Head, won the Kaiser's Prize four times at Grünau [a suburb of Berlin] under his leadership. As sport began to put out its first shoots in Germany, and as this Professor spoke cultured English and perhaps even better French, he came to His Majesty's notice, and was summoned to Plön to prepare the princes I mentioned for their Abitur [school leaving] certificate.

My mother was a modest, educated woman. Her father owned a large estate at Ritwiany [Rytwiany], then in Russian Poland, and a house in Dresden where they spent the winter. She gave my father six children – the youngest died in Plön, but the other five of us were hard to control, especially the second, Waldemar – me!

I got my first stern warning in 1900, when I was seven, when I bombarded the princes with apples as they were visiting our garden.

At the town's high school I did not distinguish myself until I tried once to swim across the lake on my own, and was brought back by a fleet of boats whose crews refused to believe an eight-year-old boy could swim so far. After my second categorical warning came the third, the one with the most far-reaching consequences.

My family was devoted to music. My father's sister (who later married Hahndorff, the Quartermaster General in the First World War) was a star pupil of Franz Liszt's in Weimar, so I had to be musical too. I was handed over to an old lady at the Dammschen Music School who was supposed to introduce me to the ABC of music. One day I turned up to our horrible one-to-one lesson without practicing beforehand. My lack of ability was punished with a rap across the fingers. I felt hurt in my male pride and hit back, and was comprehensively barred from the course. The consequence was a broken riding-crop and a nine-year-old boy sent to the Cadet Corps School.

After a short examination I was admitted to the sixth grade. All my courage had disappeared when, late one afternoon at the old Plön Castle I had to give up my sailor suit for bleached linen drill, and after a scanty supper, took my hard night's rest in a hall with 100 beds. I really cried myself to sleep, to be 'cheered up' next morning with a jug of water.

And now began a struggle for a boy's survival. We were brought up hard – obedience without contradiction was the principal theme of our upbringing, even at that early age. Anyone who didn't obey dropped out. Anyone who did not support his comrades, even to the ultimate consequence, was mentally ruined. Anyone who told tales was 'sent to the shithouse', which meant that nobody could talk to him except on duty. The result was that this sort of traitor (as we called him) simply cracked up and had to leave the Corps.

So I too, in spite of the softer feelings I had presumably inherited from my mother, gradually learned to be rather tougher. Cowardice was the embodiment of everything ugly: once when a thirteen-year-old cadet refused to dive headfirst from a six-metre board, he was given a 'slide'. In the evening break, his comrades all got together, turned the lad over and beat him to the skin with [carpet beaters?] until he promised, shivering and crying, to reform, and next day in fact he plucked up the courage to dive. Although the supervising officer discovered the marks on his body, and a thorough investigation took place, nothing about the 'slide' came out – there was no betrayal.

Meanwhile the princes had passed their leaving exams and my father became head of the secondary modern school in Bromberg [Bydgoszcz]. To keep the family together, I was also brought to Bromberg and sent to

176

the high school there. It was a wonderful time for me. My father, an idealist and loved by all his teachers and students, worked late into the evening every day. My mother was too kind to limit my drive towards freedom. I took the opportunity to organize battles between the high school and the middle-class school which were waged tooth and nail. Armed with catapults, we went on a window hunt. Only one thing was neglected – schoolwork. Then my father died suddenly, and we were alone. My mother moved to the town of Naumburg and I had to go back to cadet school.

My entry exam in Naumburg failed to get me into the Lower Third grade. I went for five weeks to a 'crammer' at Bad Kösen with a Dr Possild who tried to correct my mistakes, especially in Latin, using brutal methods. He succeeded to some extent, though it left some bloody marks behind my ear where his red pencil would land every time I made a mistake.

The Lower Third grader Wappenhans now entered the Fifth in the Cadet Corps in Karlsruhe by way of a re-sit exam. He felt good there, as he felt superior to his comrades because of his earlier experience. After just a week an examining board arrived. German was the subject. The boy Wappenhans recited the poem.

'They told us death and disaster loomed,
But nothing of that we found
Three columns of foot, three batteries of guns,
We rode them into the ground'

It was recited with such enthusiasm that, because of the unanimous applause of both teachers and students, he was moved up a class and entered the Fourth grade.

A Fight with Hermann Göring

There I met a boy whom I found unpleasant right from the start. Why was that? – because he was better than me in every way. He stood at the board – and he drew in one line the whole of the Alps, with all the peaks, passes and rivers on it. I could not think of a comeback, however hard I tried. And what a big mouth he had! God knows I couldn't stand him. His father had a hunting lodge at Mauterndorf, and this so-and-so called Hermann Göring had such a big mouth we called him 'Mauschelsdorf' [Poor Jew's Village[1]] at once (see Plate 5). But I felt hurt in my pride that he was better than me, and one day when we were marching in to dinner together, I jumped out of the ranks, and smacked Hermann one in the gob (as we put it). The result – a challenge to a fist fight. The class gathered, formed a ring, and both of us hooligans set about bashing each other with both fists; retreat would have been cowardly so it was black eyes, bloody noses, swollen faces – and then a handshake.

We met again at Gross-Lichterfelde [near Berlin], the cadet establishment where you automatically went on promotion to Lower Second, but our ways parted at once when we were assigned to different companies. In the Main Cadet Establishment at Gross-Lichterfelde there was an explicit soldierly enthusiasm. Over a thousand cadets, all future officers, felt proud in their uniform. The unit was made up of two battalions of five companies each. Each company had a Captain, to whom four Lieutenants or Second Lieutenants were assigned as instructors: the central concern was the cadets themselves. A sword-wearing Under-Officer (or Corporal) was God Almighty, the company leader with unlimited powers of punishment. Under him were four section leaders, each with four or five room seniors.

The education was like that of a Modern High School, almost exclusively delivered by civilian teachers. Most of the cadets took their Ensign's exam in the Upper Second, and would then be posted to the most varied regiments. A small number, known as the 'swots' went on to First grade to prepare for the school leavers' exam.

The teachers didn't have an easy time with us, coming up against dogged resistance. If one of them made himself unpopular, he got a 'Whisper', that is, the whole class yelled 'Ugh!' Of course we were punished – an hour's drill with rifle and helmet till our sight and hearing went, but we stuck it out together. If a 'Whisper' wasn't enough to scare the teacher, he got a 'Horse Guard'. A pin was stuck into a piece of rubber, which was fastened into the wickerwork of the teacher's chair, so that when he sat down it would stick into a certain part of his body. When the injured offender leapt up and asked who had done it, the whole class jumped up with a bang. What was he to do? The class had to be punished, as there was no betrayal amongst us.

The Origin of the Seemann Alias

One fine summer day we were lying in groups in the cadets' garden smoking, although it was strictly forbidden. Suddenly the notorious Lieutenant Meyer of the Guards showed up. We jumped up and to attention. One after another our names were taken Lance Corporal Wappenhans of 2 Company answered 'Lance Corporal Seemann, 7 Company'. The next day Corps orders were read out. 'Cadets [there followed a list of names] will be punished with three hours detention on bread and water' – among those named was Lance Corporal Seemann of 7 Company. The 7 Company Commander thought there had been a mistake, and the enquiry that followed left no doubt that someone had given a false name. The other four who had been punished were named, but nobody knew the fifth, the alleged Seemann. How could you anyway, among 1,000 cadets? Guards Lieutenant Meyer visited every company to try and recognize the offender. This was futile – everybody knew who 'Seemann' was but no one would ever give him away.

In the courtyard of 11 Company stood the Idstedt Lion, a monument to the 1864 victory over Denmark. The huge 'King of the Wild' was made of hollow cast iron, which gave us a reason somehow to bring him to life. In a week of night-time work, the Lion was filled with water through a hole in his head, then one day it reached just there. In their break, the whole Corps formed up in front of the monument, and at a horn signal, the Lion began to relieve himself in a splendid jet of water. Though higher authority eventually stopped it, the lion was able to do his business all day long, to the delight of us cadets.

Drill, field exercises, shooting, swimming and sport took up a large space in the cadets' training. The annual autumn and spring parades on Tempelhof field were the high point to show off the training, for here the Cadet Corps marched past in front of His Majesty. Life in the huts was extremely strict. Anyone who didn't obey the rules was punished in the old cadet way. In the 'cat's paw' a hand with fingers closed and pointing upwards towards the bent elbow had to be held out. There followed a blow with a flexible ruler on the fingertips. If the offender flinched even a little, the procedure would be repeated with the sharp edge of the ruler, which naturally split the nails. A more harmless method was the 'Tangent'. Bend your bottom forward! If a certain part of your body is tense, it receives a glancing blow with the ruler. Less appetizing was 'fat swallowing' which was mostly used when a cadet's belly rumbled at meal times. A piece of fat was tied onto a thread, had to be swallowed and was then pulled out again on the thread. The result was spectacular. I was surprised one night when I was awoken by a thunderous noise, and at the same time got the feeling that I was hanging in the air. I was, too! My bed had been pulled some way from the wall. As I tried to climb out of the maze of pillows, wooden and iron parts, I got a mugful of water in the face. I had been turned upside down – this old traditional procedure sometimes took terrifying forms. People tried to surprise you, whole huts at a time, and later battles took place on company, even battalion level.

Meals were eaten by the whole Corps at the same time in what was then the largest room, without pillars, in Germany. The cooking of the food was wretched, the quality poor. Not much butter, not much sugar. If we got 'Mary Stuart' noodle pudding, it consisted of a slippery white mass. If we had 'Dead Jews' this pork consisted mostly of gristle. We often left the hall with hungry stomachs, and every one of us only enjoyed 'Tobaggy', an expression that went back to King Frederick William I and his habit of [chewing?] tobacco and had been taken over by the Cadet Corps for the canteen. Here at coffee time there was everything in stacks that a hungry cadet's stomach could hope for. Cakes of every shape, whipped cream and chocolate – well, that was when there wasn't an economic crisis, which was notorious. But mostly we were all poor eaters. Parents who had money seldom sent their boys into the Corps, and from the scanty pocket money we got we still had to pay the fare into Berlin when we got leave on Sunday. We often walked in, to save the ten pfennigs for the tram.

Every Sunday we had to go to church, and to morning prayers every weekday. Apart from the compulsion, which made us hate church, we often had sermons preached, which can only be described as the product of a total lack of understanding of a young soul. Then we often had trainee priests let loose on us, to preach their maiden sermons. We put them so far off their idea by coughing that they finally got stuck in their speech. It was only later I realized what incompetent educators were let loose on us at the time. We young people were longing for role models who were capable of training us spiritually. For the few teachers who gave us some inner strength we'd go through fire. Over the Protestant Church lay the 'mountain pub', a domed building set aside for the Catholic cadets. We Protestants went there now and then for a change, just to get some variety in our churchgoing.

However, as the frequent kneeling there was much harder work than sitting in the Protestant one, we soon gave up these excursions.

The dome of the mountain pub was crowned with a statue of the Archangel Michael, who, sword in hand at a dizzying height, was an emblem for our country. Only the poor chap was naked, which made us sorry for him as he must have been freezing in winter. So it was decided to put a shirt on the Archangel. One daring cadet was helped on to the rooftop at night by his comrades and from there the young athlete climbed up the lightning rod to the top where he managed, after monstrous efforts, to pull the shirt on over the angel's head. The return journey was successful in spite of even greater difficulties. The next day the cadets were delighted to see the shirt flying in the wind – the staff, on the other hand, were deeply depressed. Of course the perpetrator and his accomplices remained anonymous. Days passed and the shirt kept flying, so the Commandant had no choice but to have scaffolding put up and under the label 'roof repairs' have the shirt brought down – apparently they couldn't manage to find anyone willing to climb up and hang from the lightning rod the way the young sportsman had.

Fighting played a large part in our lives, so when the first snow fell, a snowball fight broke out without fail between the first and second battalions in the long break. Here at least 500 men were engaged on each side. Nobody wavered or gave up as the battle was decided on the territory lost, so we got stuck into each other. Balls of ice were hurled at the closest range, then we went for it with fists. The duty officers tried to get the battalions to fall in and cease hostilities with whistles but they had a hopeless task. Only the bell for the end of break broke off the battle. The result was a sick bay overflowing with cadets, some with serious injuries.

On Sundays after church we could visit families if we could produce a written invitation and hadn't done anything significantly wrong. Invitations were not a problem – one of our many cousins was always ready to provide an appropriate certificate. So we walked out of the gate in droves, proud in our uniforms with spotlessly polished buttons, smartly saluted our superiors and looked down sympathetically on the civilians.

I liked most to visit one of my mother's sisters in Friedenau, a Frau von Rabenau who lived there with her daughter. Her sons, a vicar and two naval officers, had left home. My dear aunt understood a cadet perfectly. She spoiled me and treated me like a man, which made me really happy. I also often went to a friend of my father's, Professor Krause, who treated me to the theatre each time, which I loved. Also, I often went to see other friends of my father's, the Friedeberg family, who owned a house on Unter den Linden[2]. There I met the intellectual elite of Berlin, though I had little idea of that at the time – if so, I would have enjoyed the great luxury of a typical Berlin salon.

I usually spent my leaves with my uncle Hahndorff who then commanded a regiment in Lahr, Baden[3]. He was my real guardian, and in his serious and worthy way always showed me the right way. His wife, my aunt, was actually closer to me than my own mother. She often knew how to break down the toughness I had learnt in the Corps and show me an example of a pure, ideal family life.

I developed further till the School Leavers' Exam – which I failed, with the added comment 'for moral immaturity'. What had happened? In the written exam I actually felt really confident. On a short and – for the teachers – unexpected visit to the 'Drummers'[4] hut' (as the staff room was known) we found a list where the subjects we would get in the exam were explained. We worked seriously through these and walked into the exam properly prepared, by God, and full of hope. We even had an exam on Sunday which was Physics. The questions were familiar. After two hours I had written the required number of words, climbed over the wall and travelled to the Berlin Hockey Club (BHC) at Dahlem, where there was the first match between the BHC and an English side. I, a young cadet, was to appear as substitute for the well-known sportsman Prince Friedrich Karl, who on that day would be made a Knight of the Order of the Black Eagle at the Imperial Palace. What did the exam matter? – I was in the team! Right-winger. Just before full time the score was 2–2, then came a tearing run from the right-winger, one, two opponents dodged, a hard cross to the centre. Evans (an Englishman who played for our club) took the cross and converted it into the winning goal, 3–2 to BHC. It was the first time a German side had beaten a British one. Proudly I went back to the Corps and back over the wall. Nobody had noticed my disappearance. On Monday I innocently returned to work, but I saw from the teachers' faces that something wasn't right. I was to be expelled. The afternoon edition of the *Berliner Zeitung*[5] was held out to me, in which I saw the beaming smile of a young man named Wappenhans with an appropriate caption, which I could be really proud of. My teachers thought differently – I was not morally mature.

Serving the Fatherland

So I had to wait another six months before I joined my regiment. But now it was 1914, and I passed an emergency exam and excitedly set out as a Second Lieutenant in the 113th Regiment [Infantry] at Freiburg in Baden. Now we were going to show that we were proper men. His Majesty had told us so at the Palace in front of an audience of junior officers. Yes, we were willing: the Fatherland could count on us. So we travelled to Freiburg with our comrades, singing:

'...and if you do not risk your life, it ne'er will bring you any gain'.

Again and again we sang this line with sincere hearts.

Then came the war. The excitement made us forget all the hardships. I was slightly wounded in my very first battle in Lorraine [N.E. France] and most of the young officers with me were either killed or similarly wounded. War definitely had its dark side. At that time we junior officers charged ten paces ahead of the front rank, sword in hand, and were automatically shot down first. In view of the heavy losses of junior leaders the tactics were immediately changed. Officers were no longer allowed to carry swords, next their shoulder-straps were replaced by armbands, and they had to advance in line with their men, but the loss of subalterns, unsustainable for the future development of the war, was never to be made up.

I had only just recovered when I became Battalion Adjutant of the 2nd/239th a reserve regiment put together at Mannheim from the 110th and 113th regiments. My commanding officer was a charming old man, a Major von Roeder-Diersburg, by his badges from the Dragoons and most recently Marshal of the Court for Grand Duchess Louise of Baden. The Major didn't know much about infantry service, so I was able with luck and a reasonable grasp (though not much practical knowledge) to set about the forming of this reserve battalion. I brought my older brother into my battalion as a volunteer – it was mostly made up of young volunteers. As far as I could I tried to keep up the spirit of excitement, and used every opportunity from our victories at the time to convince the men of our final triumph. I knew nothing about politics, and didn't want anything to do with it, as it was an article of faith in the Cadet Corps that every politician was involved with some dirty work.

The whole division was assembled at Sennelager, given further campaign training, and lined up so that it at least gave the impression of a military unit. In the criminally short training time there could, of course, be no talk of a battle-ready formation. The spirit was excellent, not surprisingly when there were so many students who had volunteered to join up.

At the beginning of October we travelled to Belgium and began our advance into Flanders. My CO, Major Baron von Roeder-Diersburg had given me permission to ride several horses at Sennelager, always remarking 'Adjutant, you must be able to ride, riding is something you must be able to do; when you get into action, nothing stands in your way'. I left him to his beliefs and rode with enthusiasm. But when on 20 October 1914 we came into our first fighting contact and we were both trudging through thick Flanders mud, I could not help reminding the CO of his warning. At once he shouted out angrily, but then reached out his hand with the curt comment 'Cheeky dog!'

21 October was my birthday. My brother must have told his comrades about it, as wherever I turned up I was heartily congratulated. On the evening of this birthday, there was not much left of the proud battalion. We marched forward from Poelcappelle [Flanders] towards Langemarck [West-Flanders]. We could see nothing of the enemy, but we came under furious firing from well-camouflaged positions. Over there were old colonial fighters who had experienced war in practice. When we gathered the remains of our battalion that evening, three quarters of the

officers were missing including my wounded CO and over half of the NCOs and other ranks. On 22 October we tried to push forward again, but in vain. We were left lying under fire. Then we dug in. We received a few replacements and a new CO, Staff Major von Benzin, a man of real quality who in just a few days got us magnificently organized. It was a real pleasure to work under this talented officer – all the men immediately realized they were now in good hands. We established communication at once with our neighbouring units, improved our position by small raiding operations and prepared positions, which were protected to some extent in spite of the Flanders swamp. However on 28 October our Major fell victim to a head shot from a British sniper. I had just been on a reconnaissance operation and came back to our position proud after a summons to the Division Commander to be decorated with the Iron Cross 2nd Class. I felt wretched to see my CO lying dead. For the first time I became convinced that probably the best and most decent men have to die in battle. Next day, on orders from Division, I continued my reconnaissance and was wounded in the lower left thigh with a shell splinter.

I recovered quickly in the Reserve Hospital in Spandau [a suburb of Berlin]. The splinter was lodged in the bone, but when I could stagger about again I went to the Reserve Battalion in Bonn and reported for front-line duty. I still had to wait two months, and I used the time to study National Economics at the University there. I returned to the battalion at the beginning of 1915, in my old job. Almost all my comrades had strange faces, except my friend 2nd Lieutenant Grüninger, who led his company as before and was regarded as indestructible. He was the only man, at that time, who wore the Iron Cross 1st Class. We stuck together as we had before. My new CO was a Captain of the reserve with a fat belly who saw the essence of war as eating the best food available – our relations were not very harmonious, but at least he happily let me run the battalion, if only for his own convenience.

In March 1915 we were getting ready for the first gas attack in world history, but the materials were inadequate. However if this material was going to be used, we had to take the consequences to try to win the war – and we could have won it! The British fell into the same error later when they didn't follow the advice of the expert, the future General Fuller, and failed to fully exploit the amazing success of the tanks at Cambrai.

We dug in our gas bottles; there were hardly any reserves available. We were only surprised that the British didn't notice what we were doing, for not once but two or three times we went forward with reserves, and still the wind was unfavourable for our action. We cursed the weather frogs, which in fact had been able before to tell us clearly which way the wind was blowing. Finally, at the beginning of March, it was time. We let out the gas and advanced wearing our first gas masks (they consisted of a gauze bandage over our noses and mouths) against the enemy trenches. No shots rang out.

The trenches were full of dead British soldiers. It was only when we reached an artillery position that we had a revolver fired at us. Hundreds of guns were overrun without loss. We were advancing on Ypres over Pilckem Ridge, and our reconnaissance units had already got there. Then we got orders – fall back to Pilckem Ridge and dig in there. We understood. Without substantial reserves we could achieve nothing. We got two days to dig in completely undisturbed and then came an attack from other crack British troops to manoeuvre us out of these new positions. We held our ground, but losses on both sides must have been huge.

A Chilling Premonition

Our battalion was now pulled back into Houthulst Forest to rest up for 14 days. Ten days of rest had passed and we were sitting in our billets in the evening, drinking good Burgundy and singing. My friend Grüninger was sitting next to me. He sang 'Three horsemen out of the gate did ride, farewell! My darling there from the window spied, farewell!' loud and badly out of tune, then suddenly he grabbed me by the hand and shouted 'Hans' (he always called me that, Wappenhans was too long for him) 'I'll be killed tomorrow!' An icy chill ran down my back, for I somehow felt at that same moment 'The guy's right!' but I couldn't admit it. I contradicted him, 'You are crazy,' I said 'We've still got four days rest'. 'Fair enough', said Grüninger. 'You're a good fellow, but I'm still right'. Without a word we went to our tents, and I had only just fallen asleep when our stupid field telephone rang. 'This is the Adjutant of 2nd/239th. Write this down. 2nd Battalion 239th is to be ready at 05.30 hours tomorrow to support a section attack to improve the front of such-and-such a regiment as required. You will put three companies in the front line and keep one company in reserve to be deployed as the situation demands'. 'Yes sir!' – orders repeated. No further questions.

I hung up the phone and summoned Company commanders to a conference where I gave them their respective orders. Then the thought went through my head like lightning 'Stop! Grüninger! You stay in reserve with your company, the other three are detailed to the front line'. Next morning, an attack on the enemy positions took place after a short and weak bombardment. Two companies reached their objectives, the third stalled under fire. The reserve company – Grüninger's – was sent in. I worked my way forward with him. In the last charge, in front of the British trenches, came a soft 'Phut!' Grüninger collapsed, shot in the head. We leapt into the trenches, cleared them with grenades, secured our front, made contact with our neighbouring units, and moved on into the British shelter trenches. After a few hours' rest came a crashing bombardment which left us deaf and blind. Our shelter took a direct hit. I was lying crushed under a pile of planks and felt a raging pain in my left leg. My battalion bugler Willi Honschopp, the only survivor, freed me from this wretched position, cut the boot off my left leg, made a tourniquet with the strap of his bread bag and a makeshift bandage with some field dressings – he did all this by the light of only a pocket torch.

We couldn't get out of that trench. The shelter was full of earth, the Tommies were back on top of us. The day passed, then the night. The pain was getting worse all the time. Then we were shot at again, and the shelter shuddered under the hits. And suddenly it seemed we could hear voices. We yelled for help. The pain was raging now, and the air was foul with the stench of corpses. Then we noticed someone was digging. Timbers were carefully pushed aside, earth fell in on us and stopped our breathing. Then, after an unspeakably long time, a body slid towards us. A torch flamed – we couldn't recognize anything but we knew we were rescued. Carefully I was pulled out and laid on the floor of the trench. A doctor gave me a tetanus injection, put a bandage round my mangled lower thigh and I remained lying there till it was dark. The pain was excruciating, but I felt happy that it was Germans who now held the trench, so I wasn't a prisoner. The firing had died down. I was packed on a stretcher and given a morphine injection. These days I can understand a morphine addict – the pain vanishes, and you are tired, you want to sleep. The ambulance clattered towards Houthulst Forest, and the sound of men singing echoed in my ears 'Three horsemen out of the gate did ride, farewell! Three horsemen out of the gate did ride, farewell!' Then something hot fell from my eyes, there was a choking in my throat, and I was sobbing. I bit hard on the blanket. Yes, Grüninger, you're gone. Your premonition of death was right! Bless you, my dear chap!

A Torturous Route to Recovery

I'm lying on a stretcher in the dressing station, looking at a leg being cut off with a huge pair of scissors. An orderly put it in a corner of the tent. From the remaining stump a piece of white bone can still be seen. I feel so wretched. The completely exhausted doctor washes his hands:

he pulls on rubber gloves and puts his finger into my wounds. I yell with pain, but he's already found the big splinter. 'Doctor, you mustn't take this leg off" I beg him. 'I don't need to', says his weary voice. But I am sedated and breathe the chloroform in deeply, and as I count I only get to fourteen. I wake up in a small hospital behind the front. I'm lying in a real bed with clean linen. I feel quite well. In the evening, I'll be put on a hospital train. I'm on the lower bunk. We're moving, where? We don't know. The morphine injection sent me to sleep. Suddenly I woke up tormented by pain – I'm lying on the floor of the compartment. It's creaking and splintering. I hear groans and shouts, and then a strange silence in the darkness. I realize that we have collided with another train. The groans of the wounded in the shattered hospital carriage are appalling. Torches appear in the dark and somebody shouts 'Put the fire out!' Fear creeps into us all – are we going to burn to death? Axe blows hammer on a door, and then everything goes very fast. We're unloaded from the stretchers, laid down on the embankment and in an amazingly short time we're lying in another hospital carriage. We never discovered exactly what had happened, except that somewhere near Brussels we had to be transferred to another train.

Now we steamed on. The doctor said the train was going to Stettin [now Szczecin, North West Poland]. That would be fine by me.

I wanted morphine to be free of the pain, and then there was this constant feeling of fear. At Aachen I looked out of the window. The train was tilting right over. I saw a high embankment and hung tightly on to the bed. I had the fear in my bones that the train would tip over. But these were just feverish delusions. The doctor checked the thermometer – I had to be offloaded in Cologne, the fever was too high for me to go further.

For me the Protestant hospital in Cologne is a palace. I'm lying in a room for two people. The wound has opened up again. Now there are tubes in it and the pus is draining out. Every evening I get an injection, the pain goes away and I travel quite changed into dreamland.

My wounds begin to heal. Now I was cheerful again. My room-mate with a leg amputated played chess with me – he'd been put on my bed, facing me. The game had been going for two hours. And we'd told the Sunday nurse we didn't want to be disturbed. Then we found ourselves in the soup. One of us had touched a piece but not moved it. Hard words flew back and forth, we were angry. We didn't even look at each other, though we were lying on the same bed. The nurse didn't come back, she didn't want to disturb us. The situation grew more intolerable all the time, as neither of us wanted to give way, until at last supper arrived and we were released from this painful predicament.

Now I was taken out every day in the fresh air in a wheelchair. Cologne is a lovely city, and I wanted to get to know it – I especially liked Opera House Square, but the avenue leading to my objective is such a long way. I challenged my amputated – and by now reconciled – comrade to a race. Both our attendants agreed to take part. The first prize was five Marks, the second three Marks, and we charged away like wild beasts. The public joined in our enthusiasm, and day-by-day a bigger crowd attended our race.

Then the wounds began to fester again, and it was back to the operating table. When I woke up I had a splinter of bone in one hand, and a piece of shrapnel in the other. This was repeated twice, and then it was done! I'd had to spend three quarters of a year in that hospital and already thought I couldn't do any more for my Fatherland.

Flying Corps

When I was discharged, I arranged an evening show for my hospital comrades and then went to a replacement battalion. But with a problem in my calf bone and the calf nerve paralyzed I could only just manage to train recruits, and that badly, because I couldn't walk much despite my orthopedic boot. So in a roundabout way I applied for the Flying Corps, travelled to Königsberg [now Kaliningrad] and joined an Observers' course.

Sixty or seventy officers, all veterans of the Front, in one group. Man, what more can you ask for? Atmosphere, enthusiasm – which we needed a lot when we were stuck in an uncomfortable 'crate' to learn navigation, photography, signaling and artillery spotting. We eagerly did our duty: four planes crashed in front of us and caught fire. We couldn't help the poor fellows, we just heard them scream – the air claimed victims. We were preparing for our first observed examination.

With the help of my old fellow-cadet, Lieutenant Felmy, I went straight to Vilna [Vilnius, Lithuania] to his big brother Captain Felmy, Commander of the Flying Corps in the East. There I got to know the front-line planes. I flew mostly with Georgie, the younger Felmy, later the famous 'Eagle of Palestine'. In 1916 there were still no fixed machine guns which fired through the propeller, so we flew alongside our target which I had to rake from the back seat with a machine gun. We varied this with signal traffic 'Aboard – Ground', photo reconnaissance and evaluating tactical and strategic targets.

Between these, Georgie tested the durability of the planes in looping – because it seemed doubtful if a manned two-seater could resist the monstrous air pressure in completing the turn. It didn't disturb Georgie that I was to be just the second experimental guinea pig in the plane. I only heard a shout 'Buckle up tight-looping!' Then came the roar of the engine, the plane was pushed to its top speed and we climbed vertically upwards.

For some moments I felt a strong pressure on my skull, and then we roared into the dive. Foot off the gas, and we were flying normally. The two-seater had survived the loop. In the Western corner of the airfield, a Captain was drilling his recruits. When we fliers encountered him there was usually a row. Either it was our silk field caps that upset him, or he thought our salute was non-regulation and deserved a complaint. Georgie made short work of him; in a one-seater he swooped down on the airfield like a hawk and flew straight at the drilling recruits and the Captain, up on his horse. In complete confusion at the thundering plane, the soldiers threw themselves on the ground, while the Captain's horse bolted. This procedure was repeated three times, till the Captain finally chose to evacuate the field. The complaints and investigations went on for weeks, and have not been concluded to this day [30 years later].

Now we were ready, I came to the front at Soly East [White Russia] to Flying Section 55. Deputy-Officer Holst was assigned to me as my pilot – a shopkeeper apparently, a calm, practical pilot whom you could trust. From his side there was naturally a slight doubt about my capabilities – but that was overcome right away on our first flight.

Our duties were varied. In 1916 we faced each other in a static trench system. The fronts were relatively lightly manned on our side, and it was to be expected that the Russians would mass troops and try to break through at any point. So it was up to the airmen to find out where in good time, so that opposing forces could be deployed on our side. To achieve this objective, flights were detailed for:

1. *Close Reconnaissance*
(a) Regular photographing of trenches and artillery positions.
(b) Monitoring of all close activity (columns, accommodation, anti-aircraft guns).
(c) Contact with our batteries by radio.

2. *Long-range Reconnaissance – monitoring of*
(a) Enemy railway traffic
(b) Enemy unit movement
(c) Enemy airfields

3. *Attacking Flights – bombing of*
(a) Railway junctions
(b) Bridges
(c) Industrial targets
(d) Enemy airfields

On my first flight we were on close reconnaissance, and managed to carry out our task in reasonable weather. The Russian AA fire was heavy but extremely inaccurate. The flight back ran into problems, as rainclouds had formed below us. In those days there was no flying blind on a bearing, so I set a course for our airfield, had the pilot drive through the clouds at the given time and came straight out over our airfield in pouring rain. You've got to be stupid sometimes.

My pilot had kept his trust in me.[6]

Now we were flying almost every day and got good results. The photographic section under me worked smoothly led by Corporal (and artist) Ivo Hauptmann, Gerhart Hauptmann's[7] eldest son. The Russians' preparations for an offensive south of Smorgon [Smarhon] were continuously reported so, because of our opposing concentrations, the Russians had no success. For the first time in the East I found the opportunity to use the 'series camera' [a type of film], which was later successfully used on the Western Front.

Another success of ours was spotting for the experimental firing of the giant cannon, which later shelled Paris. 2nd Lieutenant Poelschau of the 15th Hussars was given this task, but was shot down by a French fighter that was presumably helping the Russians. So I took over the task, and was able to confirm with satisfaction that even at this enormous range accurate results were achieved.

While my pilot, Holst, was on leave, I flew quite often with 2nd Lieutenant Pernet, a stepson of General Ludendorff. Pernet was a brave little guy, but quite untalented as a flier. He often crash-landed. Flying at the front, he never went above 2,000 metres, so the Russian flak came dangerously close. Normal flights over the front had to be carried out at a minimum of 3,000 metres. It was a scary trip sitting in Pernet's crate: one day we flew to the army airbase in Kowno [Kaunas in Lithuania] to bring back a new plane. We were both ordered to have lunch at Headquarters, and I had the honour to sit opposite old Field-Marshal von Hindenburg and Pernet's stepfather Ludendorff.

As we were all former Cadets, reminiscences of the Corps were exchanged. We felt we were back in the old times, and realized that, in Hindenburg and Ludendorff's day, the old habits and customs had been exactly like ours in the Cadet Corps.

As time went on, the East was too peaceful for me. I was hungry for success – it had been drummed into me in the Cadet Corps. As the Russian fliers were nowhere to be seen, I took a poke at a stationary balloon moored near Smorgon. We went down to 600 metres, circled the balloon and from the back seat I shot off the whole magazine. The thing refused to burn, and on the ground they wound in the cable like madmen. The balloon sank lower and lower. Suddenly I felt a blow on my head, the machine gun was ripped out of my hands, and blood ran into my eyes. The balloon was almost on the ground. We turned for home, chased by shots from all the Russian machine guns and flak – but we made it home. Meanwhile I'd taken off my crash helmet and found it was torn and a small shell splinter was stuck in my head. As if the damned cold weren't enough – 30 degrees below zero. When we landed I passed out, and was taken to hospital. They soon took out the splinter and I hoped I'd be back in action after a few days. I had to rest up for fourteen days in a convalescent home in Wilna [Vilnius]. Then I got such severe earache that I immediately had to be transferred to the ear clinic. The ear was infected. It was matter of life or death, for a blood clot followed, but the magnificent doctor found ways and means to get me back on my feet.

With my head still bandaged I went to the Inspectorate of the Flying Corps in Berlin, to find a new posting. I was promised one – if I went to Berchtesgaden to convalesce for four weeks first. I did, and spent a wonderful time in the well-appointed Geiger's Guesthouse.

As well as the Hessian and Saxon ambassadors [to Bavaria?] von Bregeleben and von Salza, with their wives and daughters, Princess Emine, the daughter of the Turkish ambassador to Germany, was also staying there. We spent happy hours there in good company, we danced together, though the Koran forbids it, and I promised faithfully to visit her soon in Constantinople [Istanbul]. And soon I managed to keep my promise.

After a short detour to Stuttgart (the Inspectorate of the Flying Corps ordered me to talk sense into the Turkish officers who were supposed to be learning about engines at the Mercedes factory but were using the time for other purposes) I got orders in Berlin to kit myself out for the tropics in eight days and then travel via Constantinople to Palestine, and report to Air Group 300 'Pasha'. 'Fine', I thought 'at last a sensible order! Now you'll see a bit of the world'.

The kitting-out was complete, and Berlin was unsafe once again. We planned a great prank at our airmen's hostel on the corner of Kurfürstendamm and Joachimstalerstrasse. There were five of us, and each one agreed to invite ten young ladies to meet him on the same corner that morning. So we did, and then sat down cheerfully for coffee on the veranda, from which we could watch the results of our efforts in good cover. We certainly reached the number of fifty ladies. But the beauties' suspicious glances at each other were soon interrupted, when a policeman, who thought it was a gathering of extremists, ordered passers-by to clear off.

And then I was on the Zoo Station with my comrade 2nd Lt. Bartenier, waiting for the Balkan train. We took our places in a 1st class sleeper (of which we were particularly proud) and greeted our only travelling companion, an Austrian naval officer. Then each of us said a tearful goodbye to his absolute favourite girl. This happened again at Friedrichstrasse station. Our Austrian comrade wore a bittersweet expression, but very nicely helped us pack away our loving gifts. When this was repeated at Alexanderplatz[8], he couldn't resist remarking. 'Now look, comrades, a man could just die of envy!'

From Constantinople to Ramleh

The trip to Constantinople on the Balkan Express was a pleasure. We had a short break in Budapest, as our Austrian friend thought we should get to know the 'Pearl of the Danube'. Besides, we'd been detained once at Kospoli where everything was done with a stoical calm. He got us released. So we got off in Budapest, our Austrian comrade arranged all the rest. We were driven in an ambulance to a hospital, well looked after, and again met the charming Hungarian nurses in a delightful café on the Danube. The gypsy musicians put us in a mood which I simply can't describe. Next day we could hardly drag ourselves away from our hosts.

At Constantinople a Hamburg-America steamship, the *Corcovado* lay moored at the Galata Bridge, and we were accommodated on board. Excellent service, and nothing to do. This didn't suit us, and we asked to proceed, but we had to wait at least fourteen days. Then the station at Haydarpasha on the Asian side burned down. We saw a sea of flames and heard explosions. The British had hit a sensitive place, the starting-point for traffic to the Near East. However we got assurances that we would start in eight days. We used the time getting to know Constantinople. I went over in a government boat to the Princes' Islands[9] where His Excellency Muktar Pasha lived in a palatial mansion. I was received like a prince. My enquiries about the daughter, Princess Emine, were mostly passed over. And it was only after a meal of countless courses that I was led into a yellow drawing-room and stood face to face with her. The Princess, who at Berchtesgaden had from her outward appearance made no impression on me, now struck me very differently in these surroundings. She wore a flowing deep blue silk robe. The contrast with the yellow carpet made the deep blue colour appear even more intense. A golden belt encircled her hips and on her feet were narrow gold shoes with high heels. Her face was covered with a veil, through which I could only make out the oval of her face, from which two enchantingly beautiful brown eyes shone. I could hardly say 'Wow, Emine, how you've changed!' in my best Berlin accent. So I said nothing, shook her hand and left, quite overcome by so much beauty.

Finally it was time to go. A box of gold coins was pressed into my hand, which I had to deliver personally in Aleppo, then I took the steamer to the Asian side past the enormous barracks[10] near Haydarpasha Station. The work of clearing up [after the fire] was in full swing. The train stood ready, and knowing Asian conditions I proudly boarded a first-class carriage and made myself comfortable. Surprisingly, no other passengers came. We puffed away and after no more than an hour I'd been so badly bitten by bugs that I preferred to get out at the next station. The soldiers, who had travelled that way before, laughed at me and invited me into their goods wagon. Camp beds with mosquito nets stood there, nice and clean. Each bedpost stood in a small tin of petrol, which was exactly what the bugs didn't like. The bed I'd brought with me was put up and on we went at a cheerful speed towards the Taurus Mountains. In Eskishehir we had to change to a branch line, with only wooden benches.

A senior Turkish officer who spoke fluent German adopted me, provided food and raki, the absinth-like Turkish schnapps which takes on a milky appearance when you dilute it with water. The rattling train gasped its way painfully into the Taurus which, in its wild gorge-like valleys gave us wonderful views from the train. We cheered up when we got to the summit but clearly realized, when the train picked up speed on the downslope, that our sight and hearing was weakening. Every moment you had to be careful not to be shaken off on a curve and into the abyss. The wheels were running hot, and some wagons began to smoke – we could see a dreadful end before us. When the train finally halted, the otherwise calm Turk bellowed at the driver. We then saw a fierce confrontation, in which the Turkish officer's riding-crop played a significant part. Coming back to us in our section he gave us the news, once again in his unruffled way 'What do you say to this driver? He says he's in the right, he wanted to make up for the delay and he's been letting the train run without actually using the brakes. Inshallah – God willing – we'll get down all right'. And we did – what can you say against that? We kept quiet, and were happy, and the rest of the journey to Aleppo went without any more incidents.

We stopped over in Aleppo for two days. I handed over my box of gold, and enjoyed the hospitality of the Austrian consul, who showed me at chess what advantage a master has over an amateur.

We went on using wood for fuel. The last cedars of Lebanon had to put up with it. We panted up to the ruins of Baalbek for hours. An engineer and airman. Reserve Lieutenant Kaskeline told us about the size of the huge blocks of stone which were dragged up on to this hill hundreds of years ago. It was only with the help of ramps, and the use of thousands of labourers. These days it would be impossible to build up a store of blocks of such size, given the enormous cost. Carved into the ruins was an ancient swastika, whose meaning I am not sure of to this day.

We stopped again at Damascus. We were guests of little Meissner Pasha, the builder of the Turkish railways. The splendid life in his villa, contrasted with the misery of the rest of the people pricked my conscience. In the Damascus bazaars I bought glorious examples of Damascene art, silver-inlaid daggers and vases that looked like mother-of-pearl. We shuddered on, and the train often had to stop, as the wood couldn't generate enough heat. But finally we reached Samach, on Lake Gennesareth [the Sea of Galilee] and travelled via Afule to Ramleh, my destination.

Ramleh is a typical Arab village, though it is described as a town, with palm groves and fields surrounded by cactus hedges. The one building worth the name, the monastery, was where Air Section 300 'Pasha' lived. I was kindly greeted by my comrades especially Captain Felmy and Georgie, and immediately instructed in my range of duties.

It was now 1917, and in this year a front line of positions had been established from Beersheba to the Mediterranean coast. It was manned by Turkish units, with only small specialist [German] units and a number of officers. In command was Colonel Kress von Kressenstein, a gaunt, talented and tireless officer who enjoyed great popularity with the Turkish soldiers, because he shared their good and bad times and turned up in person at threatened hotspots. Kress had given the British plenty to do. In an incredibly bold stroke, in spite of logistic difficulties (at the time there was no railway yet), he had advanced as far as the Suez Canal. The British got a proper fright. But Kress had to retreat. Without ammunition or supplies it was impossible to continue the fighting. So he pulled back to the Gaza-Beersheba line, dug in (as far as you could in the sand) and tried to hurt the British with individual operations. General Allenby, who meanwhile had been ordered to

Egypt as commander of the combined British armed forces, for his part proceeded methodically. In an amazingly short time a railway was laid along the coast from Egypt to near Gaza. And, as if that wasn't enough, a water pipeline was laid continuously parallel to it. Then Allenby attacked. The battles of Gaza went into history as bloody fights in which the Turks performed wonders in its defence.

Air Section 300

Air Section 300 'Pasha' was the only air unit then in Palestine. It consisted of nine two-seater crews and two fighters.

Editor: The aviation squadrons of the Ottoman Empire (a Germany ally in WWI) were named 'Pasha' units after the Empire's Minister of war, Mahmud Shevket Pasha. Some German officers including Hans Joachim Buddecke (the third flying ace to be awarded the Blue Max – Germany's highest honour in WWI) and Waldemar Wappenhans were sent to Ottoman air bases. Eventually Germany transferred over 450 planes to the Ottoman Empire split roughly 50-50 between Ottoman and German units.

At that time the equipment of the planes couldn't match the British. Anyone who had the honour to serve in Air Section 300 had to be in perfect health and have successful front-line experience behind him. The British were green, daring in dogfights but without front-line experience. They lost over twenty planes, without any loss to us except a few wounded. But that changed in 1918. The best planes and crews were shipped over from England, Captain Bell[11], the famous VC, appeared on the scene with his fighters, and soon the page turned. In the cemetery at Nazareth alone lie twenty-four of our comrades: in the last year we lost seventy per cent of our crews in three months. In 1917 our task was mainly to provide a picture of the enemy's unit distribution, and from this their attack objectives. This could be done with a well-completed flight.

We flew out to sea near Jaffa, again enjoyed the scent of the orange groves, which one could smell as far as 250 metres up, and then set course for Port Said. There you nosily stuck your head out to discover what nice little ships the 'Tommies' had gathered there. That was then confirmed by photographs. After a detour over the Pyramids of Gizeh we went along the coast to Ballah, the British air base. On the way we counted the supply trains. From Ballah to the front we continually snapped and noted everything there was to see. In that terrain without cover, nothing could stay hidden. We could count one battalion camp after another, and the same with the cavalry regiments. Three squadrons formed a regiment, three regiments a brigade and three brigades a division. When these cavalrymen turned up at any point along the front we were warned, because these were the units intended to overrun the whole front in the event of a breakthrough – which was what they did later. Then the British batteries not far behind the front were photographed, and – back home to Ramleh. A short report on the phone, then into the photographic section. The results of the evaluation were immediately passed on to Command.

Not long after starting on a bombing raid, I found rather a lot of British warships at sea off Askalon. I attacked at once and dropped my bombs on them. I was amazed how the ships moved like a swarm of bees. They must have laughed at my bombs because the biggest were [only] 50 kg, which can't have done much damage to armoured vessels. For my independent action I was brought before Captain Felmy to justify myself. This meant we had missed a useful opportunity – I should have come back and landed at once, then all our available aircraft could have been loaded with heavier bombs. We could then have attacked the warships close together, and had a better prospect of success. So the ships were warned and did not come back.

During a flight near Beersheba, I succeeded in forcing a Tommy to land after a sharp dogfight. Soon after we dived on a captive balloon, but once again it would not catch fire; however, it had taken so many hits that it didn't reappear for some time.

As a reward I was supposed to take a riding trip the same day with several comrades to the Degania Jewish settlement near Jaffa. As we rode into the village we were ceremoniously greeted by the Mayor and invited to a dance. Our Arab escort had notified them before, introducing me as 'His Highness Prince Koke von Anthrazite'. As I walked grandly into the hall, in a white uniform with a large decoration at the collar, there fell out of my pocket a little packet of a certain silk paper, whose purpose was devious, and this fact came to light on this occasion. The little sheets were picked up by the wind and blown through the hall. Everybody jumped up at once, tried to gather the sheets, in order to return them to their owner with a straight face. My princely dignity was shattered.

I left my comrades and rode to the German colony in Jaffa on my own. My cousin von Rabenau was working there as vicar, and lived with his young wife Elisabeth. Before eating, my cousin read a long text from an improving book. Apart from Karl May[12], who has left brilliant descriptions of lands and people, we also read the Bible a lot to familiarize ourselves with the holy places it mentions. So I understood the text. During dinner I innocently asked my new cousin to tell me once more the essential point of what [her husband] had read out. My poor little cousin blushed and couldn't find a way to answer. She was quite put out. When the British later took Jaffa, my cousin stayed with the rest of his congregation and was interned in Egypt. His wife made her way to Samach on the Sea of Galilee, where our Air Section was later stationed. I met her ceremoniously at the station and arranged accommodation for her in my own billet.

In our club, a special dinner was held in her honour. We had not seen a German lady for a long time and were really pleased with her visit. As we rough soldiers didn't bother to pray before meals, my heart stopped when my cousin suddenly pulled out an improving book and read from it with folded hands. We sat there as quiet as mice, and breathed in with relief when we saw the book disappear and the CO wished us a good appetite. We had brewed a powerful punch, to which my cousin helped herself liberally after making sure from me that there was no alcohol in it. 'A flier never drinks alcohol' I promised her, and then all was fine. My cousin was delighted – the improving book went round under the table and everyone signed it. When I took my cousin to the station the next day, she muttered that I had sinned against God. I'm not quite sure why. Anyway, I had a hangover and wasn't feeling very bright. So sadly we didn't part in complete harmony.

In Palestine everything was being reorganized. The Asian Corps was moving up, more infantry regiments, artillery even four new Air Sections and a fighter squadron gradually came on the scene. General von Falkenhayn took over command and the Chief of Staff was Lieutenant Colonel von Papen [see Plates 10, 11 & 15], who was later to play some part in politics[13]. HQ was at Nazareth. The British were better informed than we were – a captured Major once told me what forces we were advancing with. At the same time he told me that in a very short time he would be in British territory – and in fact eight days later he had disappeared and was never seen again. As a result of the wretched communications to the rear, the operations of the Asian Corps were only possible in stages, and were never fully developed. Allenby[14] had seized the initiative, attacked during the build-up and unfortunately with great success.

The British made our regular reconnaissance flights really unpleasant. We seldom got through without fighting or without losses – yet we managed to bring in the vital material to be processed. We usually flew in from the sea pushed along the coast and vanished when things got hot. We were stationed at Samach on the Sea of Galilee. We were starting at 250m, below sea level, and in the thin air the planes often sank as much as 50 metres. With sweat pouring we laboured to bring the crates up to 1,000 metres, where the situation was calmer. Then we often went up to 7,000 metres, where we felt the bitter cold, and without oxygen. Coming home we were often dangerously tired.

Even so it was only then that the work began. The results of our reconnaissance had to be summarized and passed on to Nazareth immediately. Then the work began in the photo section. The first prints were evaluated while still wet. Concentrations of infantry, cavalry and convoys behind the front were captured on film – and sometimes discovered for the first time. New artillery positions had to be passed on to the front, and new trench outlines should not be missed.

In the midst of this work a General Staff officer often turned up to confirm in person the facts reported by phone on the now developed photos. Even the Chief of Staff and General von Falkenhayn came to see us, and all this in a heat it was hard to get used to.

We had serious losses from malaria, but I was spared. Maybe I owe that to my Turkish batman, who took care of me with rare loyalty, and made sure that there was no whining insect under my mosquito net. I didn't often swallow quinine – the effects, the constant buzzing in the head were too unpleasant for me.

Early one evening I was coming home from a reconnaissance flight. In spite of a fight with a tough lad, I managed to get important shots of Tommies landing at Ballah. Gliding we went back over the sea, then the pilot switched on the emergency tank. The engine stalled, the propeller stopped – we realized that the emergency tank had been hit, which we had not noticed. We turned as fast as we could towards the airfield. We were right over the sea [of Galilee] and the propeller still wouldn't start. On a normal glide we would have landed in the sea; this meant flipping over and a miserable death by drowning, so as far as possible we went into a shallow glide. When we got to the shore we were barely 10 metres from the ground. I felt a heavy blow on the head, and woke up in a hospital in Tiberias. I was tortured by crazy headaches and felt seasick. The doctor stuck a needle into my spinal cord and drew off water – this was very painful, but the headaches seemed to have been blown away.

After two days I went up to Bhamdun on Mount Hermon to convalesce. Wonderful surroundings, healthy air and good food gave the required boost to my recovery. Then came news that I had been awarded the *Order of the House of Hohenzollern with Swords*[15]. I had to get back to my comrades, but first a short detour to Beirut, possibly one of the loveliest cities in the world. Here you can forget everything, the evil on Earth, yes, even the war. Here you can laugh or cry, you can fold your hands and forget the wild life you had got into. I had myself taken out in a boat into the bay under a starry sky whose light was so intense that you could read by it. Below me was the greenish water, through which you could almost make out the bottom, in front were the snow-white silhouettes of the houses that clung to the hillsides, and in the background the snow-covered mass of Mount Hermon. It was an atmosphere to make one soft again, but I should stay hard – there was a war to win. I visited the Jewish University, one of the most modern buildings I'd ever seen. It had sports grounds, gymnastic and swimming halls, everything provided.

I had dinner with a Turk in a hotel garden: he took a piece of bread and threw it from the terrace into the street. A fight broke out at once over this one small piece of bread. The people's poverty was unbearable, and as the Turk explained, the Turkish governors, especially Djemal Pasha[16], were to blame. They often intercepted the caravans of grain on the way to Beirut, bought the grain cheaply and then put it on the market for high prices in the city.

When I came back to the Sea of Galilee I was tasked, with a comrade, to take two British flying officers back to Haifa and ask them some questions about the British air force. We put our British comrades on our home-built motor rail-car and set off. On the car we had mounted an old aero-plane engine with a propeller and all. A brake was attached to the back wheels – these had to be worked by two men. Our two British fliers were excited about our vehicle and enthusiastically detailed themselves for brake duty. The propeller gave us a pleasant temperature, but we had to hold on tight, so as not to be sucked into it. On straight stretches of rails we could reach a speed of 100 km/h. The Turkish railways (especially at stations) were not best pleased with our trips, but with appropriate bakshish, a small, clinking compensation, we always got by.

In Haifa we went to the German settlement, inhabited by Swabian farmers, who by hard work had made it very prosperous, where we were – as always – given a splendid welcome. We spent a happy day there with our British comrades, swam, ate and drank. When we passed the tennis court, I regretted that we could no longer play: we didn't have any more tennis balls. Next day a plane starting on a recon-flight carried a note from both the Englishmen [to their own comrades], and dropped it over Ballah. The very next day a British [plane] appeared over our airfield and dropped a backpack on a parachute. The accompanying note to the German Flying Corps read 'Thanks for the good treatment of our pilots, hope we can soon return the favour on our side. Kit enclosed for our comrades, and a dozen tennis balls for you'. Yes, it was war, but we fought it chivalrously.

From Haifa we made another trip by sailing boat to Akko [Acre]. The famous fortress that once stopped Napoleon when he tried to invade from Egypt – the same way that Allenby came later. The visit was disappointing. We stood in the market place and saw women draw water from wells, fill up clay jars and carry them home on their heads. Then my eye fell on a young girl who walked past in such a regal manner that one couldn't help staring. She had fine, aristocratic features with great dark eyes. Her ragged clothes left her perfectly formed body, like a bronze statue, free – firm, finely shaped breasts, slim hips and long legs like a thoroughbred's. As we stood looking, dumbstruck, we heard a voice nearby, 'Do the gentlemen wish to buy the girl?' I assumed the man was crazy but when he repeated the question I asked the price. Two gold sovereigns didn't seem much and each of us four chipped in. The deal was done, and she was brought to the boat, and the money handed over. We sailed off, but now we were beginning to feel uneasy – what were we going to do with the girl? She seemed happy but we could not be slave owners! Making ourselves understood didn't really work. She didn't want to return to Akko on any account, we understood from her gestures. We took care to land in the Arab quarter of Haifa. There our 'Kospoli' as we called her was sent for a bath, she got new clothes and plenty to eat. Kospoli was excited, it was quite clear. Through our interpreter from the railcar we found out that Kospoli had already changed owners twice and anyway wanted to stay with us. With a soldier's coat on, Kospoli didn't stand out. We got to Samach, rented a mud hut there, gradually made it cosy and got Kospoli to do our laundry. We always went there in a group, as nobody really trusted another. She was friendly to everyone. She didn't really understand that we weren't, or even that we wanted something else.

An end was on the way for this delusion, for I was transferred from Samach. My departure came so quickly that I never got to say goodbye. I've never heard any more of Kospoli.

In Samach we lived in the Jewish settlement, which lies right at the point where the Jordan flows out of the Sea of Galilee. Here 2nd Lieut. Kaskeline, an engineer with Siemens had built a suspension bridge over the Jordan, by which we ran traffic to Tiberias, Tapka and Capernaum and also ensured communications via Tiberias through Cana to Nazareth. From a certain spot you got the most beautiful view over the lake and its surroundings, with a backdrop of snow-covered Mount Hermon. It lay well hidden in a cypress grove called 'The Double

Eagle'. It was far and away the favourite place to visit and the visit lived up to expectation.

We often had philosophical discussions with the leader of the Zionists on those wonderful nights. He was an idealist who wanted to create a homeland for his people – and he hated his co-religionists who were always willing to send money but would not come to their homeland themselves. Again and again he begged us not to give the Jewish settlement books, for then they just read and didn't work.

At the airfield we had even organized a horse race. We did have horses, some of them of fine Arab bloodstock, which Djemal Pasha had presented to the officers of the Air Section. Of course the winner was the older Felmy's magnificent stallion.

Later I had to bring a director of Opel to our home. (We didn't get many guests at that time). He was leading a convoy as a Reserve Lieutenant. The Chief of Staff, Lieutenant Colonel Von Papen, on his way to the front, met this man halfway there and received an official report that the convoy had been captured by the enemy. Papen drove on and found the convoy camped peacefully with some Turkish soldiers. What had happened? When the convoy approached, the Turks had cautiously fired one shot. It was something they usually did. Opel ran for it and escaped with his life. von Papen held a court-martial, and he was given a severe reprimand on his record.

We went round the lake in a motorboat and landed in all the pleasant places. A few kilometres North of Samach there were hot springs, supposed to have great healing qualities. Our doctor, a Bavarian, wanted to set up a sanatorium there after the war, and maybe he did. In Tiberias, in the German House, lived the King of the Fleas. If you sat on the terrace in the evening, fleas in swarms would crawl up your mosquito boots. Now and again you took a brush and swept them off. In a pine grove at Tiberias, surrounded by exotic plants and wonderful flowers, there was a crystal-clear pool, about ten metres deep. We bathed in it, threw in rose petals and imagined ourselves back in the time of the ancient Romans. In Capernaum an old monk had lived for many years, keeping busy by digging up the ancient ruins and feeding white doves. Did the old centurion [captain] of Capernaum do the same? We didn't know, just as the miracles of Jesus Christ were not explained to us. We were shown the place where Jesus walked on the lake. There were shallows that must have been well known, otherwise you'd have gone under at once. In Cana we tasted the water at the well, but it didn't produce wine. Only our doctor gained the reputation of working miracles. When people, ravaged with fever, came to him they got quinine or injections, and the fever disappeared. Many children were cured of eye infections. When they came with their revolting sores and the flies sitting on them, you could only feel an indescribable pity – and when after a few days one of these children returned, cured and smiling to their parents we were happy with them. Our doctor, however, whose medical abilities we regarded fairly sceptically, but was all the more admired for his skill at cards, became known as 'The Miracle-worker of Galilee'.

Lawrence of Arabia

Now it was 1918. The rainy season was nearly over. I was at Jenin, the exit point of the Wilderness of Haran. We stayed in tents there, and the heat was unbearable. Till now, the front had held, but everything pointed to the fact that Tommy was making a serious effort, and our little Asian Corps came up only in dribs and drabs. Then in addition came bad news about the Hejaz railway[17] that was blown up again and again. At the Tebuk oasis, near the Red Sea there was a Turkish division, which lived practically solely on what it bought from the British through Bedouin middlemen – their communications with the railway were pretty well cut off. So we fitted out two aircraft, each one with a reserve tank of petrol which had to be transferred in flight using a hand pump. Instead of bombs we carried chests of gold. So off we went – desert, nothing but desert all the way. After an endless flight, we arrived in Tebuk, were greeted by the troops and the gold was unloaded. Their chief of staff, an officer of the General Staff trained in Germany, gave us his thanks and appreciation and pressed a small bag of gold coins into our hands with the express suggestion that we should use it to order gold cigarette-cases in Damascus. He also gave us a draft for the initials to be engraved on them in Turkish [Arabic] letters. The commander of the second plane, a Captain, had reservations about a gift like this, although the Turkish officer had explained, with charming sincerity, that we'd done more than enough to deserve decorations. But that flight was one of which I would keep deep personal memories. So we thanked him, ate some wonderfully sweet dates picked straight from the palm tree, drank tea made from orange leaves and flew home. The bags of gold and the initials were sent to HQ in Nazareth for further decisions, as duty required, and we heard no more of them.

Colonel Lawrence's[18] activities were getting themselves increasingly noticed. Arabs and Bedouin who had been on the side of the Turks now defected. The Hejaz railway was more or less wiped out. It was time to put a stop to this. We attacked troop concentrations near the railway with bombs and machine guns, and the Bedouin became more careful.

We had successes, as Lawrence later admitted in *War in the Desert* and *The Seven Pillars of Wisdom*. We observed British landings in the Gulf of Akaba, which we also bombed – but even in the desert the British air force tried to frustrate our efforts.

Next our airfield received a surprise attack by twenty-five or thirty bombers – a tough task for the conditions of the time, given the long distance. Although the bombs were dropped from fairly low altitude they had little effect. One plane had to be written off, three men were wounded, no-one was killed. The chain bombs they dropped were not much use. The next two British planes that stuck their noses into our area were 'rabbits' – beginners. They were shot down, without returning fire, by Lieutenant Bentäurer with a single plane. Because of this, flights in the direction of Akaba became even more dangerous – the British were flying a blockade.

Meanwhile they succeeded in breaking through on the Gaza front. Jaffa was captured and heavy fighting raged around Jerusalem. On one of my reconnaissance flights I discovered that after the breakthrough the British were only deploying cavalry, who were pushing far into the rear with incredible speed. One mounted unit even managed to push forward as far as Nazareth, but was driven off by the combined Staffs. At the time people didn't really believe my report. General Allenby (whom I met later on a visit to the British High Commissioner in Danzig, at his house – the former home of Mackensen[19]) confirmed that my report had been correct. As so often, the British didn't take advantage of their great success, so Falkenhayn was able, at least for some time, to form a defensive front.

The focus of the battle shifted towards Jerusalem, which after much toing and froing fell to the enemy. Now we held the East bank of the Jordan. I settled for a time in Amman and helped out the fighting troops: it was then that I fought the longest dogfight of my life against a tough opponent. We chased each other around for so long that I shot off all my ammunition. To this day I don't understand why he didn't crash. In my rear seat I had installed on the ring mounting a double machine gun, equipped with a trigger that would fire both barrels simultaneously – an iron contraption built by my chief mechanic, as the army couldn't supply anything like it. The gun worked well, and I shot the full load into my opponent. The shots hit home, I could see from the white tracks of the tracer bullets – but he didn't go down. I don't know how long the fight lasted, but it seemed like hours. Most shamingly, it was only when I landed that I realized I was bleeding slightly from my right ear. A bit of iodine on it, and all sorted out. But the crate looked dreadful, we counted over a hundred hits.

Repairs took a few days, which I used to look around our area. Beautiful plants grew wild on the ancient ruins of Roman times. An amphitheatre of huge proportions was still quite well preserved. Columns from the days of the Empire stood everywhere. I was even shown the outline of a stadium where the Romans held water shows. Civilization at the time must have reached unimaginable heights, but today this Transjordan region was neither culturally nor agriculturally developed.

I was now flying against Lawrence. An Englishman who was flying a blockade run on the Hejaz railway hadn't seen me. I came out of the sun and stayed there long enough to shoot him up from point-blank range. He crashed, but went down in flames a long way from the railway. Were we going to be denied recognition of the kill? No! We went down to pick up at least a piece [of the plane] to prove our kill. But we crash-landed and the propeller came loose. What now? The Englishman's plane had burned out and there was not much left of him. We had to get away, as in the burning sun and with no water, we'd be finished. We unshipped our rear guns and the compass, then off on foot towards the railway, sweating in streams. In the end we reached a hill; the line could not be far – then a couple of shots whistled past our ears. It was the Turks guarding the railway. We waved our handkerchiefs and they ceased fire and welcomed us beaming with delight. Did they have to fire at us? But now we weren't angry any more. We were glad of the lukewarm water and even more of the delicious watermelons. One Turkish officer spoke a little French, which was enough for us to understand each other fairly well. We had to man the position because British armoured cars had been reported to the East – that is, coming out of the desert. I didn't want to believe this – it was another trick of Lawrence's. But in fact three smallish cars, like today's Jeeps, but armoured, showed up. We let them come close, though it was hard to stop the Turks opening fire at once. My double machine gun was in good cover, and then it was time – we opened up. The armoured cars turned sharply round and vanished.

In the afternoon, a motor carriage came along the line. We stopped it and were taken aboard, and came back to the airfield after two days' travelling.

There news reached me of my transfer to the Western Front, as Commander of the 27th Battle Squadron. Great! Wonderful! A farewell party with lots of raki, and a hangover next morning, I thought – but I was shivering all over and couldn't get out of bed, and felt as if the small of my back was broken. The doctor came. I had a temperature of 40 degrees (104°F) – Pappataci's [sandfly] fever. In the evening my temperature was normal but all my limbs ached. By chance a hospital train was reported at Jenin station. I was carried in, put in a proper bed and felt quite well, as long as I didn't move. We steamed off to Damascus and stopped there in a loading bay in the goods depot. Darkness fell quickly, I tried to straighten up, but fell back on the pillows groaning. Outside we heard raised voices, torches flashed, then the noise died away and a healing silence reigned. A wounded comrade reckoned they were fetching ambulances so we could be unloaded. We dozed off, but then I heard a gentle sound like the buzzing of planes. I called for quiet and now we could hear it clearly. Bloody hell! British planes, you could tell by their sound. Then it was show time, there could have been twenty to thirty British craft attacking the station.

One plane after another dropped its bombs, there was a deafening crash and splintering – a section of the train had been hit, and you could hear the screams of men who'd been wounded twice. Then above us on an embankment continuous banging started – the infantry ammunition stored there had caught fire. When the planes were long gone, the explosions went on for hours. It was only in the middle of the night that the Medical Corps arrived and took us to hospital.

Next day the Chief MO appeared in our ward, very energetic and decisive, but he didn't stay long. So we were examined much more thoroughly by an older doctor. He was in fact a junior MO, but a specialist in tropical diseases from Eppendorf Hospital near Hamburg. He told me from the start 'In two days you'll be on your feet again, and ready to travel on in eight'. And so it turned out, but I still wasn't sleeping too well – the fleas and bugs gave me too much trouble. Next day I begged the Chief MO to get rid of the pests, and offered him my two-year experience in combating such things. I was ungraciously turned away, so I went on to help myself. I gave each patient two test tubes with cork stoppers – the hospital had plenty available – and we collected the bugs in one and the fleas in the other. The haul was a generous one, and it ended up being emptied into the Chief MO's bed while he was away at the officers' club. The next day he appeared after a sleepless night, followed by a convoy of orderlies who set about the war on the pests themselves. We were quite moved by the hospital boss's willingness to help.

My German batman took me to the station. We old Palestine hands had got the message by now – through bakshish we'd got hold of a goods wagon where our camp beds were put up after clearing away some crates. Off we went and arrived at Haydarpasha [station, in Constantinople] without incident.

We still had no idea of how serious the situation had become at home. It wasn't till Constantinople that we found out that the Balkan Express had been suspended, and we were to travel by cargo steamer to Braila, [in Romania] then try to exit via Bucharest and Budapest to Silesia, [now Southern Poland, then German] and this we did. On the steamer we sat packed together like herrings and sailed by night in case of submarines. Life jackets? 'Yok, efendim' [There aren't any, sir] said the soldier next to me. But we got safely into the Danube, and found a connection straight away, a train to Bucharest. My batman was waiting with my kit on a leave train that was supposed to be going direct to Berlin. I've not seen him or my kit since. Kismet! [That's fate].

We didn't stay long in Bucharest – the stopover was disgusting. In the German Club we weren't thought much of in our not exactly dressy uniforms. I hadn't seen so many elegant officers in one place for years. In the city it was swarming with Romanian[20] officers and their ladies – even the men were wearing makeup! We caught a train to Budapest, which looked very different from our outward journey – yelling soldiers everywhere, ripping the cockades (with the Emperor's initials on them) off their Austrian comrades' caps. As we changed to a train for home, my last suitcase was stolen. A pity – [it contained] my photos and my diary, which I'd really have liked to keep.

The Western Front – WWI

After a short stay in Berlin it was straight off to Flanders. My 27 Squadron had just been fully reinforced. Our first order was to move the squadron back. The second, to move back further. Then we had eight days rest. Pouring rain, then our first mission – the infantry fighting in Sector X must be supported by all possible means. That meant flying in really low, dropping bombs and engaging the enemy with all weapons on board.

We assembled over the airfield and flew to the front in close formation. We saw a fierce bombardment falling on the sector in question. Down to near ground level, shoot up the enemy positions with all we'd got, and bomb their artillery positions and reserves – then further to the rear to shoot up their convoys. Turn around, and then the same again. We landed at the airfield, pursued by British fighters – the result, only four out of nine planes made it home, and these were useless for next time, they'd been badly shot up. My pilot died of his wounds next day. I hadn't imagined how crazy the war on the Western Front was.

206

I had to go to the Air Corps Inspectorate in Berlin to try and get new planes and replacement crews, but I was put off, I had to wait – but I pushed for them every day. It said in the morning paper 'The Kaiser has left the army and gone to Holland'. We didn't want to believe it. After all, we had sworn loyalty to him, and we had kept our oath. Did His Majesty now want to leave us in the lurch? We couldn't even imagine it. And now, when we heard of the revolution at Kiel[21], we declared ourselves at the Inspectorate's disposal to put it down. We were refused: we couldn't understand our High Command any longer. Wasn't there a 'real man' available? Hindenburg's orders, people said. In the end, he <u>must</u> know the war was lost. We walked back to the airmen's hostel, and were jostled in the street. People wanted to tear off our shoulder straps – but we were six old warriors who could look after themselves. Our short side arms [daggers or pistols?] played a part in this. We got back to the hostel in a roundabout way, but now it was time to get out and we wanted to stay together. We put on civilian clothes, and went off on the railway towards the Harz [mountains].

So ended this 1914-18 War, whose outcome we thought would have been different. We'd been brought up in the Cadet Corps to be obedient, to love and be loyal to our Kaiser and Empire. We'd fought in this war, and bled and fought back. We were very young and wouldn't let ourselves be broken so easily. Our happiness and stupid impulses were still there. We understood nothing of politics. For us, there were only decent men and bastards. We were struggling for clarity, but we were alone, and lonely inside. We lacked experienced men, who knew life, and real men we could trust. We old cadets were used to obeying orders without arguing – but who was there to give us an order now? Nobody.

We old fliers from different fronts stayed without orders for some time. The mob in Berlin wanted to collar us – we didn't know why. What crime had we committed? We had done our duty, like any other decent fellow. Was that any reason to hate us, just because we wore shoulder-straps [showing they were officers]? Sure, there were enough bastards among the officers, especially in rear postings. We'd got to know these 'gentlemen'. But with the best will in the world, we couldn't identify with them. Of course illness and hardship had taken their toll on us too, and the many wounds were no sign that we'd held back. We always got on well with our men, and they went through fire for us. But they weren't with us anymore, they'd have to be demobbed first.

The Workers' and Soldiers' Councils were mostly made up of riffraff, deserters and pen-pushers. We got to know them often enough. And why did working people follow these characters? After all, they were at home and didn't usually risk their skin. Yes, the food situation was bad, but hadn't the troops at the front often gone hungry, when daylong bombardments made supplies impossible? Thinking of this made our heads reel – we couldn't find any explanation. Something must have gone very wrong at the top.

Halberstadt was our next objective and on the way there we agreed to travel to Braunlage [in the Harz]. In the station restaurant at Halberstadt we sat at the same table as an elderly couple. They had come from Braunlage, and were very enthusiastic about Dr Barner's sanatorium; we could recover there from all the hardships of the war. We soon made up our minds – to go on to Dr Barner's: we had plenty of money, we felt like millionaires. We airmen were paid an unreasonably high salary, and our savings were well above average.

Our reception at Barner's was rather chilly, but when we individually expressed our regrets and said we were prepared to pay in advance for eight days we were shown into the sanatorium building for accommodation. And now a happy process began – I haven't often done so little as I did then. The food was still pretty good, and in other respects we had nothing to wish for. Dr Barner and his assistant were really very kind to us, and his daughters, dressed as nurses, looked after us splendidly. Walks in the Harz, and trips to the Brocken [the highest mountain in the range] strengthened hearts and lungs. We were ready for new exploits.

In the evenings we were usually invited to the small social facilities of the sanatorium, and I think I can say with a clear conscience that we made a considerable contribution to lifting the mood of the patients. Anyway, Dr Barner was pleased when joy and fun reigned in our rooms and all the patients were infected with it. Sadly the time for these small pleasures was short, for order reigned here. We had to be in bed early. But I think many patients woke from their lethargy and found some sort of drive because they felt their sufferings were as nothing compared with what we had been through.

We were still so young and overflowing with strength, and when we came to know that a Soldier' Council had been formed in the Braunlage area, we decided to dissolve it in short order. We left on the train early in the morning. At our destination we then investigated the situation. We had only three hours for our expedition, because we had to catch the train back to Braunlage.

The leader of our squad walked into the so-called office of the Workers' and Soldiers' Council[22]. A big red flag hung in front of the building. There was no sign of public activity. The single room looked deserted – beer bottles stood on the table, the stink of bad tobacco hung in the air. Three men in tattered soldiers' coats without badges were sitting around a table, a fourth was lying on a bed. They were arguing about money, which lay in bundles on the table. Our comrade made out that he was a soldier, and needed money to travel home again – he was shouted at and thrown out. In a park nearby we held a council of war. It was still too early for action, so first we had some breakfast. Then it was time. We barged into the room one after another. 'Drop your weapons, hands up, shut up!' The four men were tied up and laid on the floor. Each one was gagged. Everything written that was lying about was destroyed. We took the money with us – it came to a pretty penny – and went back to the station. The Red Cross was glad of the large sum that an unknown donor stuck through their door wrapped in newspaper. We steamed home and came happily back from our 'outing'.

Transfer to Silesia

On December 10th I got news. 'You're being transferred to Hundsfeld in Silesia. Mission against the invading Poles. Requested to be there in 14 days. Report to the Air Force commander in Breslau'. My comrades wanted to go to Silesia too, so we decided to set off together after a visit to our families at home. At the station we got a parting song with lute accompaniment.

'Farewell, my love, farewell, adieu.
And if again I don't see you, it's been a lot of fun'.

Yes, it had been a lot of fun, but now duty called again. I had orders and would carry them out.

I visited my mother in Naumburg-on-the-Saale. She had lost a terrible amount of weight. To greet me she'd prepared some horsemeat and I forced it down. My older brother was trying to rebuild his business life in Hamburg. He'd spent the whole war with my old regiment, the 239th on the Western Front. My second brother had been killed as an active officer. The third was in a British PoW camp. At 17 with an emergency school-leaving certificate, he had gone to war, as an ordinary infantryman. When he finally came home, there was something broken inside him – serious and introverted, he did his duty. He learned agriculture from a farmer and was deeply attracted to it. After two years he was deputy manager on a big estate in Thuringia. When Max Hölz[23] with his Communist gangs came burning and looting through Thuringia, he took up arms with his comrades from the front.

209

They protected the estate, but all the thanks he got was to be fired. Discretion is the better part of valour, thought the owner – the regional government is still Red. Now my brother was studying for two years at a small bank, got his first paid job, but was fired after the inflation crisis. Later the bank took him back. He married and led a quiet, peaceful life. My sister died after a brief marriage. My mother had to be very economical with her small pension. We were glad that we children could help her a bit now.

Early on December 24th 1918 I arrived in Breslau [now Wroclaw in Poland]. All catering places were closed, so what was I to do in a strange town on Christmas Eve? How nice it would be at home! I looked for a small hotel, checked in and lay down to sleep. I woke up with burning bites – God, not bedbugs here as well! I went and bought a few things, a tiny tree with candles, a bottle of red plonk and something to eat. Then I wandered through the streets. The church bells rang and woke memories – it sounded so solemn. My heart ached somehow. I let myself be carried along by the crowds of passers-by and found myself back in church, pushed myself into a back pew like an outcast, who had no reason to be there. *Silent Night, Holy Night* the organ began. I sang along but the notes stuck in my throat. Hot tears came to my eyes – I could have burst out crying. Quietly I got up and pushed my way out. The snow crunched under my feet – the icy air did me good. From outside I looked in through windows where so many Christmas trees were glowing: I felt abandoned by my world. In my hotel room I drank my bottle of wine, and went on a bug hunt. On the first day of the festival, I had at least one objective. My air force comrade Baron von Gregory, the reporter, had invited me to a meal (I found his number in the phone book) but after that there was nothing to keep me, so I wandered out to the airfield at Hundsfeld [a suburb of Breslau].

The Lieutenant who commanded the section had not been told I was coming, but that could be cleared up tomorrow on the phone. He showed me a room in a hut. I had to light the stove myself, fetch coal, and tidy up. Those were the orders of the Soldiers' Council. What? Was there one here too? It actually sat in the main office, a comfortable fat sergeant in mufti. We quickly came to an understanding – one can get anything for money and polite words. We flew again and checked the Poles on the Eastern border – that was no longer a danger. When a Polish convoy crossed the line it was shot up for so long that they threw all their material away as they retreated. The booty was then gathered up by the border guard. We very rarely took a hit to our plane.

Now in the year 1919, our government was negotiating – they hoped in this way to get their rights. We were not to annoy the Poles any longer. We came to Brieg [now Brzeg] in a strict organization, to Captain Stahr, an able officer who later went to Russia and built up an enormous air force.

My first mission was to produce a topographic survey of the Glatz [Klodzko] mountain district. The area in question was photographed with the serial camera, the photos were evaluated and the old one in 100,000 maps updated.

The airfield was full of planes, but the Allies wanted them. Their 'snooping commissions' were already active. The best planes were got ready to start, the good ones were marked on maps. We landed and drove the planes into a shed, where they had to stay camouflaged. Nothing to report about these 'emergency landings – the snoopers had to keep on searching. I left my 'crate' standing at Hirschberg [Jelenia Gora] and went on the electric train to Agnetendorf to see Ivo Hauptmann, the artist. He wasn't at home, but Gerhart Hauptmann's youngest son, Benvenuto, gave me a friendly welcome. We sat by the fire with sparkling red rosé wine. Frau Hauptmann and her daughters-in-law delighted us with their violin playing, while the great poet came in and out. Then he stood at his desk and wrote a poem – *And Pepita dances.*

Civilian Employment

Soon we got our 'blue letter' – we could no longer be employed [in the air force]. After over five years of war I was now a Lieutenant [retired]. What now? I had no one to advise me about my future occupation, and nobody could give me any more orders. So I must handle things myself. I had saved plenty of money, so – off to Breslau, rent a room, and look in at the University. The semester had already started and I couldn't register, but nobody stopped me going to lectures. Somehow, everything would turn out right. Inshallah [God willing]!

I also took up sport. I rowed and played tennis, though my shot-up leg didn't help. It was all right for minor tournaments. I met a lot of people, received many invitations, danced and had fun, but inside there was an empty feeling. I didn't have an aim.

One morning I was in bed when somebody knocked. It was a police detective. 'Are you retired Lieutenant Wappenhans?' 'Yes, officer'. 'Do you know a Lieutenant L....?' 'Oh yes, I do business with him'. I added. 'Ah, very interesting. May I ask in what area that business takes place?' 'I've no idea – I've just invested all my money with him. He's the owner of a large transport company and his father's a Surgeon-General. I should do well out of it'. 'Have you got the relevant documentation?' 'Of course, here you are'. The detective looked at the papers and paused for a moment. Then he said, in a fatherly tone 'Lieutenant, I'm afraid your money's no good. I've had the sugar trucks that L. wanted to move impounded'. Goddamn, that's the end of my splendid life! I'd be able to stay afloat for a few months, but then what?

That was my first contact with the police. It saved me from further investigations. I saw Lieutenant L. once in Berlin – I jumped off a moving tram to stop him but he disappeared in a taxi, never to be seen again.

Now I had to work for my bare life. So far, my luck had not run out, and it didn't this time. I was hired as an apprentice in the Malpaus cigarette factory. I moved from one department to another – I had to learn it all. The factory was a finely built modern facility. Through my many new acquaintances I gained the trust of a good number of young men for improving their knowledge of English, French, mathematics and even of religion. I have to say frankly that we made these private lessons a lot of fun. In spite of my own sketchy knowledge, I was successful. The young fellows trusted me and showed me great respect. I started my lessons right after the factory closed. My conditions improved, and after seven months' work I was transferred to Danzig [Gdansk]. Malpaus had set up a branch there, whose real aim was to export to Russia. Other big cigarette companies were also establishing themselves in Danzig at the same time.

On my way through Berlin I met two old comrades. One of them lived in a smart six-room flat on the Kurfürstendamm, and begged me to join his firm. Money was no object. Apparently it was an alcohol-smuggling operation, from Scandinavia to Germany in a yacht. However, in spite of the tempting offer, I thought my own life was more secure. I met my other comrade just as he was getting into his Mercedes coupé. In his villa at Grünewald[24], which his wife had brought into the marriage with two daughters (she came from a family of publishers), I met the Crown Prince. We had a long conversation about war experiences, the Kaiser's HQ at Stenay, lucky charms and women.

I stayed in and around Danzig for ten years. I led the life of a good middle-class citizen who makes his way through rough and smooth. I wasn't obsessed with hunting for money, though I got through with a bit of luck. I was well paid as a general representative for Malpaus Cigarettes, then left them for Hasse's tobacco factory, a branch of C and G Schmidt of Altona, Hamburg.

Then I became a buyer for the Danzig-Russian Trading Company, a typical new post-war foundation, made myself independent by buying out the owners of the coal and haulage company, Schulz & Co. The buyer I hired was so efficient that I felt surplus to requirement in my own business – I let him work on his own, but he repaid me by bringing

212

the firm to the brink of ruin. In the meantime I set up, in collaboration with my old company Hasse, a big tobacconists', the 'Wappenhanse' which was mainly intended to represent the South German [?] Lottery. But it took so long to get the concession that I had to close the shop again.

I took over agencies for some good Danzig firms – wine from Karl Keller, liqueur (Danziger Goldwasser) from the famous Lachs, coal from Giesche Co., and also a coffee and a soap firm. My target was all the big estates in the old Corridor, i.e. in Poland. My area stretched from the Baltic to Upper Silesia. There might have been 600 – 700 estates, which I visited in month-long trips in my Studebaker. I was welcomed as a friend and did good business. The estates formed a core of German-ness in the corridor – the area which was awarded to the Poles in the terms of the Versailles 'Diktat'[25]. These holdings were thoroughly well run, and produced high yields in contrast to the Polish estates. The Agrarian Reform [redistribution of land] forced the German landowners to give away land, which was settled with Polish peasants, but the result of these measures was the same everywhere. Total production went down, as the settlers only produced what they needed for their subsistence. In those days we in Danzig lived under the pressure of the Versailles Diktat: we didn't feel free in the 'Free City of Danzig'. Cut off from our mother country, we longed for union with Germany. The cutting-off of East Prussia by the Polish Corridor, together with passport problems with the Poles' troublemaking, was a thorn in our side. Then we were told, by a former U-boat commander I made friends with, that the [Masonic] lodge 'Unity' was made up of patriotically-minded men, who were working towards reunion. We visited the lodge. Among us was Arthur Greiser, well known as a naval airman and later President of the Free City Senate. In time he became Gauleiter[26] of West Prussia.

The lodge was a disappointment however, because there was no sign of any activity connected with annexation to Germany. It was all good, satisfied citizens who came here, respectable and uncomplicated. The food was good, the drink even better. People were optimistic and jolly, helped each other mutually in business connections, and also helped other people – not to name names. But there was no great cause, no aim. We asked about it, and were told, it would only be explained in the higher grades. We had no time for half-measures. We cleared the lodge, i.e. we left it.

To protect the Free City of Danzig from communist takeover the Danzig Resident Force was formed. Their task was to prevent strikes and terrorism, or at least mitigate their consequences. The military instruction was conducted by the police under Colonel von Heydebreck. The organization was entrusted to me. We recruited engineers and students from the Technical College to keep vital facilities like gasworks and power stations working. Workmen were prepared to come into action in an emergency. But as no serious disturbances came at this period, interest fell off. But it was only later that the Resident Force made its appearance in action against Poland.

In my free time, I met my air force comrades. We longed for activity in the air. In the end we founded the Danzig Flying Club, whose immediate purpose was gliding. As chairman of this club I went to a conference in Berlin with [Gerhard] Milch, the Director of Lufthansa, later a Field-Marshal; this meeting gave us the chance to use Lufthansa's planes free of charge, and to work in the airline's workshops.

Meanwhile I had got married. My wife, Mania Zamboni, was Swiss. When I met her she was nineteen, a serious, intelligent and attractive girl. She had escaped from Warsaw during the Russo-Polish war [1920]. Her father lived in Warsaw, as a businessman and the Swiss Consul. He died before the war. Now the mother and daughter lived alone with relatives in Zoppot [Sopot, just north of Gdansk], till I came into her life. Mania gave me a son, whom I loved very much.

Now it is worth pointing out that I was busy in my work too. I was often on the road for a month on end in Poland. I was successful – however, the manager in my own shop met with setbacks. I hid these worries from my wife, as I sincerely would not begrudge her opportunities to travel. Then one day came the blow that threatened to tear me apart. My wife asked me to let her go. I didn't want to admit to myself that we had drifted apart. I loved her, but she appealed to my generosity, which she believed in. So I let her go and took the blame myself. We got divorced, she went to Berlin, married again and then went with her new husband and our son to Barcelona. Something had broken inside me, I didn't have anybody now that it was worth working for.

So I lived for a time as if in a dream and I let myself drift. At the beginning of 1931 I met Herr Himmler (see Chapter 10 Note 2 and Plates 3, 6 & 15) – at the future SS Obergruppenführer [Lieutenant-General] Lorenz's estate on Holy Mary Lake near Danzig. Himmler gave me the impression of being a village schoolmaster – small, unassuming, bespectacled; no outward sign of any particular intelligence, but with a didactic manner of speech. And yet there was something special about him, Lorenz remarked, when I described my impressions to him.

Joining the SS

Himmler suggested to me that I joined the SS [NSDAP No: 465090, SS Civil Badge No: 13779, SS No: 22924] and as Chief of Staff of the DD –

the Danzig branch of the SS – I built up the organization. That meant forming a defence force from the best male Germans, that meant, the kind of men who were in top physical and mental form and racially pure. This organization was to be built up from a purely military point of view, as a foundation for the restoration of the whole Reich. Himmler was looking for an efficient former active officer, and Lorenz, who was in charge of Danzig and East Prussia at the time, had recommended me. A new task, a new order. I grabbed the chance, happy to have an aim in front of me – the build-up of a soldier-like force. I had had nothing to do with parties until now, not even the National Socialists, and I really thought this should not be a party but a Movement to renew the whole German Reich. I was given an office at regional HQ and immediately set about getting a general picture of the SS. In Danzig it was still small – on paper there was one 'Standarte', which was equivalent to a regiment of three 'Sturmbann' [battalions], each of three to four 'Stürmen' [companies] distributed about the city of Danzig and its country areas. The leaders of these formations were mostly former servicemen. They were old party members and had distinguished themselves in bar fights and riots against the Communists. What they didn't have was leadership qualities.

So I set up more leaders' courses, which were conducted on farms in the country, raised money from collections, and produced a unit-training plan for military and physical exercise. Apart from that I also recruited among my former comrades and filled these leaders' posts with them as time went on. The success of this became noticeable in a short time. We got plenty of recruits, and the military appearance of the SS was recognized. But jealousy was aroused too, in the SA [Brownshirts] and the Party.

At the time I had distanced myself from the Party's programme. The idea of uniting the then divided German people in one single movement was brilliant. Workers with brains or hands, both with the same aim – a united Germany – what could be better? And only with this unity could the threatening storm of Communism be held off. All other questions were unimportant to me. The Party leader, Adolf Hitler, seemed to have been sent by God to save the Fatherland from ruin. And I wanted to follow him.

In March 1932 I was transferred to Königsberg [now Kaliningrad] to build up the SS simultaneously in East Prussia. I managed to do this in a relatively short time. Here I found generous support from SS leader Litzmann, son of a famous general. In collaboration with the SA, we inspected all the SA companies in East Prussia and the best men, suitable for the SS, were picked out.

Meanwhile I heard Hitler speak at Elbing [Elblag] and Königsberg for the first time on his election tour. I was deeply impressed by what he said and how he behaved. I can also not forget a speech by Goebbels at the Kommick Factory in Elbeing. The hall was packed – 10,000 people sitting and standing. Most of these were Communists who wanted to break up this Nazi event. But Goebbels had a masterly knowledge of how to bring people under his spell. He described the sad fate of the unemployed, so graphically that there was dead silence in that massive hall. You could even hear women sobbing. Then, as Goebbels realized that his audience was with him, came his rhetorical question. 'Who governs in Prussia today? Why is Minister Severing unable to solve these problems, he and his Marxist friends? Today you have the power, you could show it. But you aren't capable of that, as long as you only think of yourselves, and not of your people'.

At the end of his speech, Goebbels even appealed to the Communists 'We're not asking you to change your colours and join the Nazis. That would do no good. We do ask you, as thinking people, to consider the words that I've spoken to you today'. The result was not just that people left that mass meeting peacefully but also a big breakthrough into the morale of the Communist Elbing Front.

Things didn't always go as gently as in Elbing. We fifty-five men, who were brought in to protect the speakers, often got involved in fights with the Communists. In fact in Königsberg the mounted police were set on us, in full awareness of the situation. The SS were also used to break up opposing rallies or protect our speakers in debates. So one day we turned up at a Communist rally, bringing with us a twenty-stone man, a publican, who had such a booming 'laugh' that nothing could be heard above it. We put the fat guy in the middle, and every time the Communist speaker produced one of his attacks on the Nazis, we tickled him in a sensitive place. He burst into noisy laughter that was so infectious all the people attending the rally had to laugh with him. Now everyone waited for an attack on the Nazis and that was that: the audience, mostly Communists, began laughing even before we'd started tickling the fat guy.

On an election trip of Prince Auwi [August Wilhelm] through East Prussia, about 200 cars were gathered in a small 'nest'. It was mostly the larger landowners who'd come to this event. In his speech the Prince expressed his gratitude for the great interest in the Nazi rallies, but said he had realized beforehand that this interest was not so much in the Party message, as curiosity about hearing a son of the Kaiser speak. He was quite happy to put up with that, he said, as he saw in them, his audience – who had made a fine name for themselves in his grandfather's time, and that of his ancestor 'Old Fritz', and loyally served the Hohenzollerns[27] – the pedigree of a class of rulers. No government could deny their intelligence and strength, for this reason the audience needed to realize once and for all how important it was for them to get involved in the ideas of the National Socialist Party. 'We believe firmly and unshakably', said the Prince 'that we will come to power in Germany. We <u>will</u> govern. And then, gentlemen, we will need you, for you were born to lead. If we had only known before that some day in the future we would elect incompetents to rule – simply because you did not think it important to take action yourselves at the right time to save Germany from the Communist menace'.

Regional Leader Koch in Königsberg, a quite capable campaigner for Hitler, was excited then about the rapid growth of the SS. Later he fell out with Hitler, and left the SS. In August 1932 I got a new task, to take over the SS in Northern Westphalia as Standartenführer [Regimental Commander]. I changed places with [Hans-Adolf] Prützmann, an intelligent, ambitious young leader, politically skillful and all you could ask for – but no soldier. Later in the war he became an Obergruppenführer [Senior Group Leader] and my superior. In any case he was one of the few leaders at his level to have had a good childhood and education as well as spirit and intelligence. In the following years, I unfortunately came to recognize the lack of these essential requirements for higher leadership in most of my superiors. As a result of my criticism in this area I was treated with caution, and not admitted to the internal discussions of the SS high command.

Gelsenkirchen was the seat of Regimental HQ. From this out-of-the-way spot, working on North Westphalia was inconvenient, so I asked for it to be moved to Münster, where Regional Leader Dr Meyer was based. We moved in the summer of 1932. Here I worked together with the future Obergruppenführer Heissmeier, an old air force comrade. In 1935 he was put in charge of all National Socialist schools, and after his wife's death married the Women's League leader Gertrude Scholz-Klink and, what's more had eleven children to provide for from both marriages.

In December 1932 we were preparing the election campaign for the tiny state of Lippe-Detmold. Here the future of Germany would be decided – for if it proved that the National Socialists were making a comeback after their losses at the last National Parliament elections [Chancellor] von Papen wanted to persuade President Hindenburg to hand over power to Hitler, and thereby the Nazis. This was an aim we had to achieve, and we did achieve it. We swamped little Lippe country with a flood of rallies. Hitler spoke in person several times each day, propaganda was distributed to the last cottage. I was invited to dinner at the Count's Castle, where Hitler was staying at the time. The conversation was about our election prospects and what would happen if we were successful. I heard for the first time a more detailed account of Hitler's conference with Papen in the Rhineland. The campaign came to an end, the Nazis won, and on 30 January 1933 Adolf Hitler was appointed Chancellor by Hindenburg.

From then on the development of the SS took on a purely military character. Wittge [von Wittgenstein?], a former active officer in the Reichswehr [German Army after 1918], was appointed Chief of Staff of the whole SS. He gave clear orders that there should be no doubt that the SS was to receive army training. So in my new posts as Standartenführer in Nienburg-an-der-Weser and Oldenburg, I made contacts with the police and the army, to familiarize myself with modern training. I very much enjoyed developing the small country regiment at Nienburg, where a healthy sort of people lived, strong, loyal lads who were happy to give up their free time to the SS. I got important fresh ideas from my contacts with the Stahlhelm[28], with whom I got on well. The field exercises, which were normally held at weekends, got plenty of support from the locals – they were carried out without any weapons, but were designed from the point of view of tactics, already solidly based.

The regiment in Oldenburg, which I took over at the end of 1933 became the largest in numbers in Germany. At an inspection by Reichsführer Himmler, I could report to him a strength of 8,000 SS men. In recognition, I was promoted to Oberführer [Senior Leader] but before I took up a new appointment in the SS I requested a short training course with the Army.

As in 1934 there was no Flying Corps in the Army[29], I was sent to Osterode in East Prussia. I was to go as an ordinary rifleman in the battalion of one-armed Major Hube [Hans] – later a famous [4-star] general. I reported in and was declared fit for duty after a short medical examination. The doctor did not appear to notice that I was fifty percent disabled, with a damaged calf in my left leg. All night, I did my duty with gritted teeth, drilled, marched for hours with a rifle or machine-gun on my back. My wounded leg swelled up and often I could only stand to attention with the help of my comrades.

Hube was inspecting the company on a small field-exercise. A loud order came that the NCO in my platoon had fallen. I took command, '560 enemy planes in sight!' I shouted 'Take cover!' 'Who shouted that?' came Hube's voice suddenly. 'Here! I did, Private Wappenhans'. 'Where did you come up with that number – are you taking the mickey?' 'No, sir. In the next war we'll have to deal with even more'. 'Report to my office after the exercise!'

The consequences of this discussion were these; I left the office door as Private Wappenhans. I shouted to the sentry in his box 'Why don't you salute, you [so-and-so?].' 'Make sure you come back', came the reply, 'or you'll get a kick in the....' 'Right, lad, just take a good look at my face!' I came back from town as a Lieutenant and the sentry saluted, quite oblivious. I went up to him 'Recognize me?' – A bemused expression – 'Put a dollar [five marks] in the box'. I got the same surprised reaction in my old hut – then I was back on duty as an officer. I was leading a company, this time mounted. I never did any more marching.

I met the Medical Officer in the mess. He didn't recognize me from the examination. We had quite a good time, and on the second bottle I asked quite innocently if he would pass a man fit for field service who had suffered paralysis of the peronaeus superficialis in one leg caused by a shell splinter. 'But, my dear chap', said the doctor 'a man like that's just a cripple, and can't run any more?' 'Look', I told him 'I couldn't agree with you more – and yet you <u>have</u> passed a cripple fit for field service.' 'Who, me? What do you bet me?' – So we made the bet, and the bucket of champagne gave us a cheerful round.

In September 1934 I was sent to Tilsit, where I commanded a training company in the Army. I spent Christmas on my own in Königsberg, then I was off to my new job in Würzburg as leader of the [SS] brigade there. The three regiments there at Ansbach and Nuremberg were under my command. I got in touch with the army straight away, and managed to get support everywhere for my SS training programme.

As the air force was appearing again now, I reported for practice in long-range reconnaissance at Würzburg. Flying and working in the new, faster planes was a complete change – but once I'd got used to and mastered it, I was enjoying flying again. In the first manoeuvres around Würzbug and Gravenwöhr we brought back recon-results that were of decisive importance to the command.

In the critique by the commanding General von Stuttgart, the then Colonel Guderian was severely rebuked for breaking through with his tanks and operating far in the rear. At this time this performance was regarded as impossible – but the French campaign proved Guderian right – he showed that you could achieve even greater things by surprising your opponent. Guderian's tactics were also successfully used in Russia till the extreme cold stopped the tanks. The Americans later adopted these tactics too, when Bradley, after crossing the Rhine by the bridge at Remagen, thrust hundreds of kilometres into our rear without regard for casualties, shut off any retreat for Model's army and finally surrounded it.

A Reunion with Goering

At the end of 1935 I was promoted to Captain in the Reserve. On the same day I was ordered to arrange road-blocks for a visit by Göring to Rothenburg-on-the-Tauber[30]. The day of the visit would be a holiday for the whole city. Medieval costumes were cleaned, knights and their ladies dominated the scene – you felt you'd been taken back to the Middle Ages. I was ordered to attend a dinner at the well-kept Eisenhut Hotel for Göring and his wife Emmy. There was nothing left of the Göring of my cadet days, he was just an old comrade. He encouraged me to re-join the air force – I said that I would be happy to, but had to ask Himmler first, which obviously annoyed him. He didn't mention the offer again. I felt at once that I had thrown away the chance of my life, and I believe I must admit today that it was pure cussedness, not wanting to have to beg Göring – so for this reason I didn't make any attempt to become an active air force officer. However, I remained loyal to it, but only as a reservist.

During the dinner, carried away by the excellent wine, I couldn't resist asking Emmy (or was it his niece? I can't quite remember) to toast Hermann, who sat opposite us with the title 'Mauschelsdorf' in memory of his nickname in the cadet corps [see Note 1 page 266]. When 'Here's to Mauschelsdorf!' died away, Hermann banged his fist on the table and shouted 'Wapps, you bastard!' at me. We parted quite calmly, but I was left feeling depressed. My big chance had gone.

In the meantime I'd got married again. My wife came from Hanover; I'd met her at a hockey tournament. Neither she nor her family had anything to do with National Socialism – on the contrary her father was an outspoken opponent. That didn't interfere with my love for my wife. I was always of the opinion that a matter-of-fact criticism could only do good. A movement that is strong can resist any attack. I also never put my wife under pressure to join the Party. For me politicized women were a horror.

I saw very little of my superiors at Würzburg. It was only when I had to take over the Augsburg sector in 1936 that it became noticeable how close Munich, the capital of the Movement, was. The Führer turned up at official events. The House of German Art was inaugurated, it was solemnly celebrated on 9 November, and Mussolini was received in Munich with great pomp. And I had to be present everywhere to set up road blocks, which were the SS's responsibility.

We even had to go to Essen[31] to take care of the security for Mussolini. It wasn't easy to keep my leaders and men at the barriers when they were giving up all their free time, and besides that often putting their livelihood at risk, because they were never paid anything for this service.

In the leaders' conferences which I regularly held at Augsburg, Pfaffenhofen, and Lindau on Lake Constance, I insisted time and again that this state of things was only temporary, and that now the Armed SS was going to take over a large part of our duties. Now I was not quite sure exactly what our area of responsibility was. In any case, I shared my thoughts with Obergruppenführer von Eberstein. He was evasive. Although he spoke approvingly of my activity not long afterwards on the occasion of a big sports meeting of my SS in Augsburg, I was suddenly transferred – and, as I later heard, transferred as a punishment – to Stettin, to work as Chief of Staff for the main sector.

Meanwhile, Hitler had made an official visit to Augsburg. Carrying out the security arrangements had gone smoothly, and the Führer himself expressed his appreciation. I sat opposite him at dinner in the Three Moors Hotel, the food and drink were first-class. Hitler himself had a cup of coffee in front of him and ate a few biscuits – that was all. I suppose it was understandable how this man's simple tastes impressed me [Hitler was a vegetarian and virtual teetotaler]. From time to time Hitler got up and inspected the plans for the modernization of Augsburg, came back to the table, talked to Speer[32] and corrected the plans.

Before much else happened, I heard something about mobilization in Southern Germany. I rang Air Force HQ in Munich, and was told by an officer friend that it was true – we were going into Austria. I requested a mobilization order, got one by telegram and flew with my [air force, not SS] comrades to Vienna. When we landed at Aspern airfield, the situation was crazy – planes stood in rows, the Austrians were much too surprised to defend themselves. The airfield was sealed off and secured. Major General Wolff[33] took command and I was appointed his ADC and given the job of driving into Vienna and finding accommodation for the air-force staff. This worked out really quickly – I was lucky. The first man I saw from the car in the city was an SS leader I knew. I pulled up and checked out the situation. No danger in Vienna, he said the people were excited. The SS Security Service had things under control. Accommodation for Air HQ? No problem! We drove to the Astoria Hotel and commandeered it, set up telephone links with Aspern, and the Staff was in already.

These were busy days and nights, and we had to keep working. All Austrian airfields and material had to be taken over, along with factories and anything else connected with air force equipment. German and Austrian units were merged. Austria's national currency was united with ours. For days on end I spent most of the time on a plane with General Wolff. I will never forget flying over the peaks of the Alps, always in glorious sunshine. But nights meant work – I got very little sleep.

We were on our way to Wiener Neustadt[34] with Göring in his special train. The higher General Staff had retired to the dining car and were holding a conference with the blinds pulled down. The train passed slowly through every station. Everywhere there were children carrying flowers, units of all descriptions on parade, bands playing, marches and shouts ringing out, 'We want to see Iron Hermann!', but the blinds stayed down. That rather upset both of us ADCs who'd been left alone in Hermann's private carriage. The new Austrian general – Lohr's cap fitted me as if it had been moulded on, and Hermann's cloak looked impressive over my uniform. With a couple of cushions stuffed under it and his short Marshal's baton in my hand, I could prove to the public, during the slow passage through the stations, that Hermann was showing his gratitude for these enthusiastic honours. My conscience was clear – I thought I was acting in the spirit of my Supreme Commander by doing his job for a while. But when the call 'Brass coming!' came from our lookout, the 'old disorder' was restored.

At Wiener Neustadt airfield, a new air force regiment was on parade, for Göring to present its colour. Everything was ready; two regiments, one old German and a new former Austrian were standing facing each other. The band was playing marches as Hermann walked along the front rank. Then General Wolff angrily walked up to me. 'Herr Adjutant where is the colour for the new regiment? It isn't there!' Oh hell, how do I know? I thought 'I will fetch it at once'. I shouted to the furious general. My search was in vain – the colour had magically disappeared. What next? Göring had just reached the centre and begun his speech, which had to end with the presentation of the colour. Time was pressing. I made a snap decision, went over to the old Air Force regiment, and marched up to Hermann with <u>their</u> rolled colour. He ended his speech 'So I dedicate you – One People, One Reich, One Führer!' The old colour received its second presentation. I never had any news of the new one.

My general, Wolff, was extremely angry when this small correction came to light. I stayed as far away as possible from him and the crowd of generals like Sperrle [Hugo][35], Bodenschatz [Karl-Heinrich], Löhr [Alexander], Stumpff [Hans-Jürgen], Jeschonnek [Hans] and Loerzer [Bruno]. I was watching with interest the performance of an Austrian formation flying team that was doing astonishing things in French planes, when Hermann suddenly tapped me on the shoulder – I hadn't heard him coming. 'Well, how are you, old Wapps?' We chatted for a while, General Wolff was being polite to me again. The matter of colour presentation was not mentioned again.

When I arrived in Stettin, I was very ungraciously received by Obergruppenführer Mazuw [Emil], commander of the main sector. I tried to clear up the situation with my friend Obergruppenführer Wolff, Himmler's chief aide, but he was also rather evasive. Mazuw needed a man at his side to help him with organization. I did this, and after a short time he had to acknowledge my achievements. The security arrangements for Hitler's visit to Stettin worked well, although at one place the crowds had broken through a cordon of guards. We got the resulting gap plugged with reserves we'd held ready. There was also the marching detachment from Main Sector North which I put together and drilled for the Party Day in Nuremberg, which was appreciated. So it lasted hardly six months, and then I was again given an independent posting, as leader of the Mecklenburg sector, based in Schwerin.

The annual Party Days held in Nuremberg in September placed a heavy demand on the strength of the 'General SS'. Each marching detachment of a Main Sector consisted of about a thousand men. These were trained in advance in their local bases, assembled a few days before leaving at a camp, and drilled, and then travelled by train to a big temporary camp near Nuremberg. Then a day-long joint drill was held with the other units. The next day we marched off at 04.00 hours, stood for hours in the arena for the SS roll call. A speech of about fifteen minutes from the Führer, the dedication of flags to the roar of cannon and then standing still for about an hour. Then, after a short break on the field, a march past the Führer and a march back to camp, which was reached around 18.00 hours. Travel home overnight. We never got to see any more of the other big events.

Himmler did not pass up the opportunity in his great days to give an evening reception with a military tattoo to follow, which was attended – apart from prominent German guests like Goebbels and Ribbentrop – by visitors from abroad. I sat at a table with some English people and we had a good time. The well-known writer of the unusually gripping film *Bengali* (probably one of the few in which no women appeared), Mr Brown sat next to me. He had just written a book *Anti-Comintern*. We had a fascinating conversation, and continued to write to each other later. The cheerful atmosphere was infectious. Ribbentrop, then our Ambassador to Britain, came over to us. He invited me to visit England, but unfortunately nothing more came of it.

Regional Leader Hildebrandt [Friedrich] was in charge in Schwerin, a fanatical follower of Hitler; he had worked his way up from a simple farmworker because he had a certain intelligence and speaking ability. At heart he remained a simple man of the people with no sense of his own importance, a social conscience and honesty. We got on well. But he had no real understanding of the concerns of the great landowners, whom he saw only as reactionaries. He did not recognize their strengths and leadership qualities. I tried to bridge this gap where I could.

When General Count Schulenburg, the Crown Prince's former Chief of Staff, died, his body was brought back with honours to his estate and buried, with Himmler present. The old nobleman, a splendid soldier, was well known for his manly behaviour towards Kaiser Wilhelm. Always a loyal servant of the Hohenzollerns, Schulenburg did not want to let the Kaiser leave the troops who had sworn loyalty to him in the lurch in their greatest need, and escape to Holland. With all the respect required of this nobleman, he left the Kaiser in no doubt that the existence of the Monarchy was at stake. 'At a time like this', he said 'a Hohenzollern has to put himself at the head of his Army, and should he fall, it is only his person, not the Monarchy, that falls'. The relevant documents for Count Schulenburg's memoirs were, at his request, not to be made public until after Kaiser Wilhelm's death. When an attempt was made, through the army, to 'acquire' the documents, the Count had handed them over to Himmler's trustworthy hands.

One of my best SS companies was in Rostock. It was mainly made up of workers from the Heinkel factory – fine lads, decent fellows, who were genuinely pleased when I came to visit them. When I went there during the [Second World] war, as an air force officer, they presented me with a model of the Heinkel 111, which they had made especially for me. Professor Heinkel, driving his own Tatra car, took me to the factory's airfield to meet a Japanese delegation that was interested in its latest model. On this occasion, a fighter plane was displayed, which in speed far outstripped the Me 109. However, it was not yet developed enough to be put into mass production.

I had a lot of contact with the leader of the agricultural community in Mecklenburg, Count Grothe. I accepted his invitation once to visit him at his humble farmhouse, the next time I had any duty near his estate. The 'farmhouse' was a large mansion, full of the most beautiful works of art, and my accommodation there included a sitting-room, bedroom and a marble bath. Grothe's wife was American. Sadly he was killed early in the war, after being director of agricultural policy in Holland.

Reconnaissance

Meanwhile time was ticking away towards war. It was 1939. Immediately after the occupation of Czechoslovakia I spoke to Himmler, asking him to tell me clearly what my employment would be in the event of war. The answer was not clear. We SS leaders were to stay at home for now and ensure peace and order, in control of the police. I could possibly join the Armed [Waffen-] SS at a later date. As it seemed contemptible to be serving at home, and not at the front – because of the thinking I had absorbed in the Cadet Corps – I asked Himmler for immediate permission to complete my Major's course in the air force. In the end I got his approval, and immediately went to see my old commander in Palestine, Air Force General Felmy, who now commanded the 1st Air Fleet, to deliver my request. Next day I was able to report at the airfield in Goslar to the then Major Kreipe [Werner], later Chief of Air Staff. I was to be Squadron Captain of Reconnaissance – this was five weeks before the war broke out.

Now our time was spent in intensive training – Kreipe gave us no presents. We learned a lot in this time, in which we flew to the last drop of fuel. We flew long distances over the whole Reich – from Goslar to the Ruhr district, up the Rhine to Lake Constance, along the Alps to Vienna, from there to the Baltic and the North Sea, then back to Goslar. High-altitude flying alternated with the filming of strategic targets. The planning exercises Kreipe led gave us a picture of war waged in the most up-to-date way. They were not one-sided and didn't exclude the possibility of setbacks. In a personal conversation, Kreipe made it clear that we were absolutely on the brink of war. To take our men's minds off it, he organized a big sports meeting, in which each sport showed to advantage. In tennis, we won the finals. Then it was time – the mobilization order came through.

We flew, as per orders, with two squadrons to Waggum an airfield near Braunschweig [Brunswick]. The third was detailed for long-range reconnaissance in the Polish campaign. For the duration of this; which was estimated at only a few weeks, only short flights were to be made in the West. Apparently, however, there was still hope of a peaceful agreement with Britain and France. First we had to get used to flying over the sea, for which we'd never been trained. These tasks had so far been confined to the Navy's air Arm, and one squadron from Air Force High Command, which even before the war had systematically photographed the British coast from high altitude.

Long range reconnaissance, one of the most important of all functions of an air force from a strategic point of view, had been seriously neglected in connection with equipment, armaments and pilot training – even Kreipe, in his elegant manner, let it be overlooked. Of my pilots, only a single man held the 'Blind Flying B licence' which qualified him to fly out of sight of land, and in emergencies to carry out blind take-offs and landings. Nobody held the 'Blind Flying C Licence', which authorised any action.

Even so, we were burning to get at the enemy. Major Kreipe dampened our impetuousness and only required duties which did not involve serious losses right from the start. As soon as every crew from Waggum had completed several flights over the North Sea, we went over to real reconnaissance work. We usually flew in the late afternoon to Air Base North, which was sheltered by Norderney Island, had a short night's rest, then took off in the grey dawn, exactly over Juist Island – anyone who went over Norderney or Borkum was bound to be fired on by our anti-aircraft guns. The only tasks on this route were photographic surveillance of the South and East coasts of Britain.

In the middle of this work we were moved to Loddenheide near Münster. Our third squadron had meanwhile come back from the Polish campaign. They had hardly suffered any losses. All of our comrades were wearing full beards – they felt they were great warriors, and declared that after their victory, the half-time score was one-nil. Colonel Kummhuber, General Felmy's Chief of Staff, had little sympathy for jokes like this and reprimanded them in a serious officers' briefing. An hour later, the beard (or rather beards) came off.

General Felmy inspected the LRR group, and decorations were awarded. I received a bar to my Iron Cross 2nd class from my old Palestine commander. Then came a total reorganization. Two squadrons stayed at Loddenheide for operations on the Western Front, while mine was moved to Ütersen, near Hamburg, brought up to twelve full crews, put under the command of Tenth Flying Corps and tasked with long-range reconnaissance over England. The transfer took one day, but the reconnaissance work was not interrupted. The planes took off, and landed back at Ütersen. We reported to Ten Flying Corps in Hamburg, which was damned dark, and without a guide or an exact knowledge of the place I couldn't find the hotel. General Geissler and his Chief of Staff, Major Harlinghausen introduced me to our new duties. I got it right away. A fresh wind was blowing here, we would proceed without regard to casualties. I felt it my duty to tell them about the low level of training of my pilots, but Harlinghausen dismissed that with a contemptuous gesture. Oh well, we'd do our duty – and it wasn't my decision.

THE MILITARY & POLICE CAREER OF
SS-GRUPPENFÜHRER WALDEMAR WAPPENHANS (ALIAS HANS SEEMANN')

HEER (H) – ARMY (A), LUFTWAFFE (L) – AIR FORCE (AF), POLIZEI (P) – POLICE (P) & SS RANKS

Date	Rank	British Translation
July 1914	Leutnant (H)	Lieutenant (A)
1914	Bataillonsadjutant (H)	Battalion Adjutant (A)
1918	Kommandant 27th Schlachtstaffel (L)	Commander of 27th Battle Squadron (AF)
1923	Oberleutnant (P)	First Lieutenant (P)
July 1932	SS-Sturmbannführer	Major
December 1932	SS-Standartenführer	Colonel (Regimental Commander)
November 1934	SS-Oberführer	Senior Colonel
December 1935	Hauptmann der Reserve (H)	Captain of the Reserve (A)
May 1937	Hauptmann der Reserve (L)	Captain of the Reserve (AF)
July 1939	Staffelkapitän der Fernaufklärung (L)	Squadron Captain of Reconnaissance (AF)
October 1940	Major der Reserve (L)	Major of the Reserve (AF)
September 1941	SS-Brigadeführer und	SS Brigade Leader and
	Generalmajor der Polizei (P)	Major General of Police (P)
November 1943	SS-Gruppenführer und	SS-Major General and
	Generalleutnant der Polizei (P)	Lieutenant General of Police (P)
January 1945	Batallion Kommandant (H)	Batallion Commander (A)

Plate 1

WALDEMAR WAPPENHANS – ARMY, AIR FORCE & SS HONOURS & AWARDS

Iron Cross (1914) Class II and Class I

Knight Cross of the Royal House Order of Hohenzollern with Swords (1918)*

Knight's Cross of the Order of the Zähringer Löwen Class II and Class I with Swords*

Wound Badge (1918) in Silver (awarded for three or four wounds)

Iron Crescent (Ottoman War Medal)

Silesian Eagle Class II & Class I (awarded after 3 and 6 months respectively for exemplary service in defence of Silesia)

Prussian Aviation Observer Badge

Observer Badge (1938) (Could be awarded to active soldiers of the Air Force after 5 enemy flights or wounding sooner)

Clasp to the Iron Cross (1939) Class II

Clasp to the Iron Cross (1940) Class I (Repeat of Iron Cross awarded in WWI)

War Merit Cross (1939) Class II in 1942

War Merit Cross (1939) Class I in 1943

Ehrendegen (Dagger of Honour) of the Reichsführer SS (Personal award of Heinrich Himmler to members of the SS Protection Squad of the rank of Unterführer – NCO – and above)

Totenkopfring of the SS (Ring of Honour) (Personally awarded by Himmler – was highly coveted among SS members)

SS Service Awards

*Knight's Crosses were Germany's top decorations and were awarded by the Royal Houses of Prussia and Saxony for leadership, distinguished service or, like Britain's Victoria Cross and the US Medal of Honor, for military acts of outstanding bravery – especially those awarded with swords.

Plate 2

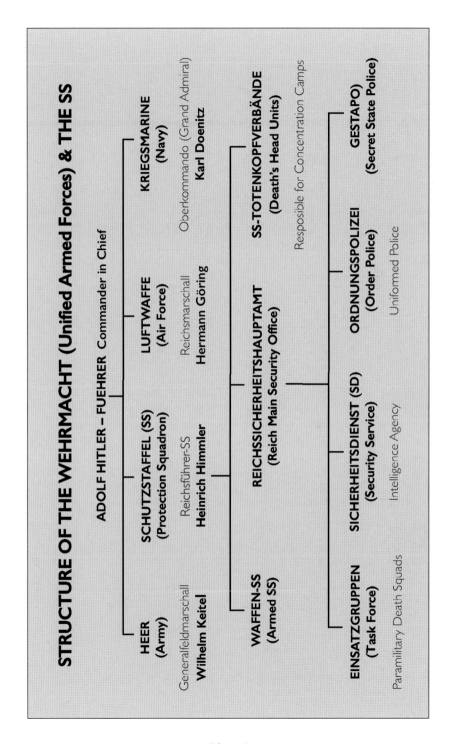

Plate 3

SS RANKS WITH GERMAN ARMY & BRITISH ARMY EQUIVALENTS

SS Ranks	German Army	British Army (US variations in parenthesis)
Reichsführer-SS	Generalfeldmarschall	Field Marshall
SS-Oberstgruppenführer	Generaloberst	General
SS-Obergruppenführer	General	Lieutenant-General
SS-Gruppenführer	Generalleutnant	Major General
SS-Brigadeführer	Generalmajor	Brigadier (US: Brigadier General)
SS-Oberführer		Senior Colonel
SS-Standartenführer	Oberst	Colonel
SS-Obersturmbannführer	Oberstleutnant	Lieutenant-Colonel
SS-Sturmbannführer	Major	Major
SS-Hauptsturmführer	Hauptmann	Captain
SS-Obersturmführer	Oberleutnant	1st Lieutenant
SS-Untersturmführer	Leutnant	2nd Lieutenant
SS-Sturmscharführer	Stabsfeldwebel	Sergeant Major
SS-Hauptscharführer	Oberfeldwebel	Warrant Officer (US: Master Sergeant)
SS-Oberscharführer	Feldwebel	Staff Sergeant (US: Sergeant 1st Class)
SS-Scharführer	Unterfeldwebel	Sergeant (US: Staff Sergeant)
SS-Rottenführer	Stabsgefreiter	Corporal
SS-Sturmmann	Gefreiter	Lance Corporal
SS-Schütze	Schütze	Private

Plate 4

Mauterndorf in Salzburg, Austria – where Göring resided from time to time at the family home or in the castle: Wappenhans and Göring 'enjoyed' a life-long love/hate relationship that commenced when they were at cadet school together. Wappenhans records. 'His father had a hunting lodge at Mauterndorf, and this so-and-so called Hermann Göring had such a big mouth we called him 'Mauschelsdorf' ['Poor Jew's Village' – see Page 266, Note 1] ... I smacked Hermann in the gob (as we put it) ... and both of us hooligans set about bashing each other with both fists; retreat would have been cowardly so it was black eyes, bloody noses, swollen faces – and then a handshake'.

Plate 5

Reichsmarschall Hermann Göring announces the appointment of Reichsfürer Heinrich Himmler as Head of the Gestapo in 1934, a position originally held by Rudolf Diels (see Chapters 25, 27 & 32 and Plates and 10 & 11). Waldemar Wappenhans was held in high estimation by both Göring and Himmler. Having directly served the two most powerful men in the Third Reich after Hitler, Wappenhans at times had to be extremely careful not to be seen to be favouring either of the two rivals over the other. In June 1936 Hitler decreed the unification of all police forces in Germany under Himmler thus merging the police into the SS (see Plate 3). Wappenhans, following an order from Himmler, went underground in January 1945 and assumed the identity of the civilian Hans Seemann. His cover was eventually blown in the autumn of 1949 when his true identity was revealed to Wolfe Frank by Rudolf Diels (see Chapter 25).

Plate 6

A Luftwaffe flypast on 'Party Day' held annually in Nuremberg between 1933 and 1938 – usually in September. If during these events Wappenhans wasn't involved in the flypasts as an air force officer, he was one of the SS officers responsible for organizing the parades (see page 223).

Plate 7

Above: Reichsmarschall Hermann Göring inspecting the aerial machine gun of a bomber or a large reconnaissance plane. In addition to being Head of Reconnaissance Waldemar Wappenhans was also a prolific machine gunner and he designed and had built his own unique double machine gun fitted with a trigger that enabled him to fire off both barrels simultaneously. He first used the gun with great effect in Palestine in 1918 against Colonel Lawrence 'of Arabia' (see pages 202/3). He had a similar transportable unit specially built for his personal use in WWII (see page 232).

Right: Göring as Wappenhans would have known him during their days together at Cadet School (see page 177 & Plate 5).

Plate 8

The tasks were clear – they were divided into:

1) Watching the North Sea (shipping movements)
2) Watching the English coast, and photographing:
   a) Loading and unloading, shipping movements
   b) Airfields and industrial sites
   c) Air defences (AA and fighters)
3) Escort flights (patrol and reconnaissance)
   a) Reporting troop locations
   b) Location of fighter units
   c) Discovery of opportunities for raids
4) Royal Navy (as under 3)
5) Special operations, co-operation with our Navy (light buoys, harbour approaches)

To carry out our tasks properly, we fine-tuned our training. The photographic section was in the capable hands of Lieutenant Büefernich. Our maps were excellent, and were carefully compared with our photos. My adjutant, Lieutenant Grollmann, worked tirelessly to keep the squadron active (both these officers died soon afterwards – shot down.)

Any of the crews who weren't flying were training – navigation, astronomy, compass use, radio, encoding and ship recognition were the main areas. We had models of all warship types so we were soon able to identify each ship at a long distance. The Heinkel III[36], which we flew, was a reliable 'bird'. They were a bit faster than the British fighters, which therefore had the advantage that they were hard to attack from behind. The British had a machine gunner behind the cockpit, who had a complete view and field of fire backwards, a good defence against attacking fighters. Our He IIIs were therefore equipped with 'armour' which prevented fires caused by hits from tracer bullets, as the incendiary element automatically went out under the pressure of the cork-like material the 'armour' was made of. At the same time it prevented fuel leaks from punctured tanks. So it mostly happened that planes that had been hit in the 'armour' had no difficulty making the long flight home over the North Sea.

The British airfields, even at the beginning of the war, were so well camouflaged that they were often missed with the naked eye. Only with precise examination of the film strips could hangars, individual planes and finally the whole site be made out. All the buildings were painted to match their surroundings, planes that weren't under cover were held off the airfield in good camouflage, and false roads ran over the roofs of buildings and even the airstrip itself. It was amazing how well-prepared everything was. Because of the photos we sent to Air Force HQ, a furious order came down from Göring to camouflage our own sites better. At Ütersen all the buildings were painted in a few days by bringing in thousands of helpers. The camouflage colours were good, you could only make out the buildings from above with difficulty. Just like the Tommies we did the same to our buildings and the airfield. We'd learnt something from them.

The Tommies' air defences were strong in the South of England, especially round London. The further you went Northwards up the coast, the weaker it became. Photos showed Scapa Flow and the Firth of Forth where stronger AA and fighter numbers gradually appeared. You could fly extremely low over the Shetland Islands in the first few months without even being fired at, but already at the beginning of November an anti-aircraft cruiser turned up there, which seriously disturbed our peaceful contemplation. At Scapa Flow, the Tommies had stationed units with Spitfires at St Mary's on Mainland [Island], which flew regular blocking patrols when we got near the coast. Apart from the warships' AA, the ground AA was also very strong.

Along the entrance to the Firth of Forth, a great number of barrage balloons stood at irregular heights (I estimated fifty to sixty), which made flying in cloudy weather agony for us. The balloons were up to 2,000 metres from the ground. If you had to fly lower because of the visibility, you could count on zooming into one of these stupid cables at any moment. A short time later, I attended a research project at Rechlin, where a plane fitted with a frame like an umbrella collided with a wire cable without crashing. Air Force HQ however refused to introduce these protective measures generally, for balloons were only a secondary form of defence.

Along the East coast there lay, at regular intervals between ten and thirty kilometres out to sea, British observation vessels, mostly trawlers, which reported the approach of any aircraft. In this way we were usually intercepted by fighters as soon as we reached the coast. To avoid a dogfight, that would prevent us from carrying out our mission, we escaped out to sea, where they were not keen to follow us, and flew back to the targets assigned when the fighters ran low on fuel and had to land. Fighters couldn't stay up for more than an hour in this first year of the war.

The British were already at a respectable level of radio technology. They often broke into our wavelengths and tried to pass orders or intelligence to us. On one flight over the Wash bay my radio operator passed on through the individual throat microphone the report he'd just received 'in map square XPZ'. We knew perfectly well that map square was a part of the North Sea. PZ meant tanks [Panzer] – so we were meant to drop tanks around in the North Sea! On our return I had the code changed.

As you approached the coast of Britain, radio use became steadily harder because of their jamming. In fact you couldn't even make out your own words on the individual microphones – a transmitter was booming out 'Ladies and gentlemen! Ladies and gentlemen!'

Shipping movement in the North Sea was extremely slight. It was mostly directed up the coast via Scapa Flow to the Shetlands, from where it went in convoys to Norway or Russia. Naturally, the British tried to cover the most dangerous part of the voyage by night, that meant the stretch between Scapa or the Shetlands and the Norwegian coast – but you couldn't complete this stretch in one night. So I set up a patrol or fan reconnaissance[37] with all my available crews. They reached the probable convoy routes in the grey dawn. Then if enemy units were reported, we didn't take our eyes off them. Then the attack units which had meanwhile taken off 'on suspicion' would be guided in and attack the convoys with bombs or their guns. After the attack units had flown away, we took photos to check their success, evaluated and reported them on our return. These flights often lasted eight to ten hours. The same thing happened with the Royal Navy. We wanted to know exactly where the 'Home Fleet' was – mostly we could pin them down in Scapa Flow, but also off the extreme North coast of Scotland in Loch Eriboll, and on the West coast in Loch Ewe.

The night attack by our attack force on Scapa Flow gave us, out at sea, an enchanting sight. The Tommies had set off a magic fire; any firework display paled in comparison. Countless searchlight beams lay like a bell over the islands. Hundreds of shells of all sizes were bursting in the air. The result was that all our efforts on both sides [i.e. reconnaissance and attack] achieved very little.

In order to carry out our missions more practically, we now usually flew in the evenings to Westerland, on Sylt Island where part of the Lion Squadron was also based. From there we took off at two or three in the morning to reach our objective in the early dawn. The winter of 1939/40 was very severe. Coastal waters froze, which left our capable Navy fliers a job to do. Their planes couldn't take off – they were frozen in. So we welcomed them like good comrades and they often came with us on our flights. It was amazing [to see] how a seaman can do anything. Every ton of shipping that swung past the coast of England, whether it was blown up or not, was greeted with enthusiasm. We learned a lot from those old seadogs – they could do a good deal more than we could.

The internal working of my squadron went on smoothly thanks to my adjutant, Lieutenant Grollmann (later killed). He was really annoyed with me because he got to fly so little. We got on well with our men, and I never had to arrest anybody. I only came near doing it once with my 'friend' – as I called my Warrant Officer. He was a clown by trade, short and stocky and uncannily strong – but with only daft ideas in his head. Putting the WO on a charge wouldn't help any more – I had to step in. My conversation with him ended with him swearing 'Never again, sir!' And there actually <u>were</u> no complaints for a fortnight, but then he put his foot in it properly again. Nothing but stupidity. So I called in the whole hut. 'If you can't sort your comrades out to the point where I, as your boss get lumbered with this petty stuff – and God knows I've other things to worry about – then from now on you'll all have to suffer. Going out dancing on Saturdays just won't be on your agenda'. Next day my 'friend' asked me to lock him up, but I didn't. His mates made sure that everything went right.

My fears that the pilots I'd been sent weren't well enough trained to meet the demands on them properly came true. As long as the weather was clear all went well – but then came orders, despite my warnings, to take off and land in the lowest cloud cover. Just then too we began cold take-offs, that is we no longer let the engine warm up for half an hour before take-off, but took off immediately after ignition. This was made possible by adding oil to the fuel.

My planes were standing ready for take-off. I would take off first, and gave explicit orders that nobody was to follow me until, after a successful take-off, I gave the relevant order by radio.

We rolled towards the take-off point. Faust, my pilot pushed down the gas pedal and we roared away. The crew started singing 'And we're flying against England'. We were almost at the end of the runway but Faust didn't pull the joystick back to his chest. 'TAKE OFF!' I yelled – Faust only pointed at the lighted control panel; the speedometer showed 100 kph, and one can only take off at 140. But I felt that the plane was doing more than 100. I pulled on the joystick, and then Faust did. We took off. Then came a violent jolt and then another. The glass pane in front shattered, and an icy draught pushed against us. We were in total darkness in the clouds. 'Swing left, carefully', I shouted to Faust 'we've got to try and get a view of the ground!' Lehmann, the on-board fitter, had to crawl forward along the bomb bay. When he came, we stopped up the hole in the canopy as best we could with our parachutes and the sailcloth of our rubber dinghy. The icy blast slackened. To one side below us we could see lights – it was the airfield. Thank God! But we were only fifty metres up – right now landing was out of the question. We wouldn't let the airfield out of our sight, despite being so low – we were disappearing into the clouds now and again, but the plane was being pushed further down all the time. Emergency measures – out with the aerial – first radio message. 'All machines – do not take off'. Second radio message – to 10ᵗʰ Flying Corps – 'Take-off for today's flight aborted. Cloud cover too low. On our take-off ground contact and damage to machine. Will try to land at dawn'. Reply from 10ᵗʰ Flying Corps. 'Emergency landing place, Lübeck'. I set a course for Lübeck, in case we needed to land there. After flying round in circles for two hours, we landed. We'd had to lower the landing gear by hand, as the electric controls weren't working. We found out that our landing gear had taken the lightning rod of a house with it, and the canopy had broken when we hit the top of a tree. That evening we, the crew, celebrated our 'birthday'. My wife, whom I called on this occasion, didn't quite understand what the birthday had to do with re-birth. I must unfortunately admit that she thought I wasn't absolutely sober.

At a meeting the same day with Flying Corps E, I categorically demanded the training of my pilots for their Blind Flying Certificate (and was assured of this). Sadly we would suffer losses before the problem was solved.

Five planes were due to take off – it was 05.00 hours. There was cloud 200 metres up, and on the return flight we could expect no change. At the briefing I'd asked all the pilots individually if they had any reservations about this flight. I said they should give their opinion openly and honestly. It would not be cowardly to say 'No', but their duty was to their whole crew. 'We've flown in worse weather before', was their answer. The first plane took off and vanished into the clouds, the second followed. The third made a sharp turn straight after take-off, came down on one wing, hit the ground and caught fire. We had never seen anything like that happen. The pilot of the fourth plane who was following right behind, apparently lost his nerve on seeing the crash, didn't see the Heinkell 111, crashed and caught fire the same way. A crew failed to come back from a flight over England – they were shot down. In another plane that <u>did</u> come home there was a man dead from lack of oxygen. That was thirteen comrades lost in one day. I have seldom felt so depressed as when I had to say a last farewell to them at my comrades' funerals.

I was ordered to report to General Milch in Berlin to give an account of this. I soon noticed the General intended to shift the blame onto Major Harlinghausen. 'No sir, I alone am responsible', I said, so I went before a court-martial. I was acquitted on all counts. Now, when the horse had bolted, something was done for Long Range Reconnaissance. The pilots were immediately relieved and went on a blind flying course. In their place arrived the best fliers in the Air Force, the Condor Legion[38] men. Major Petersen, their leader, flew his men to Ütersen himself in the new four-engine plane. He was a man with a sixth sense for flying – he found his way to the airfield in the dirtiest weather, even without a radio bearing. His crews, two pilots for each plane, were kept together. All that was missing were the Condors[39] – they were not ready yet, so his splendid men came aboard with us. There were men there with famous names who had surveyed the Amazon in difficult flights, and won reputations for themselves in Franco's war in Spain. The lift that they gave my squadron was noticeable, and when these comrades left us after two months' activity – though after losing some of their best men – the band played rousing tunes on the runway where Major Petersen's four-engine plane stood ready to collect them.

As I took another look inside the Condor, I happened to see, well packed up, my twin machine gun, which I'd got my chief mechanic here to develop, as I had earlier in Palestine. Petersen, who was interested in any new gadget, wanted my guns to go with him, it seemed. Wait a minute, old chap! Everyone picks up an extra saddlebag on campaign. The band played 'Mussi' den zum Städtle hinaus[40] and in the confusion of departure, I had the guns and Petersen's case unloaded from the Condor. After it landed in Bremen, our counter-attack was discovered – an apologetic phone call from Petersen, we made peace and his case was sent back.

We were given the task of photographing the Grim Ness entrance to Scapa Flow from the lowest possible altitude. This was in order to find out where the minefields were. Around midday our plane was 5,000 meters up in the clouds just in front of the entrance. Then the Spitfires came roaring towards us. We quickly dived into the nearest cloud, turned, then stuck our nose out again. The Brits had shot past, and we made for the next cloud before they could find us again. This game was repeated till the Spitfires ran out of fuel and had to land. Now we flew to the entrance, down to 800 metres, and just as we flew over, the cloud cover parted and blazing sunshine poured over the entrance. The film ran, and then it was back into the sheltering clouds and away home. After developing the film, the minefields could be clearly recognised. We'd given Prien a good basis for his Scapa Flow exploit

[U-boat commander Günther Prien sank *HMS Royal Oak* in Scapa Flow].

On 23 December 1939 we came back to Westerland after a successful 'fan' reconnaissance. The Christmas festivities, which we had carefully prepared at Ütersen, were almost upon us. It was snowing – QBJ [take-off forbidden] for all planes. There was no question of taking off on the 24th either. There were hundreds of men to clear the snow off the runway, so we boarded the train, rode over the Hindenburg Causeway to the mainland, and then to our home base; here too everything was under deep snow, and they had to work all day just to make flying possible. At the beginning of January 1940 I was in my plane 9,000 metres above the North coast of Scotland. By the time the Tommies wound themselves up to this height, my photographic work would be almost finished – or so I thought. It was bitterly cold – the thermometer always froze up at 40°C below, and we'd no way of knowing how cold it was now. The oxygen masks then had only one tube to breathe in and out through – so it was easy for ice to build up in the mouthpiece as a result of the saliva released when speaking. So you had to knead the mouthpiece at the same time, to prevent the ice from forming. I don't know if I'd failed to do this, but anyway I suddenly felt completely stupefied – all I could do was shout 'Down', and then I lost consciousness. When I came to, I saw we were heading for home ten metres over the drink. For a short time I clambered through the bomb bay to the radio operator's seat, and let the fresh air up my nose, but when I got back to the cockpit I already realized something was wrong with me. As it later turned out, my heart had developed a muscular weakness through the violent strain put on it.

To begin with I kept flying. One Saturday I was coming back from a flight over the Southeast coast of England. Then we ran into a pig of a storm. We were skimming over the drink at fifty metres, waves as tall as houses with crests of white foam. The rain was lashing down, so hard that we were wet to the skin despite the glass canopy. We were looking forward to getting home and the weather clearing, it was getting on for midday. I'd given my crew leave and we were meant to be relieved. No further missions were expected for the rest of that day. Feeling good, I was standing under a warm shower, when a messenger appeared. 'Telephone, sir – urgent call from 10th Corps. It's the General himself on the line'. Bloody hell! Do we never get a rest? On with my bathrobe, off to the phone. 'Hello, Captain Wappenhans. Good job you're there. Have a plane ready for take-off at once. You'll have to reckon on landing by night on return. Orders for the flight follow by courier'. It was General G's voice. 'Yes, sir!' Then I went cold – where was I going to find a qualified pilot for a night landing? Hadn't I just sent them on leave? The reserve crew on duty was not suitable for this purpose. I phoned round all the billets, got dressed, rushed into the mess. There was just one person there, my rescuing angel, Lieutenant Kowalkowski, one of the best Condor pilots. I explained the situation. He was ready to go, although he wanted to manage his young, newly-married wife.

Kowalkowski had the plane prepared for take-off. I put the photographic section on standby, who were responsible for the relevant equipment. The courier arrived, and we read the orders. 'British destroyers have forced the German steamer *Altmark* to enter a fjord in Norwegian territory in map square X. There it was fired on by the destroyer *[HMS] Cossack* – without regard to territorial borders. Your task is to bring back the relevant information while avoiding overflying what you know to be Norwegian airspace. If you sight British forces you are to attack them with bombs with the permission of your garrison'.

We flew out over the North Sea and approached the coast of Norway. It was a glorious day – for now the flight was pure pleasure. We spotted the *Altmark* in the fjord reported; it was clear in the picture through angled shots. It lay quite a long way inside the fjord. There was no sign of British destroyers and even our searches produced no result. A pity! We turned for home: by now it was getting dark, and the weather was getting worse. We flew at low altitude parallel with the coast. Our radio bearing was constantly interrupted by the Copenhagen transmitter. Then, diagonally below us a brightly lit barracks appeared, – it must be in Denmark [then still neutral] – we must not fly over the land, as it would lead to diplomatic developments. Our radio bearing began to work again, and we landed smoothly at Ütersen. For Kowalkowski his navigational feat was just 'small potatoes'. In the mess afterwards, he played the latest hits with the band he had formed. After the consumption of numerous cocktails it ended in a slurred rendering of the Volga [boatmen's?] song.

Western Front – WWII

Now spring was approaching. New attack plans were circulating, new orders arrived, with these as their objective. I was awarded a bar to the Iron Cross 1st class [awarded to recipients of the 1914 Iron Cross subsequently awarded the 1939 Iron Cross], and transferred to the Western Front. I handed over the squadron to my successor, Staff Captain Caesar. This intelligent officer came loaded with plans for the forthcoming operations. Coolly calculating, with no regard for his own safety in action, he was killed right at the beginning of the Norway campaign.

The numbers that Caesar had given me of the air forces available were not very encouraging – the French and British forces were in no way weaker. In the coming engagement we would have to operate with surprise and increased risk, in order to get air superiority from the start. This would lay the foundations for the breakthrough of the armour and the advance of the infantry divisions.

The preparations for the French campaign were in full swing when I arrived in Bremen to take over my new Reconnaissance Squadron. It was on the point of moving to Wunstorf near Hanover. When I reported to the Commander-in-Chief at Münster, it was no longer to General Felmy. He and his Chief of Staff had been relieved of their posts: a Luftwaffe courier plane had lost its way/broken down and landed in Holland. The crew had not been able to destroy the vitally important secret documents (plans for the invasion of Holland). In Münster I was let into the plans of the forthcoming operations as far as my long-range reconnaissance was concerned. The area assigned to me consisted of Holland and Belgium first, and later more over to Northern France.

In view of my earlier experiences, I didn't rest until all my crews were trained in blind flying. The invasion of Holland was now practiced to the last detail in planning exercises. Now we had about five weeks rest in front of us. As I had been working without a break so far, I got a fortnight's leave. I flew to Schwerin, where I had a lively reunion with my wife and three children. But then I had to go straight into hospital – with flu, heart trouble and blood pressure of ninety-four! Now it took a long time for me to recover – the doctors insisted that from now on a front-line posting for me was out of the question. The inspecting Surgeon-General took me in his car to Alt-Rehse in Mecklenburg. Now it's a convalescent home for the wounded, but it had been the Imperial Medical College. It stood in an idyllic setting on a lake, in a park-like garden. At the beginning of the war the Führer wanted to settle his HQ there, but now I was lying in the bedroom that would have been his. I wasn't discharged for two months, and then went to Brieg, as an instructor in tactics and artillery direction. How I achieved this honour I worked out from my own [army] records. These held entries only until 1919, and there was a note 'Excellent at artillery direction' (the long Paris gun)! In fact I owed this to coincidence more than anything, and besides, it was quite a long time ago. But the Luftwaffe Personnel Department had no new documents available and were reaching back into the old ones, which had once been sent to me at Ütersen with the note 'Update, with conduct report to the present, and return'. As I could not review them with the best will in the world, I sent the documents to 10th Corps, where they could still be today.

In Brieg there were about forty young officers training for reconnaissance. The instructors were mostly older officers with no front-line experience in this war. We made these activities really enjoyable, and I worked hard to expand my knowledge of artillery direction as soon as possible, took part in range exercises in Silesia and tried to fit theory and practice together. My highest superior, the Head of the training service was now my commander at Goslar, now Colonel Kreipe. I went to him with a request for a frontline posting again, but he had to say no – first I would have to improve my health. I went to Kudowa Spa for some weeks, drank the waters, took baths and felt on top form again. A new move to get to the front failed. Meanwhile I'd been promoted to Major; was I going to spend the war in this post at home? No! I'd been indoctrinated as a cadet that a real man belongs at the front, not at home.

I turned to Himmler with help from my friend Obergruppenführer Wolff. Himmler offered me a posting as an SS and Police commander – after basic training in his department. In autumn 1940 I began my assignment in Berlin. At that time the SS Reichsführer and Head of German Police (Himmler) had under him:

1) The SS
    a) The general SS with its Main Sectors, which corresponded more or less to the provinces. All men qualified by official standards for the SS, and who had mostly completed their military service.
    b) The Armed SS, which were considered first on the list, apart from the Adolf Hitler Guard Regiment and the Death's Head units. [Commanded by SS-Oberst-Gruppenführer Jüttner and the Command Staff].
    c) The Race and Settlement Office which found plenty to do in resettling Germans expelled from Russia, Lithuania, Latvia and Livonia [now parts of Latvia & Estonia].
    d) National Socialist schools [under SS-Oberst-Gruppenführer Heissmeier].

2) The Police
    a) The regular Police, with the Gendarmerie under them [under SS-Oberst-Gruppenführer Dalugue and Regional Police Chiefs].
    b) The Reich Security Office [Obergruppenführer Heydrich] [killed while Governor in Prague]

c) The SD [Sicherheitsdienst – Security Service]
d) The Security Police
e) The   Reich   Criminal   [Investigation]   Office   [under
    Gruppenführer Nebe] – [Chief of the Reich Criminal Police
    Office]

From these organizations I was to spend five to six weeks basic training
in the first line: of the regular Police, the Security Service and the Armed
SS.

From the outset the Central Police HQ in Berlin gave the impression
of a well-organized, strictly militarily trained operation. The leading
officers and officials of individual departments soon gave me an
overview, which I took down in writing and studied. Trips to the
Provincial Council at Wesel and the SS and Police Commander's HQ at
The Hague widened my overall picture of the work of the police and
Gendarmerie.

My first impression of the Security Service was that they had little
time to spare for me, and were always happy when I moved to a new
department. I was greeted with suspicion, in spite of their politeness.
Apparently I was regarded as Himmler's snooper. This situation came
to a head when I explained to Heydrich[41] that I had to give Himmler a
regular report on my impressions of what I was doing. Heydrich
demanded to see these reports before I sent them. I was happy to agree
to this, as well as his request for relevant proofs. A room was shown to
me with an aide and two women secretaries working – I declined this
as an office. Heydrich insisted, I complained to Himmler and was
supported.

From then on Heydrich was transformed; he made my duties easier
in every way, took me out to his hunting lodge near the Nauen radio
tower, treated me like a regular host in his family circle, went with me
to the fencing hall (where he showed he was one of the best in Germany
with foil and sabre), drove me to Tempelhof from which he flew me –
at the controls of his own two-engine plane – to a fighter training base.
Then he got into a Me 109 and went through battle practice manoeuvres.
On the way home he asked me not to tell Himmler about his flying
activities. He was too young to survive the war (Himmler said) without
frontline experience. In spite of Himmler's ban, he wanted to be a
fighter pilot.

I shared his point of view and was pleased for him when he flew
against England, and later Russia. There he missed being captured by
a whisker, when he was forced to land in enemy territory after being
hit on a low-level attack. He was rescued by an armoured scout unit.

Some days I got to take part in Heydrich's morning routine in his office. He was an early riser. He talked to me between issuing important orders on the phone and dictating to his secretary for the records, the talks, word for word, that he had had the day before with VIPs such as Hitler, Goebbels, Göring, Himmler or others. His mental energy was astonishing. As far as I could make out from Heydrich's remarks, it was all about the positions of power of the individual Nazi leaders. The differences that arose between them were dissected and used to suit the increase in Himmler's position. The leaders of the Security Service compared Heydrich with a doctor who feels the pulse of his patient (the German Reich) and then on the basis of his observations gives suitable instructions. The SD was deployed throughout the whole Reich. Apart from Head Office [paid] staff, SD operatives were active in every larger concern, in factories, offices, ministries, right down to district and parish councils, even in the Party organization down to local associations. They had to make regular and truthful reports on the mood of the people. These reports were never dressed up and had nothing to do with the sloppy praise of many party leaders who just wanted to show themselves to their superiors in a favourable light.

I remember very well how there was talk in these reports of the watering-down of the party programme – that meant the social programme, for which Hitler had done more at the beginning than any statesman in the world, was now beginning to tread on people's feet; that Party leaders who should, according to the programme, be leading by example, were starting to get too high and mighty; that Göring lived a life of gluttony, that Ley[42] was a boozer who often appeared with his dolled-up women, that Goebbels the 'cripple' (as they called him) was running off with film actresses. In the same way individual regional leaders were accused of beginning to get delusions of grandeur.

The summary of these reports, which in any case I never got to see, was passed on to the Propaganda Ministry and other places, according to Himmler's political opinions. If on Monday morning Goebbels didn't find the SD reports on his desk, he made an impatient call to Heydrich. I was present at some of these myself.

How far Hitler was kept informed by Heydrich, I have no idea. Heydrich told me when I asked him that Hitler was kept informed of everything, but with all his great concerns, people should not bother him with affairs that would be fundamentally sorted out after the war. And that included 'mucking out' the Party.

In the Anti-Jewish Department lists were being drawn up in which every Jew was registered on a card index, divided into full Jews and half-Jews. In Berlin I never heard of any kind of [anti-Jewish] measures or shootings.

I worked for a fortnight in the Reich Criminal Investigation Office, which was headed by SS Senior Leader Nebe. Here I really did get a picture, even in this short time, of the work that went into fighting crime. Statistics showed that organized crime had fallen to a minimum. The penalties for burglary, robbery with violence and murder were so severe that international gangs, who were proved to have been active in Germany earlier, had now moved abroad. Typical high-crime districts, like those in Hamburg, where murders had previously been a daily occurrence, were torn down and redeveloped. The level of [personal] security for German citizens had risen significantly. When I asked how far the CID would proceed against attacks by the SA or SS, which had featured in the Security Service reports, Nebe skilfully evaded the question, saying these had to be assessed case by case.

The technology used in carrying out murder investigations, the methods of tracing criminals, the statistics and their legacy for the future, ways of investigating and monitoring all made a great impression on me. At the Vice Squad I was shown films that had been seized at the homes of rich Jews: they showed a level of perversion which made your hair stand on end. One fact was undeniable – Nebe had brought the CID to a very high level of effectiveness.

I never got a full picture of the organizations of the Security Service and Security Police. When I asked Heydrich about it, the answer I got was that it wasn't necessary, as I would have nothing to do with their activities as a future SS and Police Chief. Heydrich suggested that I should go to France and Belgium to get to know how the Security Police were used. I had a wonderful reception in Paris, was given a room in one of the best hotels and enjoyed the beauty of this unique city. I did very little actual work. The SD leaders assigned to instruct me were so overloaded that I rarely got any grounding in what they were doing. Some of these SD leaders in Paris were awarded the Iron Cross, First Class, a rarity in that branch of service[43]. They told me about their raid on the Secret Service in Holland, where even before the invasion two of the leading members of the British Intelligence Service were brought out with their documents, put into lorries and driven across the border into Germany.

I was packed off to Bordeaux to broaden my knowledge, and then travelled down to the Spanish border. In the seaside resort of Biarritz, I came to know a little of the atmosphere of spying, in company with an SD officer (in plain clothes, of course). In a bar people were pointed out to me who worked for the British and [Free] French, whom we were watching. We talked to an extremely well-dressed lady who was highly paid by both sides – she said she was Argentinian, and lived in splendid style. In these surroundings there was no sign of hardship. There was everything you could want, wine, champagne and gourmet food. In a French lady's elegantly furnished flat we met one of our people, who was sending reports from Britain via Spain. There were similar visits in Bordeaux too.

Then I went back to Paris, where they explained the various strands in the internal politics of occupied France. Resistance organisations, collaborators, Bonapartists, Royalists all played a part. I was taken to a club where open political discussion was going on. The powers of the security service to prevent sabotage were limited – this was mainly due to the different areas of authority of the SD and the Armed Forces. Admiral Canaris[44], the director of Military Intelligence [Abwehr] considered the occupied territories as under military authority. The SD was strictly barred from advancing into Holland, Belgium and France with the German armies. Heydrich found a way of evading this ban by attaching his SD men to the Armed SS. Once they had got their foot in the door and could carry out their work successfully, areas of authority seemed from outside to have been defined; in practice, however, things didn't change. Saboteurs picked up by the SD had, by order, to be handed over to the army. It turned out that after a while they had to be arrested again, because they had been released after a short interrogation by the military authorities. These problems really annoyed me – after all, the army and the SS had the same aim, we wanted to win the war. So a way had to be found to come to some agreement.

In Brussels I met Security Director Canaris, a nephew of the Admiral. He took the time to discuss the problems thoroughly with me, and assured me that in a very short time Hitler in person would order a unified regulation of all security matters. We stayed in one of the Rothschilds' villa in Brussels – it was like a museum. Rows of priceless paintings hung on the walls – wonderful pictures by Dutch old masters were surrounded by Cubist and Surrealist works: in spite of explanations by some whizz-kid expert in this area, I couldn't stand them. This young man was there to complete a list of the collection that, just like the inventory of belongings found in every house, would be nailed up at the inner door. It was SS orders that not even the smallest object should be stolen in foreign countries[45].

In Berlin I got hold of the programme for the Armed SS. The Command Staff in the Kaiserallee [command bunker] gave me a rundown of existing units at the front, of those included in the List, and of replacement units at home. It was amazing how a cadre of troops like this had grown in the short time from 1939 to 1940. The Armed SS was recruited mainly from the general SS and the Hitler Youth. Enlistment was voluntary and achieved by advertising. The requirements for acceptance into the Armed SS were stricter than the Armed Forces: Minimum height of 1 metre 70 (5'8"), perfect health, no wearers of glasses, mental alertness. You could make a good start with lads like that. There was a good spirit in SS barracks, you must admit. The training was hard, but comradeship was encouraged above all. I felt I was back in my cadet days. Stealing from comrades was severely punished, and was more or less unknown. The lockers were always left open – they were not allowed to close them. The lads had been brought up from childhood to value service to the Führer and Fatherland most of all. They would fight in the same spirit – it could never be said of the Armed SS that they ever refused a mission. On the contrary, they were feared by their opponents. The Armed Forces High Command, to which they were operationally subordinate, always sent in the SS at hot spots, so they were jokingly known as 'the Fire Brigade'.

Deficiencies in senior command, which were noticeable in the earliest days, were ironed out in a short time by the High Command. SS leaders were selected for training as staff officers, and a number of talented senior army officers were seconded to the SS.

The young leaders, the future SS Sturmführers [lieutenants] were trained in the Officer Schools in Tölz and Braunschweig. The spirit of these young men was particularly fine: occasionally I gave lectures on flying there, and could see for myself the high level of training of the officer cadets. The credit for bringing these schools to such a rare height in organization and training is due to SS Obergruppenführer Hausser, a former army general who was still to make a name for himself in this war as an Army Commander. He was a selfless fighter for his country, an example for the whole Armed SS. In spite of losing an eye, he stayed at the front. He was one of the most popular senior SS leaders and countless stories about him went around.

Eastern Front

My training period was over now, but the police units I was to command were not yet ready. So I was sent for a few more weeks to Potsdam, to the Chief of Police there von Dolega-Kozierowski, an old friend of mine since Nienburg days. I studied the duties of a Chief of Police in detail, and discovered they were more or less representative. The Security Service here too was a power in the state, over whose activities the Chief had practically no influence. Contact with the authorities here took place only on a social basis, but I did on such occasions get to know the head of the [Prussian regional] government, von Bismarck, an extremely efficient public servant, in whose house I have spent many happy hours.

Time was marching on, and I wanted to be of some practical use at the end. I went ahead with preparations for assembling my Staff, obtaining equipment, arms and motor vehicles myself. When holdups occurred, I got help from the army and the Armed SS. In 14 days my Staff was ready to leave.

Himmler had asked the Führer meanwhile to promote me to SS Brigade leader and Major-General in the police[46], and appointed me SS and Police commander in Volhynia and Podolia[47]. Under me I had a police Colonel in command of the regular police and a Major commanding the Gendarmerie. The police commander would be detailed to me only after my arrival in Brest-Litovsk. I could get no clear definition of his responsibility for my authority over the Security Service, especially as there were serious differences between Heydrich and Daluege[48], and so my area of responsibility might be confined to the police.

The tasks of the SS and Police Leaders were allotted through Daluege. They consisted in maintaining calm and order in the part of occupied Ukraine under civilian administration (including my Volhynia-Podolia section) and guaranteeing smooth co-operation with the civil authority. The Security Service had already kept me informed about internal political events in the Ukraine, in Berlin – the army had at first been greeted as liberators by the population when they invaded, and we could have capitalized on this mood. But the civilian administration ruined this by their clumsy handling of the population. These freedom-loving peasants had had enough of the Kolkhoz [Collective farm] system and could have been our best friends with the introduction of an intelligent policy, and suitable propaganda. Sure, our troops had to live off the land, and at home people expected supplies that were urgently needed. But why did these measures have to be taken in the most brutal way possible? Mistake followed mistake. The Ukrainians were embittered, they formed gangs and began to harass us. In the Polish-controlled areas of Volhynia this mood dominated – the first partisan groups had been formed. Attacks became a daily event. I had to intervene.

Ukraine was ruled by Reich Commissioner Koch and the individual provinces were administered by General Commissioners, to whom District Commissioners [equivalent to Regional Councillors] were responsible. The GC for Volhynia/Podolia was SS Obergruppenführer Schön, a decent man who worked exceptionally hard to live at a fair understanding with the [local] people. He thought of himself as my superior, and I let him think so – we got on fine with each other.

The regular police commander divided his men systematically between all the larger settlements, and had Gendarmerie units of six to ten men posted about the countryside. In Brest itself, apart from the Staff, a company was held, to move in to fight partisans. Weeks passed while I toured the whole district, inspected the posts in their garrisons and got to know conditions from the District Commissioners. We clearly realized that Brest was not suitable as my HQ. I had to work from a more central point, and Schön agreed. We went ahead with a move to Lutsk.

Meanwhile the partisans had made their appearance. We lost our first men in the Brest area. Cars travelling alone were shot up. In regions full of marshes, which were hard to keep under surveillance, a planned campaign was impossible, given the weak forces available, so I worked with surprise, popping up suddenly with my company and any other forces we could put together from the police and army, and got good results. The first bomb attacks on the railways gave us the incentive to clear the forests to a fifty-metre distance along the tracks. Now it was possible to counter an attack from a moving train, and the railway patrols found their work a good deal easier.

I made my trips mostly in a Volkswagen, which proved indestructible and allowed us to stay out of trouble even on the worst roads. I was usually at the wheel, with my driver crouching beside me and my batman in the back, both with submachine guns with the safety off. In spite of these precautions we often came home with holes in the car.

The Security Police commander came to see me in Brest-Litovsk. He had set up his garrison in Rovno [Rivne], and wanted to move to Lutsk just like me. From the start he told me that in his missions he was in contact with my superiors in Kiev, but would be quite happy to do as I wished. This was not what I wanted, because if the SP Commander was under my command, I would also have the power to give him orders or at least to have information about his activities. I did not intend to give him a clear answer. It came out in the SP Commander's explanation that there had been executions of Jews in my area, and that more were intended. I asked him to give me a written report of this. When I reminded him of this later I was told, by the Commander of Security Police in Kiev, that written reports of the measures taken by his department must not be issued – and in any case the treatment of Jews was none of my business.

243

In spite of this I decided to write to Heydrich and ask for a comment: this brought me unfavourable notice. I had not followed service protocol for senior SS and Police officers. This was the opinion of Obergruppenführer Prützman [Hans-Otto], who summoned me to Rovno, and told me in friendly terms that I could be glad not to have to worry about these matters. He was right – and anyway, his explanation amounted to an order.

In autumn 1941 we moved to Lutsk; now I could move my work to Podolia, where reasonable district commissioners got on well with the local population. Here I started to get some return from the fertile soil of the Black Earth – with intensive cultivation in this region, it must be possible to harvest bumper crops. Previous experience showed that the collective system could not be abolished immediately – the peasants could no longer work independently, and equipment could not be obtained at once. So it was slowly revived enough to improve the workers' living conditions, and ensure they had farms, if they showed goodwill by working hard.

I received an order to go to Rovno and make arrangements for a visit from [Alfred] Rosenberg, the Minister for the Eastern regions. He arrived by special train, with Reich Commissioner Koch. The two enemies stood facing each other – Rosenberg, the highly-educated philosopher, and Koch the brutal 'gangster,' as we called him. A great drama was to be staged for the Ukrainians: the band played, Army and Party guards of honour lined up. Rosenberg drove through the little town with Koch, protected by a mounted escort. The people ignored them. In Rosenberg's retinue was his deputy, Dr Meyer, who remained loyal to the founding principles of National Socialism till his death, lived simply and modestly and never fell into the megalomania of many of his colleagues. I handed him two of the Ukrainian newspapers that were printed here under German direction. In the first there was a photo of Rosenberg with an appropriate welcoming text on the front page, and under it a smaller photo of Koch. Furious that his picture was not at least the same size as that of his rival Rosenberg, Koch had the whole print run pulped and a second paper printed in which this criminal error was corrected. Outside people were standing around, numb with hunger, not far from the gates of Rovno sounded the shots of the partisans, and here a monkey show was going on which they ought to have been ashamed of.

Some months later I was invited to meet Rosenberg in Berlin. In front of Dr Meyer, I openly told him my opinions and what I knew. Rosenberg agreed, and told me Koch would be relieved of his post, but it never happened. The Führer demanded that both men should be reconciled.

Through the Security Service commander I found out a few months later that shootings of Jews had been carried out in Rovno – by a Special Unit of the SD from Kiev with a company of the regular police taking part. These were said to have gone in drunk like madmen, and fired into the crowds in a blind rage. I sent in a report about this and requested punishment and condemnation of the officer involved. The result was that I was transferred to Nikolayev[49] as SS and Police Leader with immediate effect (1942).

Here things were relatively peaceful. The police led a quiet existence, from which I gave them a rude awakening. I had the Commander of the police relieved for incompetence. I brought the leader of a Ukrainian battalion before a court-martial for profiteering from the rations of the men he commanded. I told my subordinates that we could not win the war if everyone did not do his duty to the utmost in his post.

Nikolayev in its beautiful setting, reminded me of Palestine. From the building we were stationed in, you could look over a garden onto a huge landing stage. Beyond that you looked over the bay where the River Bug flows into the Black Sea. The tropical heat tempted you to go swimming. There were rowing and sailing boats you could use. One might even forget that we were fighting a war.

In the shipyard what looked like a Russian warship under construction stood on the stocks. It was supposed to be the biggest battleship in the world, but now it was to be scrapped. It was not worth completing in view of the costs.

A lot of German air force units were stationed at Nikolayev airfield. I met a lot of old acquaintances there and spent some happy hours in their company. I also got to know the most successful pilot in the German air force, then Captain [Hans-Ulrich] Rudel. He was a simple, modest man who neither smoked nor drank and just got on with his dive bomber flying. No pilot in the world came near the successes scored by this excellent officer, who had destroyed hundreds of [enemy] tanks. Rudel lent me one of his planes for a flight to Dniepropetrovsk [the site of a huge dam]. On the return flight we were taxiing along the runway when an unscheduled Romanian two-engine plane came roaring at us. Just behind us it lifted off the ground. We realized that it was too late and threw ourselves on the floor of our plane. We felt a violent shock, glass shattered, and we heard the noise of the roaring propeller in the distance. We picked ourselves up and looked at the mess. The Romanian's landing gear had hit the glass canopy of my rear seat and smashed the propeller. Bad luck – but lucky too! It could have ended worse.

Meanwhile the senior SS leaders were given a new and unusual task – to build a road in collaboration with the Todt organisation. The supply route the army needed was to run from Lemberg [L'viv] via Tarnopol, Proskurov and Uman to Dnepropetrovsk. Old roads would have to be included in this. Nobody had the confidence to tackle the monstrous difficulties involved in its construction. Then Himmler stepped in, got the full powers necessary, divided the whole distance into separate building sections and put the SS leaders in charge of them. Now construction firms were brought in from Germany and engineers were hired. No question of difficulties, they must be overcome. The district commissioners were made responsible for collecting carts, horses and materials. Stone often had to be brought from over 100 kilometres away in constant movement back and forth. Thousands of workers toiled day and night, but the road was completed. I was not involved in this work myself, but I was able to convince myself of its usefulness.

All SS and Police leaders were ordered to attend a conference at the Führer's HQ in Berdichev (Berdychiv), which lay scattered and well camouflaged in the forest. It was a series of small thatched buildings, modelled on the local peasants' cottages but the furnishing inside was splendid. Himmler's and Ribbentrop's staffs lived next to each other. At the same time a number of SS replacement battalions were accommodated there.

Prützmann[50] discussed with us what was to be done in the immediate future. Himmler only made short appearances. In the evenings we were shown Russian films. One story was especially interesting – it was set at the bottom of the sea: two states, living under the sea, were in a feud. One was capitalist (the prince looked like King George[51]), the other socialist. The capitalists overran the socialists but the battle came to a standstill: then little lights went on behind the capitalist fighters and burst into bright flames. It was the partisans: then horns of plenty on the socialist side spewed out tanks, guns and soldiers. The socialists pushed forward and threw the capitalists to the ground. End, full stop – kitsch: but it was a serious warning for us. The film had been made before the war. How serious the partisan threat was we would discover in a very personal way. On the way back, I passed my grandfather's estate near Berdichev: the house was almost totally burned out, the sugar factory was working again.

My neighbour in the Crimea at Simferopol was 'Bubi' von Alvensleben (this one metre ninety-two [6' 4"] giant was never called anything else by his friends). He was also one of the famous road-builders. As a former aide to Himmler, he was known for his conscientious and skillful conduct. King Michael of Romania himself recognized this and gave Bubi a huge decoration. I enjoyed two days of his hospitality, had various discussions, and got to know the unusual beauty of the Crimea.

Alvensleben had a passion for hunting: he went in a plane and shot birds like albatrosses from it. His hunting bug came within a hairsbreadth of destroying him. One day he arranged with some comrades from the Customs to fly out over the Black Sea to shoot some kind of rare bird (if it even existed). Because of bad weather he didn't cross the mountains of Yalta.

The Customs men flew out to sea on their own … and were most politely invited by a Russian submarine to come aboard. The Russian Intelligence HQ had done a good job.

My friend Jürgen Rieske, Permanent Secretary at the Ministry of Food, asked me in a long letter to appear as a witness in a trial before a military court in Bucharest. Reserve Captain Dr Schmidt-Manski was to be sentenced to six months in prison for insulting the highest leaders of the [Nazi] Party. Rieske had appealed in the highest places, to Field-Marshal Keitel, and asked me to take his place as a witness, as he was not free to attend. I knew Schmidt-Manski well from Münster – he had been in China for years as a representative for IG Farben, a gifted chemist and businessman. Even now he didn't mince his words – but he was right in his criticism. I liked him for his straightforward, open personality and we got on well.

A Romanian plane took me to Odessa, where I received splendid hospitality from the Romanian city commandant. I went on to Bucharest by train, passing the big oil rigs at Ploeşti. Bucharest had grown a lot since my first visit in 1918, and had become a fine, modern city. The life and activity cheered me up like a different world; peace seemed to have come here. Car after car rolled along the main streets. The shops were full of fine food that we hadn't seen for years. I drank in the atmosphere with longing – but I <u>did</u> have a job to do. I was solemnly greeted at the trial, then the charge was read out, Schmidt-Manski was alleged to have said in front of some citizens of German origin that Goebbels and Ley did not conform in their appearance to the guidelines that the Party had established in its racial theories.

Because of this insult to Party leaders of the highest merit, they requested a sentence of six months imprisonment for Schmidt-Manski. The counsel for the defence was, unfortunately, under the influence of a good deal of alcohol – so much so that I had to take the liberty of asking a few questions. It then came out that the counsel for the prosecution, a lady of German ancestry, had not turned up for this appointment, and that the present court consisted only of non-members of the Party. I emphasized the absolute necessity, in such special cases, of bringing in experts in Party affairs. In reply to the court's question how I as an expert, regarded the remarks made by Captain Schmidt-Manski, I replied, 'There can be no question of insult, as his remarks are nothing but the truth. A criticism made in a confidential situation is not a matter for legal proceedings'. The Captain was acquitted.

Returning to Nikolayev I found an order to report immediately to Obergruppenführer Prützmann at Dnepropetrovsk, to take over the post of SS and Police Leader there. Pack quickly, driver and batman ready to go. Off we went in the car, into the huge distances of the Ukrainian countryside. The hard clay soil was flat as a pancake. Now we could do seventy kph, and left an enormous cloud of dust behind. God help us if it starts to rain – we'd be sure to get stuck – how often had that happened on our trips across the Ukraine! Then you'd put up the hood and stay sitting, while somebody had to go hiking to fetch a horse. 'When will you be back?' It could take twenty-four hours. But this time we were lucky and soon arrived in Dnepropetrovsk.

Obergruppenführer Prützmann received me on his private train. He was as pleasant and smart as ever. My job would be to keep order in this large region. It seemed that the 'behind the front' atmosphere had crept in here, even in the SS and the Police. Prützmann told me more of his worries – Partisan activity was growing to dangerous levels. There had been a real battle at Obrisk, near Kiev, in which crack Russian troops, landed by parachute, had taken part. They were well armed too. I advised Prützmann to come to a standing agreement with the army for a unified command of all our forces in the rear area. It would be a good thing to secure an order from the Führer to this effect. Prützmann agreed, and promised I would soon be employed in fighting the partisans.

The new district was soon brought to order. I had the commander of the civil police up before a court-martial. His most distinguished action had been getting Russian parachutes collected and sending the silk home. The rest of the staff were thoroughly revised, the female helpers accommodated separately, then I was ready to go on an inspection tour of every single post.

We made a brief stop at Zaporozhye. The dam with its huge electric power station serving half of Ukraine had been destroyed by the Russians, but had now been rebuilt by the Todt organisation. We gaped at the sheer size of this construction. That evening we were at the German settlement south of Zaporozhye. German-ness had survived here intact despite years of difficulty. For decades they had been forbidden to speak German, and now we were listening to German songs – about a hundred boys and girls were serenading us. I inspected a cavalry regiment that was in the process of training – fine strapping lads who were used to Russian conditions. I was able to make good use of them later against the partisans.

We drove along the coast of the Sea of Azov. The heat was oppressive. Clothes off, jump in! Although the sea is very shallow, the waves were surprisingly big, but the sea temperature was like a warm shower.

At Berdyansk, a spying organization was being built up: night flights were made into Russian territory, agents were landed and picked up again. It was also actively producing propaganda and supplied Russian troops with suitable reading-matter.

Back in Dnepropetrovsk I allowed myself a bit more rest. My heart needed it. I was given glucose injections by the doctors at the SS hospital and also visited wounded comrades, took note of their requests and took the trouble to get them fulfilled. From the balcony of my house I could look across the Dnieper – on an island opposite there was a flourishing beach life: I got into a canoe, paddled across, jumped into the river and let myself float with the current down to the next island. The beach there was white sand – it was just like the seaside.

In the hall of my house hung a painting, *The Slave Market*. The individual figures were shown in life-size – it was so brilliantly done that you kept having to look at it – even today I can see it in front of me, in all its detail. The Russians have produced some great artists.

Towards the end of the summer of 1943 I received a radio message from Kiev: SS and Police leaders to hand over business to their deputies. Report to the senior SS and Police commander. I flew to Kiev in my Storch [a light plane used for reconnaissance, etc].

Kiev, once a beautiful city with wide streets lined with trees and buildings, had suffered heavily: the city centre, where tall modern buildings and large shops had stood, was a pile of rubble. In their retreat the Russians had planted dynamite in the whole district, dug into cellars where it wouldn't be noticed. Two weeks after the German troops marched in, the whole district blew up. The time fuses had their effect – hundreds of German soldiers, including many Staff personnel were buried under the ruins. In many other buildings like the NKVD [People's Commissariat for Internal Affairs] the detonators were made safe in time and the explosives removed.

The Opera House was re-opened by the Germans, and I went to a performance of the ballet *Coppelia*. It was excellent. In the box where I sat, an attempt was once made to assassinate the Tsar during his visit to the Ukrainian capital.

Various generals of the army were with Prützmann. The situation was discussed – progress must be made against the bandit menace.

There were already orders for bringing rear units under command. The Higher Field Commands were instructed to put all available forces at the disposal of the Commander of Anti-Bandit Operations at the same time, to protect the railways from dynamiters and to smash the enemy.

My GSO 1, a young Staff captain, was at the conference. We were ordered to take over immediately a task force already involved in chasing a partisan group near Proskurov. Their leader, was well-known to us through his daring movements, had broken through from the Russian front line and so far managed to get hundreds of kilometres into our rear by day-long marches, without letting any decisive fighting take place – this in spite of the efforts of the army, police and task forces. He always struck hard at his pursuers – my predecessor had driven his car over mines laid by the bandits and been wounded. It was believed that they had overtaken the armoured vehicles attached to the task forces, so we could be sure that they had pushed forward even further. Hundreds of horses (were found) ridden into the ground, but the gang was already moving further with newly-requisitioned horses.

On the flight to Proskurov in the Storch, I was thinking about the best way to get at this crafty partisan leader. It was said he was making for the Carpathian [mountains] to stir up revolution. Out with the map – which routes could he choose? He must bypass obstacles such as rivers and larger towns, so he could only advance slowly. I started preparing a plan, and before we landed at Proskurov it was ready.

When I took over, the task force consisted only of the three battalions I had available here in Proskurov, with eight armoured cars and supply vehicles. The police battalion I commanded was still in the Lutsk area, along with two more police battalions – and two artillery battalions of Latvians were still being trained. These forces would have to do – the partisans were reckoned to have about 2,000 men, well-armed with automatic weapons.

In Proskurov I got a radio message that one gang had already moved into the Carpathians. It couldn't be 'our friend', as one battalion had still been in contact with him the day before. I got someone to show me this position on the map – it looked as if the route I'd guessed the gang planned to take was the right one. I sent off a battalion at night to block his route, and ordered its CO to mark out a landing strip for the Storch near his objective.

At first light I had the other two battalions move forward, towards the forest where we thought the gang was. I flew over it as low as I could, but couldn't find anything. So I searched the area once more, and then I thought I could see carts in a clearing. We flew over again, and this time I clearly made out the carts, well camouflaged with branches, and men who stayed there motionless as the Storch came nearer. Now I had information – I landed right away near the two battalions advancing into the forest. I told them to leave one company with the armoured cars as a reserve, and to seal off the wood with the bulk of the force. Then it was off to the other battalion. The landing strip was awful, but no problem for my fine pilot. I ordered the CO to attack without delay and destroy the gang to the last man. The CO objected, saying the situation was unclear. I had no time to get into an argument: Prützmann had described this gentleman before as being 'soft as a plum'. I relieved him of command on the spot, handed it over to a brave Captain, and the attack went straight in. The gang had to abandon their carts, so they weren't able to get at their machine guns. They hadn't been expecting an attack from this side, so they turned back, ran into the fire of the two other battalions, and were wiped out. All their equipment fell into our hands, and maybe about 100 men got out of the 'pocket'. Our losses were slight. We sent the armour and the reserve company to pursue the remains of the gang. These men were trapped in a wood near Proskurov and more or less annihilated. Individuals could always go to ground in the larger villages, of course, without us being able to stop them.

Wappenhans Battle Group

I then flew to the Carpathians to see that all was well. A large-scale operation was in progress there, and I was able to see it concluded. Here too the gang was surrounded and wiped out. Now we had a free hand in the South, and after reporting in Kiev I flew to Kremenets on a new mission. Most of my task force had been ordered there: each battalion was now equipped with radios, so orders would come through quickly. Now the units under my command got the name 'Wappenhans Battle Group'.

We were allotted three more Storchs, armed with machine guns, but we could only carry small bombs. We set up the command post in a barracks in Kremenets, and our airfield was a meadow next to it. Here we fought with different methods. After attacking German convoys or blowing up railways, the bandits scattered into the villages and more or less resumed their peaceful occupations. Here the District Commissioners had to step in. Surprise house searches for weapons were carried out, and also every building had to show a list at the entrance with an exact inventory. The Security Police were working for the Intelligence Service, which knew very well how to take advantage of the hatred that existed between Poles and Ukrainians, and collect intelligence from both sides. It was time to gather in the harvest right away, and so we did. After I left the district, the passions of these two deadly enemies ran out of control. During a later flight to Berlin I could see, in the Vladimir Volynsky area, twenty or thirty Polish villages burning – torched by Ukrainians. Neither women nor children were spared in these conflicts – a brutal murder without compunction.

The task force was distributed, by battalions, over our 'harvest' area of Lutsk – Dubno – Zaslav – Proskurov so that the bandits found it difficult to carry out major acts of destruction. If they tried nonetheless to attack with the support of Russian paratroopers, motorised forces were sent there and did not rest until the gang was eliminated. We had enough set-backs on our side too, especially when we had army or SS units sent to us which were still unfamiliar with gang fighting. Fegelein's SS cavalry division, a unit with front-line experience, was amazed when they ran into such stiff resistance in the sector South of Kovel (assigned to them for recovery and supervision of the harvest) that they suffered serious losses, and it gave them quite a headache. There wasn't much you could do with cannon, tanks and cavalry in the trackless terrain – here you needed experienced bandit fighters, infantrymen with sub-machine guns, grenades, machine guns and mortars. Here, the Storch had to do the reconnaissance and attack with machine gun and bombs and here one achieved more success with the reports of the Intelligence Service than with tactical measures only suitable for the front. Yes, it was a different kind of warfare, but a very important part in relation to the overall situation.

This was becoming steadily more unbearable for the fighting front. The main railway line from Lemberg via Dubno, Zdolbunov, Krivin, Shepetovka to Berdichev had been blown up so often that there was no longer any question of maintaining a regular supply route. Field-Marshal von Manstein demanded that order should be restored (in a message) to the Commander-in-Chief of the rear districts. He then went to Prützmann, who gave me and my task force the job of securing the railway. Shepetovka was my HQ, with an airfield for the Storchs. The whole force was distributed along the railway, which was divided into sectors, and these at the same time assigned to a commander responsible for each. Girder bridges and viaducts had already been turned into fortified strongpoints, so our job was to guard the line between them, especially at night. In the daytime we went up with the Storchs and prevented attacks from the air.

In addition I asked, in my position of command of rear units, to have all available units put under me for night patrols on the railway. This always led to resistance from the Field Command centres, which was only overcome after angry orders by radio from Rovno.

The attacks with explosives were significantly reduced, but not completely stopped. I found out that the material used by the gangs mostly came from Russian shells: as the SD told me they came from a big dump which lay, almost unguarded, in the forest near Slavata. So I put some good scouting troops in an ambush, and they managed to surprise the Russians who broke into the dump. We were able to trace the railway bombers' HQ through skillful interrogation, and we cleaned it out: the haul was amazing – apart from a workshop for preparing the explosive devices, we found thousands of shells/grenades, machine guns, submachine-guns, trucks and horses. This operation was carried out almost without loss by a Latvian[52] battalion which we'd brought in to fight the partisans. They crept through the forest and swamps like cats and didn't rest till they had achieved success. The bombings were as good as finished, and the Army could guard the railway with locally-based units.

In October 1943 I took my battle group on a new mission, to Lutsk. In the forests round Sokol and Kolki on the [river] Styr something was brewing which might seriously threaten the retreating front. In the Pripet Marshes, where there were no motor roads or other transport facilities, the partisans had built up gangs, with the arrival of Russian paratroops, who apart from their usual weapons (rifles, machine guns etc.), boasted mortars and anti-tank guns. Apart from blowing up railways, they were ready to attack smaller communities occupied by our troops. We would have to put a stop to their activity. By regular air reconnaissance and with the help of our efficient Intelligence Service we could always find the HQ of the main gang – but the enemy was also aware of our own movements, and the main group didn't let itself be lured into a trap. They got away. It was only by spreading disinformation about our supposed withdrawal that we were able to locate them. It came to a fierce battle, in which the Storchs made a great contribution. We shot up their supply train of horse-drawn carts which carried their ammunition and food. Without ammunition, the gang could not carry on. We were already in a difficult situation because they greatly outnumbered us, and they also fought like the best Russian guards units. Even when shot in the stomach, the wounded kept firing – but now it was no good: they were overrun and lost their precious material. But we had noticeable casualties too, including one of our best batalion commanders.

At the beginning of 1944 I was asked to undertake a large-scale cleaning-up operation around Vinnitsa [Vinnytsia], and I asked for a situation report. In the rear of Colonel-General[53] Hube's army gangs of partisans had formed in a wide wooded area. With the support of the Russian air force they had set up a training camp for the local population, where they were calmly and cheerfully drilling. Bakery and butchery units had been set up. They were terrorizing the rear areas.

I asked the local Field Command centre for a report on the forces available to fight them – they seemed more than enough, about 2,000 men. We could also count on an artillery repair unit with a well-trained crew. From my own forces, I sent up one of my motorized battalions, and I also ordered an SS cavalry regiment to join the line-up. They were locals of German descent. When I reached the 'bandit country' of Slomerinka, I flew over the camps with my GSO 1. We were fired at by AA guns, a sign that this was a force that had to be taken seriously.

I visited General Hube[54] at his HQ, and he agreed with me that the large-scale training of partisans in his rear showed that he could expect heavy attacks on his front. Strong concentrations of partisans always meant that the Russians were going to attack.

I arranged with the commander of a bomber squadron in Vinnitsa that on the day of our own attack he would lend us one flight to bomb the camps, after his planes returned from raiding the enemy front. When I had assembled and inspected my new battle group, I attacked. My own police battalion was repelled with losses: the SS cavalry pushed forward too far in their enthusiasm, so I couldn't use them as a reserve, as I'd planned. So I had them swing to one side and take the enemy positions in the flank. I flew over the enemy camps in the Storch, and guided the bombers to their targets with red tracer bullets. They dropped heavy fragmentation bombs from no great height and caused serious damage – the camp was wiped out.

On returning to base I found a new order, to report to Obergruppenführer Prützmann in Rovno, and move all the forces of my battle group there. My GSO 1 transmitted the order by radio, then it was off to Rovno in the Storch. And now I began to work round the clock. With this strain, nerves were often shredded, but the work got done. On my staff the former Ambassador to Argentina, Baron von Theermann was serving, and he did some very useful work. He told me about the partisan cavalry raid in which they managed to kidnap a general from the Army HQ without being discovered.

I was ordered to fly immediately to Minsk, to try to obtain police units for our use from there. The Senior SS and Police Commander (North), a former officer who had carried out some very difficult operations with success, despite losing a leg, explained the situation there. The Commissioner-General, Kube, had been murdered by partisans: in the northernmost sector, all the Corps and Divisional staffs behind the front were raided, and some generals were even taken to Russia by plane – a daring exploit, troublesome and shameful for us. In this way, any controlled command of the forces when the Russians attacked could not be considered. We had to retreat. The release of any forces to our sector would not be possible in this situation. Obergruppenführer von dem Bach-Zelewski, who had just been appointed head of all anti-partisan operations, confirmed the release of troops to me, but also assured me that a strong armoured formation under his personal command would shortly thrust towards us from Brest-Litovsk.

A Tragic Return to Berlin

Things got better in Rovno. Lost territory was recovered. The gap [in the front] was closed. I was ordered to move the whole main sector to Lutsk, and from there to Lublin. In Lutsk I got orders to fly to Berlin, to try to arrange for the transport of material to be speeded up. At the same time news came that our fourth child, a little daughter aged two, had suddenly died. In Berlin I saw the destruction at home for the first time – our flat in Hanover had been destroyed too. My wife had brought a lot out with the four children and was eventually evacuated to Hahnenklee [near Goslar] with the help of General Bichler, with whom we were friends. We buried our little ray of sunshine, and then I went back to work.

The march from Lutsk to Lublin was like a retreat. A Hungarian division blocked the road – they didn't want to fight at the front. In Lublin I took up my duties. One of my functions was signing the documents for the award of the Iron Cross. I was glad to be able to thank my old fighting comrades, including my GSO 1, whom I was even able to bring the Iron Cross First Class at the front, where he was now commanding a battalion.

In Lemberg [L'viv], that beautiful city, I had to requisition cars and trucks for the front, and the civilian administration had to believe me. They often thought they were living in perfect peace, and had no idea how serious the situation was.

I went to see Prützmann. The troops had pulled back further, and the atmosphere was depressing. The partisans were operating with such skill that the rear was never safe. I was ordered to go on leave to recover – Himmler had a new posting for me. The position of Senior SS and Police Leader would be abolished. Something here didn't fit, and

I later realized I'd be left out in the cold. In the tensions between the Armed Forces and the SS people didn't trust me not to take sides. I said goodbye to my driver and batman in Breslau – on the way there we'd been seriously shot at by partisans once again. The old Mercedes had a few holes in it. Now I went on by train. In Hahnenklee I had a happy reunion with my family and a week's rest – my teeth needed repairing, so the SS doctor in Goslar sent me to Dachau, where there was a well-run hospital and I had a good time with wounded comrades. In two days I had 14 teeth taken out – I suppose it had to be done. There was little sign of the notorious concentration camp, although we were inside its perimeter. It was only when I went for a walk that squads of prisoners went past 'Caps off!' ordered the SS guard in charge.

I had a feeling of depression and in future looked away if a column came in sight, or turned off the path. How was I supposed to greet them – with a 'Heil Hitler'?! They'd have laughed in their minds. The camp commander, whom I happened to meet, couldn't understand my opinion.

A Sister Pia came, in a car. What her job was, nobody knew. The doctors kept out of her way, the nurses ran off. She was wearing the Blood Order[55] and ordered people about like a sergeant. She ordered some bedroom furnishings from the prisoners' carpentry shop, and I asked her if that was really in the spirit of our Führer. She avoided me after that.

The famous heart specialist Dr Fahrenkamp examined me and sent me up to Nauheim. After the cure I was supposed to report to Himmler.

The Führer's Headquarters were between Salzburg and Berchtesgaden. Obergruppenführer Wolff and his wife welcomed me at the Habsburg Inn in Salzburg, and Ambassador Hassel was there too. Wolff was always a lively host and his wife was pleasant too. But I never managed to feel really at ease. I asked Wolff to get Himmler to give me a proper job.

Around Himmler there was always a hive of activity. I was invited to lunch but never got to a serious talk. In the afternoon he asked me to come with him to Berchtesgaden to meet the Führer – we could talk on the way. Himmler was at the wheel of a small Mercedes. I sat beside him and in the back were two aides. Behind came an unoccupied car for me. Himmler praised my service record. I would get back my grandfather's estate near Berdichev [in the Ukraine] – but anyway, I must get my health back first. If Dr Fahrenkamp would be kind enough to send him a certificate of health, he would look at the future. He didn't need me urgently, only in good health. I ought to brush up my English, we are forming a British Legion [SS] at this moment and I want you to take charge of that when you are fit again.

On my way back, I searched for a way out of these fantastic plans: the Russians had been back on my grandfather's estate for ages – and weren't we at war with the British? I thought. Should we be recruiting PoWs for that? Maybe all this gossip about the new, war-winning weapons was right. I cheered up again, as the optimism infected me.

In Salzburg I phoned Dr Fahrenkamp at once: he was head of a nearby research institute. He welcomed me into his family circle like an old friend, and showed me the successful results of his work. Digitalis [foxglove extract used for heart conditions] not only regulated the heart, but also improved the growth of plants and even showed effects in conserving food. Fahrenkamp had proved this in practical experiments. Chemists would discover why plants, vegetables and cereals grew faster and better after treatment with Digitalis, and how it came about that bread, for instance, stayed fresh for weeks after the same treatment (and was already being supplied to U-boat crews), and why meat and butter did not go off. Fahrenkamp showed me the facts: two professors from the University of Strasbourg were visiting him, and wanted to find the chemical answer to this puzzle.

Editor: Himmler himself confirms Wappenhans' account. In his carefully maintained card index system and the elaborate set of records he kept on his senior SS officers he wrote, as Peter Longerich records in his account *Heinrich Himmler: A Life*: "The Reichsführer showed himself concerned about the health of the SS. He prescribed medical examinations, read the diagnosis, and gave his men tips on nutrition and lifestyle … The constant pressure and ceaseless 'deployment' led to numerous members of the SS leader corps, although only in their late thirties or early forties, suffering considerable physical wear and tear, and above all psychological and psychosomatic problems, during the war years. In the medical reports the same keywords recur: fatigue, exhaustion, problems with 'nerves', depressive conditions. For example, the report on GruppenFührer Waldemar Wappenhans from April 1944 read:'He seems agitated and exhausted. Purely physically his heart and circulation are no worse than at the last examination. […] But I was unhappy about his state as a whole. I think that from a medical point of view he urgently needs some mental rest to regain his equilibrium"'.

My medical report required five weeks' recuperation. Obergruppenführer Wolff invited me to Merano[56], and my wife came with me. In that wonderful region, we recovered our energy. Life in the hotel was like peacetime. Many Japanese were staying there, as well as the wives of Prützmann and Heydrich (who had died in an assassination in Prague). Todt's successor Speer also came there for a 'refurbishing' by Professor Gebhardt.

We travelled back to Hahnenklee, experiencing a raid from the enemy's air force in Munich. In Hahnenklee I felt like an outcast from society – life had lost its meaning. For hours I walked around in the woods of the Harz [mountains]. My lame leg wasn't coping any longer and at Christmas 1944 I sustained a fracture. The SS doctor in Goslar sent me to Hohenlychen, the well-known sports college that had been converted into an SS hospital. Professor Gebhardt was to operate on me, and he performed the small procedure. In a week I was feeling better.

The Russians were advancing on Berlin. The commander of [Hitler's] Life Guard Regiment, SS Brigade-leader Wisch lay seriously wounded in the hospital – we both thought the situation was hopeless. Himmler came several times for talks with Gebhardt – nobody took any notice of us. Then my patience snapped, and I went to Berlin and demanded an explanation at the Personnel Office. Telephones buzzed. Himmler transferred me to the Western Front. I was to take over a Battle Group in Field-Marshal Model's sector, reporting to the Senior SS and Police Commander in Kettwig, near Essen.

The Bridge at Remagen

Travelling by train in January 1945 was a real adventure; the railways weren't running properly any more. We were constantly attacked by fighter-bombers, had to walk for some stretches, and climb into the nearest goods wagon. Finally I reached my destination. The [Ruhr] industrial region was a mess, Essen just a sea of rubble. We were briefed on the situation in Kettwig.

The Rhine must be held, that is, until the most recent weapons were operational. There was talk of jet fighters, U-boats with snorkels and the atomic bomb. One of Model's orders of the day also gave information about the new weapons. Then the news came that the Americans had pushed across the Rhine on the un-demolished bridge at Remagen, and formed a bridgehead [see Chapter 24 Note 3]. Aircraft were sent in to destroy the bridge afterwards, but they failed. Bradley advanced with his army, hundreds of kilometres into our rear, and in time linked up with the British who had pushed across the Rhine at Wesel. Model's army was now totally encircled.

My battle group was scattered about the area – the battalions were sent in like plugs on different fronts. The pocket became smaller and smaller.

I thought 'This is the end'. My whole soldier's life passed before my mind's eye – the hard years as a youth in the Cadet Corps, my time as an infantry officer in 1914-15, fighting as a flying officer in the East, West and Palestine, my efforts against the Polish invasion of Silesia, the ups and downs of my first marriage and its consequences, my time as an SS officer, my gratitude for the happiness my present wife gave me, the radiant faces of my children, I couldn't forget all this. And was this the end of everything? All right – I'd led a soldier's life, so I wanted to end it like a soldier.

With one battalion, we drove the Americans back from a position they had broken through. We dug in, and with two volunteers and an aide I fired away in the dark with RPGs[57]: there was an American artillery convoy coming up to a crossroads. We crept up and fired, and set fire to three heavy self-propelled guns [tanks]. Now the end must be coming – we were behind the enemy's line, being shot at from all sides like rabbits. But nothing – absolutely nothing – happened to us. We got back to our fighting position, and I got a radio message 'Report to Berlin' to let myself be overrun and get through in civilian clothes.

Were the new, war-winning weapons still going to have an effect, and did they need me there? I felt new hope run through me. I quickly found civilian clothes, had my old alias 'Hans Seemann' written on my identity card and surfaced, as a refugee, at a farmhouse. The farmer didn't quite believe me – I might be Regional Leader Florian, I looked like him. 'Sure', I said 'and my whole staff's coming after me!' He laughed, but he still didn't believe me. In this area, far from main roads, thirty km NE of Cologne, no Americans came past. I disappeared, walking off the road, suitcase in hand, heading east. At a farmhouse I exchanged my suitcase for a rucksack. I spent the nights in the open: the March sun burned by day, but nights were really chilly. In the Ebbe Hills I met some soldiers in civilian clothes who were going the same way as me – home, not to captivity. We must not go out onto the roads, every man would be checked and carted off to prison camps without fail. Truck after truck, chock full of German soldiers raced below us at dangerous speed. For my comrades, walking off the road through woods and streams was too hard – they'd hardly reached the main road when they were caught. I was left on my own, and it was just as well.

I ran out of food, and my belly was rumbling. In the dark I made for a house. The farmer was afraid to put us up – the Yanks were making strict checks. I greedily wolfed down the food, then onwards. My wounded foot burnt like tinder, and was badly swollen. I cooled it in a stream and lay down in a meadow. I wanted to sleep, but with no blanket it was too cold. My thin overcoat didn't keep me warm. So, onwards again. I crept into a shed with hay in it and sank into a dreamless sleep. Early in the morning [I heard] voices and barking, crept out of the hay, and got lucky. It was a smallholder, who asked me in for breakfast, and gave me bread and sausage for the journey.

I went on through the Sauerland[58], past Meschede and Warburg: on the 8th day of my march, I saw Hof-Geismar lying below – I couldn't manage the long detour over the hills, in my condition, so I walked along the road. Soon a group of soldiers came around me – but they knew the district, and took me to a camp where refugees were put up. These were anti-communist Bulgarians, who gave us a friendly welcome. We lit fires in the huts, dried our clothes and boots, which were soaked through from the snowdrifts which had recently fallen, and enjoyed the good pea soup. We marched on, and ran into a long drawn-out check by the Yanks. We were taken to the Mayor: I claimed to live in the next village. I blinked at the Mayor, and he nodded. I was free to go.

Whether it was the cigarettes I gave him, or whether I'd had a decent German in front of me I don't know. In any case, I was lucky. I could stagger on, but now down off the road. A one-in-100,000 map and compass showed me the way more or less. Now every evening I found shelter in the straw in barns, my main nourishment was milk, there was oodles of it. The dairies were not yet back in full production.

The [river] Weser came in sight: here I had to get across. The bridges were strictly checked, but the ferry at Vaka was working. I watched it for a good while – no sign of the Yanks: so I went across, it worked! I came past a pretty family home: on a fine ceramic sign it said Dr X, veterinarian. A woman was looking out of an open window, and I asked her for something to eat. She found me a piece of bread and a sausage – I'd have a plate of soup too. Then the husband came home, yelled at me and his wife, 'This tramping has to stop – damned Nazi's running around, and bloody officers who've been messing us about all through the war!' Without a word, I put the bread and sausage in his hand and left.

On a farm track I met a fellow-sufferer, who wanted to go west. We exchanged identity cards – his was good. A jeep drove right across a field towards me, so I crouched in a ditch and did my business – the crew of the jeep showed no interest in what I was doing.

In a wood I was stopped by Polish refugees who robbed me of everything – the rucksack was lighter, and without an overcoat I could move further – then it started to snow again. My clothes were soaked and the slush squelched in my boots. Again I was lucky: a farmer's wife took me in – I got a real bed to sleep in, in her son's room – she didn't know what had become of him. Her husband had been taken prisoner as a Volkssturm [Home Guard]. I tried to comfort her, as far as I could. I was able to rest up for two days, then I was on my way again, fresher and stronger.

The Harz were in front of me. The farmer, whose barn I'd stayed the night in, warned me about walking over the mountains. The Yanks were shooting at anyone who moved, and SS units were still supposed to be making trouble thereabouts. But I had to get to Hahnenklee, I wanted at least to see my family before I went on to Berlin. 'You'll never get into Hahnenklee', the farmer said 'the Yanks have requisitioned every house. Some top brass are billeted there.' I walked on all the same – the snowdrifts were keeping people indoors – and up diagonally through the forest. I knew the Harz well from many walking trips. At the top of the hills you could only walk slowly through the snow.

A jeep far below me buzzed into first gear along a forest road. I got behind a tree, so the submachine gun fire wouldn't hit me. The Yanks didn't feel like coming up and congratulating me in person.

I left Clausthal-Zellerfeld on my right – now I knew every tree and bush. I had to cross the main road once, and so came past a house. I knew that the family of a young comrade had been evacuated there. I walked in and asked them for food 'I'll pay for it' I said. This was indignantly refused, so I got some soup. The wife didn't ask many questions; she didn't know me, and was deeply worried for her husband. She made sure that I could leave the house unobserved.

I had to make one more big angle, then through the branches I could see [the village of] Bischofswiesen. Trucks with Americans were driving through on the highway. A couple of bounds and I disappeared into the thick fir plantation. To reach the boarding-house where my family lived, I'd have to circle round the whole town. I couldn't use the roads, and would have to avoid the Yanks' sentries. Now and again I heard a shot – what for? At whom? No idea. Maybe the Yanks were firing from anxiety, to calm their nerves. I went up and down, over fences and through gardens. Finally I saw the house standing there, but – how could I get in? It wasn't dark yet. If the fat lady who owned the boarding house saw me, it was all over – I shouldn't even let the children notice anything – their happiness would too easily give me away, and they shouldn't have that weight on their shoulders.

Now and then people came past: in my hiding-place, behind the hedge in the snow, I was safe. Finally I saw my wife with another lady, carrying shopping bags. Behind them was my oldest daughter. Damn it! I mustn't move. In the cold, wet snow the chill was creeping further up my body. Then chance came to help me – I was lucky again. My wife came out of the door again, she was wiping her feet. I gave 'our' quiet whistle, she hesitated, leaned on the railing, righted herself and walked slowly towards me. I called to her 'I'll be here again after dark'. She understood: I could see her sob, then pull herself together and quietly vanish into the house. I ducked back into the woods, and walked till I was standing in my old hiding place. The light went out – now there was only a light in the neighbour's room. Out of the house came Krysia, our Polish maid, whom I'd once sent to my family from Brest-Litovsk, I knew she was loyal and wouldn't give me away. I crept up the stairs behind her. I was 'home'.

I stayed in bed there for two days. The danger was serious. The American Secret Service was looking for me, and had already searched the house twice. They had gone through all the cupboards and suitcases, and taken away photos of me. But their officials behaved properly – only among our dear Germans were there beasts who let their hatred of all that was called Nazi run wild, even against women and children. Our landlady was one of these so I couldn't move anywhere.

My wife wanted to go back to Hanover anyway, to her parents who had found refuge in our old flat when their house was bombed out. This environment was unbearable, and she couldn't get by here financially either.

As a destination, Berlin was pointless now for me. The Russians had marched in, Hitler was dead: what did life have in store for me now? How could I help my family? We calculated that our savings could last a year or two, if devaluation did not increase. The Property Control allowed my wife a regular withdrawal from the bank.

Meanwhile I would try to find myself a job which would enable me to make my family secure. The rest I must leave to fate. I agreed with my wife that I would look for her in Hanover in a month or two – or I'd leave news with her parents. I would have to appear to be a refugee and would go straight to Braunschweig. From there I would look further away.

My clothes were dry, my boots waxed, now I also had a coat and even spare underclothes and some provisions which my wife gave me from her own meagre stores. Very early in the morning I crept out of the house, and along the well-known route into the forest.

Two shots rang out nearby, the unpleasant signs of self-reassurance. Later my wife told me how she'd listened out from an open window, and how frightened she was to hear the bangs. Those shot had nothing to do with me. I walked down the mountains, took my old path off the road, spent only one night staying with simple working people, and on the second evening came into Braunschweig. I tiptoed the final stretch along the railway tracks. (Rail traffic had not yet begun again). In Braunschweig I looked for an old air force comrade. His house was burnt out and he was living alone in the cellar, trying to rebuild his life from there. I could sleep on the bare boards but my comrade advised me to find a firm floorboard under my feet first. I had to get some sort of work, so that I could register with the police.

During our conversation in walked a Police Auxiliary with a white armband. He yelled at me from the start – was I trying to hide here, was I one of those Nazi bastards, or a militarist? Then his nerve seemed to go. I yelled back – was he one of those bastards who wanted to hand over frontline soldiers to the Yanks on a plate and get them sent away to a PoW camp? He said no, suddenly became friendly and promised to help me find work. He gave me a note to a foreman at the Lower Saxony Motorworks in Waggum, where I took off on my first flight against England.

Next day I reported there – the foreman wasn't available, but his deputy advised me to find a job in the country right away – then I would at least have enough to eat. Here at the factory everyone was still going hungry.

In the evening I arrived at a village after a twenty-kilometre walk. I talked to the head of the local Farmers' Association. He sent me straight to a farm across the road. There they were delighted to meet me, especially the daughter of the house, strong as a bear, who managed the farm. I got a room to myself, and ate all I could of country delicacies we hadn't seen for a long time.

Just before 05.00 hours I was un-gently pulled from the feathers. I had to pump water and then muck out the cowshed. I took off my shoes – had to save a good pair, so I still had to go barefoot. Of course, I was always being told off – the tough daughter helped out. After breakfast we went to the field. There we lifted turnips with a machine – I drove the horses. Early potatoes were piled up, fertilizers were spread, until your hands burned from the acid material. Wood was cut in the yard, and cleaning was always my job. It went on from early morning to late in the evening. The physical strain didn't do much for my weakened body. The first days I was still well treated by the Valkyrie[59], but when she saw that I didn't respond to her unsubtle messages, she became brutal. She began to harass me, but this certainly changed again.

In the evening an American truck drove up. Soldiers with automatic weapons jumped out. We were all herded together into a hut, and had to get out the schnapps. I answered them in English, that we couldn't let them have any unless they had brought a bottle for us. This led to a fairly long discussion. They searched the place from top to bottom, but left us in place – I even got a pack of cigarettes, which I honourably shared out. The daughter of the house was polite to me again.

I went to see the commanding officer, showed him my papers and police registration in this village and asked for a certificate, allowing me to travel to Hanover in the British [occupation] zone. I had the prospect of a job there. The commandant gave me the relevant document after a doctor had given me a certificate declaring me unfit for agricultural work.

So I could travel to Hanover without any trouble. I had a police registration and deregistration paper in my hands, and the American document as well. But the trains were still not running. I had to walk to the autobahn, catch a coal truck there and in this unusual way for me, arrived quickly in Hanover. I sat on a bench in the Eilenriede [?park] and thought about how I could get into our large block of rented flats unobserved. A pretty young girl was sitting beside me: she asked if there was anything she could do for me. I took a chance and explained my situation. She went to the flat and returned with my father-in-law. My family was still in Hahnenklee – I wrote down the phone number and promised to ring soon. The girl took me to some relatives for a few days. Yes, there were still unselfish people who were ready to help in the homeland.

Property Control Board

The Labour Exchange couldn't find me a job. There was no work for a businessman – but without a job there was no support money, so I was forced to go back to farm work as a substitute for the Poles, who still lived on the farms but didn't want to work.

I continued with this work for five months. In the meantime I had learned from a comrade how you can get by in spite of the long hours, by conserving your strength. I kept my eye on my objective, and regularly talked to the local council office, looking for a way out. An attempt to get into the cigarette industry failed, and I then had no success at the Military Government. Then I had some luck again. Chance came to my rescue. One Friday in September when I presented myself at the Regional Council office. I overheard an angry discussion. It seemed that the Military Government had set a deadline on Thursday morning for the appointment of a specialist in Property Control. How, in such a short time, could they find a man with 1) a command of the English language, 2) a school leaving certificate and 3) legal and business knowledge, with special reference to Martial Law (article) 52? The Council had missed the first deadline, and the second, set for next Thursday, could not be disregarded. I appeared like a 'God from the machine'. When I told them I met all these requirements: I was appointed with immediate effect, they gave me a car to collect my things, found me a room to live in, and by Thursday morning I was already working on the material. My first report to the Military Government took place with the British commandant of the Hanover Rural District. My poor knowledge of English didn't become obvious after my explanation that my grandmother had been English avoided any further questions.

Now my Property Control superior from Hameln showed up, with his secretary. He was still a Captain in September 1945, a bank manager in civilian life, a small active man, intelligent, decisive and generous. We got on well from the start. He completely agreed with the plans I showed him for the seizure of wealth to be taken under the Property Control [regulations] as per Martial Law article 52. He tactfully avoided mentioning my weak knowledge of English.

The provisional seat of the Regional Council was a large school in Ronnenberg. As a specialist for the Military Government, I sat in a hall-like room with seven or eight other employees. There was incessant coming and going of visitors, typewriters clattered and you couldn't hear yourself speak. Also the pay, paid in arrears, was so meagre that I could hardly live on it myself. Something had to change. I suggested to my boss [I should have] an office of my own, an English-speaking secretary hired, and a car provided for me to carry out my duties. This was approved, and very soon I moved into my own office. I bought the car out of my own pocket – with money lent by friends. My position at the Regional Council was abolished and I now became the Military Government's expert for the whole Hanover District. I rented a large office, hired a second expert and a second secretary.

At first I worked myself as administrative trustee for the wealth to be checked: later I appointed four trustees to carry out this work, and provided them with cars. My own financial situation was now healthy enough for me to be able to help my family.

If I have to account today for my actions and decisions, I am completely convinced that fate / chance which shows us our path, often leads us to heaven, but often drives us to ruin.

I have often looked death in the face and even sought it once, during the suicidal sortie on the Western Front. But it was God's will that I should live to fill other tasks.

If I had been taken prisoner in 1945 by the Communists or the Poles I would have been hanged – as have many other comrades – without reasonable justice. Today [1949], when the senseless hatred for Nazism and the military is apparently draining away – when people are beginning to think objectively again, I no longer need to fear the light of day.

Now I shall be free among my beloved family and ready to work and live with a happy heart and cheerfully get on with my work!

Waldemar Wappenhans aka Hans Seemann

Editor: The Wappenhans Confession was taken and transcribed by Wolfe Frank following his meetings with/interrogations of Wappenhans between August and October 1949. Frank then discussed the contents and the case with the intelligence services of Britain and the USA and negotiated, or perhaps decided (discussed in the following chapters), the final outcome. Having been informed that the authorities had agreed to spare his life and guarantee his long-term freedom the former SS-Major General then added the final three paragraphs of the document before signing it as both Waldemar Wappenhans and Hans Seemann. Two identical copies of the testimony were produced: one was handed in to British Naval Intelligence, who then spent six weeks interrogating Wappenhans; the other was retained by Frank and remained amongst his papers, uninvestigated and un-translated, until it again saw 'the light of day' in 2015.

Notes:

1. 'Mauschel' (the equivalent of the pejorative, anti-Semitic use of 'Yid' in English) is a term in German for a 'poor Jew' with implications of fiddling and cheating, particularly when applied to someone who has a big mouth (physically or metaphorically), speaks loudly and gesticulates with their hands – perceived by some, particularly in Germany in the early 1900s, as being characteristics of some German Jews – for Göring's appearance at the time the epithet was first given to him at Cadet School see Plate 8.

In a paper entitled *Why was the ideology of Zionism associated with chauvinist nationalism and imperialism?* Nuray Bamanie of Faulkner University, using quotations from Theodor Herzl (regarded to be the founding father of modern Zionism) explains the use of the term as follows:
'Herzl like Freud and other assimilated western Jews, resented the uncultured Jew who they called mauschel (English 'yid'): Herzl clearly states in an article in a German newspaper, *Die Welt* in 1897: "We've known him for a long time, and just merely to look at him, let alone approach or, heaven forbid, touch him was enough to make us feel sick. But our disgust, until now, was moderated by pity; we sought extenuating, historical explanations for his being so crooked, sleazy, and shabby a specimen. Moreover, we told ourselves that he was, after all, our fellow tribesman, though we had no cause to be proud of his fellowship … who is this Yid, anyway? A type, my dear friends, a figure that pops up time and again, the dreadful companion of the Jew, and so inseparable from him that they have always been mistaken one for the other. The Jew is a human being like any other, no better and no worse … The Yid, on the other hand, is a hideous distortion of the human character, something unspeakably low and repulsive". It was necessary for early Zionists such as Moses Hess and later Theodor Herzl to overcome European prejudice by splitting the Jew into two distinct personifications. One type of Jew was the enlightened cosmopolitan who carried his Jewishness in the same way an Austrian or a Frenchman bore his national origins. The other, the un-favored Jew is the mauschel, which Herzl suggested that "at some dark moment in our history some inferior human material got into our unfortunate people and blended with it"'.
Mauschelsdorf it seems, as a play on the word Mauterndorf (his home town) was being used by Göring's fellow cadets as a derogatory, mocking nickname to describe one or more aspects of his demeanour, features, appearance or characteristics and, in later life, Wappenhans was not afraid to publicly remind the Reichsmarschall of his epithet (see page 220), in spite of Göring being the second most powerful man in Nazi Germany.
(Until this publishing of the Wappenhans Confession Göring's sobriquet, and how and why he acquired it, may have been lost in the mists of time, but – and these are perhaps questions for criminal psychologists – did the cruel, deliberately offensive use of the word mauschel to contemptuously describe a young, and perhaps impressionable, cadet – especially in view of what Herzl suggests was the general understanding of the term in those days – be a root cause of Göring's anti-Semitism? and did this trigger in him the hatred that later led to him becoming the chief architect of the 'Final Solution to the Jewish Question' – the Holocaust?).

2. One of the most select avenues in Berlin, East of the Brandenburg Gate.

3. A region in the far South-West, bordering France and Switzerland.

4. 'Drummer' is the German slang for teacher.

5. The *Berliner Zeitung* is a German daily newspaper based in Berlin.

6. In a two-seater aircraft the observer was in command.

7. Gerhart Hauptmann was a German dramatist and novelist.

8. These Berlin stations are less than a mile from each other!

9. The Princes' Islands are off the Asian coast of greater Istanbul (Constantinople).

10. Florence Nightingale's Hospital during the Crimean War.

11. Probably the naval airman Richard Bell-Davies, later an admiral.

12. Karl May was a German writer of hugely popular Western novels in late 19th Century.

13. Franz von Papen was Chancellor of Germany in 1932 and Vice-Chancellor under Hitler from 1933-1934. He was one of the defendants at Nuremberg who Wolfe Frank later interrogated and for whom he interpreted (see also Plates 10, 11 & 15).

14. Field Marshal Edmund Henry Hynman Allenby, 1st Viscount Allenby, GCB, GCMG, GCVO was an English soldier and British Imperial Governor. During WWI he led the British Empire's Egyptian Expeditionary Force in the conquest of Palestine.

15. The Order of the House of Hohenzollern was a dynastic order of knighthood awarded to military commissioned officers and civilians of comparable status (see also Plate 2).

16. Ahmed Djemal Pasha was an Ottoman military leader and one third of the military triumvirate known as the Three Pashas (also called the Three Dictators) that ruled the Ottoman Empire during WWI. He was also the Mayor of Constantinople (Istanbul).

17. A narrow gauge railway that ran from Damascus to Medina.

18. Colonel T. E. Lawrence (of Arabia) was a British archaeologist, military officer, diplomat and writer. He was renowned for his campaigns against the Ottoman Empire during WWI.

19. Anton Ludwig August von Mackensen was a German field marshal. He commanded with extreme success during the First World War and became one of the German Empire's most prominent and competent military leaders. He was Commander in Chief of the Eastern Front 1915-1918.

20. Romania had attacked Austria in 1916 and been quickly defeated by Germany.

21. The Kiel revolution started with widespread mutinies in the Navy. Eventually the Keiser's government collapsed.

22. The Workers' and Soldiers' Councils were almost entirely made up of SDP and USPD members. Their program was democracy, pacifism and anti-militarism. Apart from the dynastic families, they deprived only the military commands of their power and privilege.

23. Max Hölz was a German Communist, most known for his role as a 'Communist Bandit' in the Vogtland region.

24. Upper-class suburb of Berlin.

25. The Treaty (or Diktat) of Versailles ended the state of war between Germany and the Allied Powers. Signed on 28 June 1919 the treaty required Germany 'To accept the responsibility of Germany and her allies for causing all the loss and damage' during the war. This article (231) later became known as the War Guilt clause. The treaty forced Germany to disarm, make substantial territorial concessions, and pay reparations to certain countries that had formed the Entente powers. Germany had to recognize the independence of, and cede certain territories to, Poland including Pomerelia (Eastern Pomerania) which was transferred to Poland so that the new state could have access to the sea – this became known as the Polish Corridor.

26. Nazi regional leader.

27. The Hohenzollern family, from SW Germany, ruled Prussia for nearly 400 years and were Emperors 1871-1918. The Prince probably meant his great-grandfather, Kaiser Wilhelm I; 'Old Fritz' was Prussian King Frederick II 'The Great' (1742-1786) whose victories made Prussia a great European power.

28. Stahlhelm (Steel Helmet) was the war veterans' organization.

29. The Versailles Treaty forbade Germany to have an air force.

30. A wonderfully-preserved medieval city in SW Germany.

31. Essen was a long way from Wappenhans Bavarian district, in the Ruhr.

32. Albert Speer was Minister of Armament & War Production in Nazi Germany – who, during the Nuremberg trial, requested and was granted a private audience with Wolfe Frank.

33. Obergruppenführer Karl Wolff was Chief of Personal Staff Reichsführer (Commander) and SS Liaison Officer to Hitler until sometime in 1943. At the end of World War II, he was the Supreme Commander of all SS forces in Italy and negotiated the surrender of all German forces in Italy, ending the war on that front in late April 1945. At Nuremberg, Wolff was interrogated by Wolfe Frank and allowed to escape prosecution by providing evidence against his fellow Nazis.

34. Wiener Neustadt – an important industrial city SW of Vienna.

35. Hugo Sperrle was a German field marshal of the Luftwaffe during World War II. He was previously commander of the Condor Legion in Spain.

36. The Heinkel 'He 111' was a German aircraft designed by Siegfried and Walter Günter at Heinkel Flugzeugwerke in 1934.

37. A reconnaissance patrol leader selects a zone from which to operate and then selects routes out from and back to the Objective Rally Point (ORP). The routes form a fan shaped pattern and must overlap to ensure that the entire area has been reconnoitered.

38. The Condor Legion had served on Franco's side in the Spanish Civil War 1936-9.

39. The Focke-Wulf Fw 200 *Condor* was a German all-metal four-engined monoplane that saw service with the Luftwaffe as long-range reconnaissance and anti-shipping/maritime patrol bomber aircraft. The Luftwaffe also made extensive use of the Fw 200 as a transport plane.

40. Folk song used by Elvis Presley for the chorus of *Wooden Heart*.

41. Reinhard Heydrich was a high-ranking Nazi official and a main architect of the Holocaust. He was a Senior Group Leader and General of Police as well as chief of the Reich Main Security Office (which included the Gestapo and SD). Many historians regard him as the darkest figure within the Nazi elite and Hitler described him as being 'the man with the iron heart'. He was directly responsible for the 'Einsatzgruppen' – the special task forces that travelled in the wake of the German armies and murdered over two million people, including 1.3 million Jews, by mass shooting and gassing.
Heydrich was critically wounded in Prague on 27 May 1942 and died from his injuries a week later.

42. Robert Ley was the German politician during the Nazi era who headed the German Labour Front from 1933 to 1945. He was interrogated by Wolfe Frank at Nuremberg but committed suicide while awaiting trial for war crimes.

43. The Iron Cross was normally a (higher) combat decoration.

44. Wilhelm Franz Canaris was a German admiral and chief of the Abwehr (the German military intelligence service) from 1935 to 1944. Initially a supporter of Hitler by 1939 he had turned against the Nazis as he felt Germany would lose another major war. He was executed for high treason as the Nazi regime was collapsing.

45. In Western Europe: the 'subhuman' East was considered to be fair game, and systematic looting began after D-day.

46. In German-speaking countries a Major-General commands a brigade.

47. Now Belarus/Ukraine. Much of modern Poland had been Prussian territory since c. 1790. Polish names often crop up in the German army and civil service.

48. Kurt Max Franz Daluege was the chief of the national uniformed Ordnungspolizei (order police) of Nazi Germany. From 1942 he served as Deputy Protector for the Protectorate of Bohemia and Moravia.

49. A shipbuilding centre between Odessa and the Crimea.

50. Hans-Adolf Prützmann was a high-ranking German SS official during the Nazi era. From June to November 1941, he served as the Higher SS and Police Leader in the Army Group North Rear Area in the occupied Soviet Union.

51. Wappenhans probably means King George V, who looked very like Tsar Nicholas, his cousin.

52. Latvia was occupied and annexed to the USSR in 1939-40. The SS raised two divisions in Latvia and one in Estonia.

53. The rank below Field-Marshal.

54. Hans-Valentin Hube was a general in the Wehrmacht of Nazi Germany during World War II. He commanded several panzer divisions during the invasions of Poland, France and the Soviet Union.

55. A civilian decoration for Nazis.

56. In the German-speaking Alpine region of Italy.

57. Rocket propelled grenade – German: Panzerfäuste – 'Tank fist'.

58. Hilly district south east of the Ruhr. It contains the Dambusters' reservoirs.

59. In Norse mythology a 'valkyrie' is one of a host of female figures who choose those who may die in battle and those who may live.

60. Frank Mercer MA (Oxon) DTEFLA (Diploma in the Teaching of English as a Foreign Language to Adults) (born 1944) who translated this Testimony, like Wolfe Frank, is a gifted linguist. He took a Classics degree at Oxford in 1966 and taught Latin, History and French in state schools until 1982 and English as a foreign language in Sweden, Turkey, Denmark, Spain and England until his retirement in 2011. He learnt German at school, on a BBC course and from colleagues and students throughout his teaching career. Always fascinated by military history Frank Mercer has been a member of the English Civil War Society since 1974 and is a regular war-gamer.

AFTERMATH

'I have faced death often and even sought it once – but it was God's will that I should live to fill other tasks. I would have hanged most certainly, as have many of my comrades, without reasonable justice, if I had been made a prisoner in 1945'.

Waldemar Wappenhans, October 1949

WOLFE FRANK
1913 - 1988
At the Nuremberg Trials in 1945/6

Plate 9

Plate 10

CONNECTIONS

1. **Wolfe Frank:** As Chief Interpreter at the Nuremberg Trials in 1945/6 Wolfe Frank interrogated, translated and announced the Tribunal's verdicts and sentences to Göring, von Papen and Schacht. He also interrogated Rudolf Diels who provided him with much information about Nazi war criminals. In 1949, following a tip off from Diels, Frank tracked down and apprehended SS-Gruppenführer Waldemar Wappenhans, then handed him over to Allied authorities after having taken from him what has become known as the Wappenhans Confession (see Parts Three and Four of this book).

2. **Hermann Göring:** Reichsmarschall, the most senior Wehrmacht officer, Commander-in-Chief of the Luftwaffe and Hitler's designated deputy was the superior officer of Wappenhans, Diels, von Papen and Schacht. He was found guilty on all counts at Nuremberg and was sentenced to death by hanging (announced by Frank), but he committed suicide the evening before his scheduled execution by ingesting cyanide.

3. **Waldemar Wappenhans:** SS-Major General and Lieutenant General of Police had known Göring since their days together at Cadet School and he served with him in both world wars in the air force. They had a fist fight in their cadet days and seemed to have had a love/hate relationship throughout their careers. He also served under Himmler, and Von Papen was one of his commanding officers during WWI. Wappenhans, Diels and Schacht were fellow members of a debating forum that met regularly in the post war years and it was Diels who betrayed Wappenhans as described below.

4. **Rudolf Diels:** Was related by marriage to, and was the protégé of, Göring who had appointed him to be the first Head of the Gestapo. In 1933 when the Reichstag Building was set on fire, Hitler, Göring and von Papen informed Diels that 'this was the start of the Communist Revolt and that every Communist official should be shot'. Believing him to not be ruthless enough Göring relieved Diels of his office and handed it to Heinrich Himmler (see also Plates 3 & 6). Diels was later implicated in the assassination attempt on Hitler's life but his own life was spared following Göring's intervention and he was instead sent to fight on the Eastern Front where he escaped and surrendered to the British. Following the war the British Property Board stripped Diels of his home and farm and placed it under the control of Hans Seemann who denied Diels's request to visit his property. Diels's subsequent enquiries, via his former police and Gestapo connections, revealed that Seemann was in fact Wappenhans and this led to Diels revealing the fact, firstly to Wolfe Frank and then, almost certainly, to an investigative journalist of *Der Spiegel*.

5. **Franz von Papen:** As Chancellor of Germany (and Deputy Chancellor under Hitler) von Papen worked closely with Göring, Schacht and Diels but was acquitted at Nuremberg (see Plate 15). He had been Wappenhans superior in WWI in Palestine.

6. **Hjalmar Schacht:** Economist, banker, centre-right politician, and co-founder of the German Democratic Party, Schacht was never a member of the Nazi party but served as President of the National Bank (Reichsbank) and Minister of Economics under Adolf Hitler. He was tried at Nuremberg, but was fully acquitted (see Plate 15). He, along with Diels and Wappenhans, (as Seemann), was a leading member of the group that eventually revealed Wappenhans true identity to Wolfe Frank.

Plate 11

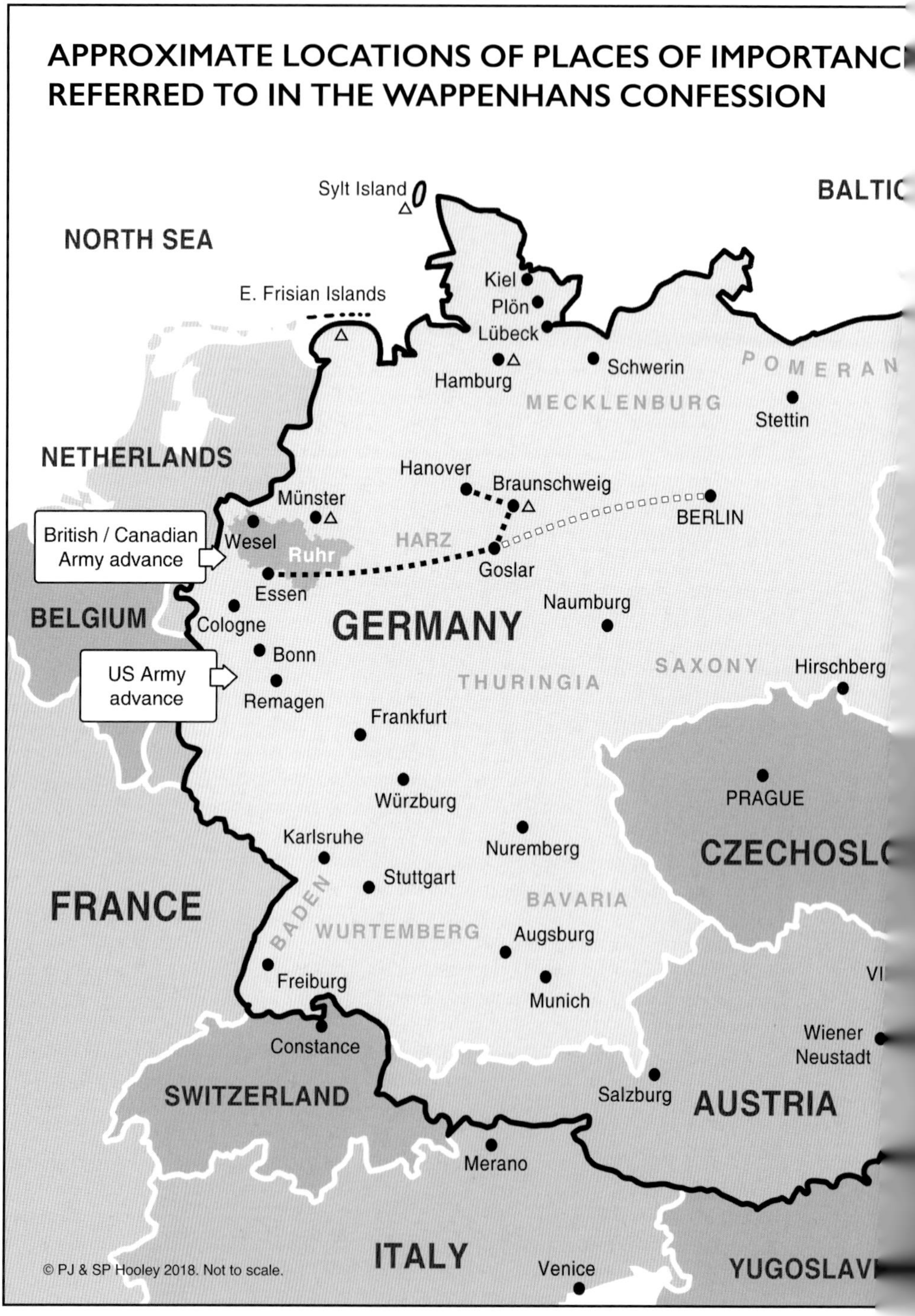
APPROXIMATE LOCATIONS OF PLACES OF IMPORTANC
REFERRED TO IN THE WAPPENHANS CONFESSION
Sylt Island
BALTIC
NORTH SEA
E. Frisian Islands
Kiel
Plön
Lübeck
Hamburg
Schwerin
POMERAN
MECKLENBURG
Stettin
NETHERLANDS
Hanover
Braunschweig
Münster
BERLIN
British / Canadian Army advance
Wesel
Ruhr
HARZ
Goslar
Essen
Naumburg
BELGIUM
Cologne
GERMANY
Bonn
US Army advance
Remagen
THURINGIA
SAXONY
Hirschberg
Frankfurt
PRAGUE
Würzburg
Karlsruhe
Nuremberg
CZECHOSL
Stuttgart
FRANCE
BADEN
WURTEMBERG
BAVARIA
Augsburg
Freiburg
Munich
VI
Wiener Neustadt
Constance
Salzburg
SWITZERLAND
AUSTRIA
Merano
ITALY
Venice
YUGOSLAV
© PJ & SP Hooley 2018. Not to scale.

Plate 12

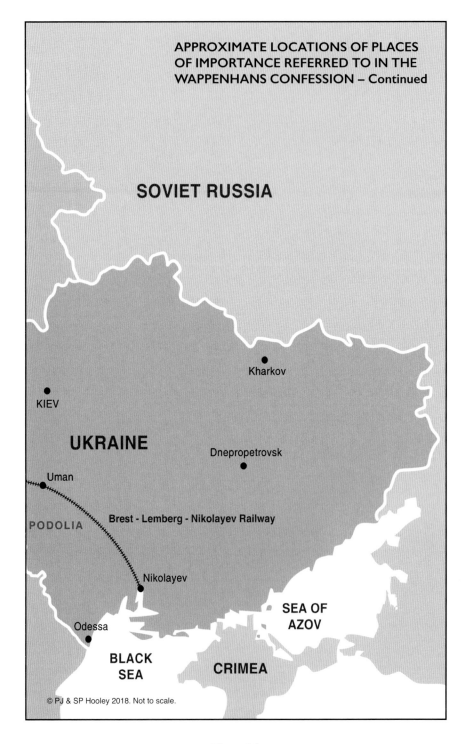

APPROXIMATE LOCATIONS OF PLACES
OF IMPORTANCE REFERRED TO IN THE
WAPPENHANS CONFESSION – Continued

SOVIET RUSSIA

Kharkov

KIEV

UKRAINE

Dnepropetrovsk

Uman

Brest - Lemberg - Nikolayev Railway

PODOLIA

Nikolayev

SEA OF
AZOV

Odessa

BLACK
SEA

CRIMEA

© PJ & SP Hooley 2018. Not to scale.

Plate 13

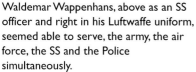

Waldemar Wappenhans, above as an SS officer and right in his Luftwaffe uniform, seemed able to serve, the army, the air force, the SS and the Police simultaneously.

He went straight from Cadet School to an Infantry Regiment at the outbreak of WWI and was badly injured a number of times. No longer able to lead his men into battle he transferred to the Flying Corps where he became head of aerial photography, reconnaissance and a machine gunner. Later he was transferred back to the Western Front as Commander of the 27th Battalion. After the war he joined the Police before taking up civilian positions. Later Himmler persuaded him to join the SS.

At the outbreak of WWII, he returned to the air force as Squadron Captain of Reconnaissance where he carried out many of the most important aerial photographic missions of the war and was awarded bars to the Iron Crosses (1st & 2nd Class) he had received during WWI.

Following further woundings and a heart condition Wappenhans was posted back to the Western Front before returning to a role that saw him serving in both SS and Police simultaneously where he rose to the ranks of SS-Major General and Lieutenant General of Police.

Early in 1945 Himmler transferred him back to the army to take over a Battle Group on the Western Front defending the Ruhr before ordering him to walk the 450 miles from the Ruhr to Berlin. En route, he learned of the Fuehrer's death and that the war was lost – at which point SS officer Waldemar Wappenhans became the civilian Hans Seemann.

Plate 14

Above: Himmler, Wappenhans and other members of the SS leadership.

Below: Franz von Papen, Hjalmar Schacht and Hans Fritzsche at a press conference held in the Palace of Justice, Nuremberg immediately after Wolfe Frank had announced their acquittals.

Plate 15

THE REVEALING OF THE NAZI
GENERAL'S TRUE IDENTITY

Editor: Following publication of *A High Nazi Officer is Run to Earth* (Chapter 24) Wolfe Frank sent Waldemar Wappenhans a copy of the article he had written and in return he received the following letter, handwritten in German and dated 4 January 1950 – as translated it reads:

Dear Mr Frank

With my thanks for sending your most interesting article in the *New York Herald Tribune* I add my sincere good wishes for the New Year. And these really come from the heart as you have kept your word in every respect.

Your treatment of my case in the *NYHT* confirms this yet again. You mention no names, no places and write in an elegant, objective and remarkably gripping manner.

Today I'd have preferred it if you <u>had</u> mentioned my name, so as to counter what was written in *Der Spiegel*. In any case you don't need to be careful with my name any more from now on.

As I've told you already, I cannot understand at all why Herr Diels and Herr Wendt told Mr Augstein [chief editor] from *Der Spiegel* about my case. It was definitely not in their interest to do so. Could you shed some light on this for me?

The Press has now quietened down. What is going to happen to me? I do not know. The local State Attorney thought giving a false name came under the Amnesty, and from the Bielefeld Appeal Court I've heard nothing.

In spite of all the gloomy prospects for the future, I trust in my luck. Somehow there will be a way out of the present misery.

Kind regards also from my wife.

Your very devoted

Waldemar Wappenhans.

Der Spiegel is a German weekly news magazine published in Hamburg that was founded in 1947 by John Seymour Chaloner, a British army officer, and Rudolf Augstein, a former Wehrmacht (unified armed forces of Nazi Germany) radio operator. The magazine was (and still is) renowned for its investigative journalism and for revealing political misconduct and scandals.

Frank confirmed in his own memoirs that, following his interrogation in London by the Admiralty, Wappenhans 'went through his de-Nazification trial and was sentenced to serve one year in some camp'. The above letter therefore was written by Wappenhans before he knew what his sentence was to be and after he had been 'interviewed' firstly by the Admiralty and then by the Hanoverian Criminal Police who, according to *Der Spiegel*, had been instructed by British Intelligence not to arrest him.

Der Spiegel goes on to report that Wappenhans spent fourteen days in Herford and moved into a cottage in the village of Harsewinkel, where he was interviewed by two 'English gentleman. They caused him to write plans on partisan control in Russia and on enemy combat in Germany'. Following this further interrogation the 'two Englishmen' handed Wappenhans over to British Police who in turn instructed their German counterparts to issue Wappenhans with a new passport and a driving licence in his own name.

There were only two copies of the Wappenhans Confession produced, one was handed to the Admiralty, the other was retained by Wolfe Frank. It is quite clear from what *Der Spiegel* published in issues 51/1949 and 1/1950 that at least some of the information contained in the Confession had been leaked to them by people closely associated with British Intelligence – whom Wappenhans names in his letter to Frank as being Wendt and Diels (who is mentioned by name in the article).

(In separate notes, written whilst he was undercover in Germany, Frank records: 'Went to Hembach by train. I had a long talk with Diels, who agreed to do the following things for me: (1) To enable me to contact a certain war criminal wanted by the Poles for murder at Hanover; (2) Through one Dr Wendt, to enable me to get into the Volkswagen plant; (3) To arrange a talk with Schacht; (4) To play along with me if [I said] I wanted to go to the Argentine … Has given me reason to believe that at least in the higher regions the former big Nazis, though perhaps today without being organized, are backing each other up').

It is important here to take a closer look at the 'illustrious group' with whom Frank met prior to his confrontation with Wappenhans (Chapter 25). They were indeed men of considerable standing and importance:

Dr Heinz Wendt, the host, was a close friend of **Rudolf Diels** (who had arranged for Frank to attend the meeting). Wendt was a world-renowned authority on icons and was considered to be 'one of the three great experts on the subject'.

Hjalmar Schacht[1] had been President of the Reichsbank, co-founder of the German Democratic Party, Minister of Economics from 1934–37 and Minister Without Portfolio until 1943. As one of those put on trial at Nuremberg (acquitted) he was already well known to Wolfe Frank.

Wilhelm Roepke[2] was one of the world's leading economists. He was an adviser to German Chancellor Konrad Adenauer and was described by biographer Russell Kirk (and others) as being 'the principal architect of Germany's recovery at the end of the Second World War'. Frank indicates that Roepke has 'talked to and advised the Americans a great deal on German affairs'.

Count Gustav Westarp was described by Frank as being 'a German politician, ex-SS member, questionnaire forger, in touch with British Intelligence … one arm, dark moustache, very quiet, very cold'. Frank goes on to say that Westarp was in frequent touch with the British and had opined 'The Allied policy of handling Germany is nothing but an almost uninterrupted series of blunders'.

Herr Kroenn was, according to Frank's notes, 'Argentine President Juan Peron's envoy who had orders to collect Dr Schacht'.

Of this group Rudolf Diels had already told Wappenhans he knew who he was and had passed that information on to Frank and Wendt – who Frank states had 'agreed to help me in every way'. Count Westarp was speaking frequently with British Intelligence and Roepke with the Americans. John Chaloner, the joint founder of *Der Spiegel,* also worked with the Foreign Office and with Field Marshal Bernard Montgomery. There is no doubt that Wendt and Diels had revealed Wappenhans' identity to Rudolf Augstein, one of Germany's top investigative journalists and that he, via Westarp, Roepke, Chaloner, or some other source connected with British Intelligence had been given access to, or sight of, at least parts of the Confession. Included with the article were two photographs of Wappenhans – one of him as an SS officer, the other in Luftwaffe uniform. As Wappenhans indicates in his memoirs the authorities had taken all photographs of him from his home – someone in British Intelligence must, surely, therefore have also supplied these images to Augestein.

Wappenhans' great concern, of course, was that any information at all had been 'leaked' to *Der Spiegel* not only by those he would have considered to be friends but also by those connected with British Intelligence – his anonymity had been compromised and his life put at risk from the Russian and Polish authorities still seeking his extradition. Wolfe Frank would, no doubt, have been furious that *Der Spiegel* had been able to publish parts of his story and name Wappenhans on the very day (15 December 1949) that his own column appeared in the *NYHT* – a feature in which he had, as promised, so carefully concealed the identity of the former SS officer. Whether this had any impact on their relationship is unclear, however Frank does record that after these events he never saw Diels again.

In a further intriguing twist to the leaking of information to *Der Spiegel* and Diels, Wendt and Westarp's involvements with BI, on the 4 November 1949 E. B.

'Crash' Abbot, Head of 13 Niedersachsen Intelligence Staff and British Military Governor of Hanover, in a hand-written letter to Frank included the following:

Dear Wolfe

Our friend [Wappenhans] has retired from circulation for the time being. Presumably he will be putting his case to the German authorities in the fairly near future.

I have seen Dr Wendt several times since our meeting on the race course and I find him a very interesting and charming person … If Dr Wendt is seeking to find a party which will rally the Right Wing the sooner he drops Dorls [Diels?] and Westarp the better! They can only make the group still-born.

Drop me a line sometime,

Thine, 'Crash!'

Notes:

1. Hjalmar Schacht (1877–1970) was the former President of the Reichsbank (central bank of Germany) and co-founded the German Democratic Party in 1918. Although never a member of the Nazi Party, he was Minister of Economics (1934–1937) and a Minister without Portfolio until 1943. He was dismissed from office after clashes with Hitler and Goering and was arrested in 1944 by the Gestapo as having been implicated in the 20 July attempt to assassinate Adolf Hitler. He was interned in Ravensbrück, Flossenbürg and Dachau concentration camps. Because of his previous involvements in the Third Reich, Schacht was put on trial alongside Goering et al. at Nuremberg where he was charged with conspiracy and crimes against peace. Frank had interrogated him, acted as interpreter during the trial and had announced to Schacht that he had been acquitted (see also Plates 10, 11 & 15).

   Whilst on his undercover mission for the *Hangover After Hitler* series Frank met up with Schacht to discuss, amongst other things, the German economy and the refugee crisis. They also exchanged a number of letters in which Schacht confirms that he agrees with Frank's assessment of the facts and opportunities for Germany and urges the Allies to give West Germany religious freedom and the chance to achieve a decent level of prosperity, through its own efforts, that will act as a 'magnet' to attract East Germany so strongly that no politics will be able to prevent eventual unification (it took forty years and the collapse of the Soviet system for Schacht's vision to come to fruition).

2. Wilhelm Roepke (1899–1966) was a professor of economics of world standing. Although German by birth Roepke was opposed to the Nazi regime and this led him to move to Turkey in 1933 and then to Geneva in 1937 where he became professor of economics at the Graduate Institute of International Affairs. There he wrote a number of acclaimed works including *Civitas Humana*; *The Social Crisis of Our Time*; *Economics of the Free Society*; and *The Solution of the German Problem*.

  Post-war and until the late 1950s Roepke was a personal adviser to West German Chancellor Konrad Adenauer and Minister of Economics Ludwig Ehard. Biographer Russell Kirk (and others) consider Roepke to have been 'the principal architect of Germany's recovery at the end of the Second World War'.

WHAT HAPPENED NEXT

From the documents Wolfe Frank wrote about his discovery of Wappenhans and his handing him over to the British Authorities it is clear that it was he, Frank, who decided: what was to be done with the SS General; who he should be turned over to; and, having extracted his life story, what should and should not be included in the Wappenhans Confession – as Frank's following record demonstrates:

'I told him to attach to the manuscript of his military story a piece of paper giving his correct name and address, since up to that time, no one on the British side knew as yet who he was. This he did at exactly the time and in exactly the manner which I had told him to adopt, saying to me that he had been trained all his life to obey orders, and that it seemed that he was now taking his orders from me, and that as always, he was taking them, unable to question them, although it might well be that I was doing him a bad turn'.

Frank also records, presumably referring to events after Wappenhans death –

'Der Spiegel on that occasion interviewed Frau Wappenhans who made some pretty vitriolic remarks about some deal her husband was supposed to have worked with one Wolfe Frank'.

It is clear that Wappenhans and Frank did indeed have 'some deal' and that their intention was to, at some appropriate time, publish the testimony – one of only two copies of which, signed by Wappenhans, had been retained by Frank.

It is also clear that it was Frank who typed up the final document, decided what its content would be and (following Wappenhans' death) that he would press ahead and include the document as part of the book he intended to publish. This is all confirmed in a document, discovered amongst his papers, written by a senior partner in a firm of French specialist copyright lawyers – whose opinion had been sought regarding the ownership of the testimony. That opinion states[1]:

'W. Frank was the confidant and author of an eye-witness account of events in Germany during the war. The person recounting the story was involved in the Nazi regime and preferred to keep his name withdrawn, and he has since deceased.

'It would appear that W. Frank is the owner of the copyright of his manuscript and his relationship to the deceased Nazi gives rise to the assumption that the latter had joint rights in the manuscript. In the circumstances [W. Frank's] liability in this regard may be difficult to prove without some definite evidence showing joint authorship by the deceased Nazi. Under French law it is the person who writes down the story who is 'prima facie' and author and the 'raconteur' does not automatically have a share in the copyright'.

Notes

1. Opinion, dated 15 February 1977, from a senior Barrister-at-Law with Bodington & Yturbe (founded 1825).

IRONY

There are a number of remarkable coincidences and ironic twists in the intertwined stories of Wolfe Frank, Waldemar Wappenhans and Rudolf Diels and it seems they were destined to come together in the circumstances that they did.

Had Frank not protected and befriended Rudolf Diels during and after the Nuremberg trials, it is unlikely Wappenhans would have ever come to the notice of the authorities, or if he had, his identity and freedom would have been protected by his friends within the British Military Government. By the same token had Frank not dealt with matters in the way that he did, and engineered a deal on Wappenhans's behalf with the British and Americans, the former Nazi SS officer would have been handed over to the Russians or the Poles – and, as one US lawyer confirmed, 'The Poles will certainly kill this guy, and can you blame them?'

It is clear from his memoirs that it was Frank who decided what the content and format should be. However Wappenhans concludes his testimony – which is more the autobiography of a brave warrior who unquestioningly obeyed the orders of superiors than the 'confession' of a Nazi wanted in connection with war crimes – with the following added admission:

'I would have hanged most certainly, as have many of my comrades, without reasonable justice, if I had been made a prisoner in 1945'.

And here is the irony.

Had he been captured in 1945 Wappenhans would have stood trial at Nuremberg alongside his former friend and colleague Hermann Goering and the other Nazis, where he would have been interrogated by Wolfe Frank, who was well skilled in drawing out and recording damning confessions from the accused[1]. It would then have been Frank who interpreted for him, and it would have been Frank who would have announced to him that his fate would be 'Tod durch den Strang' (death by the rope).

When Wappenhans was eventually tracked down and cornered in 1949, it was the very same Wolfe Frank who interviewed him, interrogated him, recorded what he said and acted as his translator and interpreter. In the changed times it was Frank, and Frank alone it seems, who had the power to decide to which authority Wappenhans should answer, and it was Frank who decided what should be included as evidence, how it should be presented and, perhaps, even how it should be interpreted and dealt with.

The Voice of Doom had become the Voice of Hope.

It can truthfully be said that the man who had been most involved in the prosecution and intermediary stages of the Nuremberg trials and who would have announced the death sentence, was indeed the man who, just four years later, saved Wappenhans's life and spared him a lengthy prison sentence – by gathering the same information and carrying out the same duties of interrogation and interpretation but presenting the evidence in an entirely different way to the authority he thought would be most sympathetic towards the apprehended SS officer. No wonder Wappenhans signs the personal letter of thanks he sent to Frank (Chapter 27) as 'your very devoted Waldemar Wappenhans'.

Having been informed by Frank of his eventual fate the utter relief that ensued is clear in the very last sentence of Wappenhans's epic eighty-four page testimony:

'Now I shall be free among my beloved family and ready to work and live with a happy heart'.

It was Wolfe Frank who alone had made that possible and having read Wappenhans's testimony it is easy to see how he arrived at the conclusion: 'We [British and US Intelligence] dug out the file on Wappenhans and, with our very thorough knowledge of SS activities in Poland, we decided that Wappenhens, in the positions he had held there could not, under normal circumstances, have perpetrated atrocities'.

I will not comment, or attempt to pass judgement, on what Wappenhans records in his Confession. Readers of this important document and future historians will make up their own minds. I would ask however that the following observations be taken into consideration.

Bearing in mind it was written under the instructions of Wolfe Frank, the testimony avoids going into detail about a number of matters, areas and situations from which it might have been difficult for Wappenhans to disassociate himself – whether he knew about them or not. At the same time the former SS officer puts distance between himself and the atrocities that took place in locations for which his positions within the Third Reich would have made him ultimately responsible – especially those matters the Russians and the Poles were so anxious he should answer.

It should also be borne in mind that Wolfe Frank was a man whose fairness and dedication to duty had so impressed those, at all levels and on all sides, who had witnessed his performances as Chief Interpreter at the Nuremberg trials – perhaps best summed up by The Office of Chief Counsel for War Crimes: 'Wolfe

Frank … superlative scholarship and administrative assistance … and intellectual integrity … satisfactory alike to the bench, the defence and the prosecution'.

Having spent so much time researching and analysing Wolfe Frank, I am of the opinion that – with his integrity, honesty, commitment to duty, his quest for justice, his knowledge of the Holocaust, Nazi officers and their methods, and his renowned skills as an interrogator – had there been the slightest doubt in his mind, he would have reached an entirely different conclusion and taken an entirely different course of action.

I also believe that few will disagree with Frank's statement that: 'Wappenhans was a brave man and, first and foremost, a soldier'. This cannot be denied. Yet some of the few sparse biographical reports that have appeared about Wappenhans (on the Internet and elsewhere) indicate that he deserted in January 1945. This is untrue and does the man a great injustice. Such a suggestion would have mortified this courageous and dedicated warrior, however it is easy to see how such a misconception might have been arrived at as January 1945 was the point where his SS records seem to come to an end – and he didn't reappear on the radar until the autumn of 1949, and then under the alias of Hans Seemann.

What actually happened in January 1945 is explained in the final pages of the testimony. Himmler, who only shortly before had indicated that he had earmarked him to be 'Commander of the SS British Legion', transferred Wappenhans back to the Army where for the following two months he had, with distinction, commanded a battalion in General Model's sector defending the Ruhr. Following this, and obeying orders, Wappenhans had then attempted to reach Berlin.

The fact is Waldemar Wappenhans gave truly astonishing service to his country. He entered both World Wars on their very first days and he was still involved in the thick of battle on the days those wars came to an end.

In his first involvement in 1914, at the age of twenty, he was wounded leading his men, from the front, in a battle charge. Then during the final days of WWII, having recently further proven his bravery in one of the war's last great battles (where, with the only three survivors of his unit, he had taken out three US tanks) he attempted to walk from the Ruhr to Berlin to further support the Cause to which he had devoted (and fully expected to lose) his life. In his own words 'I'd led a soldiers life, so I wanted to end it as a soldier'.

Between 28 July 1914 (the start of WWI) and the end of WWII Wappenhans had bravely and selflessly served his country in the way he had been trained and commanded to do – without question. Awarded the Iron Cross in both wars and, amongst other distinctions (see Plate 2), two Knight's Crosses, he was seriously wounded many times – one spell in hospital lasting nine months. As a soldier he had led from the front in the great battles of WWI at Poelcappelle, Langermarck, Lorraine, Ypres, Pilckem Ridge and elsewhere and he had been involved in the world's first ever gas attack in which, once again, he was badly injured. Following every discharge from hospital Wappenhans was back in the thick of things at the earliest opportunity and when his injuries prevented him from leading his troops on foot he took to horseback or transferred to the airforce. He further distinguished himself in both wars as an airborne machine gunner and head of the reconnaissance sections where he was again shot down and wounded a number of times – on one occasion his plane was found to have sustained over 100 hits.

In March 1945 surrounded by General Bradley's 12th Army of 1.3 million men Wappenhans took his final instructions from the Third Reich – 'I found that there were orders for me to get through to Berlin. I was to let the Americans overrun that area, and I was to get out in civilian clothes'.

With Germany now being overwhelmed by Allied forces, Wappenhans donned his disguise, assumed the alias Hans Seemann and although suffering many injuries and ailments including a badly damaged leg and heart problems, he began his long, tortuous and arduous trek from the Ruhr to Berlin – presumably to help Hitler defend what remained of the 'Thousand Year Reich' and then go down with the ship.

The battle of the Ruhr Pocket[2] in which he was involved, was concluded on 18 April 1945. Wappenhans indicated he received his final orders and started walking sometime in March. He was still walking towards Berlin when, having called off to see his wife and family en route at Hahnenklee (a suburb of Goslar), he heard of Hitler's suicide (30 April) and that the Russians had captured the city. Only then did he realise all was lost. It seems, suffering from his injuries and heart condition, via many detours and crossing difficult terrain, including the Harz mountains, whilst avoiding American troops, it had taken him a month to cover the 250 miles from his final battlefield to his family's home.

Wappenhans was no deserter. It was only at the point that he learned the war was lost and he was high on the Allies Wanted List that he permanently assumed the identity of a civilian, mingled with the crowd and faded into obscurity.

Regardless of allegiances and the rights and wrongs of the two world wars, few, if any, other combatants from either side, would be able to match the extended period of bravery, fortitude and endurance or the long, distinguished and devoted service to country (on land and in the air and through some of the greatest battles of both wars) as that shown by Waldemar Wappenhans, who was perhaps, until now, the forgotten man of The Third Reich.

Notes

1. Amongst the many statements used at the Nuremberg trials that came directly from Frank's probing was that made by the Chief of Special Action in the East, Otto Ohlendorf who, as Frank records:

'He [Ohlendorf] avowed, without hesitation, that he had ordered the "humane" killing of some 90,000 people. His pride and joy, he told us, had been the mobile gas chambers, which he then described in great detail. They were vans, disguised as transport vehicles, which were driven to the scene of the murders. There, the victims were asked to board. Ohlendorf's claim to humanitarian fame, he felt, was his special system of loading and unloading these gas chambers in such a way that the victims never guessed what was awaiting them. Even more important, and this is where his listeners began to reel in horror, his staff were spared undue mental suffering. They had, so he explained, been very severely emotionally affected by the struggles and screams of the dying until he had designed his new solution for the Final Solution'.

2. The Ruhr Pocket was a 'battle of encirclement' that took place between the last week of March and 18 April 1945 in the Ruhr Area of Germany. Some 317,000 German troops were taken prisoner along with 24 generals. The Americans suffered 10,000 casualties including 2,000 killed or missing. On 7 March the US 12th Army under General Bradley had crossed the Rhine at Remagen (see Chapter 24 Note 3) and together with the Allied 21st Army of Field Marshal Montgomery in the north had, by early April, surrounded Model's forces to create a massive encirclement of 370,000 German troops. It was from this theatre of war that Waldemar Wappenhans, under orders, left the battlefield with the intention of walking 350 miles to Berlin to continue his contribution to the defence of the Fatherland.

A HAPPY CONCLUSION TO THE
HANGOVER AFTER HITLER SERIES

The main objective of Frank's *Hangover After Hitler* mission, as directed by the *NYHT*, was 'to obtain an entirely new approach, a fresh appraisal of the German question; and to present the resultant highlights, constituting a summarized report in human terms, as a useful contribution to the understanding of one of the great key problems of the post-war world'.

In undertaking the project, Frank showed the continuing courage that had already marked him out as an exceptionally brave man. His enquiries and some of the people and situations with whom he became involved put him in danger, which is why, where necessary, he carried a loaded revolver. As it turned out he never needed to use that gun, but he wasn't to know that and even the *NYHT* thought his life was at risk – as one executive wrote to another: 'He might not come back; but that would be his and our bad luck'.

It is through these articles and his reports on his discussions with various authorities that Frank had come to the conclusion that the Allies, with the possible exception of the Russians and Poles, were losing their appetite for hunting down and bringing Nazi war criminals to justice – even those such as Wappenhans who would have been executed for their crimes had they been caught earlier.

The *Hangover after Hitler* series was undoubtedly a revelation and a huge success, not only in Europe and America, but around the world – as a telegram from Geoffrey Parsons Jr. in January 1950 clearly illustrates:

'NEW YORK – "Please advise Wolfe Frank Six article series circulated ninety papers last week but too early [to] evaluate response – stop – no luck yet on book deal but will try personally on return from California next week – stop – hope return Ile de France sailing February tenth." Parsons'.

This was a hugely encouraging message that would have pleased Wolfe Frank. However, because of the changing situation and relationships between Britain, the US, Germany and Russia at that very time, as highlighted in his observations, the intended 'book deal' was shelved. Frank himself explains why:

One thing had gone wrong with the project: the articles came out too late. As the reader will, no doubt, remember, a great deal was happening on the Russian front at the end of 1949. Put into very simple terms, we [the Allies] were busy understanding what Mother Russia was all about and we didn't like what we were discovering.

Unfortunately for my series, interest was swinging away from Germany, rapidly becoming the 'good guy', towards Russia, the 'bad guy'. The bad guy is always more spell-binding than the good one. Not that this took anything away from the reception the articles got from those who cared, or those who knew.

Some European publications paid the highest-ever syndication fee for them. But the US let us down: eleven articles appeared in the New York edition, but syndication stopped short of expectation, and, in consequence, so did my revenue. Alas. But (so says the undocumented views of many) money isn't everything and I am today as proud as ever and as glad to have done it.

WAS FRANK WORKING FOR BRITISH INTELLIGENCE?

To suggest that Wolfe Frank conjures up images of the Scarlet Pimpernel or James Bond is not to exaggerate the lifestyle, charisma and appeal of this twentieth century adventurer and lothario. In the years leading up to the Second World War, Frank gave the impression of being little more than a pleasure-seeking philanderer with a somewhat cavalier attitude who managed to regularly take refreshment in the presence of Adolf Hitler without ever giving the Nazi salute[1]. However this persona camouflaged the true character of a man who, in reality, was involved in an underground resistance movement, centred on those who met at the Carlton Tearooms in Munich, and who was risking his life smuggling Jews and large amounts of money out of Germany.

Likewise, during his pre-war years in England as an escapee and his transition into a businessman, and then a British Army Captain – as well as during his undercover operation for the *NYHT* – Frank could have passed as the model for Ian Fleming's archetypal hero. An astonishingly handsome man irresistible to women, he was suave, chivalrous, cultured, charming, a gifted raconteur, a gambler, a risk taker, highly intelligent and a unique linguist who spoke five languages. He was also an intrepid adventurer who was prepared to risk his life for his adopted country or a worthy cause and he could move flawlessly between all levels of society, never looking out of place in whatever role he adopted – he was as convincing as a German nobleman, an English aristocrat, or a British Army officer, as he was as a squaddie, a factory hand, a farmer, a schools' inspector, a Bavarian coal miner or a refugee.

As a peerless translator, interpreter and interrogator he was one of the stars of 'history's greatest trials' and as an undercover investigative journalist he undertook a unique and dangerous challenge that delved deeply into some of post-war Germany's most pressing issues. These included the refugee crisis, anti-Semitism, de-Nazification, morality, nationalism, black marketeering and, most importantly, Germany's widespread willingness to protect the whereabouts and identities of wanted Nazi war criminals.

Whilst it is clear that Frank's enterprise was to a great extent being supported, directed and financed by the *NYHT*, was it possible he was also in some way involved with one or other of the British or US Military Intelligence services?

There are a number of clues and circumstantial evidence contained in Frank's memoirs, archives and in other evidence to suggest that he could have been.

Firstly, there was his pre-war friendship and associations with Major Humphrey Sykes[2] whom Frank first met in the Italian Alpine resort of Sestriere in February 1937. Frank was on holiday with his then fiancée Baroness Maditta von Skrbensky and he had explained to Sykes that because of his Jewish ancestry it was impossible for him and Maditta to marry in Germany or another European country. In spite of having only just met them Sykes offered to arrange for Wolfe and Maditta to be married from his home on the British Army base at Tidworth in Wiltshire. The offer was accepted and the marriage took place at Andover Register Office in April.

After a brief honeymoon in Tidworth the Franks returned to Germany where Wolfe was tipped off, by a friend in the Gestapo, that he was to be arrested the following morning and interned in Dachau concentration camp. With little money and few clothes he fled from Germany, leaving behind his bride of six days – whom he did not see again for almost ten years.

Frank suggests in his memoirs that it may have been Maditta's father, Baron von Skrbensky, who had reported him and his non-Arian background to the authorities, stating that the Baron 'belonged to the "Herrenclub" in Berlin – a sort-of political, social, sinister assembly of nobles, industrialists and political grey eminences of Germany who were of considerable importance to Hitler.' Frank also indicates that his involvement with the underground group may have come to the attention of the Nazis. They may therefore have been watching him, and his meeting with a British Army major in Italy at a sensitive time and his subsequent marriage in England and stay at the major's home on a British Army base may also have heightened their suspicions.

Frank managed to escape in the nick of time just before the Gestapo arrived to arrest him in the early hours of the following morning. He fled to Switzerland where Humphrey Sykes sent money for his passage to England and then allowed him to live at his family home. After a short period of integration, during which Frank learned the language, Sykes appointed him to be CEO of several companies and introduced him to many acquaintances in society, the theatre, to friends at Scotland Yard and members of both houses of Parliament. Sykes also arranged for Frank to work with a development scheme in Cape Canaveral and advised him how to completely disassociate himself from his former homeland to become 'a stateless person'.

During Frank's period of internment as an 'enemy alien,' he and Sykes engaged with a number of parliamentary members and camp officials including Sir Timothy Eden, brother of the then Secretary of State for War, Sir Anthony Eden (later Prime Minister). This led to Frank's release and to him joining the British Army where he gained a commission and rose to the rank of captain.

Sykes may of course have just taken a fraternal or comradely interest in Frank or he may simply have acted as a Good Samaritan. However following Frank's death Sykes, by then retired, travelled down from Scotland especially to go through Frank's papers, some of which were very sensitive documents that Frank should not have had. Mike Dilliway, the beneficiary of Wolfe's estate was careful not to let Sykes see Frank's memoirs, but the former army major did leave with a number of other files, at least some of which, no doubt, pertained to the army, Nuremberg and Frank's undercover operation for the *NYHT*. Amongst all the many documents retained in Frank's archives, and apart from what he has written in his memoirs and a single photograph (see plate 10), there is not one record of his years of service in the British Army. Frank was a hoarder, yet there is no trace of his army records, any medals, awards or achievements. There were no discharge papers; identification, medical or grade cards; service record; pay book; certificate of transfer to reserve; or any other document connecting him to his years of service in the British Army, or indeed anything that linked Frank to Humphrey Sykes[4].

Leaving aside Sykes's desire to get hold of documents that may have caused him concern, any official or unofficial association Frank may have had with Military Intelligence is more likely to have been in connection with his undercover operation for the *NYHT* – the resultant information clearly being of as much value to the intelligence services as it was to Frank and the *NYHT*.

Such an arrangement, if one existed, and the way it was conducted would therefore have benefitted all concerned. If Frank was captured and interrogated, especially by the Russians, MI could have distanced themselves from any involvement by pointing out Frank was simply working as a journalist – which he was. The *NYHT* in turn could claim that they only had an arms-length agreement to print anything Frank, as a freelance, might put their way. Frank on the other hand was, in reality, being financed and supported by one of Europe's top newspapers and he was able to get into places it would be difficult to penetrate without the cooperation of senior intelligence and military personnel.

Amongst the most compelling evidence to consider in this context is the following:
- The degree of subterfuge involved in Frank's cover story, his assuming of another German's identity and the involvement of the former French Resistance workers who prepared his forged documents.
- The readiness of Sir David Maxwell Fyfe[3], soon to become Home Secretary and then Lord High Chancellor to support Frank's proposal.

- The *NYHT*'s belief that Frank's life could be at risk on the mission and that 'he might not come back'.
- The fact that prior to commencement Geoffrey Parsons Jr., the *NYHT*'s European Editor, discussed the project with, and had the support of, Senator Foster Dulles the Republican nominee for President the previous year, who later became the 52nd United States Secretary of State. At their meeting on this matter Dulles indicated 'no American correspondent could get underneath the surface' and Parsons affirmed Frank had 'the highest recommendations from top British and American officials'.
- Prior to the final go-ahead, Parsons had flown to Heidelberg to get the whole project cleared personally by General Huebner the Military Governor of the American Zone in Germany and to get the General's assurance that Frank would be ' bailed out of jail' if he got caught. Parsons had also received approval from General Lucius Clay, the senior US Army officer responsible for the administration of occupied Germany after World War II.
- The relative ease with which Frank gained access to: refugee camps, high ranking politicians, bankers, industrialists, economists, government ministers, judges, lawyers, black marketeers, former SS officers and their families, and a prisoner on death row.
- The help he received from British Intelligence officers. He had discussed every aspect of his proposed investigation with the British Military Governor and other high ranking British and US officers, all of whom went out of their way to assist him in his mission.
- Whether or not he was 'licenced to kill', Frank was armed during his period in Germany.

Perhaps the most compelling evidence that Frank may have had some connection to MI, however, was the level of authority he seemed to have been given or assumed which gave him access to military and intelligence personnel and records. This allowed him the freedom to negotiate the terms of a high ranking SS officer's surrender and then decide what should be done with him, who he should be turned over to, what he did and did not include in his testimony and what would happen to him following his arrest. Quite simply, it seems, Frank alone had the power to decide whether Wappenhans lived or died.

Notes:

1. In his memoirs Frank records 'Whenever the Fuehrer was in Munich and had some time on his hands, he would arrive at the Carlton for coffee after his presumably vegetarian lunch. His arrival was signalled by a quickly gathering

crowd outside and the shouts of 'Heil Hitler'. I would get up as rapidly and as inconspicuously as possible and disappear into the washroom. The other guests would rise upon Hitler's entry and would stand, facing his route of progress, with their arms raised until he had sat down. His party was usually small, perhaps four to six people and would invariably include his adjutant, Brückner, with whom I sometimes played tennis. Once Hitler had sat down at his table in the left corner of the second of the Carlton's two rooms, I would return to my seat. This I usually managed to choose in such a way that I could also pretend to miss his departure which was always over very quickly since he left the place with fast long strides before anyone had time to get up and 'Heil' him. Thus, during my three years of visiting the Carlton, unlike all the other guests, I never once gave the Hitler salute as the Fuehrer went by'.

2. Humphrey Hugh Sykes was born in 1907. He was the son of Major Herbert Rushton Sykes and Hon. Constance Harriet Georgina Skeffington. He married, firstly, Grizel Sophie, daughter of Air Vice-Marshal Sir Norman Duckworth Kerr MacEwen, in 1936 – from whom he was divorced in 1948. He married, secondly, Muriel Hooper, daughter of Colonel John Charles Hooper, in 1958. He was educated at Rugby School and gained the rank of Major in the service of the 9th Lancers. He died in 1991 after having travelled from Scotland to the home of Mike Dilliway in Mere in search of Wolfe Frank's manuscript and other documents.

3. Sir David Maxwell Fyfe (1900-1967) was a Member of Parliament, lawyer and judge who variously held the offices of Solicitor General, Attorney General, Home Secretary and Lord High Chancellor. He later became the Earl of Kilmuir. At Nuremberg he was Britain's Deputy Chief Prosecutor and his cross-examination of Hermann Goering, which was translated by Wolfe Frank, is regarded as having been one of the most noted in history.

4. In a further development, and following the publication in 2018 of *Nuremberg's Voice of Doom* (see Preface Note 4), a close friend of Frank's came forward and attested that, late in his life, Wolfe had asked for assistance in destroying a quantity of documents and photographs from his past. The witness duly provided that help and further confirmed that following Frank's death they had, late at night, been interviewed at length by police and that soon after that Frank's home had been broken into and searched by a person, or persons, unknown. Whilst the witness to the destruction of the evidence and these events wishes to remain anonymous I can confirm them to be a highly respected citizen of uprightness and integrity who, in my presence, signed a statement confirming the above to be a true record and an eyewitness account of events of which they had personal first-hand knowledge – *Editor*.

EPILOGUE

Waldemar Wappenhans

After his release from custody, and again with help from British Intelligence, the German authorities were instructed to issue Wappenhans with new papers in his real name and he went to work for the coffee importer Heimbs & Co in Brunswick (his wife was a Heimbs). In spite of his identity having been revealed it seems that no attempt was made by the Russians or the Poles to put him on trial to face the charges for which he believed he would be convicted.

Waldemar Wappenhans died on 2 December 1967, aged 74, in Hanover, having spent seventeen years of freedom 'among his beloved family'. He is buried there in the Friedhof Engesohde – the City Cemetery.

Rudolf Diels

Following his last meeting with Frank in 1949 Rudolph Diels served in the post-war government of Lower Saxony and then in the Ministry of the Interior. He retired in 1953 and died on 18 November 1957 when his rifle accidentally discharged while he was out hunting.

There may be no more to the demise of Diels than that. However one cannot help wondering how the son of a farmer, a veteran of two world wars, the former head of the Gestapo and, as confirmed by Frank, 'a keen hunter and an excellent shot' – in other words a man who had been around firearms his whole life – 'accidently shot himself with a hunting gun'.

Wappenhans had a long memory and his Confession indicates that he was a man who found it difficult to forgive and forget. In this context, and bearing in mind it was Diels who had broken his promise not to reveal the true identity of the former SS-Gruppenfuehrer – and then made it publicly known through *Der Spiegel* – that Wapppenhans' comment in his private, previously unseen, letter to Wolfe Frank raises a more chilling possibility:

'As I've told you already, I cannot understand at all why Herr Diels and Herr Wendt told Mr Augstein from *Der Spiegel* about my case. It was definitely not in their interest to do so'.

(Klaus Wallbaum in his book on Diels – *Der Überläufer* (The Turncoat) – seems to agree there may be more to the officially recorded verdict. In his on-line introduction he records: 'He [Diels] died in 1957 supposedly after a hunting accident, but many, including Erik Larson, author of *In the Garden of Beasts* question this, as does this writer').

Wolfe Frank

The full story of Wolfe Frank's own, astonishing life, including all that happened to him post *Hangover after Hitler*, is told as a biographical epilogue to *Nuremberg's Voice of Doom*[1].

The following is a brief résumé of some of the more important highlights.

It can certainly be said that Frank was a unique character of extreme contrasts. On the one hand he spent a lifetime in the fast lane thoroughly enjoying himself – even during the most difficult of times – and it cannot be denied that he was a lothario, a playboy, a risk taker, a serial adulterer, a heavy drinker, a participant in (sometimes an organizer of) orgies and he was an opportunist who liked nothing more than a challenge – even if that meant risking his life.

For most of his adult years he stayed on just the right side of whatever laws, rules and regulations were applicable, or he managed to avoid getting caught or severely punished if he ever broke them. In short Frank seems to have been a mixture of Casanova, with whom he had much in common, Cary Grant, the aforementioned Scarlet Pimpernel, James Bond, and Oliver Reed.

Irresistible to women, he was married five times – to a German Baroness, an American actress, a suspected Russian spy, an Italian hostess and an Austrian interpreter – and he had countless affairs and casual relationships.

His other side showed him to be a man of immense courage, charm, good manners, honour and ability. He was highly intelligent, a gifted linguist and raconteur and one who, at times, moved in the highest circles of society and the theatre. His handling of the translations and interpretations at Nuremberg sets him apart from all other interpreters of his time, perhaps of all time. He was asked to undertake the toughest of assignments imaginable and he was perhaps the only man in the world who could have so satisfied all concerned.

Throughout a packed lifetime Frank was at various times an engineer, a financial advisor, racing driver, theatre impresario, broadcaster, journalist, salesman, businessman, restaurateur, skier and property developer.

Until the end of his days he drew nothing but admiration from the fairer sex – 'You are still totally recognizable as one of the most attractive men I have ever seen' –wrote one casual acquaintance shortly before he died.

In his final years however he had became something of a recluse and he had fallen on hard times financially and emotionally. He was also suffering from a number of debilitating illnesses, including Parkinson's Disease, which had put an end to his means of earning a living as an interpreter for the European Union.

On 10 March 1988, reflecting on his situation and, in spite of what the above mentioned admirer had written, upon what he had once had and had lost for ever, this proud man prepared himself to look his immaculate best, dressed himself in his best clothes and went to his favourite local restaurant. There he indulged himself in the hostelry's finest cuisine, which he washed down with a bottle of vintage champagne, before getting into his car and driving off into the night. The following day his body was recovered from his smoke filled vehicle. On the seat beside him was his final will and testament in which he left all he possessed to his friend Mike Dilliway. His estate consisted of a few less than valuable chattels and several boxes of documents recording his life story together with his records detailing his mission in Germany where he became the Undercover Nazi Hunter. Mike Dilliway, not realizing what he had, placed the boxes in his loft where they remained un-investigated for twenty-five years.

Frank, with his privileged background, came into the world in style. He lived every moment of that life in style and he died with style in his own way, in his own time and by his own hand. There was however one final terribly sad twist to his story. After a lifetime of being surrounded by beautiful women and having had more friends, acquaintances and admirers than any man has a right to expect – and having, as the Voice of Doom, once been listened to by an estimated world wide radio audience of four hundred million – just five people were in attendance at his funeral service in Salisbury.

Two quotations that stand out in Wolfe Frank's memoirs are worth repeating as a fitting conclusion to the life and times of an exceptionally brave man whose achievements on behalf of his adopted nation and the free world should not, I hope readers will agree, be allowed to fade into obscurity. These quotations also, perhaps, sum up what drove Frank to undertake his *Hangover after Hitler* mission and assume the role of the Undercover Nazi Hunter:

'As long as there are orphans who remember the extermination of their families, as long as there are men and women mentally or physically crippled by the faithful servants of Hitler's Third Reich, we should not afford ourselves the luxury of burying such ghastly memories.

'I had been involved in the writing of a chapter of human history that would be read, talked about and remembered forever. I had been more totally and decisively immersed in recording the horrors of the war [and its aftermath] than most of the millions who had fought in it'.

Note:

1. *Nuremberg's Voice of Doom: The Autobiography of Wolfe Frank, Chief Interpreter at History's Greatest Trials* (edited by Paul Hooley and published by Frontline Books).

APPENDIX
A FINAL CONUNDRUM – 'FAKE OR FORTUNE?'

Amongst all the *Hangover After Hitler* material were four documents that stick out like a sore thumb and are so at odds with everything else in the Wolfe Frank archives as to make one wonder what on earth they were doing there.

These documents consist of the three original drawings shown here and two typed original scripts purporting to have been produced and signed by the renowned American writer, illustrator and playwright James Thurber.

A number of leading experts on the life and works of Thurber have been shown the drawings (some have been known to fetch up to $10,000 each) but none are prepared to confirm or deny that they are originals.

The drawings bear Thurber's distinctive signature and are illustrations that go with two of his well known Proverbs: *The Bear Who Could Take It Or Leave It* and *The Owl Who Was God*. They are accompanied by original (i.e. typed and not photocopied) versions of the text that goes with them. All 4 leaves have been produced on sheets from the same ream of paper strongly suggesting the texts were produced at the same time as the illustrations – which is exactly how Thurber liked to work.

Both Proverbs were first published in the *New Yorker* on 29th April 1939 and appeared in Thurber's book *Fables of our Time and Famous Poems Illustrated*

produced in 1940 and in other books. From what can be seen the versions used in the different publications are not always exactly the same.

There is a connection between James Thurber and Frank – through Maxine Cooper, the second of Wolfe's five wives.

Maxine was an actress (see Note 2, Chapter 1) who, at the very time Frank was undercover in Germany working on his *Hangover after Hitler* series, was starring in a Thurber play[1] alongside his collaborator and life-long friend Elliott Nugent. In her letters to Frank she makes it clear that Nugent is pursuing her and trying to seduce her. On 20 June 1949 she wrote: 'The great Elliot Nugent asked yours truly out twice. The first time was oh so lovely after I talked about you for most of the evening and he praised my "great Acting." The second time was fine until riding home in the cab I had to remind him that he really shouldn't break up a happy home. Thank God for mother then, because all he got out of the evening was a hot cup of coffee. Before I went out the second time I asked Ferdy's[2] permission which was granted because he deemed it in the line of business. I have another name for it and I have now called the whole thing live and learn and never go out with authors or producers period punkt'.

The professionals to whom the illustrations have been shown include:

A leading expert on British cartoonists who did express some doubt 'I feel uncomfortable about them … carefully crude instead of stylish'.

One of America's leading experts on Thurber illustrations, opined: 'Sometimes I can tell readily, but in the examples you've sent, I'm afraid I cannot go out on that limb. But, I would not dismiss them outright either: there is nothing about the "hand" that looks wrong to me, despite the ineptness of the drawing … We do know of different versions of Thurber drawings, for a couple of reasons: 1) it might be a preliminary version that the editor asked him to adjust; 2) he sold or lost the original but could readily re-create it for a fan. I would tentatively say that, if you do find a published version of the Bears that differs from yours, it is still quite likely you have an original Thurber'.

A Thurber biographer who also worked for the *New Yorker* and knows more about Thurber, his life and works than all others: states – 'Thurber was notoriously careless with his completed material and could well have given his ms to anyone who asked for one … if the drawings date to 1939 it is very likely they could be genuine'.

Keny Galleries, specialists in Thurber works, *The New Yorker* and Thurber House[3] are unable to confirm one way or the other, and Ohio State University, which houses a vast collection of Thurber's work, will not authenticate or comment upon Thurber drawings but does state the illustrations found amongst Frank's papers are 'similar to many others in the vast collection we [OSU] possess'.

There are therefore a number of matters that should be taken into consideration when considering the provenance of these works, which are as follows:

• There were three people prominently involved with Thurber and the promotion of his writing and drawings – the aforementioned writer, Hollywood actor, director, producer and playwright Elliott Nugent – whom Thurber met at university and who became his mentor, lifelong friend and collaborator – E. B. (Andy) White and Harold Ross (editor) his colleagues at the *New Yorker*. Thurber was a writer who doodled as he considered his subjects and would then throw all the illustrations into the waste paper basket. White retrieved, in his words, 'thousands' of discarded drawings which were done in pencil. White then inked over the images to enable them to be used for printing – fifty two in Thurber's first book alone – and in doing so established Thurber as an artist of merit. Hundreds if not thousands of drawings were subjected to this treatment before Thurber was persuaded to produce his work in ink and there are several versions of many of the illustrations in their entirety or as separate parts.

- Thurber did not believe there was any value in his drawings and ended up owning very few. In 1946 he wrote 'Such good drawings as I still possess were caught up in London by the war and are still there … I sent forty to an art gallery in Hollywood who sold ten, paid me for five and could never find the remaining thirty … a great many of my [published] drawings, say one hundred, have disappeared'. Others were cut up and reused in other ways and many more were just given away to people who asked for them.
- It seems Nugent pestered and no doubt tried to impress Maxine as some of her letters to Frank indicate. Frank was at the time on his dangerous undercover assignment for the *NYHT* but he was flown in and out of London by the Paper for the opening night of Thurber's play.
- I have found a different part version of the 'bears' illustration' in *Further Fables of our Time* and the 'birds and animals on the branch' in *Lanterns and Lances*.
- Apart from one person, none of the authorities to whom I have submitted the work, including the Thurber Museum, Ohio State University, Thurber House. A Thurber expert, a leading biographer and Keny Galleries, are prepared to say the Frank owned drawings are not Thurber originals. Two experts suggest they could be authentic and OSU confirms the drawings are similar to many they hold in their archives.
- Throughout his career Thurber was steadily losing his sight and was blind by the age of about forty-five. He also developed a 'tremor' in his hands that made it impossible to always trace accurately – so he just did them again and again until he was satisfied – discarding all his 'preliminaries' into waste paper baskets from where they were retrieved by White and others.
- Versions of the three Frank owned drawings appear in different books with slight variations.
- Thurber would draw and give away up to thirty cartoons for guests at a single dinner party and would draw on anything – walls, tablecloths, napkins, etc., but favoured bond paper (of many makes) similar to that used for the cartoons in the Frank archives.
- The Frank owned drawings were found in the same box as Maxine's letters informing Wolfe that Nugent was pursuing her.

Whether these illustrations are original Thurber's or not may never be known.

The best that can be said about the drawings are the words used by a Thurber expert 'there is nothing about "the hand" that looks wrong to me' and a Thurber biographer – a man who spent half a lifetime studying Thurber's life, times and work – 'They could well be legitimate … I have no idea of their legitimacy, nor probably would anyone else at this late date'.

Notes

1. Thurber and Nugent together wrote the play *The Male Animal* for Broadway which was later turned into a film starring Henry Fonda and Olivia de Havilland. The play opened in the UK in 1949 starring Nugent, Barbara Kelly and Maxine Cooper. After a run at The Arts Theatre the play opened at The New Theatre London in June 1949 before moving on to Brighton.

2. The Ferdy Maxine is referring to was her, and Wolfe's, close friend and confidante the actor Ferdy Mayne, known privately as 'The West End Stallion,' who starred in over 230 films and countless West End theatre productions.

3. Thurber House is a literary centre in Columbus Ohio for readers and writers and is based in the historic former home of James Thurber.

ACKNOWLEDGEMENTS

As with *Nuremberg's Voice of Doom,* the mine of information contained in the records that Wolfe Frank bequeathed to his friend Mike Dilliway has made this book possible. I would once again therefore like to put on record my gratitude to Wolfe for the vast amount of time, care and effort he put into recording the events he included in his *Hangover After Hitler* series of articles and in taking and transcribing the Wappenhans Confession. I am also grateful to Mike Dilliway for entrusting me with the task of editing Wolfe's work and Martin Mace and Frontline Books for encouraging me to bring this book to fruition. I especially thank Frank Mercer (see Chapter 26 Note 60) who painstakingly and zealously translated the Wappenhans testimony. As a life long enthusiast of military history in general, and the two World Wars in particular, Mr Mercer was also able to provide highly pertinent details (included amongst the Notes to and in the square brackets of Chapter 26) which have significantly added to a number of explanations that enhance this important historical document.

I also thank my son Simon for his considerable help with some of the graphics and my wife Helen for her proof reading skills, and for her continued understanding of the months that I spent two floors above in my man cave sorting, researching and producing this work.

Others whose help and kindness I gratefully acknowledge include: Amanda Sadler for her skills in typing up the translated version of the Wappenhans Confession; Fran Hill of Vale Secretarial; The British Library; Gillingham (Dorset) Library; Allan Bishop and Connor Drewitt of Gillingham Press; and Rob Hopmans (ww2gravestone.com) for allowing me to use two of his photographs of Waldemar Wappenhans.

I also take this opportunity to once again pay tribute to Sir Tim Berners-Lee and his colleagues for inventing the World Wide Web and for making the 'Internet' available to all free of charge – an act of monumental generosity that has benefitted mankind in general and every computer user in particular, especially historians and researchers at every level. Credit must also be given to the countless experts and amateur enthusiasts who so willingly share their knowledge via the information super-highway. Without this technology and the wealth of resources it has made available to us all, books such as *The Undercover Nazi Hunter* would have been more difficult to produce and would be far less substantial in content. Whilst there are too many to name individually, and many anonymous sources fall into this category – I am grateful to them all. I do however make special mention of *Wikipedia* and its contributors for the direct service provided and for the invaluable other reliable sources, links and references that they gather together for the benefit of the millions of daily users of this wonderful innovation.

Finally, I apologize unreservedly for any names I have inadvertently omitted from these acknowledgements or for not giving proper credit in any instance where it has not been possible to verify authorship or ownership. If any such occurrences are found and brought to my attention I will ensure appropriate permissions are sought and that any future editions of this book are amended accordingly.

Paul Hooley

GLOSSARY & ABBREVIATIONS

AA	Anti Aircraft
Abwehr	German Military Intelligence Service
Adjutant	Military officer who acts as an administrative assistant to a senior officer
ADC	Aide de Camp (personal assistant)
AFN	American Forces Network
Allied Power / The Allies	Those countries opposed to the Axis Powers during World War II
Anti-Semitism	Hostility to, prejudice, or discrimination against Jews
Axis Powers	The nations in World War II who fought against the Allied forces
BBC	British Broadcasting Corporation
BHC	Berlin Hockey Club
BI	British Intelligence
BMW	Bayerische Motoren Werke (in German) or Bavarian Motor Works (in English)
Brownshirts	Sturmabteilung (SA) – Storm Detachment
Bundeshaus	Parliament House of the Federal Republic of Germany 1949 – 1999
Bundestag	The German federal parliament
BWCE	British War Crimes Executive, The
CEO	Chief Executive Officer
CIC	Counter Intelligence Corps
CID	Criminal Investigation Department (or Division)
CO	Commanding Officer
DC	District Commissioner
DDT	Dichlorodiphenyltrichloroethane

De-Nazification Programme to eradicate National Socialist thought from political, economic, intellectual and cultural life.
DVP   Deutsche Volkspolizei (German People's Police)
DNB   German News Bureau
Dogfight   An aerial battle between fighter aircraft
DP   Displaced Person

Endloesung   Final disposition of a problem
Erznazi   Arch-Nazi
ERP   European Recovery Programme, The

Fluechtling   Refugee

GC   General Commissioner
Generalleutnant Lieutenant General
Gestapo   Geheime Staatspolizei (Secret State Police)
Gruppenführer   Group Leader
GSO   General Staff Officer
Great War   World War I

HQ   Headquarters
IMT   International Military Tribunal
JEIA   Joint Export-Import Agency
KC   King's Counsel
KPH   Kilometres per hour
KdS   Komandeur der Sicherheitspolizei (Chief of SS and Police or SSPF)

Lèse majesté   A crime committed against a sovereign power
LRR   Long Range Reconnaissance
Luftwaffe   German Air Force, The

Mauschelsdorf   Poor Jew's village
MG   Machine Gun
MI   Military Intelligence
MO   Medical Officer or Orderly
MP   Member of Parliament or Military Police

Nazi Party /   Nationalsozialistische Deutsche Arbeiterpartei
NSDAP   (National Socialist German Workers' Party more commonly known as the Nazi Party)

NATO	North Atlantic Treaty Organisation
NCO	Non Commissioned Officer
NKVD	Narodnyy Komissariat Vnutrennikh Del (the interior ministry of the Soviet Union).
NVOD	*Nuremberg's Voice of Doom*
NY	New York
NYHT	*New York Herald Tribune*

Oberfuhrer	Senior Leader
SS-Oberst-Gruppenführer	Supreme Group Leader
Obergruppen-führer	Senior Group Leader
Obersteiger	Under manager
OCCWC	Office of Chief Counsel for War Crimes
OCTU	Officer Cadet Training Unit
OMGUS	The Office of Military Government, United States
ORP	Objective Rally Point
Orpo	Ordnungspolizei (Order Police)

Panzerfaust	Tank fist – a high-explosive anti-tank warhead
Polizi	Police
Polizeiführer	Police Leader
POW	Prisoner of War
Putsch	A secretly plotted and suddenly executed attempt to overthrow a government

Reich	Realm
Reichsbank	German National Bank
Reichsführer-SS	Reich Leader of the SS
Reichsmarschall	Marshal of the Reich (highest rank in Nazi Germany)
Reichstag	Parliament
RKU	Reichskommissariat Ukraine (Civilian occupation regime)
RPG	Rocket Propelled Grenade
Rt Hon	Right Honourable

SA	Public Limited Company in USA
SA	Sturmabteilung (Storm Detachment)
Schatzkammer	Treasure chamber
SD	Sicherheitsdienst (Security Service)
SDP	Social Democratic Party

SED	Socialist Union (Communist) Party of East Germany
SP or ST	Subsequent Proceedings or Subsequent Trials
SPF	SS and Police Leader
Spruchkammer	De-Nazification Court
SRP	Socialist Reich Party
SS	Schutzstaffel (Protection Squadron)
SSPF	SS and Police Leader
Stahlhelm	Steel helmet
Standarteführer	Regimental Commander
Strafkompanie	Penal Unit in Nazi concentration camps
Sturmbann-führer	Lowest Officer Rank of SS
Tommies	Slang for British soldiers (Tommy Atkins in WWI)
UK	United Kingdom
USPD	Independent Social Democratic Party of Germany
US/USA	United States/United States of America
USSR	Union of Soviet Socialist Republics (The Soviet Union)
VC	Victoria Cross
VD	Venereal Disease
VIP	Very Important Person
Volk	People in the ethnic sense
VP or VoPo	Volkspolizei (People's Police)
Waffen-SS	The armed wing of the Nazi Party's SS organisation
WAV	Wiederaufbau Vereinigung (Economic Reconstruction Party)
Wehrmacht	The unified forces of Nazi Germany
WO	Warrant Officer
WWI	The First World War (1914–1918)
WWII	The Second World War (1939–1945)

BIBLIOGRAPHY

Brandon, Ray and Lower, Wendy, *The Shoah in Ukraine (The Mass Murder of Jews under German Nazi Regime During 1941–5; The Holocaust* (Indiana University Press, 2008)

Bourne, et al., *Germany off the Beaten Track* (Globe Pequot Press 1989)

Cimino, Al, *The Story of the SS: Hitler's Infamous Legions of Death* (Arcturus Publishing Ltd, 2018)

Cooper, R.W., *The Nuremberg Trial* (London 1947)

Der Spiegel, issues 51/1949 and 1/1950

Frank family records and official documents

Gaiba, Francesca, *The Origins of Simultaneous Interpretation* (University of Ottawa Press, 1998)

Hasek, Jaroslav, *The Good Soldier Schweik, (Penguin Books)*

King, Henry T. Jr, *The Nuremberg Context from the Eyes of the Participant* (Military Law Review 1995)

Longerich, Peter, *Heinrich Himmler: A Life* (Oxford University Press 2012)

Maxwell Fyfe, Sir David, Personal correspondence to Wolfe Frank

New York Herald Tribune

New Yorker, The (7 September 1946 edition)

Oregonian, The

Francis, Patricia (née Leonard) biographical notes

Persico, Joseph, *Nuremberg: Infamy on Trial,* (Viking-Penguin New York 1994)

Rosignoli, Guido, *Army Badges and Insignia of World War 2 part 1* (Blandford Books 1972)

Sigel, G. A., *Germany's Army and Navy,* (Bracken Books 1989)

Speer, Albert, *Inside the Third Reich: Memoirs of Albert Speer.* Translated by Richard and Clara Winston, (Macmillan 1970)

Taylor, Telford, *Anatomy of the Nuremberg Trials, The* (Knopf Doubleday Publishing)

Taylor, Telford, *Final report to the Secretary of the Army on the Nuremberg War Crimes Trials*

Time Magazine – Germany; The Defendants (29 October 1945)

Tusa, Ann and John, *The Nuremberg Trial* (Skyhorse Publishing 2010 & London, Macmillan, 1983)

U.S. Library of Congress, *War Crimes Before The Nuremberg Military Tribunals – Volume IV* (1949)

U.S. Library of Congress, *Military Law Review, Volume 149* (summer 1995)

Washington, DC: Government Printing Office

Wikipedia

INDEX

INDEX

United States Zone, 85, 95
Ütersen, 226, 228, 232–4, 236

Vaka, 260
Vatican, 66
Vaughn, Robert, 163
Venereal Disease (VD), 43, 87, 90–1, 110, 115, 167
Ventner, Shirley, 44
Versailles Treaty (Diktat), 269
Vice Squad, The, 239
Vickers Machine Gun, xxiv, 8
Vienna, 221, 225, 270
Villa Frank, xxii
Vilna (Vilnius), 188
Vinnitsa (Vinnytsia), 253–4
Vladimir Volynsky, 252
Vogtland, 269
Voice of Doom, The, xxii, xxv–xxvii, 1, 283, 296
Volhynia-Brest-Litovsk, 242–3
Volkswagen, 44, 47, 49, 54–5, 59, 92, 119–22, 125–6, 132, 134, 137, 243, 276

Waffen-SS, 68, 77, 225
Waggum, 225–6, 263
Wallbaum, Klaus, 295
Walther, Dr Ernst, 46, 153
Wanted List, The Allies, xiii, xv, xxi, xxv, 55, 158–9, 163, 167–8, 171–2, 285
Wappenhans Battle Group, 251
Wappenhans Confession, The, xv, 266–7, 276, 280, 283
Wappenhans, Professor Friedrich, 175
Wappenhans, Waldemar, xiii–xiv, xvi–xvii, 43–4, 158, 161, 163, 165, 167–75, 177–8, 182, 185, 195, 211, 218–19, 233, 257, 266–7, 270, 272–3, 275–8, 280, 282–7, 292, 294, 303, Plates, 1, 2, 5, 6, 7, 8, 10, 11, 12, 13, 14, 15
Wappenhanse, The, 213
War in the Desert, 203
Warburg, 260
Warsaw, 214
Wash, The, 228
Washington, 79
Washington Post, The, 13
Watts, 43
Wavell, Field Marshal Lord, xxiv
Weare, Buel F., 13–14, 16, 18, 20–3, 26, 29–30, 48, 241
Weber, Herr, 47, 144
Wehrmacht, The, 77, 133, 174, 272, 276

Weigl, Dr, 41
Weimar, 56, 176
Weimar Republic, The, 33, 35, 54, 56
Weinert, A. J., x–xi, 39, 71–5
Wendt, Dr Heinz, 43, 167, 170, 275–8, 295
Wesel, 237, 258
Weser, The
    see River Weser
West Sector, 46
Westarp, Count Gustav E., 43, 132, 167, 277–8
Westerland, 229, 233
Western Front, The, 160, 162, 190, 204, 206, 209, 226, 234, 258, 265
Western Zones, 24, 53, 59, 95, 101, 113, 134
Westphalia, 88, 217
Whatever Happened to Baby Jane?, 3
White, E. B., 301
Wichmann, Lotte, 91
Wiederaufbau Vereinigung, 129
Wiener Neustadt, 222
Wiesbaden, 66
Wiessler, Herbert, 40
Wilderness of Haran, The, 202
Wilna (Vilnius), 191
Winkl, Camp, 107–109
Wisch, SS Brigade-leader, 258
Wischmann, Johannes and Otto, 44
Wise, William H., 14, 24, 31, 34–5
Wolff, Obergruppenführer Karl, 222–3, 236, 256–7, 270
Wolfsburg, 39, 44, 120, 125, 132
Wooden Heart, 270
Workers' Council, 49, 122, 147–8
Wulkow, 175
Wunstorf, 235
Wurzburg, 219–20

Yalta mountains, 247
YouTube, xxvii
Ypres, 185, 284
Yugoslavia, 102, 111

Zamboni, Mania, 214
Zaporozhye, 248
Zaslav, 252
Zdolbunov, 232, 252
Zehlendorf, 155
Zhytomyr, 172
Zoppot (Sopot), 214
Zurcher Zeitung, 9, 12
Zwickau, 115, 117